Marketing Commu

The Marketing Series is one of the most comprehensive collections of books in marketing and sales available from the UK today.

Published by Butterworth-Heinemann on behalf of the Chartered Institute of Marketing, the series is divided into three distinct groups: *Student* (fulfilling the needs of those taking the Institute's certificate and diploma qualifications); *Professional Development* (for those on formal or self-study vocational training programmes); and *Practitioner* (presented in a more informal, motivating and highly practical manner for the busy marketer).

Formed in 1911, the Chartered Institute of Marketing is now the largest professional marketing management body in Europe with over 22,000 members and 25,000 students located worldwide. Its primary objectives are focused on the development of awareness and understanding of marketing throughout UK industry and commerce and on the raising of standards of professionalism in the education, training and practice of this key business discipline.

OTHER TITLES IN THE SERIES

STUDENTS SERIES

Behavioural Aspects of Marketing
K. C. Williams

Business Law
A. A. Painter and R. G. Lawson

Economics Frank Livesey

Effective Sales Management
John Strafford and Colin Grant

Financial Aspects of Marketing
Keith Ward

International Marketing
S. J. Paliwoda

Marketing Communications
C. L. Coulson-Thomas

Marketing Financial Services
Edited by Chris Ennew, Trevor Watkins and Mike Wright

Marketing-Led, Sales Driven
Keith Steward

Mini Cases in Marketing
Lester Massingham and Geoff Lancaster

The Fundamentals of Advertising
John Wilmshurst

The Fundamentals and Practice of Marketing
John Wilmshurst

The Marketing Primer: Key Issues and Topics Explained
Geoff A. Lancaster and Lester Massingham

The Principles and Practice of Selling
A. Gillam

Strategic Marketing Management: Planning, Implementation and Control
R. M. S. Wilson, C. T. Gilligan and D. Pearson

Marketing Communications

COLIN J. COULSON-THOMAS

MSc(Econ), MA, MSc, AM, DPA, FCA, FCCA, Dip M

Published on behalf of
the Chartered Institute of Marketing

For Yvette and Vivien Coulson-Thomas

Butterworth-Heinemann Ltd
Linacre House, Jordan Hill, Oxford OX2 8DP

 PART OF REED INTERNATIONAL BOOKS

OXFORD   LONDON   BOSTON
MUNICH   NEW DELHI   SINGAPORE   SYDNEY
TOKYO   TORONTO   WELLINGTON

First published 1983
Reprinted 1984, 1985, 1986, 1987, 1990 (twice), 1991

ISBN 0 7506 0418 2

Printed and bound in Great Britain by
Redwood Press Limited, Melksham, Wiltshire

Contents

Acknowledgements   x

Preface   xi

1   COMMUNICATIONS   1
1.1   Communication   1
1.2   Systematic Communications   3
1.3   Messages   6
1.4   Channels   10
1.5   The Evaluation of Communications   13
        Examination Question   14

2   PEOPLE   15
2.1   Behavioural Concepts   15
2.2   Values   20
2.3   Leadership   23
2.4   Job Satisfaction   24
2.5   Groups   26
        Examination Questions   33

3   ORGANIZATION AND COMMUNICATION   34
3.1   Organizations   34
3.2   Behaviour in Organizations   35
3.3   Organization and Communication   41
3.4   Structure, Function, and Communication in Organizations   43
3.5   Types of Organization   45
3.6   Technology and Tasks   50
3.7   Organization Design and Development   53
3.8   Setting Up and Adapting Organizations to Changing
             Technological and Market Conditions   57

3.9	Formal and Informal Systems	59
3.10	Management Control	60
3.11	Marketing Organization	61
	Examination Questions	63
4	MARKETING MANAGEMENT	65
4.1	Managing Staff	65
4.2	Managing Marketing Specialists	67
4.3	The Product Manager	68
4.4	Managing Organizational Change	69
4.5	Computer-based Modelling	71
4.6	Specialists and Communication	74
	Examination Questions	76
5	INNOVATION	77
5.1	The Management of Creativity	77
5.2	Innovation	78
5.3	New Product Development	83
5.4	The Management of Diversity	85
	Examination Questions	87
6	MARKETING COMMUNICATIONS	88
6.1	Marketing Communications Strategy	88
6.2	Image	91
6.3	Persuasion	93
7	BUYER BEHAVIOUR AND MOTIVATION	96
7.1	Consumer Behaviour	96
7.2	Consumer Preferences	99
7.3	Assessing Preferences	102
7.4	Demand Management	104
7.5	The Industrial Market	105
7.6	The Industrial Purchaser	106
	Examination Question	109
8	THE PURCHASE DECISION	110
8.1	Information	110
8.2	Behavioural Factors and Influences	111
8.3	The Purchasers	113
8.4	High Risk Purchasers	114
8.5	Analysing Purchasers	115
8.6	The Large Purchase	116
8.7	The Industrial Seller	118
	Examination Question	119

9	THE PROMOTION MIX	120
9.1	The Promotional Mix	120
9.2	Promotional Mix Testing	121
9.3	Packaging	122
9.4	Advertising	123
	Examination Questions	125
10	SALES MANAGEMENT	126
10.1	Salesmanship	126
10.2	Sales Function and Organization	128
10.3	Managing Salesmen	133
10.4	Reporting and Information	135
10.5	Assessing Salesman Performance	136
10.6	Sales Staff Remuneration	138
10.7	Salesman Stress	140
	Examination Questions	141
11	BRAND/PRODUCT MANAGEMENT	142
11.1	Branding	142
11.2	The Product Manager	145
11.3	Brand and Functional Management	148
11.4	Managing Brand Managers	148
11.5	Brand Issues and Strategy	153
11.6	Brand Performance	155
	Examination Question	160
12	DISTRIBUTION	161
12.1	The Distribution Output	161
12.2	Channel Selection	165
12.3	Channel Evaluation Techniques	169
12.4	The Productivity of Distribution	172
	Examination Question	179
13	RELATIONSHIPS WITH EXTERNAL ORGANIZATIONS	180
13.1	Allies and Associates	180
13.2	External Communications	184
13.3	Establishing and Managing Service Relationships	188
13.4	The Marketing Control System	193
	Examination Questions	193
14	PUBLIC RELATIONS	194
14.1	Public-relations Function	194
14.2	Marketing and Publicity	195

14.3	Public-relations Responsibilities	196
14.4	Systematic Public Relations	197
14.5	Publics	198
14.6	Public-relations Channels	204
14.7	Public-relations Planning	208
14.8	Evaluation	209
14.9	Corporate Identity	210
14.10	Crisis Communication	212
15	ADVERTISING	214
15.1	Types of Advertising	214
15.2	Economics and Advertising	215
15.3	How Advertising Works	217
15.4	Advertising Objectives	221
15.5	Agencies	223
15.6	Advertising Research	227
	Examination Questions	237
16	MEDIA	238
16.1	Mass Communication	238
16.2	Media Characteristics	239
16.3	Print Media	240
16.4	Electronic Information	246
16.5	Outdoor Advertising	247
16.6	Broadcast Media	248
16.7	Film	251
16.8	Telephone Selling	251
16.9	Media Credibility	252
16.10	Media Conventions	253
16.11	Media Culture	254
16.12	The Multi-media Approach	255
17	THE ADVERTISING CAMPAIGN	256
17.1	Campaign Elements	256
17.2	Advertising Strategy	257
17.3	The Advertising Message	258
17.4	Advertising Expenditure	259
17.5	Media Planning	264
17.6	Effective Advertisement	268
18	SALES PROMOTION	272
18.1	Sales Promotion	272
18.2	Sales Promotion Publics	272

18.3   Consumer Promotions   273
18.4   Trade Promotions   280
18.5   Sales-force Promotions   282
18.6   Promotion Opportunities   282
18.7   Character Merchandising   283
18.8   Sponsorship   285

19   SOCIAL MARKETING   288
19.1   The Scope of Social Marketing   288
19.2   Public Programmes   290
19.3   Non-profit Marketing   292
        Examination Questions   293

20   MARKET RESEARCH   294
20.1   The Marketing Information System   294
20.2   The Information Input   298
20.3   Research   300
20.4   Presentation   306
20.5   Market Research Organization   307
20.6   The Value of Market Research   307
20.7   Changes in the System   308

21   COMPETITORS   310
21.1   Competition   310
21.2   Competing   311
21.3   Market Dominance   314
        Examination Questions   316

22   COMMUNICATIONS FROM THE MARKET   317
22.1   Interests in a Company   317
22.2   The Changing World   317
22.3   Marketing During Shortages   319
22.4   Criticisms of Marketing   322
22.5   Consumerism   326
22.6   Criticisms of Advertising   329
22.7   The Social Aspects of Marketing   332
        Examination Questions   334

Bibliography   335

Index   336

Acknowledgements

I would like to thank Elsie Thomas, Julia Hill and Martyn Bittleston for their assistance without which this book would not have been completed.

Colin Coulson-Thomas
Mullion, Cornwall

Preface

The purpose of this book is to outline the major components of the marketing communication process. It presents an introduction to the theory of communications and those aspects of the behaviour of people as individuals and purchasers, in small groups and in larger organizations of particular concern to the business communicator. The organization and management of such aspects of marketing communication as innovation, selling, branding, distribution, public relations, advertising, promotion and market research are considered alongside their place in the promotion mix. Attention is drawn to the particular problems of communicating with external organizations and the need for organizations to be aware of and receptive to a wide range of communications from the market.

The book's aim is to give readers a knowledge of the routes and methods by which a business communicates with its market(s), and the ways in which such routes and methods may be evaluated to assist the reader inter-alia, to:

1. Explain how a company communicates with its markets and analyse the role of advertising, sales promotion and sales force in this process.
2. Plan the most effective relationship between a company's internal organization and the markets which it serves and identify the effect of any mismatch.
3. Brief and control a sales force or an advertising or research agency and evaluate the results of their work.
4. Identify and exploit buyer motivations in a given market.
5. Determine the optimum communications mix for a given company/product/market situation.
6. Plan the company response to consumer feedback, legislative action or economic developments in terms of marketing communications.

Approach

What is all this to do with marketing? While this book cannot help but deal with concepts that are at first sight academic, it will repay careful reading. Marketing

xi

performance is generally dependent upon getting the organization, and the communications within it, right. It is particularly important in this area to relate theoretical knowledge to real world problems and hence wherever possible points will be illustrated by reference to recognizable applications.

The intention of the book's approach is not to equip the reader with a doctor's bag of tricks and techniques available for reproduction or use as an examination or situation demands. Instead it is hoped to give readers an understanding of likely communication problems and an approach to possible solutions that will enable them to both tackle and take full account of the particular circumstances of each case.

The emphasis will be upon approaches that are practical and useful. It is important to stress the limitations and weaknesses of particular approaches as well as their advantages and strengths.

While for convenience the book is divided into chapters and sections, it is important at the outset to stress the interdependence of, and relationship between, various organization and communication aspects. Thus a key feature of communications is the nature of channels which are an important aspect of an organization, while one approach to understanding organizations is by examining the patterns of communication within them. There are behavioural aspects that underly communication and with which the reader must become familiar.

Readers should be able to approach communication problems with a view to taking full account of the particular circumstances of each case in order to identify the real problems and propose practical solutions that are specific to the individual situation. Employing 'standard' or 'model' solutions to real world problems can be dangerous.

There is little embellishment in this book. Major approaches are outlined briefly with sufficient qualification only to enable readers to assess their practical worth. Readers are encouraged to apply these approaches to communication situations with which they are familiar. The Test questions provided at the end of each chapter should underline and summarize key points and stress that the purpose of the book is the encouragement of approaches and attitudes rather than the communication of facts. These sections also suggest the sorts of questions readers ought to be asking in situations with which they have been, are, or are likely to be familiar in order to illustrate how techniques combine in practice and hence to reinforce their value and applicability to business situations.

1. *Communications*

It is difficult to plan a marketing programme without an understanding of the communication process. Marketing is above all a communication activity. A knowledge of the nature of communication can also help the marketor to better understand his or her own organization and a number of marketing management problems which can emerge. An organization can be seen as a network of communications. The point will be developed further in Chapter 3. This Chapter examines some basic aspects of communication of interest to the marketor.

1.1 COMMUNICATION

Communication can be informative and/or persuasive. With persuasive communication the aim is to have some effect upon the attitude or behaviour of the target audience. There are many forms of persuasive communication, a speaker addressing an audience, an institution appealing for support or parties employing sticks and carrots in negotiation situations.

In any communication situation there will be a communicator, the sender or source of a message, the message itself, the channel that carries it and the audience that receives it. There should also be some feedback from the audience to the communicator, although this cannot always be assumed.

A GROUP OF ASSOCIATED COMPANIES ESTABLISHES A BUDGET AND A COMMUNICATIONS PROGRAMME IN RESPECT OF EACH OF THEIR MAJOR CUSTOMERS. CUSTOMER PROFILES AND ANALYSES REVEAL PROBLEM AREAS THAT BECOME THE FOCUS OF SUBSEQUENT COMMUNICATION ACTIVITY. CUSTOMER INTERESTS ARE FOUND TO SHIFT OVER TIME.

1.11 Communications Strategy

Effective communication is something that does not automatically happen. It needs to be carefully planned. An organization must identify the internal and the external groups with whom it is or ought to be communicating and decide what

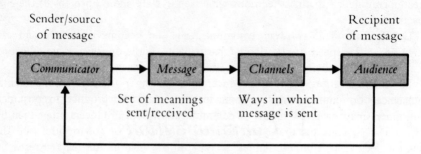

Figure 1.1   Feedback
Effect of the message

messages should be sent along which channels to reach them.

The why of communications is often overlooked. There should be a reason for, an objective behind every communication. Messages must reflect communications objectives and be tailored to the specific needs of each public.

Publics or audiences are groups having certain common characteristics with whom an organization is or ought to be communicating. Their identification and definition needs great care or the wrong message will be sent by the wrong means to the wrong people. When groups have conflicting interests, communications need to be carefully handled. A message aimed at one public is likely to be picked up by at least some members of other publics.

It is important to know one's audience. It should be segmented, refined if necessary. The more narrowly one's audience is defined the easier it becomes to tailor messages and channels.

Audiences can be subdivided in terms of interest and awareness. The awareness dimension is important as it must precede assessment or evaluation and desired action. Awareness may or may not lead to understanding or interest and subsequent audience involvement.

IN AMERICA'S ELECTIONS CANDIDATES TRADITIONALLY PAID GREAT ATTENTION TO BARBERS SHOPS. IT WAS FOUND THAT PEOPLE TENDED TO 'TALK POLITICS' WHEN VISITING THEIR BARBERS. BARBERS BECAME A KEY PUBLIC.

Question 1:   List your publics. Draw a distinction between those with whom you are and those with whom you ought to be communicating and explain what you could do to bring the latter category within the former group.

1.12   One-way and Two-way Communications

One-way communication tends to be faster and two-way communication the more accurate. With two-way communication receivers of information tend to have greater confidence in their decisions while senders are more open to off-the-cuff reactions.

Unless controlled, two-way communication can become disorderly and can function at the speed of the slowest participant. While one-way communication can appear more orderly to an outsider, its cost can be inaccuracy.

In communication between producer and consumer there is a fundamental imbalance. Communication is predominantly one-way, from producer to consumer. Consumers may have few means of communication with producers other than by letters of complaint and praise and decisions to purchase or not to purchase. The lack of feedback from consumers is the primary reason for market research. Instead of passively waiting for information to come in from the market, the company goes out and actively seeks it.

Marketing management could be defined in terms of communication between producer and consumer. This communication is the essence of marketing. Without it, commerce would die away.

Question 2:   Assess and compare the extent of two-way communication between the following organizations and their members:

(*a*)   General Motors
(*b*)   the Catholic Church
(*c*)   a local tennis club
(*d*)   an army regiment
(*e*)   a think tank.

1.2   SYSTEMATIC COMMUNICATIONS

A disciplined and planned approach to marketing communications begins by identifying and carefully defining the publics or target groups with whom one is or ought to be communicating. Which groups are included will depend upon one's strategy, for example whether the company is aiming to increase the purchasing of existing customers or to reach new customers.

When promotional resources are limited and act as a constraint, the targets should be ranked in priority. Target groups should be carefully selected and as narrow and specific as possible. A mail shot promoting an insurance magazine to a list of 1,000 insurance brokers may be more effective than an alternative mail shot to 20,000 middle managers. The ratio of responses will certainly be higher and perhaps even the absolute number of replies.

The more larger groups are broken down the easier it is to tailor messages to their particular needs. How each target group arrives at a purchase decision needs to be determined along with the information required.

Once a target group and its information needs have been identified, messages need to be devised to achieve marketing objectives appropriate to each group.

The channels of communication selected will influence the messages and vice versa. The mix of messages and channels will be such as to maximize cost effectiveness within the overall budget. Work will need to be divided between internal and external resources — between one's own marketing department and such people as distributors and agents.

A communicator must be sufficiently flexible to vary messages and channels according to the feedback received from target groups as reflected in sales, responses to attitude surveys or consumer complaints. Cutting programmes according to the results of panel recall tests or dealer surveys can often save substantial sums which are then available for redirection along alternative channels.

AN INHABITANT OF A REMOTE CORNISH VILLAGE, ON HEARING THAT A LARGE SATELLITE SKYLAB WAS ABOUT TO RE-ENTER THE EARTH'S ATMOSPHERE, WENT TO HIS ATTIC PULLED OUT A TIN HELMET THAT HAD BEEN LEFT OVER FROM THE SECOND WORLD WAR AND PROCEEDED TO WEAR IT. HE WAS MENTIONED IN NATIONAL AND OVERSEAS NEWS BULLETINS, BECOMING FOR TWO DAYS A CELEBRITY. SOME DAYS LATER PIECES OF THE SATELLITE FELL TO EARTH ON THE OTHER SIDE OF THE WORLD IN AUSTRALIA.

Question 3:   You have invented a better mousetrap. Draw up a communications programme of what you intend to say, to whom, when, by what means and for what reasons.

1.21   Analysis and Objectives

Analysing the situation to find out what the communications problem is may be far from easy. Reports can mislead. The actual problem may not be that which appears at first sight. One needs to be able to distinguish between consequences and underlying causes. If a problem is wrongly identified, subsequent communications activity will be wasted.

Specifying an objective must precede any detailed communications planning. The objective should be practical and address itself to the communications problem. An objective might be general or specific. It must be understood by those responsible for a programme and should be expressed in such a way that it can be measured. Narrower objectives are easier to achieve.

A COMPANY FACED WITH LABOUR TROUBLES IN ONE OF ITS PLANTS HAD TAKEN A SERIES OF STEPS TO DEAL WITH LOCAL 'BONES OF CONTENTION'. THEN IT WAS REALISED THAT THE LOCAL DIFFICULTIES OVER QUITE SMALL MATTERS WERE MERELY

A SYMPTOM OF A GENERAL UNCERTAINTY THAT HAD ARISEN AS A RESULT OF A RUMOUR THAT THE COMPANY HAD PLACED ORDERS ABROAD RATHER THAN WITH ITS PLANTS. THE PROBLEMS CEASED WHEN THE EMPLOYEES WERE INFORMED THAT THE ORDER WAS PART OF A RECIPROCAL PURCHASE DEAL. THE PLANT COULD NOT MAKE THE PRODUCT CONCERNED BUT WOULD RECEIVE SUBSTANTIAL ORDERS FOR OTHER PRODUCTS AS A RESULT OF THE OVERSEAS PURCHASE.

1.22   Publics

There is little point communicating with publics for the sake of it. One must be selective and communicate only with those publics most relevant to the communications problem in question. Time and money can be saved by identifying those most affected by or interested in a message.

With a little more effort most publics, even quite small ones, can be disaggregated. Complete selectivity will be impossible. There might be a deadline to meet. On other occasions one may need to trade off the cost savings of greater selectivity against the costs of achieving it.

Careful identification of publics can assist the development of messages. These should be derived from one's objective and be tailored to the requirements of the public or audience at which they are to be directed. Before transmission, a message might have to be modified to suit the needs of a particular channel. Detailed knowledge of an audience can enable one to pitch a message at the right level and select the most appropriate channel of communications.

A PUBLIC RELATIONS MANAGER INHERITED A MASSIVE 'FREE LIST' OF PERSONS TO WHOM HER COMPANY'S GLOSSY HOUSE JOURNAL WAS AUTOMATICALLY SENT. ON THE LIST WERE MEMBERS OF SEVERAL PUBLICS OF LITTLE INTEREST TO THE COMPANY. THE MANAGER WROTE TO MOST OF THOSE ON THE LIST ASKING THEM TO PAY A SUBSCRIPTION FOR THE JOURNAL. MANY DROPPED OUT. THE MANAGER ACHIEVED A CONSIDERABLE COST SAVING AND AN ADDITIONAL SOURCE OF REVENUE FROM SOME TWENTY PER CENT OF THOSE PREVIOUSLY ON THE FREE LIST WHO WERE PREPARED TO PAY A PRICE FOR THE JOURNAL WHICH INCORPORATED A SIZEABLE PROFIT MARGIN.

Question 4:   List the publics you consider would be interested in the following developments:

(a)   a new zebra crossing in the high street of a small town
(b)   an aeroplane crash involving an undisclosed number of deaths

(*c*)   a new method of moulding glass fibre boat hulls

(*d*)   a new law affecting planning permissions.

1.3 MESSAGES

Transmitting a message along a channel inevitably means its codification into a form which can be transmitted. The message must be coded by the sender and decoded by the recipient. Both stages introduce scope for distortion.

Perception is a very individual thing. Each person views the world through spectacles tinted with biasses that have grown out of their own personal experience. Images and words mean varying things to different people and must therefore be selected with care. This is why it is important that messages be in tune with the beliefs and attitudes of those at which they are directed. People are more favourably disposed to messages that reflect their own beliefs.

Needs — as will be pointed out in Chapter 2 — vary. They result from objective requirements and from personality factors. To one person being 'modern' may be important. Another may be less concerned with being 'up market' than with obtaining goods that are 'value for money'. The bandwagon effect is important for some consumers, that is, following the crowd or not being the 'odd one out'. A brand image can be tailored to customers in each of these areas, or to meet a combination of requirements. Messages must take these factors into account.

Habit in consumer behaviour can be very important. Having chosen people tend to rationalize their choices by playing up the advantages of selected options and playing down the virtues of rejected options. People will not accept new messages uncritically, but evaluate them and integrate them into their existing beliefs and attitudes. Messages that confirm existing feelings are clearly effective but it is interesting that messages initially 'opposed' or questioned tend, following acceptance, to be held onto with the great tenacity.

A message that reinforces existing beliefs then has a greater chance of achieving credibility than one which challenges existing beliefs. Unwelcome messages are sometimes denied. When not agreeing with there is a tendency to devalue the credibility of a source. It is written off as biassed or as unimportant. Alternatively individuals may consider themselves an exception. Lung cancer becomes something which other people who smoke heavily get.

The extent to which a consumer is swayed by advertising is dependent upon a number of factors independent of the quality of the advertising. It is generally easier to sell a product when a consumer is sympathetic to one's message, predisposed to act in a favourable way. The consumer may have already recognised the need. The message may have been compatible with the consumer's existing beliefs, thus reinforcing existing predispositions. An initially hostile or sceptical audience is much less likely to be influenced by a message.

Recipients of messages need to be able to 'place' the subject and should as a result of the message see it as relevant to them. The relevance point is important. To the marketor who has spent months preparing to launch it, the new product may seem the most important thing in the world. One target group might have no interest in it, another a little. Casting bread upon water can be expensive. Messages should only be sent to those who are likely to be interested in receiving them.

A MARKETING MANAGER RETURNED FROM HER HOLIDAYS TO FIND THAT A 10,000 DIRECT MAIL SHOT HAD RESULTED IN ONLY 37 FIRM ORDERS FROM MEMBERS OF A PARTICULAR PROFESSION. ON REFLECTION IT WAS REALIZED THAT ONLY ONE VOCATIONAL GROUP WITHIN THE PROFESSION CONCERNED WAS LIKELY TO BE INTERESTED IN THE SERVICE IN QUESTION. THE MARKETING MANAGER MADE A TELEPHONE CALL TO THE SECRETARY OF THE PROFESSION'S INSTITUTE AND THREE WEEKS LATER THE INSTITUTE'S MEMBER SERVICES COMMITTEE AGREED TO BULK BUY 200 UNITS OF THE SERVICE FOR THE ENTIRE MEMBERSHIP OF THE APPROPRIATE INSTITUTE VOCATIONAL GROUP.

1.31 Message Credibility

A source with high credibility is more likely to be able to persuade. Credibility results from a combination of perceived importance and trustworthiness. It can thus be built up by establishing a source as important, high in status, power and prestige or by emphasizing reliability and openness. Credibility is higher where the prestige and perceived skill and other qualities are relevant to the subject matter of the message.

Messages are frequently judged by the credibility of their sources. A message from a high credibility source has a greater chance of acceptance. There is something called the 'halo' effect, the tendency of people to impute to individuals and things the qualities of other individuals and things with which they are associated. Thus the qualities attributed to a well-known personality may 'spill over' into a cause the personality has agreed to sponsor. Well-known people are frequently paid large sums to appear in advertisements. The closer the perceived link between personality and product, the stronger the halo effect.

The process also works of course in reverse. A personality's image can be in turn influenced by the products they advertise. A politician might be linked in the public mind with a means of transport or, in one notable case in the UK, a brand of dog food. Some advertisement campaigns have launched personalities. A character in a television advertisement can be so strong as to lead to offers of further film and television work for the person portraying the character concerned. The association of personality and product may be seen as flattering or as detrimental to the individual in question.

Credibility then is a prime requirement of an effective message. The halo effect is important. Certain sources are more credible than others. A former Commissioner of the Metropolitan Police could, for some, become a very credible tyre salesman when appearing on television commercials.

Question 5:　　Identify credible sources for the transmission of messages about the following products and justify your choices:

    (*a*)　　new method of birth control
    (*b*)　　ant powder
    (*c*)　　Italian peaches
    (*d*)　　self-adhesive tape.

1.32　Structuring Messages

A message must reach its target audience, be perceived as relevant and hence lead to desired action. Audiences vary in their persuadability. Some people do not have strong feelings others do. A communicator may find women more susceptible to one message than men and the young more susceptible to another than the old.

The message that is sent may not be the message that is received. It may be distorted by the channel that communicates it and will be subject to the selective perception of the target receiving it. A message should have a purpose, a function. It needs to be structured according to the job it has to do. It should be credible, should not communicate what is already known, must not appear as an intrusion and must be clear and unambiguous.

When structuring a message, points to be included must be ordered. The strongest arguments for one's case could be put first or last. One could aim for initial impact or work towards a crescendo. A message could aim initially to attract interest and attention, then pass information and finally seek to persuade. Strong arguments tend to be wasted in the centre of messages. In the case of a two-sided message the opposing view should be stated first and then countered with one's own view.

A message need not be totally one-sided. The more predisposed an audience is to one's point of view the more effective a one-sided message is likely to be. Those who are more cynical, perhaps even initially opposed, may be more responsive to a two-sided message, one that admits to some shortcomings in addition to drawing attention to strengths. Aware educated audiences appreciate points of view, are less likely to view the world in terms of black and white and may therefore be especially receptive to a frank and open two-sided message.

Where an audience is subjected to a contrary message, counter-propaganda, the two-sided message may be necessary to prevent the two conflicting messages from cancelled each other out. A two-sided message may be able to suggest a resolution of two points of view. Admitting to weaknesses can diffuse critics and build respect.

A PROMINENT UK POLITICIAN STRUCTURED HIS SPEECHES INTO BLOCKS. A BLOCK CONTAINING HIS MAIN POINTS WOULD BE ALLOWED TO 'FLOAT'. HE WOULD INSERT IT INTO HIS SPEECH AS AND WHEN THE TELEVISION LIGHTS WERE SWITCHED ON.

Question 6: Compare the different ways in which a message about the escalation of an international crisis in South East Asia to war between the countries concerned, would be structured for transmission by the following channels:

(*a*)   a ten-second television news flash
(*b*)   a 'quality' daily lead story
(*c*)   a 'popular' tabloid inside page story
(*d*)   a monthly international relations journal
(*e*)   a Press Agency tape.

1.33   Reputation

That the effectiveness of a message depends very much upon the credibility of its source is particularly true in the case of the marketing of industrial goods. The general reputation of a company can influence demand for its goods. Salesmen from a reputable company tend to find it easier to obtain a first hearing and customers tend to be more willing to try their products for the first time.

It must, however, be pointed out that customers have higher expectations with regard to salesmen from reputable companies. Reputable company salesmen need to live up to higher expectations. A good presentation from the salesman of a reputable company can be highly effective.

Many customers are more receptive to salesmen they regard as low in trustworthiness and competence from reputable companies than to salesmen believed to be higher in trustworthiness and competence but from unknown companies. A company with a reputation may in some circumstances be able to employ relatively less well-qualified salesmen. There are limits to this policy, as a poor sales presentation can damage a company's reputation. Effective presentations a e those which put across succinctly what a product does.

INADEQUATE LIAISON BETWEEN A MEDIA BUYER AND THE SALES STAFF AT A COMMERCIAL TELEVISION STATION LED TO THIS UNFORTUNATE SITUATION. FOLLOWING A PLAY ABOUT A YOUNG UNMARRIED GIRL HAVING AN ABORTION THE ACTRESS WHO HAD PLAYED THE GIRL APPEARED IN A TELEVISION COMMERCIAL ADVERTISING A BABY PRODUCT, PLAYING ON THE LIVING ROOM FLOOR WITH A BABY.

1.4 CHANNELS

A company communicator has access to a variety of channels. Published channels will range from annual sets of accounts, through sales literature to company histories. House journals and bulletin boards might be used for internal communication. Meetings, trade-union negotiations and closed-circuit television could be used to transmit information.

There are many publics with whom a company will need to communicate, its shareholders, employees, customers and creditors, the government, local communities and a variety of opinion formers. Each will have its own preferred channels of communication. Which are selected will depend largely upon the nature of the public and the message to be transmitted to it.

Internal channels will be within the organization's control. External channels of communication may not be. Public-relations work may be initiated in the hope of stimulating favourable messages in the media. The organization might be subject to unfavourable, unexpected and unwanted media coverage.

Channels can be personal and non-personal. Among personal channels will be the salesman with a vested interest in an outcome, the objective consultant and 'social' channels, friends and neighbours. The latter channel should not be overlooked, for word of mouth influence can be strong. The non-personal channels are the media, situations and events. Media are extensive and extremely varied.

Impersonal channels generally find it more difficult to attract attention. The target group will probably be selective in what it sees and takes in, retention may be low. A target may be suspicious or cynical. Impersonal channels have difficulty in providing feedback. They vary in their longevity. Broadcast media are clearly transient, newspapers are rarely kept for more than a few hours, while magazines may be stored and a reference work kept and consulted over a period of years. Media audiences can vary from millions to hundreds. Generally the larger the audience is, the more general it will be.

> A LEADING MANUFACTURER OF MOTOR PRODUCTS OPERATES A FLEET OF THREE AIRSHIPS. EACH HAS THE COMPANY'S NAME PAINTED ON ITS SIDES. AT NIGHT THE NAME OF THE COMPANY CAN BE ILLUMINATED IN LIGHTS. THE AIRSHIPS DRIFT OVER POPULATION CENTRES IN EUROPE AND ON THE EAST AND WEST COASTS OF THE UNITED STATES.

Question 7:   Your company has just had an extremely successful year. Its financial results are due to be published in three days' time. List the channels you would use to reach the following publics:

- (*a*)   existing shareholders
- (*b*)   potential shareholders

(c)   employees
(d)   financial analysts
(e)   local communites.

1.41   Opinion Formers

Personal influence may be important in the case of the significant purchase where the purchaser is reluctant to commit money upon the basis of say an advertisement without consulting someone known to have used the product or service concerned. In the case of products consumed in social situations, such as food and clothing, obtaining advice from other people may be the rule rather than the exception. A personal opinion from a trusted source can be a potent influence but over time such a viewpoint could be eroded by frequent exposure to impersonal media.

The opinion former can be extremely influential. Communicators frequently target their messages at key individuals, perhaps the editor of a trade journal, who are known to be important influences upon the behaviour of others. The views of opinion leaders are sought by others. They may give leads that others follow. In doing this they become in themselves channels of communication.

An organization should consciously aim to build up its contacts with opinion formers. They can be reached in a number of ways, by press release for example or by invitation to events. An advertisement could be targeted at the dinner conversation of an elite group of opinion formers. Sales staff might be encouraged to join the 'right clubs' in order to reach such people.

A MANUFACTURER OF SPORTS EQUIPMENT EMPLOYED A PRO-MINENT SPORTSMAN TO PROMOTE ITS PRODUCTS. A MATTER OF DAYS BEFORE A NATIONWIDE POSTER CAMPAIGN FEATURING THE SPORTSMAN WAS ABOUT TO BE LAUNCHED A NEWSPAPER REPORT-ED THAT DUE TO POOR PERFORMANCE THE SPORTSMAN WOULD BE DROPPED FROM THE NATIONAL TEAM.

Question 8:   Identify opinion formers who would be significant influences upon the purchasers of the following products:

(a)   pop records
(b)   rose bushes
(c)   wines
(d)   hotel accommodation.

1.42   Channel Management

Channels vary in their value for communicating with particular publics and their effectiveness can vary over time. As technology changes and people 'move on', channel contacts need to be kept up to date.

The timing of a message can be a strong influence upon channel selection. A particular journal may be read by a key target group but if the final copy deadline is six weeks ahead of publication date it may be necessary in the case of a time sensitive message to select an alternative channel.

Previous experience can result in communicators falling into the trap of re-using channels with which they are familiar, regardless of their effectiveness for particular communications.

The costing of channels can be difficult. Costs can be hidden. Some form of evaluation is essential to channel modification decisions. A company does not evaluate its communications activity for the sake of it. The purpose of programme evaluation is programme modification in order to achieve more cost-effective communication.

A COMPANY HAD PLANNED A PROGRAMME OF TELEVISION COMMERCIALS. AN INDEPENDENT TELEVISION COMPANY INDUS-TRIAL DISPUTE CLOSED DOWN MOST OF THE INDEPENDENT NET-WORKS IN THE UK. THE COMPANY, THROUGH ITS ADVERTISING AGENCY, BEGAN TO LOOK FOR OTHER CHANNELS OF COMMUNICA-TION. ITS AIM WAS TO REACH HOUSEWIVES. IT DISCOVERED INDEPENDENT LOCAL RADIO AND FOUND THIS TO BE A MORE COST-EFFECTIVE WAY OF REACHING ITS TARGET PUBLIC THAN TELEVISION.

1.5 THE EVALUATION OF COMMUNICATIONS

Communications activities will need to be costed and programme cost compared with budget. At this point a management decision may be necessary on the size and direction of budget revisions.

Where programme costs exceed budget the programme may need to be cut back. In order to do this, desired activities should be ranked in order of their expected effectiveness. Having done this the least cost-effective activities can be eliminated one by one until a mix of activities is reached that is within budget.

Frequently there is no limit to the extent of communications activity that could be carried on. Hence it is usually necessary to set priorities and to be selective. A marketing manager responsible for deciding the content of a com-munication programme should bear in mind the vested interest of both internal staff and external agencies in making a programme as large as possible. Those on a commission income will seek to maximize expenditure.

It is important to establish criteria for evaluating the effectiveness of all forms of communication. In the absence of this information the allocation of resources between areas is extremely difficult. Continuous evaluation allows the emphasis of programmes to be shifted according to the response achieved. Continuous feedback allows a campaign to adapt to changing circumstances, if need be, to take advantage of sudden opportunities.

A large company may employ a mathematical or computer model to co-ordinate its communication planning. Sales response data would be fed into the model for each item in the communications mix. According to the allocation of expenditure, the effectiveness of the whole campaign portrayed in print-out sets of financial statements will vary. With such a model, a manager can experiment, trying different allocations in the search for an optimum.

In subsequent runs of the model during the implementation phase the sales-response coefficients can be altered in the light of experience. The initial allocation of resources can be checked. The effectiveness of new messages or channels can be tested on a pilot basis, the results of which can be examined using the model.

When a consumer is subjected to a battery of communications, of course it becomes very difficult to isolate individual items in order to assess their effectiveness. One might find that in practice two separate items within the communications mix cancelled each other out or that alternatively items reinforced one another, the whole being greater than the sum of the parts.

Where a manager is brought new to an ongoing campaign some attempt should be made to measure the effectiveness of individual items if this has not already been done. It may be, for example, that the campaign places great emphasis upon journal advertising when direct mail shots would be much more cost effective. It is easy to settle into a rut. Because existing methods of communication are working well, there may be a natural reluctance to experiment with other methods that might be even more successful.

FOLLOWING A GENERAL ELECTION CAMPAIGN A GROUP OF POLITICAL SCIENTISTS MET TO CONSIDER WHICH FACTORS HAD MOST INFLUENCED THE OUTCOME. THE ISSUES, THE PERSONAL-ITIES OF THE PARTY LEADERS AND THEIR TELEVISION IMAGES, GENERAL DISSATISFACTION WITH THE ECONOMIC SITUATION AND THE DESIRE FOR A CHANGE WERE ALL EXAMINED. THE GROUP WAS NOT ABLE TO AGREE UPON WHICH FACTOR HAD BEEN MOST IMPORTANT.

Question 9: Establish criteria for evaluating the effectiveness of public relations campaigns to promote the following:

    (*a*)   a new single parent family benefit
    (*b*)   a hospital's prototype clinic
    (*c*)   a company's case in an industrial dispute
    (*d*)   a village carnival.

EXAMINATION QUESTION

Discuss how existing users can influence the successful marketing of an industrial product or service. Using an industrial marketing example of your choice say how, in practice, a new product with no previous users can be marketed.

2. *People*

Ultimately all marketing communication is about the needs and interests of people as individuals and in groups. Outstanding marketors tend to have a shrewd and subtle understanding of people. Knowing what makes a person 'tick' is of particular value in interpersonal communications. Good salesmen know the people with whom they are dealing. A marketing manager, to be effective, also needs to understand the motivations of his or her staff.

Marketing is above all a study of human behaviour and of the factors that influence, condition and constrain it. The marketing manager is primarily concerned with influencing human behaviour. This requires an understanding of it. If products and services are to be developed to meet human needs then these needs must first be identified and appreciated.

2.1 BEHAVIOURAL CONCEPTS

Before turning to the behaviour of individuals in groups and in organizations respectively, the behaviour of individuals as individuals, its motivation and purpose, will first be examined.

2.11 Rewards

Rewards are basically of two kinds, extrinsic rewards such as pay and praise and intrinsic rewards such as self-esteem and professional satisfaction. People vary in the weight they respectively attach to intrinsic and extrinsic rewards.

The phrase to soldier on the job reflects one view of work as a necessary evil that one has to endure for the sake of being able to pay the rent. Work can be seen as inherently unrewarding in anything other than money terms or it can be seen as a source of wider satisfaction.

Work can be enjoyed for its own sake. Many people enjoy their work to such an extent that they become frustrated on holidays or following retirement. Work can offer challenge and companionship.

Where work is monotonous, noisy and routine or otherwise physically or mentally unpleasant then in order to motivate employees, considerable extrinsic rewards may need to be offered. Many manual workers are fundamentally interested in extrinsic rewards.

A professional by contrast may see reward primarily in terms of a job well done in the eyes of a peer group. A researcher for example may be motivated less by an increase in salary than by the opportunity to take a sabatical leave.

People's needs vary. At a basic level, most of us are interested in food, shelter and sex. Then there are the range of material goods and services many take for granted. One may have, beyond this, ambitions for a larger house or a second car. Many are driven on by the desire for more intangible and often more elusive goals such as status, prestige, power and authority. Mental satisfaction, freedom, being one's own boss, might also be important.

Efficiency is often not pursued for its own sake. A group may opt for lower production and salaries in the interests of maintaining a greater variety of work. There are also satisfactions to be gained from a job well done and the knowledge that others are impressed with one's performance. Reputation and respect can be highly valued.

Recognition is important to many people. A higher salary may not compensate for invisibility, being tucked away in some obscure location, being anonymous, not having the world aware of what one is doing. Interacting, working with others, can also be highly valued. An employee may accept a routine desk job if this results in interaction with others, in preference to the more prestigious and more highly paid but isolated life of the travelling salesman.

When handling staff, a marketing manager must be aware of the varying motivations and needs of those within his or her team. There can be enormous differences between individuals. One sales clerk may consider his salary to be a payment for an input of time while another may consider hers to be payment for output, a job done. A professional, say a consultant, may prefer to be paid for the performance of a specific task defined in a contract rather than for time spent within the organization.

The questions of encouraging creativity and rewarding sales effort will be examined in Chapters 5 and 10. Rewards should, if possible, be visible, related to effort and appropriate to an individual's needs. A senior salesman might long for a testimonial or a plaque to put on a wall while a junior salesman might be more interested in hard cash to pay off a bank overdraft.

The rewards that motivate the most tend to be those that are closely related to and meet needs. Rewards that satisfy all people at all times do not exist. Rewards should be tailored wherever possible to the needs of those individuals it is desired to motivate.

ONE MANAGER STOPPED LOOKING FOR A NEW JOB OUTSIDE OF
AN ORGANIZATION WHEN THE WORD 'DIRECTOR' WAS INSERTED

INTO HIS TITLE. HIS DUTIES HAD NOT IN ANY WAY CHANGED. THE MANAGER CONCERNED NOW EXPERIENCED A MUCH 'EASIER TIME' WITH HIS AMBITIOUS WIFE WHO HAD HITHERTO CONTINU-ALLY COMPARED HIM WITH A YOUNGER NEIGHBOUR WHO WAS A DIRECTOR.

Question 10:   What satisfactions do you derive respectively from work and play and what frustrations do each give rise to? What motivates you in work and play, distinguishing between satisfaction and rewards.

Question 11:   By reading this book, what needs are you aiming to satisfy?

Question 12:   Identify some rewards that motivate you and others that do not and explain why.

2.12   Authority

In communication, an authoritative source has credibility. Authority derives from the legitimate use of power. It can be charismatic, deriving from personality or traditional as with the boards of family companies. Authority in such instances is not necessarily related to competence.

In most organizations, authority derives from rules, procedures and agreements. There are usually checks and balances and even the Chief Executive is at risk if he goes 'too far' and is felt to be acting beyond his brief. The impersonality of such authority is an advantage, but in some cases rules assume an authority of their own and it can be forgotten that they were at some stage the creation of men. Such is the fate of the bureaucratic organization which becomes ossified by its rules.

An innovator or entrepreneur can obtain power and subsequently authority by breaking conventions. Such authority is earned rather than bestowed. On other occasions rules rather than conventions may be broken with less desirable results by those taking short cuts.

People vary in their reaction to authority. Some are more inhibited than others. Some see authority as a challenge, others are reluctant to rock the boat, becoming 'boot lickers' and 'crawlers'. When subject to more than one authority, individuals may feel a conflict between say authority based on knowledge and that based on status.

To get a favourable reaction from others some individuals are compliers. Others, identifiers, emulate and seek to become like that which they highly regard. It is easier for one individual to influence another when both have the same value systems.

The traditional view of authority is that it flows from top to bottom. Today, increasingly, authority is regarded as vested in people rather than roles and hence it could flow upwards. Marketing communications should if possible be directed at those with authority.

Authority is usually taken to imply the existence of a hierarchy and varying degrees of status. Status is a matter of reputation and standing. An individual can have authority but little respect and hence a lower status than position on an organization chart might otherwise imply. Some occupations have a higher status than others. In most societies, doctors have a high status and dustmen a low status.

IN WARTIME THOSE TAKING ON JOINT COMMANDS INVOLVING THE MANAGEMENT OF TROOPS OF SEVERAL NATIONALITIES WERE FREQUENTLY GIVEN ACTING RANKS CONSIDERABLY HIGHER THAN THEIR PREVIOUS RANKS. TROOPS OF VARIOUS COUNTRIES WERE FOUND UNIVERSALLY TO RESPECT RANK.

Question 13: Describe an 'authority system' with which you are familiar, outlining the sources of authority, whether you consider them to be firstly legitimate and secondly 'fair', and why.

2.13 Power

It is usually observed in organizations that some individuals are more powerful than others. Power is frequently defined as the ability to influence the behaviour of others. It is a relationship. It can depend upon context. A trooper may obey the order of a sergeant-major on the parade ground and ignore him during the evening at a social 'do' in town.

Experts can have power as a result of their possession of scarce knowledge. Power can depend upon control of information. Research suggests that power goes to those who control the dominant source of uncertainty or who act to reduce uncertainty. Power then can have a number of sources — rank, control of rewards and punishments, knowledge, station in a workflow, group membership or particular traditions, norms and beliefs.

The effective salesperson seeks to influence those with power. Power is relative; knowledge will not be a source of power if it is felt to be irrelevant in a particular context or if there are alternative individuals available with similar skills. Individuals with more than a certain amount of power may possess just enough of it to resist others who are more powerful.

In some situations a simple willingness to act can be a source of power. If one individual takes a lead, the uncertainty of others can be reduced. Many people first gain power by taking the initiative in situations of confusion and uncertainty.

The ability to do harm, to disrupt, can also be a source of power. The person in the marketing department that carries details of key customers' requirements in his head cannot easily be replaced and has power by virtue of sole possession of vital information.

Power is generated and lost in the course of relationships with others. Power could be said to be the ability to influence outcomes in ways that are favourable to one's interests or to one's perception of one's interests. Expertise, rank and status, control of information, access to political support, sensitivity to the points of view of others and the support of others can all create potential for power. Whether this potential is turned into actual power will depend upon the individual.

Power is influenced by and in turn determines communication within an organization. A 'gate-keeper' may achieve power by hoarding information, so becoming the 'only one who knows'. Increasing communication can lead to a wider sharing of power, reducing the influence of some individuals and enhancing that of others.

The formal structure of an organization as set out, for example, in a chart of responsibilities can be an imperfect guide as to where power lies. One manager may run a 'tight ship' while the commands of another at a similar level may be ignored by his subordinates. Trade union representatives in many organizations are high on the informal power structure.

In the marketing context, the customer that buys a high proportion of an organization's output can have great power. A tied supplier is correspondingly weak. A sole supplier can have the power not to concede special concessions to customers. A customer known to act as a market leader may be able to demand special discounts.

Uses of power can range from co-determination, through co-existence to coercion. Organizations that coerce their employees can alienate them. Involvement and creativity by contrast may be stimulated by spreading power. The more unequal power is, the more scope there is for coercion.

A SMALL GROUP OF RETIRED BUSINESSMEN IN CALIFORNIA INSTEAD OF 'WAITING TO DIE' INITIATED A 'CUT TAXATION' CAMPAIGN WHICH LED TO THE 'PROPOSITION 13' VICTORY WHICH FORCED PUBLIC AUTHORITIES TO SLASH THEIR EXPENDITURES. SIMILAR MOVEMENTS SOON GAINED STRENGTH IN OTHER STATES. THE INITIATORS BECAME INTERNATIONAL PERSONALITIES.

Question 14: What are the main sources of power respectively of the Prime Minister, a Cabinet Minister, an academic, a senior civil servant, a bishop, a trade union general secretary, a managing director, a pop star, and the director general of a trade association?

2.14 Role and Status

The terms role and status can be of value in understanding behaviour within organizations. Status can be considered the esteem accorded to positions in an organization by those within it, while role is what individuals must 'do' to justify their status. The marketor will be particularly interested in the role and status of purchasers.

Some individuals may have a number of roles and experience conflict between them or view a role differently from others. Some people do not have sufficient information to know how to perform their roles. A manager may have task roles that help a group to solve its problems, maintenance roles directed towards helping the group to function effectively and personal roles concerned with satisfying the individual's own needs.

In analysing the roles of individuals within organizations, it is useful to determine the activities and relationships associated with the role, the expectations of the individual and of others, whether these expectations are in conflict, how people adjust to these conflicts and how conformity is achieved. In any organization, there are rewards and sanctions which may or may not be appropriate to roles.

In a marketing organization, there may be a number of centres competing for status. It might depend upon the landing of a really large order, upon the initial design of a winning product, upon diplomatically handling a customer complaint or upon concluding a more favourable royalty or licence arrangement. An organization can be restructured or its objectives changed to shift the location of authority, power and status. The status implication of changes may need to be considered before they are made.

> IN THE UNITED KINGDOM PEOPLE IN POSITIONS OF POWER OR RESPONSIBILITY EAGERLY AWAIT LETTERS INFORMING THEM THEY HAVE BEEN AWARDED AN HONOUR. BEING THE LORD MAYOR OF LONDON FOR A YEAR INVOLVES THE PERSONAL EXPENDITURE OF TENS OF THOUSANDS OF POUNDS.

Question 15:   What role and status as an individual do you possess, what are their sources, how are they constrained and how might they be increased?

2.2 VALUES

Effective communicators are receptive to changing values. Traditional management values are under challenge. The young in particular tend to be more concerned with quality than quantity, opposed to uniformity and rigidity and interested in participation and self-fulfilment and decentralized organizations.

A contrast is emerging between old and new values, traditional and modern executive styles. The traditional executive style is closed, rigid and authoritarian, is concerned with absolutes, believes in roles and puts emphasis upon uniformity. The modern approach is more open, flexible and participative, admits relativity, believes in people and their individuality and emphasizes variations and tolerates differences.

Employers and employees can have quite distinct beliefs and values. An employer can become obsessed with the right to manage, the employee with the right to work, to be consulted over changes in working methods and conditions and the right to object to these. In the informal structure of an organization, there can be conflict about who actually owns a job: the company, or the particular trade union within whose territory it falls. The employer is likely to be concerned with individualism, the assessment of individual performance, while the union will stress collectivism, the need for solidarity. People within an organization can experience conflict between their loyalties to their employer and to their colleagues in the workforce.

Values can change. Groups of people can suddenly become interested in quality rather than quantity, a tailored rather than a uniform product, participation rather than apathy. Individuals can mature, accepting that people can have differing views of the world and reconciling themselves to the co-existence of different value systems.

One classic case of the conflict of values is the clash of production and marketing attitudes within an organization. Should marketing exist to sell what is produced or should production exist to supply whatever marketing identifies as a market need? Both marketing and production may be jealous of their own and each others' territory. Who, for example, should be concerned with the design of new products?

IN THE UNITED KINGDOM THE LABOUR PARTY IN OPPOSITION GENERALLY FACES THE PROSPECT OF BEING PULLED APART BY THE OPPOSING FORCES OF ITS 'LEFT' WING AND ITS 'RIGHT OF CENTRE SOCIAL DEMOCRATIC' WING. CONSIDERABLE SKILL IS REQUIRED TO HOLD THE TWO FACTIONS, WITH THEIR VERY DIFFERING VIEWS ON POLICY AND THE 'GOOD SOCIETY', TOGETHER. THE EMERGENCE OF THE SOCIAL DEMOCRATIC PARTY ILLUSTRATES HOW DIFFICULT IT CAN BE TO BUILD A CONSENSUS.

Individuals' views of the world reveal a great deal about them, the people and the organizations with which they are likely to be compatible. Viewing the world as a competitive 'dog-eat-dog' jungle, a war of all against all, in which one exploits or is exploited, is unlikely to be compatible with working within a people-centred, task-oriented culture. Those who stress order and rationality, the importance of authority and also the need for 'give and take' may be ideally suited for work within a more formal and functional organization.

While some see the world as a 'given', a set of rules to be obeyed, others see it as a complex balance struck between shifting forces and interests. Organizations can be viewed as temporary structures, a collection of loose arrangements which will need to be refined or changed to suit the demands of developing situations.

2.21 Values and Social Science

The social sciences have yielded many useful insights into how the values of different groups of the community vary. These insights are of potential benefit to the marketor. Theory can lead to more perceptive and adaptive marketing practice.

Sociology has provided marketors with useful insights into how social class is perceived, and into behaviour within families. It may be important to know that those who patronize lounge bars are different from those who drink in public bars and that while one is popular in the southern suburb the other is preferred in the northern industrial town. It is also important to know that wives are the major influencers of the purchase of certain goods.

Demographic information can be crucial in market forecasting. The fact that a population is ageing can lead to the change of a brand image and the introduction of new products. The spread of suburbs may raise the question of new marketing outlets and the rationalization of sales points in regions experiencing longrun industrial decline. Within a depressed area, points of growth might exist, perhaps a new town, offering a local market which might be profitably exploited for the first time.

Economic theory has produced some valuable insights into such questions as the tradeoff between income and leisure time, the substitution of one product for another as prices change, the potential for price discrimination assuming that it is not outlawed, and how spending is related to income. There is some evidence for example that when income fluctuates, consumers may spend to maintain a standard of living in the short term, drawing from savings if necessary, and will in the longer term adjust spending to expectations concerning long run income rather than maintain a fixed proportion of spending to income.

Game theory has allowed some understanding of competitive behaviour in oligopoly and particularly duopoly situations. Risk analysis suggests how uncertainty can be handled. The marketor lives in a world of values, within and without the organization, and must be aware of them and how they are changing.

Question 16:   Set out the predominant values of an organization with which you are familiar, separately identifying those which have influenced your own values and those with which you do not agree, in each case explaining why.

Question 17:   Explain how the values of a group with whom you are currently in contact might be of interest to the marketor.

2.22   Culture

There is a cultural dimension to communication. Different societies and groups within societies can have distinct beliefs, attributes, attitudes and behaviour that are shared by the members of the group and transmitted from one generation to another. Cultures change as generations modify what is handed on. People speak of a western culture, a materialist culture or of a certain ethnic culture.

Socialization is the process by which those joining a group steadily absorb group values and adopt group patterns of behaviour as a result of becoming what is regarded as desirable within the group.

Salesmen are viewed in some quarters as forming a distinct culture whose life revolves around fast talk, expense accounts, bright shirts, suitcases of samples and the price of petrol.

Consumption patterns can be profoundly influenced by cultural background. Fortunes have been made tailoring products to a cultural niche that has been overlooked by others. In export marketing, one has to be particularly aware of cultural differences. Lipstick cannot be mass marketed in Saudi Arabia.

Certain values may be associated with particular cultures: respect for age and tradition, desire for change, leisure or security, extravagance or sociability. A begging monk can have high status in one society, a highly-paid jet-setting executive can enjoy great status in another.

Cultural changes can have profound marketing implications. Consider women's liberation, equal pay legislation and the double income of the dual career family.

The young, ethnic and religious minorities form subcultures that can be major markets. The record, convenience food and clothing industries are heavily dependent upon the expenditure of the young. Social classes can be viewed in subculture terms.

IRAN, A COUNTRY WHICH WAS PURSUING AN AMBITIOUS WESTERN INDUSTRIAL DEVELOPMENT PATH UNDER THE SHAH, WAS TORN APART BY AN ISLAMIC REVOLUTION WHICH SWEPT ASIDE THE 'DECADENT' WESTERN WAYS AND INTRODUCED ASPECTS OF MUSLIM CULTURE. ISLAM, RIDING ON AN OIL BASE, IS EXPERIENCING A CONSIDERABLE CULTURAL RESURGENCE.

2.3 LEADERSHIP

Where individuals are free to leave organizations and tasks are done by consent, following discussion and negotiation, the location, definition and exercise of leadership or the giving of a lead becomes difficult. Arguably, in a perfect democracy there are no leaders but few organizations are democratic to this degree. In most organizations there will be a boss, a 'governor', a top man or leader. This leader may become the target of particular marketing effort.

The qualities required by an effective leader in the abstract are open to dispute though there is agreement that these qualities will vary according to the context. The qualities that are highly regarded in war may become a handicap in times of peace. Many American servicemen much decorated by their country for their war service in Vietnam have experienced great problems in — and some have not been successful in adjusting to — civilian life.

Leadership can derive from the will to dominate, an ability to be liked or to inspire confidence, or the gift of being able to persuade. Arrogance, a raging 'ego', 'smooth' operations or a plausible manner can lead to the assumption of a leadership position, but further qualities are generally required to sustain such a position.

Leaders may not be a race apart. Perhaps there are leadership qualities in most managers just as there is supposed to be a field marshall's baton in the knapsack of every private soldier. Possibly situations create leaders or just apathy, the alternatives voluntarily dropping out.

Leadership may be seized in one situation and relinquished in another. The 'driving force' at work may take a back seat in leisure activities. Some have a thirst for leadership and fight to retain it while others are only too happy to give it up.

A group may select a leader who is known to be pliable. A 'caretaker' leader may be appointed to fill a gap or as a figurehead. There will in such circumstances be a distinction between the formal 'leader' with authority and the actual seat of power exercising a leadership role.

Leadership is often dependent upon its acceptance. Leadership which does not have consent, which is not regarded as legitimate, can be overthrown. A common objective, a shared task or an external threat can build the consent necessary for the exercise of strong leadership.

A leader needs to be fully aware of the expectations of those who have granted the leadership role. Sometimes one must lead from behind and be wary of over-stepping the mark. What has been given may be taken away.

Survival as a leader in most business organizations depends upon being both liked and acceptable, being perceived as having skills and qualities highly relevant to the task in hand or to important aspects of it, and the possession of power. These 'sources' of leadership can change over time. As a business moves into further markets, new leaders will emerge whose qualities are more in tune with the needs of the moment. Those who are adaptable tend to stay on top the longest.

> A PROMINENT HEAD OF A REPRESENTATIVE BODY WITH CON-
> SIDERABLE GIFTS AS A COMMUNICATOR LOST HIS POSITION. HE
> HAD REFUSED TO DELEGATE ASPECTS OF THE ADMINISTRATIVE
> FUNCTION WHICH HE HAD FOUND TIRESOME IN ORDER TO CON-
> CENTRATE UPON THAT WHICH HE DID BEST, COMMUNICATING.

Question 18:   Describe the leadership qualities of someone you have met who is in a position of authority. How did the person concerned come to occupy a leadership role and what challenges to the leadership position did the person face?

2.4   JOB SATISFACTION

Job satisfaction can be measured indirectly by summarizing staff turnover, strike days and absentee rates, and directly by questionnaire and interview to uncover the otherwise hidden personal and social benefits of work. The factors that influence satisfaction include whether or not one works with others, one's colleagues, how many people one reports to, past experience, the nature of the work and of the workplace, the mix of duties and the recruitment and training programmes.

Studies of work situations suggest that human factors tend to be more important than physical ones. Generally, the most satisfied staff are found in locations where the organization is appropriate to the activities concerned.

Evidence suggests that intrinsic motivation such as self-development and fulfilment can contribute more to job performance than extrinsic motivation such as pay. The intrinsic rewards are the more personal. While a lack of extrinsic reward such as low pay can lead to dissatisfaction beyond a sufficiency, the extrinsic reward may do little to further increase satisfaction.

Marketing staff need to be motivated. Intrinsic motivation can be increased by building greater variety and discretion into a job. Employees could be allowed more freedom to decide how they will tackle a particular job and what skills and knowledge they will need to bring to bear. People tend to be more motivated when they are able to see how and the extent to which they are contributing to the whole, to the final product. The clearer the goal the better is performance. A job that is too easy or too difficult can reduce motivation.

Extrinsic motivation tends to be most suitable where work is routine and repetitive and the environment is stable. Conversely, where the environment is changing the encouragement of involvement and creativity will require intrinsic motivation.

A marketing department could be consciously redesigned to increase job satisfaction by means of job enrichment. This can be achieved by enlarging jobs horizontally to encompass a greater number of tasks or vertically to give greater responsibility. Too many job enrichment programmes are negative in that they aim to reduce boredom rather than positively set out to promote satisfaction.

IN A PLANT MANUFACTURING BREAKFAST CEREALS THE OPERATOR OF ONE OF THE MACHINES GENERALLY GOT DRUNK AT ABOUT FOUR O'CLOCK IN THE AFTERNOON. THE MAJOR BREAK OF EACH DAY FOR THE OPERATORS BECAME THE TEN-MINUTE RITUAL OF RUSHING IN TO WATCH 'GIANT FLAKES' COMING OFF THE MACHINE AS THE DRUNKEN OPERATOR FELL ASLEEP. SWEEPSTAKES WERE HELD ON EXACTLY WHEN TO THE MINUTE THIS WAS LIKELY TO OCCUR. LITTLE ELSE OF INTEREST HAPPENED IN THE FACTORY FROM ONE DAY TO THE NEXT.

Satisfactory jobs tend to be those that are reasonably demanding, offer a fair degree of variety, give scope for personal development, involve the taking of decisions, provide social support and recognition, relate to non-work interests and have desirable prospects. People like to communicate with others and to have some means of identifying and measuring tangible results. In general, satisfaction increases as more discretion is given and as aspects of work which are automatically prescribed are reduced.

Question 19:   Outline the ways in which your major current activity could be made more satisfying from your point of view. What prevents such changes from taking place and what obstacles would lie in the way of their implementation?

2.41   Stress

Stress can have many causes. A frequent one is a fluctuating workload, what is termed the overload, underload situation. This can lead to changing patterns of interaction between staff, and for individuals peptic ulcers, coronary thrombosis and reduced performance. Stress can also be the result of an ambiguous role or from a conflict of roles. Two individuals may overlap due to ill-defined boundaries.

When a group has advance warning of an increase in workload then duties can be redefined to cope with it. Prior experience of dealing with a suddenly-increased workload and the support of other members of a group can cushion an individual from stress. An introvert can withdraw further in a stress situation while an extrovert might become more aggressive and even thrive on pressure.

At management level, stress can lead to concentration upon a narrower area and the short term. Ambiguity becomes irritating. Under pressure, people are more likely to take up extreme positions. Rumours can spread in a tense situation: tempers can fray and some may act impulsively.

Question 20:   What is the most significant source of stress in your major current activity?

2.5   GROUPS

Collections of individuals that interact with one another in relation to a particular belief, activity, event or objective constitute groups. There are many forms of group and most individuals will belong to a number of these. The behaviour of individuals is modified by the groups to which they belong.

The family is a natural group, a historical society, a voluntary group. A group can be ongoing or set up for a particular purpose. Entry to a group can be open or closed. Groups vary in terms of the demands they place upon their members.

Important groups such as close friends, family and one's work group are sometimes called primary groups and other less-important voluntary groups, secondary groups.

Individuals who are highly dependent upon group membership tend to observe group standards rather more than those which are less dependent. Some rules of a group may be binding; a group may have the power to discipline its members.

Groups then can be formal or informal. Groups that individuals closely identify with are reference groups. Reference groups can strongly influence the behaviour of those within them. Group goals can quickly become personal goals. Individuals come to evaluate themselves according to the group's standards.

Reference groups can condition buying behaviour and levels of aspiration. Put two individuals into an identical situation and one can be frustrated while the other is satisfied, where the former's reference group is more successful.

Groups can be very useful for generating ideas and spreading information, obtaining commitment and securing acceptance and tackling open-ended problems. They are less effective when quick decisions must be taken and options compared. Problems can arise when personalities are in conflict when co-operation is required. Groups are sometimes unwilling to accept other points of view and may become incapable of dealing with change when too high a value is placed upon order and stability.

THERE WAS LITTLE INTERACTION BETWEEN MEMBERS OF A GROUP OF STUDENTS UNTIL ONE DAY A NOTICE APPEARED ON THE COLLEGE BULLETIN BOARD INFORMING THEM THAT ALL COURSE WORK FOR THE TERM HAD TO BE HANDED IN TWO WEEKS EARLIER THAN EXPECTED. FEW OF THE STUDENTS WERE IN A POSITION TO MEET THE NEW DEADLINE. THEY GOT TOGETHER AND ORGANIZED A PROTEST WHICH THEY CARRIED TO THE PRINCIPAL.

2.51 Group Behaviour

One cannot fully understand behaviour and communication in organizations without comprehending how groups operate. Groups are collections of individuals who are aware of each other, interact, share certain common values and who perceive of themselves as a group. Groups are therefore different from football crowds or bus queues.

Some groups have their origin in physical proximity, others in a shared task or function. Once established, groups tend to be held together by some task. Its extent will be limited by the task and social links.

Most people in organizations will belong to a number of groups. Such groups could include office groups, supervisory groups, project groups, professional groups, sports groups, and interest groups. Not all these groups will limit their membership to employees, and a number of them may not appear on a formal organization chart. Nevertheless, ignoring them would result in an incomplete picture being obtained of how many organizations work.

The activities of groups can be divided into task functions which are concerned with getting work done and maintenance functions which are concerned with keeping the group together. Groups pass through a series of stages as members learn what they have to do and determine how the group is to operate, exchange views, develop methods of working together and perform their tasks.

Groups have functions beyond getting the work done. Their social functions include providing emotional support and security, identity and affiliation. A group can be more resilient than an individual and can be very effective in reducing individual differences.

The more important the task facing a group, the less likely it is that it will tolerate deviant behaviour. Cohesiveness tends to vary in proportion to inter-action and outside pressure.

The behaviour of individuals is particularly influenced by the various reference groups to which they belong. Within these, opinion leaders are of particular importance. Opinion leaders are those whose opinions carry weight in the sense that others follow their lead, perhaps giving great weight to their advice.

In communications terms, an opinion leader can be a very credible source. When proposing changes in organizations it is often important to sound out in advance the view of opinion formers.

AT A SALES CONVENTION ONE SALESMAN CONTINUALLY SAT AND ATE ALONE AND SPOKE CONSTANTLY IN PLENARY SESSIONS POSING MANY ARROGANT QUESTIONS TO GUEST SPEAKERS. ON ONE OCCASION HE WAS 'SHOT DOWN IN FLAMES' BY A SPEAKER. THEREAFTER HE APPEARED FOR THE FIRST TIME AT 'GROUP SESSIONS' AND BEGAN TO PARTICIPATE AND SEEK THE OPINIONS AND ADVICE OF OTHERS.

Question 21:   List the groups to which you currently belong and the task and maintenance functions you perform in respect of each group.

2.52   Individuals and Groups

Individuals can be categorized according to their approach to problems. The least adaptive assume there is only one right answer for a given problem. The more flexible acknowledge the existence of alternatives but may still believe in a 'best answer'. Still more flexible individuals are prepared to take each case coming up on its own merits and to accept personal responsibility for developing a solution.

The most flexible individuals have their own values and points of view but recognise that others may differ. Such people can accept conflict and contradiction and are prepared to look at the world in different ways according to the context and opportunity.

The more flexible an individual the more likely is a degree of independence, self-control and individual responsibility. Individuals who believe there is only one right answer to any problem are likely to be dependent upon others and to be controlled and have their tasks carefully defined for them.

The differences between individuals have implications for group structure and performance. Too often groups put so much effort into achieving objectives, performing tasks, that they fail to keep an eye on their own internal workings, how individuals are interacting and communicating within them.

A CHILD AT SCHOOL WHO HAD NOT SPOKEN FOR TWO YEARS AND WAS LARGELY SHUNNED BY FELLOW PUPILS CAME 'OUT OF HIS SHELL' AT THE SCHOOL'S ANNUAL CAMP. THE CHILD WAS THE ONLY ONE WHO COULD PADDLE A CANOE. AN ADVENTURE TRAINING EXERCISE CARRIED OUT IN COMPETITION WITH ANOTHER SCHOOL CULMINATED IN THE REQUIREMENT THAT A MESSAGE BE CARRIED BY CANOE ACROSS A WIDE RIVER. THE CHILD BECAME A TEAM LEADER ON THE THIRD DAY.

Question 22: Give a frank assessment of your strengths and weaknesses as an employee. How far do you expect to progress and why?

Question 23: List the pressures to which you have been subjected as a consequence of the membership of a group and your responses to these pressures, examining the implications of these responses for yourself and for the organization.

2.53 Selecting Group Members

How does a marketing manager assess the competence of specialist subordinates? Track record is one approach. Other approaches are a preference for objectivity and openness, putting a high value upon the ability to see more than one side to an argument provided this is not evidence of indecisiveness.

A manager may prefer those with similar backgrounds or those with like experience. Personal empathy is frequently important — but should it be? Just because one gets on well with a person, it does not follow that the quality of that person's advice will be high.

An individual who adopts a 'nine-to-five' approach to work can slow the efforts of a group and act as a focus of discord. Compatibility is the prime requirement of group membership. It takes time to adjust to the peculiar workings of a group. New members should be able to adapt before the work of the group is complete.

Bringing in staff from outside to fill responsible positions can cause resentment among existing staff. The clerical worker may be leap-frogged by the marketing graduate or marketing diplomate who, while lacking in experience initially compared with a long-serving clerk, may be perceived as having a greater ability to learn and as having more promising long-term prospects.

Recruitment policies need to be geared not only to the filling of immediate positions but to ensuring a steady progression of staff through the organization. There may need to be good people in the pipeline who can be groomed to fill the highest post eventually.

To achieve compatibility the potential recruit could be exposed to existing group members. In some consulting firms existing consultants on teams have the power of veto on new entrants. Groups can be allowed to select their own members. If compatibility is not achieved the group then has only itself to blame.

THE DIRECTOR OF A MASTERS COURSE IN BUSINESS ADMINI-STRATION BECAME BORED WITH HIS STUDENTS. THEY WERE ALL AMBITIOUS AND RUTHLESS, ACADEMIC 'HIGH FLYERS' AND HAD BEEN SELECTED BECAUSE THEY WERE LIKELY TO DO WELL IN THE WORLD. THE REPUTATION OF THE BUSINESS SCHOOL DEPENDED UPON THE WORK PERFORMANCE OF ITS ALUMNI. THE DIRECTOR DECIDED TO CHANGE THE ENTRANCE CRITERIA AND TO SELECT IN FUTURE ON THE BASIS OF WHO WAS LIKELY TO GAIN MOST FROM THE COURSE. A MUCH MORE VARIED INTAKE RESULTED AND THE STUDENTS WERE ABLE TO LEARN A MUCH GREATER AMOUNT FROM EACH OTHER.

Question 24:   Establish criteria for the membership of a group with which you are familiar and explain why the characteristics you list are desirable.

2.54   Group Dynamics

Industrial goods are often effectively bought by groups, rather than individuals. The industrial goods marketor needs to understand group dynamics. A group will be held together by bonds. Some staff may work out of economic necessity or because of loyalty or a belief that a contractual obligation should be discharged. The desire for excellence in work or the achievement of a goal or enjoyment of work and the companionship of others can lead to dedication to the task in hand.

Group members may co-operate just because they have been told to do so. Staff may feel that sinking differences is in their own best interests. A formal system may specify group membership and how it is to be organized.

The demands of achieving an objective can force co-operation. Working together in a team can itself be a source of satisfaction. Joint effort can appear stimulating and challenging.

The group bonds may have to overcome competition for power and economic advantage, status, excellence of work, extent of contribution and individual learning. The group may consider its terms of reference to be too narrow and restrictive. Opinion may differ over how best to work internally and over 'lines' that should be adopted vis-a-vis other groups. Disputes could be settled by the intervention of a higher power, recourse to rules or precedents, by discussion, negotiation or bargaining.

Decisions in a group may emerge from consensus. The group may defer to a member who will be most affected by an outcome or who has the greatest relevant knowledge and experience. A group may leave decisions to those whose job description it is to take them. Subordinates may defer to those with higher status. Weaker staff may be reluctant to challenge those with power and authority.

Information within a group could flow from top to bottom along informal and formal chains of command. A two-way flow could be built into the system or allowed to arise spontaneously.

Information could be restricted to those closest to and responsible for the task concerned. It may originate from the centre of activity outwards rather than from authority to the point of work. In an informal system a group could consist of a myriad of voluntary relationships, entered into for mutual advantage, development and enjoyment.

Most groups will need to develop relationships with other groups. When very different categories of staff need to interact, individuals acting as 'integrators' may be needed to 'build bridges'. The integrator will need to be acceptable and credible to both groups and possessed of the necessary interpersonal skills.

The integrator role is an exposed one and integrators need to be tough. When things go wrong, the person 'in the middle' can become a scapegoat. Both groups can blame the intermediary for the failure of relations between them to develop satisfactorily.

A MANAGER WHO HAD BEEN STRUGGLING WITH AN INDUSTRIAL DISPUTE FOR WEEKS GOT FED UP WITH SPENDING HOURS EACH DAY MAKING FRANTIC TELEPHONE CALLS FROM HIS OFFICE. HE HAD RECEIVED VERY CONFLICTING REPORTS ABOUT WHAT WAS HAPPENING AT THE DEPOT AFFECTED BY THE DISPUTE. HE DECIDED TO GO DOWN IN PERSON AND 'TAKE A LOOK'. HE MET THE PARTIES INVOLVED FACE TO FACE. THE DISPUTE WAS RESOLVED WITHIN A MATTER OF HOURS.

Question 25: What are the forces holding together and tending to pull apart a group with which you are familiar? How can the former be encouraged and the latter controlled?

2.55 Group Tensions

A certain amount of tension is inevitable in any group situation. Holding a group together is the common desire to complete a task. Where skills within the group are complementary there may be mutual recognition that the whole group will sink or swim together.

Against the forces holding a group together there will usually be other forces that tend to pull it apart. There might be a struggle for the leadership of the group. Where duties and roles are ill-defined there might be confusion and the attempts of group members to encroach upon each others' territories. Within a group alliances can form and change. When membership of a group changes old tensions may ease while new sources of tensions are created.

In most situations staff exhibit a tendency to watch each other. The amount of work one person does or does not do will be assessed by others. A member of a group who is seen as a 'passenger' can be a source of dissatisfaction. A person who overworks may be admired, thought to be exploited or regarded as a fool.

Within a marketing department certain markets can attract a reputation for being interesting and others for being dull or hard work. Servicing one market may involve travel to exotic locations and meeting fashionable people while another market may be serviced from a backstreet office and involve little variety. Marketing staff are likely to watch who gets the 'plum' appointments.

Allocating marketing responsibilities can give rise to many resentments. One manager may be perceived as having greater experience or superior qualifications to another in the eyes of fellow managers, but this view may not be shared by a marketing director. Subordinates may feel that age should be an important criterion in a promotion decision, a superior may not.

A MANAGER IN A DEPARTMENT ALLOCATED EXTRA DUTIES RECEIVED A SALARY INCREASE. IMMEDIATELY SHE WAS SHUNNED BY HER COLLEAGUES WHO BEGAN TO GOSSIP TO 'SUPERIORS' ABOUT THE QUALITY OF HER WORK. THE RESULTING JEALOUSY-INDUCED TENSION WAS ONLY RESOLVED BY ACROSS THE BOARD SALARY INCREASES WHICH INCLUDED MANY WHOSE DUTIES HAD NOT CHANGED IN ANY WAY.

Question 26: Outline the major sources of tension in a group with which you are familiar. How does the tension manifest itself, is it perceived by group leaders and what is and could be done to relieve the tension?

A marketor may have to manage a group with very different backgrounds from his or her own. The marketing manager promoted from the sales function could, for example, have particular problems understanding the mentality of office-bound clerical staff. Their values may be very different from those of the free-wheeling expense account salesman and those of the production worker.

AT A COLD STORAGE DEPOT THE CANTEEN HAD A WHITE LINE PAINTED DOWN THE CENTRE OF IT SEPARATING THE TABLES 'RESERVED' FOR CLERICAL WORKERS FROM THOSE 'ALLOCATED' TO THE 'MEN' WORKING IN THE STORE ITSELF. BOTH GROUPS QUEUED TOGETHER TO RECEIVE IDENTICAL SELF-SERVICE CATERING FOOD. NO-ONE EVER 'CROSSED' THE LINE AND ATE IN THE 'WRONG' PART OF THE ROOM. THE STORE WORKERS RECEIVED SUBSTANTIALLY HIGHER SALARIES THAN THE CLERKS.

EXAMINATION QUESTIONS

1. 'Man has two different sets of needs' says Herzberg. Out of that seemingly simple observation has come a new insight into the nature of work motivation. Discuss.

2. What rewards, in addition to a salary, can people obtain from working in organizations and what contribution can the opportunity to gain these added satisfactions make to the achievement of the overall objectives of the organization?

3. What do you consider is the most likely cause of employee alienation in a modern business? Is the minimization of alienation compatible with conventional ideas of profit and productivity?

4. In what ways do you understand the concept of the manager as a leader is relevant to staff motivation?

5. Managerial authority and its acceptance by subordinates are both undergoing profound changes. Describe these changes and discuss the particular implications for the sales manager.

6. 'In business, from the factory floor to the boardroom, decision-making by consent is replacing traditional autocracy'. Discuss.

7. 'The more people a business employs the worse and more frequent the industrial disputes, or the higher the absenteeism, including obviously bogus sickness, becomes.' Comment on this statement and say whether in the light of recent experience in western industrialized nations there are any lessons to be learned about the size of working groups.

8. When recruiting staff, companies may not appoint candidates with the best qualifications or 'track records'. Why?

3. *Organization and Communication*

Marketing communication involves communication with groups within and between organizations. Man is a social animal and works together with others in groups in order to perform all but the most basic tasks. Inevitably we all belong to organizations of one form or another. Marketing personnel are no exception. A few may operate alone, perhaps selling a personal service, but the rest of us are employed within organizations.

3.1 ORGANIZATIONS

No two organizations are alike. Organizations vary in size, structure and purpose. Some are successful, others are not. Some organizations are more accountable than others. Organizations can have very differing membership criteria. Membership may be voluntary or compulsory. Organizations can strongly influence the behaviour of those working within them. Sometimes the reverse is the case. Individuals and organizations inter-react.

Most organizations are managed. They have a purpose. People within them are expected to perform and perhaps to conform. This involves organization and communication.

Where an organization is located is important. The context matters. Countries and regions differ. One industry may be subject to a higher degree of regulation than another. Organizational freedom varies. The immediate environment may be hostile or competitive. Most organizations, when they decide how they intend to act, must take other organizations into account.

An organization may ·appear to have a life of its own. Its goals may be other than appears at first sight. Some purposes may be perceived as more legitimate than others. The goals may or may not be realistic or understood. Not all within the organization may agree with them.

The structure of an organization may or may not be appropriate to what it is trying to achieve. Structure should be related to the function of an organization,

34

its purposes and to the needs of those who work within it. Structures are not always immediately apparent. The organization chart may conceal a host of informal arrangements. What ought to happen is not always what happens in practice.

It is sometimes difficult to change the structure of an organization. No one form of organization is best. It all depends upon what is being done. Certain structures, however, tend to be preferable from the point of view of those working within them. Bureaucracy has become a value-laden term. 'Red tape' is synonymous with inefficiency. 'Bureaucratic power' is regarded as unjust. Organizations can and sometimes do make unfair demands upon their members.

Organizations then exist in many forms and behave in different ways. Organization provides the structural vehicle for communication within companies. Human behaviour affects and is in turn affected by organization and communication and the relationship between organization structure, operating effectiveness, and communication.

3.2 BEHAVIOUR IN ORGANIZATIONS

A great deal is now known about human behaviour as a result of work that has been done in the fields of psychology, sociology, and physiology. The behavioural sciences are quite well-developed. The literature is extensive. This chapter will concentrate upon concepts of special relevance to organizations and communication within them.

3.21 Management Thought

There is a growing management literature devoted to the behaviour of individuals in organizations. Since the end of the second world war the individual's attitude to work has become a key concern of behavioural scientists.

Rensis Likert drew a distinction in the late 1940's between organizations that were production-centred, tightly controlling and supervising their employees in the interest of output, and those that were employee-centred, taking account of the interests of staff and in particular their need to inter-relate at the point of work, achieving performance through satisfaction rather than coercion.

Douglas McGregor related these approaches of organizations to attitudes about people. The 'Theory X' view of people saw man as naturally disliking work which hence only gets done where people are coerced and controlled, most people the view assuming are lacking in ambition and disliking responsibility, and hence preferring to be directed. The contrary or 'Theory Y' view regarded work as a natural activity to which people direct themselves in order to achieve objectives, commitment stemming from the rewards of achievement. The view assumes people to have latent imagination and creativity and an inherent desire for responsibility and advancement which, while frustrated by much of industrial life, could be released.

Chris Argyris found that workers in plants found detailed supervision oppressive and developed 'defence mechanisms' against it such as apathy, ambivalence or even aggression. These mechanisms can put strain upon individuals and organizations.

Tom Burns divided organizations into mechanistic (rigid, authoritative, hierarchical) and organismic (flexible, evolving) types, which mirrors Douglas McGregor's theory X and theory Y dichotomy. Joan Woodward greatly extended our understanding of organizations by relating their structures to the work they do. Different types of organization were found to be appropriate to different types of work. Satisfaction tended to be high when organization structure was appropriate to task.

The crucial question of motivation was tackled by Abraham Maslow who saw people as possessing a hierarchy of needs ranging from the basic needs such as food, sex, and shelter, through security and safety to recognition and self-respect, and ultimately self-realization. The earlier, more basic needs must be satisfied before an individual can progress to satisfying the 'higher' needs, the inference being that the extent to which individuals satisfy their 'higher' needs for self-respect and self-realization depends in part upon themselves but largely upon the design of organizations. To be effective organizations must take account of 'higher' needs.

Frederick Hertzberg examining the organization of work drew a distinction between two categories of motivation satisfiers (achievement, recognition, responsibility, promotion) and hygiene factors (pay, working conditions, perks, type of supervision). Hygiene factors were often largely the reasons for deciding whether or not to join or leave organizations while on-the-job performance was regarded by Hertzberg as largely dependent upon the presence of satisfiers.

The absence of satisfiers can lead to alienation. Robert Blauner found assembly-line working as much more likely than craft working to lead to alienation. William Whyte chronicled the alienation felt by the middle manager as a result of the pressures upon him to conform. J. A. C. Brown found that in practice the oppressiveness of formal organizational systems is often relieved by informal networks and contacts.

At Glacier Metal, Elliott Jacques and Wilfred Brown examined group behaviour at the point of work and found motivation to be high where reward was seen as related to the length of time that elapses between discretion being exercised and its success or failure being able to be determined. 'Fair' systems of remuneration were those felt by employees to be fair.

3.211   Further Reading

Argyris, Chris, *Understanding Organizational Behaviour*, Dorsey (1960).
Integrating the Individual and the Organization, Wiley (1964).
Intervention Theory and Method, Addison-Wesley (1970).

The Impact of Budgets on People, Controllership Foundation (1952).
Personality and Organization, Chapman and Hall (1948).
Personality and Organization: The Conflict Between System and Individual, Harper and Row (1957).

Blauner, Robert, *Alienation and Freedom: The Factory Worker and His Industry*, University of Chicago Press (1964).

Brown, Wilfred, *Organization*, Heinemann (1971).
Exploration in Management, Heinemann (1960).

Brown, J. A. C., *The Social Psychology of Industry: Human Relations in the Factory*, Penguin (1970).

Burns, Tom (with Stalker, G. M.), *The Management of Innovation*, Tavistock (1966), (in J. R. Lawrence (Ed.)).
Operational Research and the Social Sciences, Tavistock (1966).

Hertzberg, Frederick, *Work and the Nature of Man*, World Publishing Company (1966).

Jacques, Elliott, *Equitable Payment*, Wiley and Heinemann (1961).

Likert, Rensis, *New Patterns of Management*, McGraw-Hill (1961).
The Human Organization: Its Management and Value, McGraw-Hill (1967).

Maslow, Abraham H., *Motivation and Personality*, Harper and Row (1954).

McGregor, Douglas, *The Human Side of Enterprise*, McGraw-Hill (1954).
The Professional Manager, McGraw-Hill (1967).

Whyte, William H., *The Organization Man*, Cape (1957), Simon and Schuster (1956).

Woodward, Joan, *Industrial Organization*, Oxford University Press (1965).
(Ed.) *Industrial Organization: Behaviour and Control*, Oxford University Press (1970).
Management and Technology, HMSO (1958).

3.22 People in Organizations

Individuals and organizations modify each other's behaviour. Organizations select particular types of individual and vice versa. Some organizations seek to mould those within them. Some forms of human behaviour are relatively immune to the particular structures of individual organizations. Conflicts occur when individuals and organizations have differing objections. Groups of individuals come together and fragment. Some may combine and create organizations within organizations to represent their interests.

Many people have strong views of what is 'fair', 'just', or 'right'. Organizations face moral problems. There may be conflicts of values to be reconciled. These may be related to or independent of the work the organization does.

Conflict can arise over whether membership of an organization is regarded as permanent or temporary. The professional who is highly mobile between organizations may find it difficult to understand the viewpoint of the shop steward who is interested in 'protecting' jobs. The shop-floor worker may regard a job as a 'life'.

Why should one person control another? In what circumstances is an order or command legitimate? Staff obey others for a variety of reasons – position in the staff hierarchy, perception of mutual roles, bowing to superior knowledge or experience or to experience and skills that are more relevant to the task in hand. Acceptance of an order can also result from perceived self-interest. A member of staff may feel it politic or financially prudent to obey or may see compliance as contributing to individual development.

A crucial factor to bear in mind so far as people within organizations are concerned is that the capabilities of people can vary according to their workload. Heavy puressure of work can drive out long-term planning and force concentration upon the immediate. Immersed in a mass of detail, it is easy to lose track of the 'broader brush' picture. One ends up not being able to see the wood for the trees. Many people find a fluctuating workload particularly destructive. Peaks and troughs can lead to stress overload and stress underload situations. It is not always possible to spread workloads, and the capability of people to handle varying workloads must be taken into account in selection decisions.

EDITING WORK INVOLVES MEETING HEAVY PROOF READING PEAKS IN WORKLOAD. ONE EDITOR, WHILE CONCENTRATING UPON REDRAFTING ARTICLES MANY TIMES TO ACHIEVE PERFECTION, FREQUENTLY ALLOWED THE PRODUCTION SCHEDULE OF HER JOURNAL TO SLIP, WITH THE RESULT THAT IT FREQUENTLY CAME OUT LATE. CONCENTRATION UPON DAY-TO-DAY DETAIL TO IMPROVE THE QUALITY OF CONTENT CAUSED HER TO LOSE SIGHT OF THE OVERRIDING OBJECTIVE OF PUBLISHING ON TIME.

Personality clashes can prevent key people from getting together and can neutralize talent.

A TECHNICALLY HIGHLY-QUALIFIED FILM CREW RAN HEAVILY OVER BUDGET AND ULTIMATELY FAILED TO RETURN WITH SUFFICIENT FOOTAGE TO MAKE A FILM, DUE TO THE DIRECTOR AND CAMERAMAN CONTINUALLY ARGUING ON LOCATION ABOUT

WHETHER OR NOT THE DIRECTOR SHOULD LINE UP AND COMPOSE EACH SHOT.

Good news is generally preferable to bad news. Many managers identify strengths more readily than weaknesses. Defects, errors, and mistakes tend to be unsettling. They are often hidden, concealed, perhaps figures distorted or manipulated or misrepresented. People in organizations do not always tell the truth.

Question 27: In what ways have you been influenced by and your behaviour modified by the organizations to which you have belonged?

Question 28: What are the purposes of the organizations to which you belong? What are their similarities and differences?

3.23 Choices in Organizations

Organizations generally — but not always — choose who is to be within them to do what, when, and how. Many individuals are in a position to choose the organization for which they are prepared to work. Individuals and organizations make choices about each other on such questions as how much effort to put in, whom to promote, and what is a fair level of remuneration.

Choices depend upon information, expectations, rules, economic factors, and such psychological influences as aspiration and motivation. In each of these areas there is room for disagreements that can lead to charges of favouritism and discrimination.

Sometimes parties within organizations may disagree over whether a choice exists. Managements may argue that the harsh realities of the marketplace are such that they do not have a choice. A trade union might contest this claim, arguing in favour of a sales drive or even the seeking of state support as an alternative to redundancies in the marketing department.

THE STAFF OF A SHIPYARD REFUSED TO ACCEPT THE LEGITIMACY OF A MANAGEMENT DECISION TO CLOSE A PORTION OF THE YARD AND STAGED AN OCCUPATION AND 'WORK IN'. THE MEN WOULD NOT CONCEDE THAT THE MANAGEMENT HAD ANY RIGHT TO EXERCISE DISCRETION CONCERNING WHETHER OR NOT THE BUSINESS OR A PART OF IT SHOULD CONTINUE. SUCH A CHOICE, IT WAS ARGUED, COULD ONLY BE EXERCISED BY THE EMPLOYEES AS THEY WERE MOST AFFECTED BY THE OUTCOME OF SUCH A DECISION. ON SUCH QUESTIONS THE MEN REGARDED THEMSELVES AS HAVING THE RIGHT TO FULL CONSULTATION AND INFORMATION PRIOR TO DECISIONS BEING MADE. DECISIONS WITHOUT THEIR CONSENT WERE NOT ACCEPTABLE.

Question 29: What choices do you make vis-a-vis an organization for which you work or to which you belong? In what areas does the organization constrain your choices and why?

3.24 Industrial Relations

Industrial relations practice appears at times to be solely concerned with breakdowns of communication within organizations. These frequently result from conflicts of values and beliefs. People see situations through spectacles tinted with their own experience and the set of beliefs and values this has created.

No two people will take exactly the same view of a given situation. Even when two parties agree on their objectives, they may disagree over the nature of a current situation that is to form the base from which future activity will proceed.

What are these conflicts of values when employer and employee sit down together to negotiate? For a start they may have different views on rights. To the employer the most important value is likely to be the employer's right to manage. The employee will be more concerned with the rights to work, to have a monopoly of certain kinds of work, to be consulted over changes in working conditions, and to disagree if necessary over proposed changes.

A crucial question at issue is sometimes who owns the job — the firm or a union that sees the job as a part of its territory to be protected from the encroachments of other unions. Employers are often concerned with individual assessment while the union activist may be primarily concerned with the interests of workers or a group. The employer may think in terms of loyalty to the business, the employee of loyalty to the union or to fellow employees. A union shop steward may have important interests beyond the organization.

Many managers facing union negotiators do not consider the pressures under which such negotiators work. They will have members and a head office to whom they must 'sell' an agreement and the views of these two groups may be widely divergent.

ONE MANAGER IN A CAR COMPONENT PLANT ACHIEVED A RAPPORT AND UNDERSTANDING WITH A SHOP STEWARD BY BEING THE ONLY PERSON AT THE PLANT WHO FULLY UNDERSTOOD THE VIEWS OF THE UNION'S REGIONAL ORGANIZER WHICH WERE BEING 'PUSHED DOWN' THE UNWILLING THROAT OF THE SHOP STEWARD CONCERNED. TOGETHER THEY WORKED OUT A FORMULA THAT WAS ACCEPTABLE TO MEN, LOCAL MANAGEMENT AND UNION HIERARCHY.

When negotiating, one should always be aware of the process of negotiation itself and where it is leading. Are the disagreements over the discussion or a question of fact, about the problem or its solution, about questions or answers?

ONE ONGOING INDUSTRIAL DISPUTE AT A PUBLIC HOUSE IN
IRELAND LASTED SO LONG THAT IT BECAME A TOURIST ATTRAC-
TION. A LIVELY TRADE IN SOUVENIRS DEVELOPED AND THE
LANDLORD BECAME CONCERNED WHENEVER THE PICKETS FAILED
TO APPEAR. THE STOPPAGE HAD BECOME NOT ONLY A RITUAL,
BUT A WAY OF LIFE AND A LUCRATIVE ONE.

In a marketing context a manager might find that staff permanently in the office
or working in sales offices attached to factories with over 1,000 employees are
much more interested in trade union affairs and militant than salesmen 'on the
road' and operating independently or employees working in small units. In a
conglomerate some sectors, certain plants will have worse labour relations problems
than others. An attempt to confine an issue to one office may be seen by a shop
steward as a management plot to employ a divide-and-rule strategy.

In industrial-relations matters, a marketing manager must be fully conversant
with any official negotiating procedure, consulting the personnel and other
departments as appropriate. Standing alone against the tide, commendable in one
situation, may be folly in another.

One needs to look at organizations and the people within them critically. What
are their strengths and weaknesses? How long will it take to put things right? Are
there alternative courses of action and how do they compare? How does one
select from the alternatives? When tackling industrial disputes one needs to be
aware that both 'giving in' and continuing can have costs. A 'victory' may not be
possible, merely the selection of a 'lesser evil'.

Question 30: Outline a dispute in which you have been a protagonist. How did
the disagreement arise and how was accommodation reached? Did you consciously
weigh the cost of conceding against the penalties arising from the continuation of
the dispute?

3.3 ORGANIZATION AND COMMUNICATION

It is not easy to differentiate between organization and communication. The two
are related and interdependent. The patterns of communication within an organization is a crucial part of its definition and description. An organization cannot be
said to exist if its components are not communicating with each other.

The structure of an organization and the people working within it can encourage
or inhibit communication. Barriers to effective communication exist in the form of
formal systems and human attitudes.

While communication is at times difficult to suppress, its existence let alone its
efficient operation cannot be taken for granted. It needs to be directed, planned
and managed, perhaps encouraged in one quarter and suppressed in another.

Communication usually involves the transmission of information; a major responsibility of management is seeing that it is correct, 'true and fair', and timely.

What is important to bear in mind is that the mere existence of a formal system does not necessarily lead to superior performance. A great deal depends upon the quality of opportunities and of individual managers. An intangible such as the quality and quantity of communication, the extent to which a formal potential for communication is realised in practice, can vary enormously between organizations.

Managers preoccupied with their heavy immediate responsibilities may fail to get together to discuss the longer-term implications of their activities. Discussion helps to build teams. Communications questions can be overlooked in the heat of the moment.

The industrial-relations problems mentioned in the last section could be regarded as breakdowns in communication. Giving instructions, conveying information involves communication. It can be formal and informal and inevitably arises when people get together.

Most managers spend the larger share of their time engaged in forms of communication, participating in meetings, answering telephone calls and dictating letters. Communication can be regarded as the blood which flows in the organizational structure veins. Without it one has a lifeless structure, a corpse.

The structure of an organization, then, can be seen as a communications network, setting out who will communicate to whom, for what reason, when and by what channel. Communications will flow in both directions along most channels. Some communications will be supportive and others disruptive. A great deal of communication may be devoted to amplifying, qualifying, and correcting other communications.

Some communication situations such as committees and interviews require special skills. The perceptive communicator pays special attention to non-verbal communication or 'body language'. A participant leaning away from the table at a meeting may be physically expressing some doubt about a course of action that is being proposed.

Channels of communication are often vulnerable and can be disrupted or sabotaged. A trade union may purposely break a channel of communication. A manager may have a vested interest in biassing a message. The industrial spy may be looking for a 'leak' of information. An ill-considered message dashed off in a fit of temper can do lasting damage to the frame of mind in which subsequent messages are received and interpreted.

Communication is not always clear and concise. 'Noise' may be present due to the communicator, the channel of communication, or a recipient. Words mean different things to different people: an intangible image may cloud an issue. Questions of status can inhibit communication, as can physical distance. These factors must be borne in mind when organizations are designed.

ONE INDUSTRIAL COMPANY SOLD OFF ITS HEAD OFFICE AND RELOCATED ITS CENTRAL SERVICE ACTIVITIES CLOSE TO THE DIVISIONS WITH WHOM THEY HAD THE GREATEST CONTACT. THE BENEFITS OF PROXIMITY WERE THOUGHT TO OUTWEIGH THE DISADVANTAGES OF NOT HAVING A LONDON OFFICE. THE LONDON PRESENCE, WHILE USEFUL FROM THE POINT OF VIEW OF COMMUNICATION WITH EXTERNAL BODIES, WAS INHIBITING INTERNAL COMMUNICATION.

Question 31: Draw up a list of communications problems in an organization with which you are familiar and outline what is being done about them. If the problems are not being tackled, why do you think this is so?

Question 32: List the channels of communication you use in an organization to which you belong, differentiating between those which are formal and informal, and setting out why each channel is used, and the extent to which you think it is effective.

3.4 STRUCTURE, FUNCTION, AND COMMUNICATION IN ORGANIZATIONS

No two organizations are alike. They vary in their management structure, functions, and communication systems. There are a number of approaches to the analysis and categorization of organizations into types which are useful in evaluating the strengths and weaknesses of different structures and communications practices. These may appear, unavoidably, somewhat theoretical and difficult. We are daily learning more about organizations and our understanding is as yet incomplete. Some basic theory can help potential problem areas to be identified, practical solutions to which will be considered in subsequent chapters.

3.41 Effective Organization

There is no one form of organization that is effective for all situations at all times. An organization must be tailored to the job it has to do and to the people who work in it. Within the same company, different management functions may require their distinct forms of organization.

An effective organization is one that meets the demands made upon it by the technology in which it operates (e.g. plastic or agricultural), company goals (e.g. expansion or consolidation), and management culture (e.g. sales- or production-orientated), and takes into account the characteristics of those working within it (e.g. generalists, workers, or professionals), their management style (e.g. bureaucratic or entrepreneurial), the nature of their work (e.g. routine factory or varied and open air), and their relationships. When building an organization, a balance must be achieved between many factors and inevitably there will be tradeoffs.

3.42   Approaches to Organizations

The basic structure of an organization covers how work is divided and allocated and how co-ordination is achieved. This is usually set down in formal organization charts and job designs.

The basic structure is lubricated by operating practices such as rules and procedures, information systems, rewards and sanctions, and assessment methods. Informal practices often grow up to remedy differences in this formal structure and these also require consideration.

The classic organization theorists were concerned with the division of work by function, territory or product, the allocation of tasks, and the measurement of efficiency. Co-ordination was assumed to be achieved through the organization hierarchy.

A more human-centred and less mechanical approach to organization has since grown up which assumes that people are not only rewarded by money, have a number of roles and that the goals of an organization and of people within it will not always coincide.

The human-centred approach to organization concentrates upon the satisfaction of human needs through social groupings and participation at work. Much emphasis is placed upon collaboration and co-ordination. Adherents of this approach tend sometimes to forget that individuals vary in their requirements and that a shortage of information can limit participation. Nevertheless, the 'movement' has a compelling message: 'build organizations to meet the needs of people rather than modify people to satisfy the demands of organization'.

When reconciling the two approaches, one needs to remember that people in different departments can evolve distinct cultures with their own values. The division of work not only leads to economic differences but social ones and attitudinal ones as well.

The amount and type of co-ordination required within and between each group or function will depend upon what it does and its members (e.g. the degree of uncertainty the group faces and the extent to which members of the group are homogenous or diverse).

Communication between individuals and within groups must support the division of work and assist the desired co-ordination. In a sense, organization is division, allocation, and co-ordination, while communication is a means by which the co-ordination is achieved and makes possible the allocation and division.

Organizations consist of structures, functions, and patterns of communication. It is useful to consider these and their interaction in a small number of extreme and stereotyped but nevertheless suggestive organizational types.

3.5 TYPES OF ORGANIZATION

Organizations can be categorized into groups with common characteristics in a number of ways. In this section the 'pigeon-holing' will be on the basis of 'culture'. Organizational culture is a broad notion that covers both attitudes and practices.

The relationships between individuals, the types of individuals selected and promoted, their roles and their values and those of the organization will all be shaped by its culture. Hence, looking at organizations in terms of their cultures enables us to consider together both structure and communication. It also reminds us that organizations and the types of individual within them are inseparable.

3.51   The Power Culture

The power culture is a one-man-band type of organization in which a single individual, perhaps a founder entrepreneur, is dominant. This one powerful individual hires and fires, at times indiscriminately, and manages by dividing and ruling staff.

Influence within this type of organization depends upon how close one is to the big man rather than upon the logic of one's arguments. Rumours are likely to abound concerning who is in and without favour. The boss will take all the big decisions, may be temperamental, is probably charismatic, and his removal is likely to precipitate a succession crisis from which the organization may not recover.

The main function of a power culture as a whole can be to satisfy the ego drive of the leader and the desire of the led he attracts for an authority figure. The big man may crave attention and more of whatever he can get.

The division of separate functions within the organization and allocation of tasks may not be clear and may shift dramatically over time. Work tends to be given to the 'last person the big boss saw'. Job titles will not count for much: more than one individual or group may be given the same job to do. The big man may pursue a divide-and-rule policy and encourage a number of competing crown princes.

The pattern of communication within a power culture resembles a spider's web. Individuals within the organization may interact with the 'gaffer' at the centre much more than with each other. Power will depend upon closeness to and the frequency of communication with the centre. The standing of individuals within the organization can rise and fall like a yo-yo according to the whims of the boss.

The power-culture type of organization might be suitable for a subsidiary in the north of Brazil where the marketing task is to push sales of a new product and where the labour force needs to be tightly controlled. It can achieve startling results in start-up and entrepreneurial situations. Press, oil, and railroad barons built empires by means of power cultures.

Succession is the Achilles' heel of the power culture. When the big boss founder dies, the organization may fold up. Staff are not used to taking decisions and no one remaining may have an overall picture of the organization. The Ford Motor Company almost died soon after its founder. For some the power culture is 'fun while it lasts'.

WHEN THE FIRST HENRY FORD DIED HIS COMPANY ALL BUT COLLAPSED. HE HAD INSISTED UPON TAKING ALL THE MAJOR DECISIONS HIMSELF. BY THE TIME THE ORGANIZATION HAD BEEN PULLED TOGETHER AND A PICTURE OF ITS TOTAL POSITION ASSEMBLED THE COMPANY HAD BEEN OVERTAKEN AND HAD LOST ITS DOMINANT POSITION IN THE MARKET TO GENERAL MOTORS.

3.52   The Role Culture

The role or functional culture is stable, even classical. It is built upon departments with carefully-defined functions, formal and correct procedures, and power within it depends upon position within the bureaucratic hierarchy. Problems tend to be tackled by resort to precedent or committee.

This form of organization is stable, rewards loyalty, is slow to change and offers considerable job security. The main props of this sort of organization are the functional departments, and its cement tends to be the networks of inter-departmental committees.

Succession in the role culture tends to be orderly. This type of organization could manage reliably a network of established customers and products in a market area relatively isolated from change. It is ideally suited to the public sector and organizations that must work within delegated and narrow powers.

In a society, the role culture may have an important part to play in the main-tenance of order and stability. It may become an institution, a pillar of society, a bastion against change. It will attract and serve the needs of those who consider these values are important.

The pattern of communication within the role culture resembles a layout composed of chains. Forms and reports are passed from person to person up the appropriate hierarchy. The functions may be relatively self-contained with (e.g. in the case of the civil service) communication between them occurring only at the highest level.

Specialist functional expertise is rewarded as is bureaucratic skill: the ability to draft reports and abide by the rules. Considerable power may reside at the level at which key documents are drafted.

The role culture is unsuited to environments of rapid change (e.g. fast-moving consumer goods or the fashion market) and in which individuals are required to be creative (e.g. advertising agency). Job titles are important and the 'cult of the personality' is not encouraged. The restless, the 'people in a hurry', will not stay in the role culture for long. Form is sometimes regarded as more important than achievement. 'It is not what you do, but how you do it, that is important.'

THE BRITISH POST OFFICE AS A GOVERNMENT DEPARTMENT WAS OPERATING IN AN AREA FACING CONSIDERABLE TECHNO-LOGICAL CHANGE. ITS MANAGEMENT WAS THOUGHT TO BE TOO FORMAL AND BUREAUCRATIC AS A RESULT OF THE CIVIL SERVICE CULTURE. IT WAS HIVED OFF AS AN INDEPENDENT PUBLIC COR-PORATION AND GIVEN THE GREATER FREEDOMS ENJOYED BY OTHER NATIONALIZED INDUSTRIES, ALTHOUGH THE STAFF REMAINED UNCHANGED.

3.53 The Task Culture

The task or performance culture is organized upon the basis of getting the job done. Its structure can shift as multi-disciplinary project teams are established and wound up. Status and hierarchy will vary according to the job in hand, as power depends upon knowledge and its relevance to particular projects.

The ability to work with colleagues in problem-solving groups is a key requirement of staff and individuals may enter and leave the organization on an assignment basis. The decentralization of problem-solving could result in problems of control and co-ordination.

This form of organization is most appropriate for rapidly-changing markets, in which highly skilled and creative people are employed and the short lines of communication enable fast responses. It thrives upon a continual supply of problems to be solved and would thus be suitable for a marketing consultancy. It is not suitable for routine and repetitive tasks.

The performance culture may not be interested in survival for its own sake. It will continue to exist so long as there are problems for its talented and motivated staff to tackle. It is most vulnerable to the obsolescence of the specialized skills of its staff. Thus the decline of investment in the US space programme resulted in heavy unemployment among science Ph.D.'s who had been working in task groups in Houston.

The pattern of communication within a task culture may resemble a wheel or a bridge. With a strong project leader, the wheel analogy is most appropriate, the spokes representing communication with the centre and rim communication between team members. Where the centre is less dominant the bridge analogy is more appropriate, the cross-strutts and girders symbolizing the communication links between the team members themselves.

This form of organization and pattern of communication is most suitable for the exploitation of innovation, a crucial function in a developed world whose basic industries are threatened by emerging nations with their cheap labour and imported technology. The function of the organization is achievement, getting results, and it attracts individuals who are achievers.

SHOCKED BY THE PERFORMANCE OF THE RUSSIANS WHO HAD PUT A 'SPUTNIK' IN ORBIT AROUND THE EARTH, PRESIDENT KENNEDY ANNOUNCED THE INTENTION OF THE UNITED STATES TO PUT A MAN ON THE MOON. NASA WAS ESTABLISHED WITH THE TASK OF ACHIEIVING THIS. ITS BRIEF WAS TO GET WHAT IT WANTED WHEREVER IT MIGHT BE FOUND. A MULTI-DISCIPLINING TEAM OF SCIENTISTS WAS ASSEMBLED, WORK SUB-CONTRACTED, AND NEW SYSTEMS AND MATERIALS DEVELOPED AS NEEDED. THE AMERICANS WON THE SPACE RACE.

3.54   The Matrix Organization

In a matrix form of organization individual members of staff are subject to a dual authority relationship: vertically up the hierarchy of one's functional department and horizontally with other individuals from other departments working as multi-disciplinary teams on particular projects. This form is thus a combination of role or functional and task cultures in which the individual has both functional and task responsibilities.

Where the multi-disciplinary task forces become a permanent team, the selection of a leader may prove difficult but some integrating factor is usually required, normally a project manager. Communication is especially crucial to the matrix form of organization and the pattern of communication forms a net of vertical and horizontal links. Individuals at the knots in the net, at the crossover points between vertical and horizontal communication, can become extremely powerful. They are gatekeepers and their role supplies them with scarce information.

Matrix and task groups attract different individuals. Within the matrix team a variety of disciplines will probably be present and the arrangement is likely to be *ad hoc*. Members of the task team by contrast may be more homogenous, may stay together on a reasonably permanent basis and could be drawn entirely from one functional area. To be successful in both cultures one needs to be able to work effectively within and to lead and motivate groups.

Matrix teams are frequently employed to develop and launch new products and to manage major products and brands. It is found in the motor and aviation industries and there have been occasions on which a project has outgrown its host organization, a merger or government involvement being the result. In a divisionalized organization the matrix form of organization is compatible with the retention of centralized specialist services. Management consultancies frequently adopt *ad hoc* matrix teams to tackle particular assignments.

A MAJOR NATIONALIZED INDUSTRY IS ORGANIZED UPON A DUAL REGIONAL AND FUNCTIONAL BASIS. STAFF SPECIALISTS REPORT TO FUNCTIONAL HEADS WHO ARE REPRESENTED AT

MAIN BOARD LEVEL, WHILE WORK IN EACH REGION IS CO-ORDIN-
ATED BY GENERAL MANAGERS. THE SYSTEM WORKS WELL AND IS
APPROPRIATE TO THE SERVICES THE ORGANIZATION PROVIDES.
PRIOR TO NATIONALIZATION, THE INDUSTRY CONSISTED OF
INDEPENDENT REGIONAL COMPANIES.

3.55   The Person Culture

The most employee-centred form of organization, standing at the opposite end of
the spectrum from the power culture, is the person culture. In this the most
important factor is the personal needs of staff, their individual growth and development.

Decisions are likely to be made upon the basis of consensus and interpersonal
relationships are informal, with the object of giving a maximum of job satisfaction
and freedom to individuals within the group. A small design partnership might
adopt this form of organization.

The pattern of communication in person cultures represents a three-dimensional
object, possibly an amoeba, within which each individual is able to communicate
with every other individual. This is termed an 'all channel' network of communication and tests have shown it to be the most effective for creative problem solving.
Typically, a great deal of communication occurs.

Person cultures tend to be communities of equals coming together for mutual
benefit. The advantages can be shared common services and hence reduced individual overheads for each individual participant. While ideally suited for the self-
motivated or the 'inwardly directed', this form of organization is not suitable for
those who need to be told what to do and it is also much slower acting than forms
of organization that have an appointed or elected leader.

The person culture may become the predominant organizational form in the
future. As the transportation of human bodies becomes more expensive and the
costs of transporting information are brought down, it may become more cost-
effective to take work to people, rather than people to work.

Individuals may prefer to work at home and maintain contact with their
organizations via telephones and computer terminals. One can imagine a whole
community of professionals selling their personal skill services on a contract and
fee basis and buying central administration services from competing bureau-type
organizations.

A MANAGEMENT CONSULTANCY SUB-CONTRACTS A GREAT
DEAL OF ITS WORK TO INDEPENDENT CONSULTANTS. THESE
REGISTER THEIR INTERESTS AND EXPERIENCE AND ARE ALLO-
CATED TO PROJECTS ACCORDING TO THE MUTUAL SATISFACTION
OF CONSULTANCY AND CONSULTANT. THE CONSULTANCY

PROVIDES CENTRAL SERVICES SUCH AS WORK STATIONS AND INTERVIEW ROOMS. PORTABLE COMPUTER TERMINALS ARE PROVIDED FOR THOSE CONSULTANTS WHO WISH TO ACCESS COMPUTER-BASED MODELS FROM THEIR HOMES.

3.6 TECHNOLOGY AND TASKS

Effective organizations are those which evolve to match the technologies and tasks that confront them. It will be seen that technologies and tasks can be categorized and that different types present organizations with distinct challenges.

3.61 Technology

Technology, the nature of the business one is in, and its manufacturing and operating requirements, has a critical influence upon organization. One would not expect a motor-car factory to be organized in a similar way to an advertising agency. Joan Woodward, who has examined the structures of many organizations, has concluded that their prime determinant is technology.

Technology is basically the methods that are available for converting inputs into outputs, various resources into goods and services. It has been summed up as 'the state of the art'.

Stable technologies are those in which few exceptions are thrown up and changes rarely occur. An adaptive technology is one in which there are frequent changes and moreover the problems thrown up are unprecedented and require the development of *ad hoc* and novel solutions. A paper mill, retirement home or social security department would present a stable technology while the drug research laboratory, consulting firm or aerospace design team operate within an adaptive technology.

The more uncertain the business environment, the greater the amount of information that will need to be processed. For predictable routine tasks, rules or programmes can be established but as uncertainty increases, goals or objectives must be set, guidelines rather than cut and dried rules. The more difficult questions are referred up the management hierarchy.

A craft industry may have a technology in which there are few exceptions, and problems are difficult to analyse. By contrast, in engineering there may be more exceptions but at the same time techniques are available to analyse complex problems.

The existence of many exceptions and the resulting devolution of discretion and authority suggests a team form of culture. Where the technology is stable and work is routine and with few exceptions, the role culture with its rules and procedures may be more appropriate. High-discretion organizations tend to be people-centred and low-discretion organizations task-centred.

IN THE EARLY PART OF THIS CENTURY AIRSHIPS WERE DEVELOPED AND MANUFACTURED BY LARGE ESTABLISHED ORGANIZATIONS. THEN DUE TO DISASTERS LARGELY CAUSED BY THE INFLAMMABLE NATURE OF AIRSHIP GAS THE AIRSHIP WAS SUPERSEDED AS A MEANS OF TRANSPORT. MORE RECENTLY THE AVAILABILITY OF NEW NON-INFLAMMABLE GASES AND THE RISING COST OF OTHER MEANS OF TRANSPORT HAVE ONCE AGAIN MADE THE AIRSHIP A VIABLE ECONOMIC PROPOSITION.

EXISTING MANUFACTURERS OF AIRCRAFT WERE UNWILLING AND/OR UNABLE TO UPDATE AIRSHIP TECHNOLOGY. THIS WAS DONE BY A SMALL AND YOUNG VENTURE TEAM WHO, WITH LIMITED RESOURCES AND WORKING 'FROM SCRATCH', DESIGNED A NEW FORM OF AIRSHIP WHICH, FOLLOWING THE SUCCESSFUL TRIALS OF A PROTOTYPE, ENTERED SERIES PRODUCTION.

When a technology is stable, organizations tend to become centralized and programmed with a considerable division of labour, narrow functions and upwards flow of information, and strongly led. Planning tends to be detailed with frequent reporting which concentrates upon how tasks are to be achieved. Staff are given detailed instructions and closely monitored. Efficiency is regarded as very important. Work is checked frequently, orders are obeyed and mistakes are generally not tolerated.

Stable technologies breed power and role cultures. Role cultures and their communications pattern are particularly suited to stable technological environments. Power cultures are in danger when their 'leaders' become bored. The order, stability, and routine cause problems for task and matrix cultures. Their members thrive on problem solving and as the number of 'exceptions' dwindles they become frustrated and leave.

When exceptions do occur, the role cultures may not have people 'on their books' to deal with them and may need to call in specialist help from professional members of people cultures. Thus the management consultants are called in.

Effective organizations in an adaptive technology tend to be decentralized. The division of labour will be limited and co-ordination will be mainly achieved by face-to-face contact. The information flow will be horizontal rather than vertical, as groups get together to tackle problems.

The organization will be headed by flexible generalists. Planning will originate at many points in the organization and will be broad, with long time horizons and with an emphasis upon objectives and results. Participation will be high, information shared and supervision will be general, staff being assessed infrequently and by results. Learning and success will be highly valued and rewarded. Task and person cultures perform the best in fluid situations.

IN THE POST SECOND WORLD WAR PERIOD A GREAT MANY NATIONAL DEFENCE PROJECTS HAVE BEEN CANCELLED AFTER, IN SOME CASES, HUNDREDS OF MILLIONS OF POUNDS HAD BEEN SPENT ON THEIR DEVELOPMENT. IT MAY TAKE A DECADE TO DESIGN, BUILD AND TEST A NEW WARSHIP. MILITARY TECHNO-LOGY ADVANCES SO RAPIDLY THAT VESSELS CAN BE OUT OF DATE BY THE TIME THEY ARE LAUNCHED. FIRST-GENERATION GUIDED MISSILE DESTROYERS HAVE BEEN SCRAPPED AS IT WOULD NOT BE COST-EFFECTIVE TO CONVERT THEM TO SECOND GENER-ATION ELECTRONICS. NEW SOLUTIONS MUST BE FOUND, BASIC HULLS WHICH CAN BE EFFECTIVELY UPDATED AS NEW EQUIP-MENT BECOMES AVAILABLE.

3.62 Tasks

An organization, even a functional area within an organization, must perform a variety of tasks. A marketing organization may need to design and plan, research a market, advertise, distribute, service, control, and supervise. The requirements of different markets and products vary. For one (e.g. helicopter in Iran) technical support may be critical, while for another (e.g. a cheap disposable in Sweden) it may be irrelevant or virtually non-existent.

The structure of an organization (e.g. whether it is centralized or decentralized, formal or informal) will depend upon the tasks it has to perform. A routine task can lead to a stable low-risk role type of organization. Difficult tasks will require task teams with appropriate specialist skills.

For highly repetitive tasks which involve little employee discretion, a bureau-cratic role or mechanistic structure can be the most appropriate. By contrast, where variety makes the exercise of discretion important, one needs a more participative and people-centred — one could call it organic — structure.

Effective organizations and individuals are those able to participate, welcome and cope with the various tasks they are required to perform; their capabilities match the demands of the task that faces them. When allocating work it is as important to match tasks to organizations and individuals as vice-versa. The two are inseparable and part of the same process.

The pattern of communication will also vary widely according to task. Con-trollers and supervisors will be concerned with internal communication, the salesmen, market researcher and advertiser with external. It may not be necessary for salesmen to communicate between themselves but this interaction might be vital in the advertising department. In some tasks there will be a higher degree of two-way communication than in others. Moving between tasks can cause problems for individuals who require time to adjust to new patterns of communication.

A MARKETING MANAGER HAD GREAT DIFFICULTY IN UPDATING HIS MASTER PRODUCT MANUAL. THE WORK WOULD BE DETAILED AND TIME CONSUMING AND HIS STAFF SHUNNED IT. NONE WERE WILLING TO BE 'COOPED UP' IN THE OFFICE WHILE THEIR SALES COLLEAGUES WERE ON THE ROAD. THE JOB WAS EVENTUALLY GIVEN TO A RETIRED TECHNICAL AUTHOR WHO RELISHED THE OPPORTUNITY TO EARN SOME POCKET MONEY.

Question 33: Examine the organizations in which you have worked. To what extent are they:

- (*a*) task-centred or people-orientated
- (*b*) power, role, performance, matrix, or people cultures
- (*c*) appropriate to the technology within which they operate
- (*d*) appropriate to the task they are required to perform
- (*e*) in stable or changing technologies
- (*f*) adaptive to technology and task changes?

Question 34: Outline the major factors to be taken into account in organization design. What weight would you attach to the following:

- (*a*) predominant activity
- (*b*) nature and pattern of workload
- (*c*) amount of information
- (*d*) type of staff
- (*e*) company objectives
- (*f*) technology
- (*g*) competitors
- (*h*) power sharing
- (*i*) communication
- (*j*) environment?

3.7 ORGANIZATION DESIGN AND DEVELOPMENT

A business passes through many phases as it grows. It may begin as a family unit, split into departments, establish separate divisions, acquire new businesses, and sell existing ones. Moving into new markets and introducing new products can give rise to considerable organizational change.

Question 35: At what stage in its organizational development is the organization with which you are most familiar?

The design and development of an organization will, in the long run, be determined by the technologies within which it operates and the types of job it does or tasks it performs. Similarly the task the organization tackles and the technologies it moves into will in turn be influenced by its design and development.

There is no best design or most desirable avenue of development. It will all depend upon what the organization is doing now and where it wants to go. Good design is a process of matching organization to situation. The matching of organization to strategy is a dynamic or continuing process.

3.71   Organization Design

The key problem in designing an organization is to match the form of the organization to the activity it undertakes. Which form of organizational culture is most appropriate will depend upon the predominant activities. Thus the role culture might be appropriate for a steady-state situation while policy-making might require a power or task culture, depending upon circumstances.

Individuals, at various times in their careers, move from one form of culture to another. An economic graduate or holder of the DipM could start in a task culture carrying out market research projects and then move to a role culture, a bureaucratically-run customer complaints department, but is unlikely to be equally effective in both these environments. Hence the organization, to be effective, must suit the people who will work it.

A workload can be regular or fluctuating. Some slack may need to be built into the system to cope with peaks of workload. To cope with a larger flow of information, a vertical information system could be introduced. This would establish control units beyond which items are referred upwards on a management by exception basis and is likely to result in a greater volume and frequency of reporting. Alternatively, lateral relationships could be established between departments or divisions to cope with problems at the level at which they arise as an alternative to referral upwards. This could result in greater interdepartmental contacts, the appointment of liaison officers or even special multi-disciplinary task forces.

When designing an organization, one needs to be aware of personal biasses and overall objectives. Some individuals are task-orientated, their priority is getting the job done regardless of the human consequences. Others put a higher priority upon job satisfaction and happiness.

The people-centred approach to organizational design puts more emphasis upon the need to change behaviour and the impact of change upon individuals. It is concerned with the process of change, involving people to discuss what is required and encouraging them to develop their own solutions. Self-control and self-direction are important to this approach and its objective can be to share power by means of increasing communication.

Other important factors to take account of in organization design are the degree of uncertainty faced, the need for speed of action, and overall size. Where activities are diverse, a number of technologies may be found within one organization. This can cause a host of problems. An executive with an impressive track record in one part of the organization may fail when transferred to another within a different technology. Large and important units within an organization should be managed by a design tailored to their particular activity.

A MINING COMPANY HAD TO DEVELOP A NEW OFFICE IN BRAZIL. IT EXPORTED A COMPLETE UNIT FROM ANOTHER COUNTRY. THE OUTCOME WAS DISASTER.

MINING DEVELOPMENT WAS VERY ADVANCED IN BRAZIL. THE MIX OF SKILLS WAS WRONG. A PORTUGUESE SPEAKER RESENTED NOT BEING GIVEN A MORE SENIOR POSITION WITHIN THE OFFICE IN VIEW OF HIS LANGUAGE ABILITIES. TWO WIVES REFUSED TO LIVE IN SAO PAULO. BRAZILIAN LAW ONLY ALLOWED A FOREIGN COMPANY A MINORITY STAKE IN MINING VENTURES.

ANOTHER COMPANY SIGNED A JOINT VENTURE AND SLOWLY INTRODUCED PERSONNEL TO BRAZIL ON SHORT ASSIGNMENTS AS REQUESTED BY THE JOINT VENTURE PARTNER. EVENTUALLY A PERMANENT OFFICE WAS DEVELOPED IN THE NORTH OF BRAZIL CLOSE TO THE JOINT VENTURE'S ULTIMATELY SUCCESSFUL MINING OPERATION.

3.72 Organizational Development

As a company grows and develops, its organization is likely to pass through a number of stages. This section sketches the evolution of an expanding company from entrepreneurial to divisional form. It was devised by Bruce Scott, Professor in Business Policy at the Harvard Business School.

At the entrepreneurial stage, the company is likely to be a single unit that performs all the stages of whatever product or service it offers. There is no need for communications procedures between units. The major resource allocation problem is likely to be how much the owner manager will take out.

At the second 'functional' stage of the organization's development, a number of sub-units will be established based upon function or technical speciality. The relationship between these units is likely to be integrated, that is, a product or service will pass through each sub-unit in turn on its way to the market. Each of these functional sub-units will compete for the available funds.

Some formal means of measuring performance will probably have been developed such as engineering or cost criteria. Cost criteria could involve the comparison of an actual cost with a standard. Rewards and punishments within the organization will be increasingly systematic and impersonal. This is the role or functional culture.

In the organization's final divisional form, a number of separate units exist based upon product market relationships. There could be separate product divisions or geographic divisions. The relationship of these units is probably no longer according to the integrated pattern, each unit now relating independently and directly to its market. Resources could be allocated between the units upon the basis of return upon capital employed.

Within the divisionalized organization performance is likely to be measured according to market criteria such as profitability, or return upon resources invested by product or region. Rewards and punishments are allocated by a very impersonal and systematic reporting and assessment procedure. A matrix form of organization might emerge.

As a company grows, its marketing organization will also evolve through a number of stages. Initially, the staff will be composed of salesmen but as a firm expands specialists with skills such as market research and advertising are recruited.

A point is reached at which managers are required to manage salesmen and specialists. The management might be organized on a product or market basis. In some organizations, the marketing organization might resemble a mini-business. The ultimate stage is probably reached when the marketing department has grown into a division headed by a general manager.

Where products draw on similar production processes and a similar method of selling is used in different markets, companies tend to use functional marketing organizations with a sales force organized upon a territorial basis. Where the production process is common but markets are varied, marketing services are frequently centralized and the sales force divisionalized.

If the market is common but the products are dissimilar and require different manufacturing processes, then a single sales force may be used with the remainder of the marketing organization devolved on a divisional basis. Where products and markets are very dissimilar, a loose form of organization co-ordinating profit-centre divisions might be adopted.

The large divisionalized and diversified company may have, within its umbrella, a number of cultures. The senior management will allocate tasks to the appropriate cultures. This requires a considerable understanding of the characteristics of each, and of their strengths and weaknesses. Getting the allocation wrong will result in square pegs in round holes. This can cause inefficiency, stress, and breakdown.

Question 36: What are the major organizational changes occurring in the organization with which you are most familiar? Why are they occurring? How are people reacting to the changes? How are the changes being managed and with what success?

3.8 SETTING UP AND ADAPTING ORGANIZATIONS TO CHANGING TECHNOLOGICAL AND MARKET CONDITIONS

Where an organization is to be built from scratch, it should be built tailored to match technology, task people, and strategy.

A more usual problem faced by managers is the need to adapt an existing organization to changing technological and market conditions. The evidence of the need for change could be performance-based (e.g. falling sales, dwindling market shares), people-based (e.g. increasing 'illness' and resignations) or 'system'-based (e.g. collapse of a reporting system due to overloading.

A MOTOR MANUFACTUER BEGAN TO FEEL THAT ITS RESOURCES WERE BEING SPREAD ACROSS TOO MANY VEHICLES AS A RESULT OF THE ORGANIZATION'S PRODUCT DIVISION STRUCTURE. EACH PRODUCT DIVISION HAD A VESTED INTEREST IN ITS OWN CONTINUANCE. MAJOR COMPETITORS HAD RATIONALIZED THEIR LINES, PRODUCING HIGHER VOLUMES OF FEWER MODELS.

THE COMPANY WAS REORGANIZED INTO TWO MARKET-BASED DIVISIONS, HIGH VOLUME CARS AND TRACTORS AND TRUCKS. WITHIN EACH DIVISION THE NUMBER OF PRODUCT LINES WAS REDUCED SOME REDUNDANCIES WERE INEVITABLE AND MARGINAL PLANTS WERE CLOSED. THE NEW ORGANIZATION WAS MORE ABLE TO COMPETE WITH HIGH-VOLUME FOREIGN MANUFACTURERS.

3.81 Information

Where an organization is faced with the need to cope with an increased flow of information it can either reduce this flow by doing less, that is, concentrating on what is most important, or by redesigning the organization to increase its capacity for processing information.

Installing a more sophisticated information and reporting system with a plan for dealing with what were previously regarded as exceptions is one way of improving an organization's ability to handle information. Another solution is to create more lateral relationships, that is, encouraging the tackling of a problem at one level as an alternative to referral up the hierarchy.

Some organizations are sufficiently powerful within their markets to deal with increasing uncertainty by directly acting in the marketplace to reduce it.

3.82   Responsiveness

It is possible to some extent to measure responsiveness to changes in technology and task. How quickly are orders processed or crises dealt with?

Responsive individuals and organizations tend to have certain characteristics in common. There are levels of adaptability. The environment is constantly monitored by the most adaptive to identify threats and opportunities. They are pro-active rather than re-active. If an existing rule, procedure, or past solution is not applicable to a particular situation, then rather than panicking, a new response is sought. The less adaptive resort to an existing stock of responses; the still less responsive always rely upon a fixed rule or procedure for dealing with disturbances; while the least responsive are usually caught unprepared. As one moves from the most to the least responsive category one finds progressively less information being used. Communication falls in quantity and quality. It should be pointed out, however, that reliance upon rules and procedures can work where technology and the market environment is stable.

The effectiveness of people in an environment of changing technology will depend upon the extent to which they understand their environment and perceive it as changing rather than as stable and uniform. Some organization cultures are more adaptive than others.

The role culture tends not to be adaptive. The matrix form or organization can be adaptive when suitable individuals can be found within it (or supplemented from outside) to form project groups appropriate to new developments. The power culture is as adaptive as its entrepreneur leader.

As flexibility and adaptability increase, the role culture will experience mounting strain. The co-ordinating committees will tend to become overloaded. The world will not wait while new rules are drawn up. Organizational change may be forced by external forces, perhaps the bank bringing in consultants and a matrix form of organization being adopted.

In the most adaptive technologies, the task- and particularly the person-cultures will thrive on change. The skills of their members and their patterns of communication, which allow relatively free interaction between experts, are especially suited to problem-solving. Power cultures will become high credit risks. One wrong major decision of the big boss might result in the death of the organization.

TWO MAJOR OIL COMPANIES CAUSED PROBLEMS FOR THE ENTIRE OIL DISTRIBUTION AND RETAILING INDUSTRY BY FAILING TO SUBMIT DETAILED REQUESTS FOR PRICE INCREASES IN TIME TO MEET THE UK GOVERNMENT'S DEADLINE. THE COMPANIES HAD NOT ADJUSTED TO THE NEW REGULATORY ROLE EXERCISED BY THE GOVERNMENT AND ONE OF THEM HAD BEEN MISINFORMED ABOUT THE DEADLINE.

Question 38: How responsive is the organization with which you are most familiar? How could it be made more responsive?

3.9 FORMAL AND INFORMAL SYSTEMS

What happens in practice within a company, how it actually operates, may be very different from what the conclusions drawn from an examination of its organization chart and the job specifications of its staff might suggest. The informal system may in some areas be more important than the formal one.

Question 39: What are the major differences between the formal and informal systems in the organization with which you are most familiar? In what areas is the informal system more important?

3.91 Organizational Politics

Most business organizations are to some degree political organizations. Groups can form with the purpose of improving a relative power position or to change rules in order to convert informal power to formal authority.

Office politics are irrepressible as individuals jockey for status. Competitive situations can arise where, for example, two departments vie for the new typewriter that has just been delivered. Progress in an organization demands both co-operation and competition between individuals.

Staff adopt very different strategies for getting ahead. Some attach themselves to other individuals or groups they perceive as being on the up, while others seek to make a personal mark by carving out an individual niche. The former strategy might be the most successful in a power culture, the latter in a task culture in which task team members are chosen upon the basis of demonstrated individual professional achievement.

In his book *White Collar*, C. Wright Mills expresses one view of how individuals get ahead in organizations:

> "Now the stress is on agility rather than ability, on 'getting along' in a context of associates, superiors and rules rather than 'getting ahead' across an open market; on who you know rather than what you know; on techniques of self-display and the generalised knack of handling people. But the most important single factor is 'personality', which commands attention, . . . by chorus, . . . force of character, or demeanour . . . . Geting ahead becomes a continual selling job . . . You have a product and that product is yourself."

Some companies contain extensive cliques based upon networks of reciprocal obligations. These cliques may be in conflict. Considerable ties of loyalty can build up over the years; sponsor and protegees may form teams. These informal relationships must be sought out by anyone seriously intent upon analysing and changing an organization.

It is necessary to keep any such understanding obtained up to date. Power is generated, consolidated, maintained, and eroded through relationships with others. The situation in most organizations will be dynamic.

> AN ALLY OF A NEW MANAGER ABOUT TO TAKE CONTROL OF A MARKETING DEPARTMENT HELD A NUMBER OF LARGE ORDERS OVER UNTIL THE BEGINNING OF THE NEXT BUDGET YEAR IN ORDER TO BOOST THE PERCEIVED PERFORMANCE OF THE NEW MANAGER AND REDUCE THE SALES ACHIEVED BY THE OUTGOING (AND DISLIKED) MANAGER. ONE OF THE ORDERS WAS SUBSE-QUENTLY LOST, THE INTENDING CUSTOMER COMPLAINING ABOUT THE DELAYS IN PROCESSING IT.

Question 40:   In what ways can organizational politics be:

  (*a*)   constructive
  (*b*)   destructive?

3.10 MANAGEMENT CONTROL

The system of management control applied and its communication requirements will depend upon the tasks performed. The system will vary across departments and according to a company's strategy, its staff and the technology within which it operates.

There is no best form of management control applicable to all situations. This section will concentrate upon how control can be established by setting objectives and then measuring the extent to which they are achieved within the time allowed. The control system adopted must be appropriate to the objectives set and the people responsible for carrying them out.

A company that carries out its own research and development, manufacturing retailing, and distribution is more likely to require an expensive monitoring and appraisal system than the retailer able to operate on a trial and error basis. In the former case, the consequences of failure will be much more traumatic.

The more remote an organizational unit from field operations, the less it will be concerned with the detail of a strategy. A holding company may not be interested in individual product-market decisions within an agreed business area while the investment company may only examine financial performances.

Question 41:   How is management control achieved in the organization with which you are most familiar? Is it effective and appropriate to the organization's

    (*a*)   tasks
    (*b*)   strategy
    (*c*)   technology
    (*d*)   people?

3.11 MARKETING ORGANIZATION

The status and role of marketing within a company will depend upon its objectives and its approach to achieving them. The more unstable the technology within which a firm is operating, the greater the need to be market-orientated to survive. Reorganizing a marketing function by market in place of product can increase the status of marketing within a company. Marketing has the highest status in the market-centred company.

Organization, technology, tasks, strategy, and people will all influence the place of marketing within an organization.

Question 42:   What is the status of marketing within the organization with which you are most familiar? What are the reasons for this?

Having outlined some major organizational types in this chapter and established that effective organizations are those that match the jobs they have to do, a number of alternative ways of organizing the marketing function will now be examined. Marketing departments vary as widely as organizations in general but it is nevertheless instructive to categorize them into a limited number of types. Their advantages and disadvantages for particular marketing situations can then be assessed.

Marketing can be organized on a function, product, market, or project basis. Frequently, an organization in practice is a mixture of each of these. Over time, the mix is likely to change, the emphasis being at one moment in one direction and at the next in another. Each form of organization has its strengths and weaknesses and when designing a marketing organization, one is inevitably involved in tradeoffs.

3.111 Organization by Function

In this form of organization the marketing department is made up of marketing specialists (in sales, market research, planning, and advertising, etc.) reporting up a hierarchy which culminates in a sales or marketing director. The department is staffed by marketing professionals and, generally, marketing professionals alone. For ease of management they may be divided into groups, for example operations and planning. The focus of the organization is marketing skill. Specialist functional expertise is the organizing factor.

Functional organizations work best in companies having homogenous products and markets. When the differences between products and market is minimized, marketing skill becomes a suitable focus. Organization by function is particularly suited to stable technologies and tasks that throw up few exceptions. It fits in well with role cultures. The predominant channels of communication tend to be internal, as memoranda and reports flow up and down the bureaucratic hierarchy.

ONE ORGANIZATION WITH DEPARTMENTS SPECIALIZING IN PARTICULAR NARROW FUNCTIONS FOUND STAFF SPENDING A GREAT DEAL OF TIME IN EACH OTHERS' ROOMS. THE EMPLOYEES WERE FOUND TO BE DISSATISFIED AS A RESULT OF NOT BEING ABLE TO SEE HOW THEIR FUNCTIONS INTER-RELATED AND CONTRIBUTED TO THE FINAL PRODUCT.

AN OPEN DESIGN OFFICE WAS INTRODUCED. A MIX OF FUNCTIONS WERE PLACED ON EACH FLOOR. SOME DEPARTMENTS WERE MERGED TO ENLARGE THEIR FUNCTIONS. AFTER THE CHANGE STAFF APPEARED TO BE MORE SETTLED.

3.112 Organization by Product

The organization is built around a product or group of products having common characteristics rather than marketing skill. This is most appropriate where products or groups of products are dissimiliar. They are grouped, for example, industrial and consumer, or human and non-human.

In the larger company, each branch might have its own organization. Services offered by specialists can be centralized and offered to the product groups as and when required or devolved. In the divisionalized company, each product group could be run by a general manager with profit responsibility. Product knowledge becomes the focus. The organizing factor may be similar production requirements.

Centralizing certain functions such as market research and advertising can lead to benefits of specialization but, where products are unrelated and changing, the centre can become out of touch with what is happening in the field. In a mixed form of organization, central functions might only be devolved to the larger product groups. Communications problems can arise when specialists report to both the general manager of their product group and to their functional head at main office.

Product organizations are compatible with role cultures. When strongly led, a product group can develop symptoms of the power culture. In the area of new product development, product task groups are frequently resorted to, the freer interchange of information within this form of group assisting innovation. In product organization, the predominant communications channels can be those facing backwards to production managers, designers, stock controllers, and engineers.

3.113 Organization by Market

When customers fall into distinct groups with different buying practices relating to similar products and 'markets vary more than products', then the market form of organization might be the most appropriate. The organization is built around market managers responsible for groups of customers having common characteristics. Expertise about the requirements and practices of its particular market is accumulated in each unit. Market knowledge becomes the focus, a similar selling process.

This form of organization may not be practical when customers are widely spread, when a territorial form of organization would be more appropriate, or when there are no obvious common characteristics linking groups of customers. Where appropriate, it frequently evolves into a performance or matrix form of organization. The more dynamic the market the less likely it is that the organization will be a role culture.

The predominant channels of communications in market organizations are those that relate to the market. Priority may be given to information about market needs flowing inwards rather than product information flowing outwards.

A MAJOR CUSTOMER OF AN INDUSTRIAL SUPPLIER COMPLAINED THAT THREE OF THE SUPPLIER'S SALESMEN HAD CALLED UPON HIM ON THE SAME DAY. HE WANTED TO KNOW WHY HE WAS BEING SUBJECTED TO SUCH CLOSE 'INVESTIGATION'. ON EXAMINATION IT WAS FOUND THAT THE COMPANY'S PRODUCT-BASED ORGANIZATION WAS RESULTING IN MANY DUPLICATED JOURNEYS. THE COMPANY WAS REORGANIZED, IN SOME AREAS GROUPS OF RELATED PRODUCTS BEING BROUGHT TOGETHER, IN OTHERS LIAISON SALESMEN ALLOCATED TO SPECIFIC MAJOR ACCOUNTS.

3.114 Organization by Project

This is the most flexible and adaptive form of marketing organization. The job to be done, the project or task, becomes the organizational focus. The group organizes itself so as to best be able to tackle the work that must be done.

Task groups in the most changing of technologies and markets tend to perish or become performance, matrix, or person cultures. Effective performance can sometimes be directly related to the quantity of communication within the group. In adaptive groups, the channels tend to face in many directions and two-way communication is preferred to one-way.

3.115 Market-centred Organization

For a period, market-centring was in vogue. Organizations can be built around their markets rather than their production capabilities, products, or regions. The market-centred companies' market orientation is reflected in the way its organization is structured. Its various functions and divisions are constructed around the markets it serves.

Some electronic equipment manufacturers have built their organizations around markets such as health. Others have organized vertically by industry rather than geographical area. In some cases, a mixture of product and market organization is retained. A number of safety equipment companies have divisions serving separate industries. Transportation companies could organize on the basis of distribution needs having, for example, separate oil, chemical, and mineral divisions.

Companies have adopted the market-centred approach for a number of reasons. Often the step is taken defensively, following competitor action. For a large customer, the main benefit comes from dealing with one salesman concerned with all of one's requirements rather than with a number of salesmen each concerned with a piece of the whole.

Compared with organization on a branch management basis, market-centring switches the emphasis away from products and towards customers and markets. Market-centred companies can grow by selling more of their existing product range to their markets and by evolving new products to meet the needs of their markets.

EXAMINATION QUESTIONS

1. In recent years, much attention has been given to the multi-national enterprise. What are the marketing organization and communications advantages and disadvantages of such enterprises?

2. When framing their recommendations, consultants often have regard to the 'management style' of a company. What is meant by this expression and why do you consider it important?

3. Give at least one example (real or imagined) where the way in which a company is organized would seem to be incompatible with the achievement of its marketing objectives. Discuss the extent to which inadequate communications have a contributory effect.

4. 'It should be possible to assess the extent of a company's commitment to marketing by looking at its organization chart.' Discuss.

5. Suggest how a manufacturing company should be organized to ensure that on a continuing basis, its products make use of the latest advances in technology.

4. *Marketing Management*

This chapter relates what has been learned about individuals and groups to certain questions of marketing management within organizations. Subsequent chapters deal successively with the management of innovation and new products, the management of existing products, the management of sales staff, the management of relationships with bodies external to the organization, including distributors and competitors, and how one learns about the preferences of customers.

4.1 M A N A G I N G   S T A F F

A manager responsible for others can possess a variety of attributes. One manager may be firm, protective, and decisive. Another may delegate and be responsive to the needs and career ambitions of others.

Some managers reward objective performance. Others are most indulgent to those who show the greatest loyalty and deference to them. A correct manager may be a stickler for rules, taking pains to exercise only allocated authority and only demanding from subordinates what the formal system requires.

A subordinate may or may not be compatible with a manager. The compliant, hardworking, and loyal subordinate will match the strong decisive manager but may feel uncertain with a manager who delegates and allows his or her staff a high degree of discretion.

Some employees are safe, responsible and reliable, reluctant to take risks and possibly embarrass. This can irritate an aggressive, dynamic manager. A subordinate can be self-motivated and interested in individual development. This could please a manager who delegates but annoy a more authoritarian one who would prefer to be in control.

Matching staff to managers can be a complex process. Much will depend upon the overall attitude of the organization towards those who work within it. Are they expected to 'fit in' and to do what is required of them? Is more imagination required, but within the context of original duties and responsibilities?

Alternatively, the task may be put first, the ideal employee being regarded as one who is able to summon whatever skills and energy are required to complete the task. An organization could place a very high value upon the needs of those who work within it.

Creative staff are likely to resent managers who treat them as work fodder, people whose time and energy is 'there', just to be used by those who are higher up the organization chart. The manager who sticks to the 'letter of the law', constantly referring to job descriptions and the terms of service agreements, may be equally objectionable.

More acceptable would be the manager who appears as a fellow professional, contributing to and equally committed to the achievement of a common objective. Creative personnel will of course respect creativity. Staff are likely to value managers who rank highly on criteria they consider to be important.

The motivation of people to do routine work can rest upon simple economic rewards and punishment and the enforcement of established procedures and work standards. Motivating creative workers may demand a very different approach.

The objectives of the group or the nature of the task may need to be set out and a discussion held of the best way of reaching desired performance. Staff can show a high personal commitment to goals, the establishment of which involved their participation. The greatest motivation may of course be the intrinsic interest of the work being done and the intrinsic enjoyment of the way in which it is done.

> AN EMPLOYEE SUGGESTED TO ANOTHER THAT A MANAGER WHO WAS A HEAVY DRINKER SHOULD BE SHOT. 'IF HE WAS' CAME THE REPLY 'WHATEVER POURED OUT OF HIM WOULD HAVE A HEAD ON IT'.

Question 43: How should a good manager deal with staff who are respectively lazy, overambitious, frequently late, hard working to the point of being slavish, and heavily involved in political and trade union activities?

> ONE DIRECTOR OF A LOCAL AUTHORITY DEPARTMENT USED TO DEAL WITH DIFFICULT QUESTIONS FROM COMMITTEE MEMBERS BY SAYING 'THAT IS A VERY INTERESTING QUESTION. TO DO IT JUSTICE, RATHER THAN TACKLE IT HERE, I WOULD LIKE TO GIVE IT FURTHER CONSIDERATION AND COME BACK WITH A REPORT'. FEW REPORTS CAME BACK.

Question 44: Outline some action you have taken to delay the implementation of a change with which you have not agreed. What action if any did the initiator of the change take to overcome your resistance?

4.2 MANAGING MARKETING SPECIALISTS

Within the marketing area there are many who hold staff positions. Frequently, staff roles are exercised by experts, specialists who in their daily work come into contact with non-specialist line managers. In such encounters there is scope for misunderstanding.

The staff specialist may look down upon a line manager as possessing fewer specialist qualifications. The line manager in contrast might consider staff work a soft option, an ivory tower existence closetted from the sharp end. A line manager daily facing crisis situations may consider staff specialists as an expensive luxury.

Staff work tends by its nature to be fluctuating. A specialist may be involved on specific assignments of fixed duration. Between assignments, a specialist may be embarrassed on meeting line managers at not having work to do. Credibility as a specialist will depend upon the ability to influence line specialists.

Staff specialists may operate across departmental and office boundaries. Their roles are often ambiguous. A specialist and a line manager may have differing perceptions of what needs to be done. Because so much of their work may be regarded as a prelude to change, staff specialists are particularly susceptible to hostility. Those likely to suffer from change will naturally seek to prevent it.

To be effective, a specialist must be credible. This depends upon the ability to engender a positive response in others. To influence, one must know what is important to those one seeks to influence and their view of the world. Having a variety of contacts on a number of matters can assist in the building of relationships. An expert may build up credibility by successfully tackling a series of small jobs before making a play for a larger one. Timing is often crucial in such circumstances.

As an organization grows, it may establish a wider range of specialist support services. New departments may be formed, centralizing certain marketing activities. This process can result in certain functions being taken from the product manager. In some companies, liaison managers act as go-betweens, intermediaries between product managers and the managers of particular resources.

AN OPERATIONAL RESEARCHER CONTINUALLY MOVED BETWEEN EMPLOYMENTS IN ACADEMIA AND IN CONSULTING FIRMS. IN NEITHER 'WORLD' HAD HE BEEN SATISFIED UNTIL HE WAS GIVEN THE JOB OF BEING PROJECT MANAGER ON THE INTRODUCTION OF A NEW WORLDWIDE MARKET REPORTING SYSTEM. THE MANAGER PREVIOUSLY THOUGHT TO BE A 'BOFFIN' WAS FOUND TO HIS AND HIS COLLEAGUES' SURPRISE, TO POSSESS CONSIDERABLE MANAGEMENT SKILLS. HE BECAME DEEPLY INVOLVED WITH THE PROJECT WHICH WAS COMPLETED AHEAD OF TIME.

Question 45: Outline what communications problems you consider might emerge during interaction between the following specialist—non-specialist pairs:

(*a*)   teacher—parent
(*b*)   doctor—patient
(*c*)   chemical salesman—farmer user
(*d*)   public health inspector—restaurant owner
(*e*)   business graduate—'come up the hard way' salesman.

4.3   THE PRODUCT MANAGER

Organizations are rarely static and companies with a surface appearance of considerable stability may be found in practice to be in a state of considerable flux. In some organizations, the status of product managers had been eroded in recent years. Some companies have moved away from product management back to functional organization. Other, however, have adopted and strengthened product management. The effectiveness of product management has not changed, only its relevance to the tasks and strategies of organizations.

Within companies that have retained product management there has been an evolution of practice. Functions such as advertising have tended to be taken from the jack-of-all-trades product manager and given to specialists. Specialization and professionalization have become almost universal phenomena. Professionals are tending to demand more person-centred forms of organization.

The product manager role is effective so far as product market research, product planning, and monitoring are concerned. Product decisions, however, should be made at the competent level which might be higher up the management tree than the product manager.

The competent level is that at which the required information and decision-making expertise is available. Different decisions will be taken at different levels. The location of decision-making will vary according to the particular tasks the organization is undertaking and the characteristics and qualities of staff occupying positions within it.

Marketing tasks and personnel then can be grouped on a functional basis, an overall manager co-ordinating specialist contributions and applying them to the solution of marketing problems. Alternating functions can be grouped around products. In some cases decentralization may allow considerable discretion to those responsible for a particular group of products. Another form of organization is to group tasks to serve a market.

Within a product-centred form of organization, product managers may emerge in order to create a planning and promotional focus. Without product managers, products can receive uneven service.

The product manager with authority may be able to act swiftly without having to go through committees. The product-manager system can ensure that new and emerging brands are not overlooked but receive their full share of attention. The system also provides a training experience for future general managers.

A production orientation frequently leads to a stable but bureaucratic form of organization which reacts much more slowly than the more market-orientated company which has remained flexible and which has consciously invested in adaptability. The long-run survivors are those organizations which can both perform today's tasks efficiently and retain a high capacity for change.

Question 46: Outline the major advantages and disadvantages of product management.

4.4 MANAGING ORGANIZATIONAL CHANGE

Moving from a product-centred to a market-centred form of organization can present problems. Specialist sales staff may need to be trained or recruited. The market centre can form a profit centre as can a factory supplying a number of markets. New accounting skills may be required. The changeover can lead to higher overheads.

The first step is often the market-centring of the sales force or the grouping of products serving particular groups of customers into market divisions. The next stage is the allocation of both manufacturing and marketing functions to market divisions. The key to success is identifying markets that are homogenous, made up of customers with similar and related needs. Each market centre can be run by a profit-responsible manager to whom considerable authority is delegated.

Support services such as research and development, financial control, management development, and corporate public relations are frequently centralized in companies that have re-organized on a market basis. The manager of a market centre could be given the freedom to only draw upon central support services as and when required.

A company could define its markets in terms of generic-need or in terms of target groups. The teenage market could be the focus of marketing activity.

A COMPANY ADOPTING A MARKET-CENTRED FORM OF ORGANI-
ZATION BEGAN TO LOSE A NUMBER OF ITS MORE EXPERIENCED
SALESMEN. THEY COMPLAINED THAT KNOWLEDGE OF THE PRO-
DUCT DID NOT SEEM TO MATTER ANY MORE AND THAT IN
PROMOTION TERMS THEY WERE LOSING GROUND TO YOUNG
'SMOOTHIES' WHO ONLY TOOK BIG CUSTOMERS TO LUNCH AND
WHO DID NOT WANT TO GET THEIR HANDS DIRTY WITH THE
'NITTY GRITTY' PREFERRING TO KNOW A LITTLE ABOUT A LOT
OF PRODUCTS, RATHER THAN A GREAT DEAL ABOUT ANY ONE
PRODUCT IN PARTICULAR. TWO OF THE SALESMEN ABOUT TO

LEAVE WERE PERSUADED TO STAY ON IN A NEW MORE SENIOR INTERNAL CONSULTANCY ROLE.

Question 47: How appropriate do you consider the market-centred form of organization would be for a:

(*a*) supermarket
(*b*) coal mine
(*c*) office furniture manufacturer
(*d*) barber's shop
(*e*) hotel
(*f*) ball-bearing manufacturer
(*g*) advertising agency
(*h*) hospital?

Defining a business in terms of servicing the needs of its customers and adopting the market-centred form of organization can establish the primacy of marketing within a company. Market changes become the driving force of organizational change. Whether or not the organization is stable will depend upon development within the marketplace.

The greater the extent to which the marketing concept is adopted the more likely it will be that staff with marketing backgrounds and qualifications will hold higher positions within the organization. The business 'leader' may well be a marketor.

The continuance of the market-centred orientation by an organization should not be taken for granted. Specialists may yearn for more of a functional form of organization and seek through small steps to obtain it. There might be a barely perceptible shift towards a product-based form of organization.

Many employees feel uncomfortable with the marketing concept. They find it unsettling rather than challenging. To some it may appear nebulous. One is dealing with developments 'out there' in the market, rather than focusing upon the product which is known and is largely within one's control.

Unless there is lasting excess demand, a company that does not adopt the marketing concept will be in danger. Value added is ultimately created by customers. If customers do not buy, an organization will be left with so much scrap material. If the customer is not satisfied, there may be competitors eager to increase their market shares who satisfy them instead.

A TECHNICAL DIRECTOR OF AN ENGINEERING COMPANY THAT HAD EMBRACED THE MARKETING CONCEPT CONFESSED THAT HE HAD CEASED TO ENJOY BOARD MEETINGS. IN THE 'OLD DAYS' THE BOARD WOULD ADJOURN EARLY TO GO DOWN TO THE LABORA-TORY TO SEE 'WHAT WAS GOING ON'. NOW MEETINGS LASTED WELL INTO THE AFTERNOON 'WITH ALL THIS TALK ABOUT

MARKETS AND CUSTOMERS – SOON WE WON'T BE MAKING INTER-
ESTING PRODUCTS ANYMORE'.

4.5 COMPUTER-BASED MODELLING

There has been a great increase in the marketing application of computer-based
modelling. Models are employed to improve the quality of marketing decision-
making. The trend is currently away from detailed and complex company-wide
models in favour of specific applications of small, custom-built models. The
emphasis today is upon simplicity, understanding, and the relevance to a decision
situation.

Simple models are best from the point of view of building confidence along
with accuracy, and relevance to a decision situation. The best introduction to
modelling is often via mechanization of a laborious hand routine. Modelling can
force managers to think logically about a problem and to exercise judgement.

In the early stages, modelling is likely to need the support of top management.
Modelling can assist in the decision-making process, enabling marketing managers
to make better decisions but in no way replace them. Wherever possible, a model
should be tailored to a specific context and, when beginning, too much should
not be expected too soon.

Question 48: Outline a management technique with which you are familiar and
(honestly!) count the number of occasions on which you have made use of it to
tackle business problems. If the technique in question is applicable to a wide range
of management problems, explain why you have not used it more often.

A marketing manager may be faced with a choice between using an off-the-shelf
model or a tailor-made model, perhaps constructed with a user-orientated language.
By using special languages called modelling languages, non-specialist managers are
able to construct their own models. This is frequently justified where model usage
is heavy. It should always be remembered, however, that a model which is 99.99%
correct is, nevertheless, useless. A complete arithmetical check is a must. Models
therefore become cost-effective when a number of runs are envisaged, perhaps to
test the sensitivity of an outcome to various input assumptions.

An effective model should be usable by non-specialists and operated close to the
location of decisions. It should be practical, adaptable, sensible, complete, and
credible, and the user should be able to control it and to communicate easily with
it. A model does not replace the manager, it helps him to make more effective
decisions.

When building a model, it is important to capture the world to be modelled as
the user sees it. If this is not done, the user may consider the model irrelevant and
not 'his' model. A model should reflect what the user considers to be important.

One must clearly differentiate between fact and judgemental input. A manager is much more likely to make use of the results of a model if he is able to interact with it and thus 'play a part' in their generation.

A model organizes information in such a way as to make it more valuable to decision-makers. In so doing, it encourages clear and logical thought. The creative part of modelling is setting the problem out logically on paper and solving it. Once this is done, coding the resulting model in a language a computer will understand becomes a routine job which can be handled by a programmer. Models demand rigorous thinking and their use can therefore impose extra demands upon managers and one must beware of possible behavioural reactions such as an eventual return to old ways because, although less efficient, it 'used to be less tiring'.

4.51 The Use of Models

Models can serve a variety of functions, for example to evaluate the effectiveness of advertising. They can calculate the outcomes of certain events or the consequences of certain assumptions. They can both evaluate alternatives and search for alternatives. A model could generate tables showing profit and distribution consequences of different product mixes or be given the task of working out the optimum allocation of depots to territories. A model could be used to calculate the optimum number of calls for each customer.

Computer-based models can be used cost-effectively to produce marketing reports and hence can help improve the control of diverse operations. They can be employed to appraise the likely return on new investments, say the construction of warehouses. Models can incorporate probabilities, for example given a salesman's call, the probabilities of a purchase of each of the company's products.

Models offer a high speed of response, require the explicit listing of assumptions, can allow more alternatives to be evaluated, can identify new options, can allow more questions to be asked and can relate to activity. They can thus help in planning and, as a control tool, can assist in the identification of areas of weakness.

A model can work backwards from a given result to calculate the values of certain input variables which will cause this selected output. Thus, a firm could specify certain target rates of sales and profit growth and use a model to determine, given its production constraints, which mix of products would generate the desired results. The same model could then be used to generate the implications of such a product mix for whatever areas of marketing activity had been built into the model.

4.52 Problem Solving

A marketing manager is most unlikely to be conversant with such techniques as Markov-process models, simulation, queuing theory, game theory, network planning, and linear or dynamic programming to the point of being able to apply them to complex problems. There is, however, usually little need for him to possess such expertise. A larger company will have its management scientists with specialist qualifications in these fields and, wherever and whenever there is a gap in-house, recourse can always be had to external consultants.

What is more important in a marketing manager than such technical expertise is the ability to recognise when day-to-day problems are susceptible to management science techniques, and a willingness in such cases to call in the expert. Although not versed in a particular technique, it does not follow that a marketing manager will be unable to monitor and control the assignment in question. It is important to remember that, however complex a technique employed, the whole assignment is likely to be tackled in a logical sequence of steps.

The first step is to define the problem, then make sure one is focussing upon what is really at issue. Next, one must identify the variables involved and collect data on those factors that influence the results one is examining. At this stage, the data can be analysed but, before actually developing a model, criteria should be established for assessing the results.

The model employed to process the data and produce the results might be of varying degrees of complexity. Whether it is computer-based or scribbled on the back of an envelope, it is vital that it be tested prior to an operational run. This should be done using actual data on a realistic problem. The whole model should be tested, not just a portion of it. Unless a complete manual check is carried out, there is no way, as was stressed in Section 4.5, of knowing whether or not a model is working as it should.

The complete and tested package is then put to work, the results examined and, if successful, the new procedure is implemented as a normal part of the work of the marketing department. Once operational, a model application or other procedure should be continually assessed and refined as required.

A PROPERTY COMPANY REFUSED TO EMPLOY A MODEL THAT HAD BEEN BUILT FOR IT AT GREAT COST. IN A SAMPLE PRINT-OUT THAT HAD BEEN PROVIDED, ONE OF THE DIRECTORS HAD FOUND AN ERROR OF ONE POUND IN AN ADDITION OF SEVERAL AMOUNTS RUNNING INTO MILLIONS OF POUNDS. IT WAS EXPLAIN-ED THAT THIS WAS A 'ROUNDING ERROR', THE MODEL ROUNDING ALL NUMBERS TO THE NEAREST WHOLE POUND. THIS EXPLANA-TION WAS NOT ACCEPTED. THE MODEL WAS REJECTED ON THE GROUNDS THAT IT COULD NOT 'ADD UP PROPERLY'.

Question 49: Your company wishes to instal within three months a mini-computer in your sales department to produce up-to-date sales forecasts. The department is currently staffed with middle-aged women who, through years of experience, are able to decipher the handwriting of individual salesmen. The new computer will only require one operator, the salesmen filling in precoded forms.

Explain how you will be spending your time over the next three weeks.

4.6 SPECIALISTS AND COMMUNICATION

Scientists need communication with their peers if they are to remain in the van of progress. This causes problems for the security-conscious company. A management, through fear of revealing new product-development plans, can starve a scientific team of the contact with activity occurring at the boundary of knowledge which could alone ensure success. Alternatively, the scientific team with the scholar's belief in openness and the need to pass new knowledge to others could inadvertently pass to a competitor a piece of information of great value, enabling them to overcome some obstacle that has been holding them back.

Some organizations, for example a consulting firm, might find its very existence depending upon it being seen as 'up with the leaders' in many fields. The firm's competence and reputation might be enhanced by the publication of technical articles and the wide publicity given to survey results. Published booklets and books help to create confidence in the author's ability and lying on library shelves may be referred to many times, on occasions such referrals leading to enquiries and subsequent work.

Question 50: Outline what speciality-related communications needs the following specialists would have and suggest ways in which these needs could be satisfied:

- (*a*) nuclear scientists
- (*b*) transport managers
- (*c*) accountants
- (*d*) marketors
- (*e*) welders.

4.61 External Specialists

A hard-pressed marketing manager can always seek help from outside of the organization. The objectives of such help should be carefully defined and only those organizations approached with skills and experience relevant to the job in hand.

When commissioning outside help, it may be advisable to brief not only on what needs to be done and why, but on how an objective is likely to be achieved. Constraints should be pointed out and a ceiling placed on expenditure of time and money. Deadlines should be set if drift is to be avoided.

When an outside consultancy is hired, it should be made clear at an early stage that progress is to be reviewed periodically. A form of report may be specified. Some flexibility may need to be built into a brief but an organization should take care to distinguish between charges that are within and those that are without the original terms of reference. An organization must be prepared to pay for work that is required beyond that initially agreed.

When selecting an external service, one should bear in mind considerations other than cost. The cheapest service may have been cut to the bone. As a supplier may attempt to charge what the market will bear some cost breakdowns should be asked for. A large external service organization may require that such safeguards as progress payments be written into a service agreement.

Question 51: What outside help would you seek if you were charged with the task of acquiring and installing a mini-computer based reporting system? Draw up a brief for each source of assistance desired and explain how in each case you would propose to monitor performance.

An external organization offering help is likely to be primarily concerned with its own interests. Outside help may take time to organize and may not be available when needed.

A marketing manager may be reluctant to seek external help for fear that this will be seen as evidence of failure to cope with a job or just plain idleness. There is no guarantee that any activity will lead to success. The 'better the devil that one knows' approach can lead to an organization just soldiering on.

Cutting corners, lowering standards of safety and accuracy, and employing 'cheap' labour can be means of improving contract profitability. The user of an external service should keep an eye on the quality of work. It is difficult to cut corners when a brief is narrow and specific. It is generally advisable to confine outside help to those areas in which it is likely to yield the highest return.

Many marketing managers have become somewhat cynical of the slick reports and presentations delivered by external consultants. A glossy brochure may contain elementary errors of fact. Volume for its own sake is of little value. Beware of those who present long reports in order to give the impression that a great deal of work has been done. An examination of an external consultant's client list may reveal possible opportunities for confidential information to fall into the hands of competitors.

A youngish consultant may dress expensively and drop the names of prestigious clients. The more experienced consultant may by comparison appear detached and aloof, even disinterested. The personalities of consultants vary so much that every effort should be made to select those likely to be compatible with one's own staff. This requires a knowledge of who will actually do the work.

Being on the same wavelength is one thing; merely tossing back someone's own ideas, biases and preferences is another. It is easy to be lured into paying a lot of money for one's own point of view to be expressed. Independence can be valuable. The ideal consultant on experience grounds may not be available or unwilling to meet a deadline.

A BRAND MANAGER EMPLOYED AN IRON RULE OF CHANGING HIS ADVERTISING AGENCY EVERY EIGHTEEN MONTHS, REGARD-LESS OF PERFORMANCE. HE FELT THAT BEYOND ABOUT A YEAR, AGENCIES TENDED TO BECOME STALE AND SLACK, THE QUALITY OF THEIR SERVICE TAILING OFF.

EXAMINATION QUESTIONS

1. Suggest how conflict between individuals can be used creatively in a business organization.

2. Account for the emergence of companies other than advertising agencies providing specialist media-buying services for advertisers.

5. *Innovation*

Innovative situations, contexts, and behaviour give rise to particular communication problems. This chapter examines creativity, innovation, and the development of new products and their organization and management.

5.1 THE MANAGEMENT OF CREATIVITY

Creativity generally involves combining new elements in novel ways. It can be encouraged by consciously assisting cross-fertilization between areas, recognizing the needs of creative personnel and judging performance according to standards the creative personnel themselves understand and respect. Disappointment resulting from the rejection of ideas will need to be carefully handled.

Creative groups should be open to a wide range of information sources and specific techniques such as brainstorming, lateral thinking, dimension linking, task or gap analysis, and guided problem solving.

Question 52: How would you measure creativity?

5.11 Creative People

Creative people can become carried away with the creative process itself and, to take an example, lose sight of the ultimate publics which advertisements are aimed at. In the advertising world the gimmick may attract the attention of one's peer group at an international advertising festival and perhaps win a prize, while at the same time pulling in fewer extra sales than a less creative solution.

One can become stale in creative work. Alternatively, one can become obsessed with change for its own sake. Some become bored with the detailed implication aspects of campaigns once the initial creative work is complete.

An advertisement can build upon what has gone before or start afresh. The former may be more cost effective from the company point of view but less stimulating for the copywriter eager to demonstrate independence from old ideas. It is easy for a designer to become 'carried away' with the means and to forget the ends of communication.

A client should make it clear to creative personnel that they are not being judged on the basis of how imaginative their gimmicks are but according to the workability of their solutions to concrete communications problems. It is the 'what is being said' that is important, rather than the 'how it is said'.

Balance is particularly important in communication. A balance must be struck between the attention-getting, information-giving, credibility-building, and motivating aspects of an advertisement. Over-concentration upon one or other of these factors can lead to the virtual exclusion of another from consideration. Having one good practical solution is preferable to being confronted with a variety of solutions each of which has some defect.

Question 53:   Your designer, who is known to dislike working under pressure, is running late but promises to come up with a very creative solution. As your deadline rapidly approaches what do you do?

5.2 INNOVATION

Some individuals are naturally venturesome and eager to try new ideas. Others are conservative and wedded to tradition. Individuals vary in their ability to tolerate risk. Internally-motivated people tend to take the initiative more than the outwardly motivated, who rely upon others to give a lead and take their values from opinion formers.

Innovators are often highly mobile. They are explorers. They tend to have above-average numbers of contacts and to be more aware of what is going on around them. Marketing managers building teams may wish to achieve a balance between the venturesome and the conservative or to neutralize the conservative if change is needed. A good manager has a shrewd idea of the tolerance of each of the staff in his or her team for risk and change.

Those that lag behind can be of value in marketing situations. Many fingers have been burned as a result of jumping too soon into a new market with an untested product. Caution, if not overdone, is a virtue in some industries. Brand loyalty assumes a degree of conservatism.

A TALENTED DESIGNER WITH A CONSIDERABLE TRACK RECORD WAS ABOUT TO LEAVE AN ORGANIZATION TO SET UP HIS OWN BUSINESS TO MARKET A NEW PRODUCT HE HAD DEVELOPED. THE COMPANY IN PANIC OFFERED TO BACK THE NEW VENTURE. IT FLOPPED. THE FAILURE WAS A BLOW TO THE DESIGNER'S SELF-CONFIDENCE AND HIS SUBSEQUENT WORK WITH THE COMPANY WAS NOT OF A HIGH STANDARD.

5.21   Innovation, Adoption and Organization

The adoption of an innovation tends to occur over time as shown in Figure 5.1. Initially a few adventurous innovators persuade the early adoptors, often by word of mouth, before the early majority take it up. It may be some time before late adoptors, and later still laggards, take up an innovation, even though its utility has been demonstrated by the majority of users.

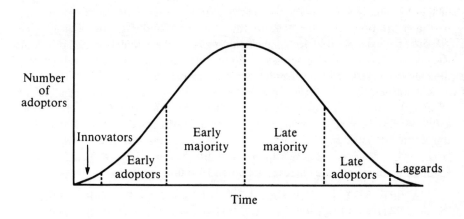

Figure 5.1   The adoption process

When introducing innovations into organizations, it is well to be aware of some of the factors that encourage and inhibit the acceptance of change. Adoption is easier when the advantages are easy to perceive. Having decided that a change is necessary it is all too easy to rush into implementation without considering whether those responsible for the implementation have been properly briefed on why the changes concerned need to occur and the reasons for them.

An innovation, whether a new procedure or a new product, should be as compatible as possible with existing behaviour, beliefs, and values. Speed of acceptance tends to be directly related to the degree of simplicity and the ease with which the reasons for a change can be explained.

Experimentation, test-marketing, trial periods, all help to build confidence and win acceptance for change. Where some resistance to change is likely, one should always attempt to first experiment on a limited basis. Once the advantages begin to be apparent, others will adapt. Seeing is beliving.

When changing organizations, it is well to bear in mind that people tend to approach problems from the point of view of what is in it for them. The advantages of change may be obvious enough from the point of view of the whole organization but may not be apparent to the team in the sales office. If their co-operation is to be obtained, it may be necessary to spend some time explaining how they as a group will benefit. One cannot assume that all employees feel that what is good for the organization is good for them. Communication then is often the key to successful innovation.

Nothing will happen unless the world is told about a new product and its advantages are explained to potential customers.

Creative personnel can be seen as threats by those who are conservative or who have a vested interest in the status quo. A stable organization may be unwilling or unable to tolerate a person who 'rocks the boat'. An innovator can become restless to the point of leaving, perhaps to found a small business. In many growing markets, for example the electronics field, many of the founders of today's giants were yesterday's salaried employees. Only by branching out on their own were they able to experience a satisfactory working environment.

A bureaucratic organization can stifle change. A hard-pressed manager will concentrate upon the short-term and not be sidetracked by the idea which, once a fortune has been spent on it, may with much effort and a great deal of luck transform an industry in ten years' time. And yet the ultimate survival of the large organization will depend upon its ability to innovate. A means must be found of holding onto the creative, the potential rolling stones.

A CREATIVE GROUP HAD BEEN WORKING FOR OVER A YEAR AND HAD FAILED TO 'COME UP' WITH AN ACCEPTABLE SOLUTION. THE GROUP WAS INFORMED THAT ITS EXISTENCE WAS NO LONGER JUSTIFIED AND THAT ITS OPERATION WAS TO BE CLOSED DOWN. THE GROUP'S LEADERS, ON THEIR OWN INITIATIVE, SPENT THEIR SUMMER HOLIDAYS IN THE BACKROOM OF A SEASIDE HOTEL AND WITHIN A MONTH ARRIVED AT THE COMPANY'S HEAD OFFICE WITH AN IMAGINATIVE SOLUTION.

Question 54: What steps would you take to encourage the adoption of the following:

(*a*)   a new seed planter by farmers
(*b*)   a revolutionary method of birth control to men in an Indian village
(*c*)   short skirts by middle-aged ladies
(*d*)   toupées by middle-aged men
(*e*)   the drinking of beer by middle-class housewives?

5.22   Organizing for Innovation

A committee may be an ineffective means of encouraging innovation. A committee may deliberate but responsibility for execution will usually lie elsewhere. Successful innovation requires the authority to both plan and execute.

A new product department unlike a venture team may drift, as a result of not being focussed onto a particular product. A department can become bureaucratic. It may be regarded as just another unit from the point of view of budgeting and reporting.

An individual manager may have great difficulty in innovating alone. A group may be required to carry an idea through to commercial launch. A team can act as a channel for ideas which cannot be pigeon-holed elsewhere and which, as a result, might otherwise be lost.

5.23 The Venture Team

A large organization could create within it a microcosm, a sub-unit whose characteristics are especially conducive to innovation. A special unit, a think tank, could be created, perhaps physically on its own and free from day-to-day management responsibilities or a venture team with special responsibility for new product development.

What are the characteristics of a successful venture team? Being physically and organizationally separate is important, as is drawing team members from a variety of disciplines. Cross-fertilization can occur in the multi-disciplinary team.

Detailed job descriptions should be avoided and authority diffused within the team. Giving team members a financial stake in their output can boost the flow of practical ideas. Deadlines, burdensome reports, and low status can all inhibit venture-team performance.

One potential weakness of the venture team stems from the high calibre of staff it is likely to require. Team members must be able to motivate themselves. They may be inwardly directed and yet able to work with others. Departmental managers may be unwilling to lose valued members of staff to the venture team. Without a financial incentive a new venture team may produce ideas and then become bored with them and move on rather than following through to commercialization.

A group is a dynamic entity. It will mature, consolidate, or fragment over time. A new venture team could have had its origins in a loose arrangement between a number of people with similar interests and perhaps meeting after office hours. Formal recognition can lead to financial support, the use of an office with secretarial help. As a project proceeds definite roles might emerge for team members. Specialisms based upon skills and experience or personal preferences could emerge.

One member of the team might be given a leadership role. More details reporting arrangements and perhaps some formal internal operating procedure could be devised as the group progressed from idea to product. At some point a product concept might be regarded by senior management as 'proved' and therefore handed over to an operating division.

The selection of a venture team leader can be crucial. A technical or commercial background coupled with some profit responsibility is desirable. As new ventures frequently fail a team leader cannot be risk averse. A highly-qualified younger business graduate might survive and learn from failure while an older manager might not be given a second chance. Managers with entrepreneurial skills may be found in small profit-centre divisions or in a business which has recently been acquired. The team leader may be more willing to serve given multiple sources of sponsorship within the organization.

A VENTURE TEAM DRAWN FROM SEPARATE DEPARTMENTS FOUND THAT ITS MOST VALUABLE IDEAS CAME FROM LONG LUNCHES. THIS WAS THE ONLY OCCASION ON WHICH ALL MEM-BERS OF THE GROUP, ALLOCATED ON A PART-TIME BASIS, COULD COME TOGETHER. THE TEAM LEADER REQUESTED A FULL TIME COMMITMENT OF MEMBERS FOR A LIMITED TIME, AND SEPARATE PREMISES. THE REQUEST WAS GRANTED AND THE TEAM'S TASK WAS RAPIDLY COMPLETED.

Question 55: Your organization wishes to develop a new hairspray, a plastic container for tomatoes, and a new radio commercial. In each case assemble whatever team you feel would be appropriate, describing the qualities desirable in team members, how you envisage the team would organize itself, and to whom and how often it would report.

5.24 Locating the Teams

Impatience can lead to a new product idea being killed prematurely. A venture team can become preoccupied with the intrinsic interest of an idea and overlook such questions as market research or cost analysis. Moving from a concept to a business appraisal can cause problems for the venture-team manager drawn from one functional specialism. A team may need to be strengthened at this point.

A really large organization might allow a venture team to hawk its ideas around a number of operating divisions in search of backing. A frequent brake upon further progress at this point can be a reluctance to order equipment required from outside of the organization. A really novel idea might require the development of a new distribution system and existing divisions may be reluctant to finance this.

The success of a venture team may depend upon lobbying to obtain government finance or upon the availability of cash due to the financial success of the whole organization. An organization short of cash could encourage outside venture capital participation in new projects. An alternative for the new venture that requires heavy capital investment is joint venture or consortium development.

5.3 NEW PRODUCT DEVELOPMENT

Most new products fail. In competitive fields the life spans of products will be very short. The cost of failure rises the further a product passes along the development process. This consists of a number of stages, points at which development can be stopped.

A new product begins with an idea. Ideas can originate with customers, competitors, sales staff, or scientists. There are a number of management techniques such as brainstorming; attribute listing, quality matching, problems analysis, and gap analysis which can be used to generate new ideas.

The ideas thrown up need to be screened. Some formal assessment procedure will be necessary. Future costs and revenues will have to be forecast and compared.

If a go-ahead is given the product will need to be produced. There will be research and development work to be undertaken, tools to be engineered, packages to be designed, names to be chosen, and promotional copy devised. A test market may be arranged ahead of full commercial launch.

Commercialization will follow a successful test market. The rate of adoption of the new product and the reorder levels will be monitored. Feedback of performance in the marketplace may suggest product improvements.

5.31   New Product Development Organization

The new product development function in a company can be organized in a number of ways. Individual product managers could be given responsibility for developing new products or this function could be given to specially designated new-product managers. A new product department or committee could be established or the task of developing new products given to venture teams.

Managers of existing products are often too busy to devote attention to anything new beyond modifications to their existing products. Different skills are required to develop new products than to run existing ones. Recognition of the specialist skills involved has led to new product-manager designations. Such specialists may operate primarily with existing managers and can find themselves in a state of limbo.

A fully-fledged top-level committee can carry more clout, can pull together people from separate specialities and co-ordinate overall new-product development. Such a committee can, however, be slow-moving and when operating on the basis of compromise can slow down progress.

A separate department can make use of professional skills and avoids some of the problems associated with committees. It can, however, be more effective as a co-ordinating body than as an actual implementor.

The nitty-gritty of new-product development may best be left to venture teams, mixed groups specifically charged with the commercial development of a particular product or business. The venture team could continue past successful product launch as a product management team but is often axed at this stage, denying the future development of the product much of the specialized expertise that has been built up.

> A GROUP WORKING ON A NEW PRODUCT WERE ACCUSED BY THEIR FELLOW COMPANY EMPLOYEES OF NOT PULLING THEIR WEIGHT. THEIR EFFORTS WERE NOT PRODUCING A TANGIBLE OUTPUT. THEIR PERFORMANCE SUFFERED. THE COMPANY'S MANAGEMENT DECIDED TO PHYSICALLY SEPARATE THE NEW PRODUCT DEPARTMENT FROM THE REST OF THE ORGANIZATION. THE DEPARTMENT WAS MOVED TO A NEW OFFICE AND AS A RESULT ITS WORK PROGRESSED MORE RAPIDLY. THE TIME GAIN- ED HOWEVER WAS LOST AT THE COMMERCIAL LAUNCH PHASE WHEN IT WAS FOUND THAT OTHER DEPARTMENTS HAD 'LOST TOUCH' WITH THE NEW-PRODUCTS STAGE OF DEVELOPMENT.

Question 56:   What forms of organization would you use to develop new products in the contexts, respectively, of a university, a hospital, a political party, and a nationalized industry?

5.32   Danger Areas

The efficiently-running marketing department can give an impression that all is well when opportunities for developing new products and for promoting existing products in new markets are being overlooked. Resources need to be allocated to both the running of existing businesses and the establishment of new ones. A manager who believes his or her future promotion to depend upon meeting the current year's budget may resist the allocation of resources to activities that may not bear fruit for another three or four years.

Marketing staff frequently prefer to work upon current projects that involve tangible output. As the majority of new products fail, association with new-product ventures may be viewed by marketing department staff as risky.

The reverse halo effect may operate, if only subconsciously. Marketing staff are aware of this and may not want to be associated with failure.

The new-product development area contains many potential sources of communications problems. A group developing new products tends to communicate with itself at the expense of communication with the outside world. This can lead to a project being overtaken by changes in the market or innovation by a competitor or a great deal of effort being expended upon the duplication of what is available elsewhere.

A divisional new-product team could work in isolation and fail to draw upon strong central research and development expertise. A strong personality can ride roughshod over wiser counsel. Parties coming together might find in the middle of a programme that their interests are, in fact, divergent. This can lead to the disintegration of a project.

Some new-product teams are very secretive. They, perhaps as a result of a lack of self-confidence, hoard information about their projects out of fear that they might be cancelled. The absence of communication might give the impression that little is happening and this could lead to cancellation. Alternatively, information might allow a person outside of the development team to inject an idea or a piece of information that could strengthen the project and ensure its continuance.

A periodic examination should be made of a product portfolio to determine where each product lies on the product life-cycle. A business, the majority of whose products are in the decline stage of their life-cycles, must clearly devote more resources to new-product development than one whose major products are entering the growth stage. The latter company may have to be very selective in developing new activities in order not to starve existing ones of vital resources.

Question 57:   Explain how you would set about discovering whether or not new-product development opportunities were being overlooked in the following businesses:

- (*a*)   a container terminal
- (*b*)   an oil refinery
- (*c*)   a small handicrafts shop
- (*d*)   a restaurant
- (*e*)   a publishing company.

5.4   THE MANAGEMENT OF DIVERSITY

A senior marketor in a diversified organization may be faced with a variety of very different businesses to manage. Managing these hetergeneous units requires the establishment of criteria for identifying and grouping characteristics that can form the core of a separate unit and the development of a common system of reporting that can cope with diversity. Separate units should be natural business units.

Strategies and objectives deivsed for each of these separate units must meet the overall needs of the organization. Strategies established must reflect the risks faced by each unit, their competitive position and whether the business is new or established. Quite different people may be required to run embryonic and mature businesses.

Rather than impose a standard strategy, a diversified company may have to develop many strategies that meet the varied needs of sub-units. Success criteria should also be flexible: standard indicators will not allow the valid comparison of very different businesses.

In terms of leadership, one unit may require an entrepreneur, an opportunist, another a manager, and yet another an administrator to keep things ticking over. Time horizons for planning can vary. A constraint could be fixed or related in whole or in part to sales. Reporting can vary in formality.

Managing a business unit requires an ability to assess a market-product situation and abstract the essence, particularly the risks involved. Bringing in an outsider on a consultancy basis can introduce a source of objectivity when the strategy of a unit is to be assessed. In the case of the embryonic venture a sympathetic ear can be welcome, someone with whom the unit manager can have 'off the record' chats.

A business unit, however small, must have a sense of identity, of where it is headed, the business it is in and what it is good at. The larger organization can set the objectives of units within it narrowly or broadly according to the maturity and responsibility of unit managements. One could aim to increase sales, market share, returns, profits, or efficiency ratios or reduce risk. A specialized unit could be given a less quantifiable objective concerned with social responsibility, prestige, or survival.

Defining what a business is good at is far from easy. A unit's resources are its productive capacity, the quality of its staff, its market position, the availability of finance, and such special factors as a monopoly granted by a patent.

Competitive advantage can depend heavily upon the performance of other units. The relative strength of competitors may encourage a unit to develop new markets and products rather than aim at increased market penetration.

Managers without product responsibilities but functional duties should have a clear idea of their function. An attempt should be made to get functional staff to approach the products with which they deal from the point of view of the businesses they are in. There is usually some common thread that can link together the separate aspects of a business. Spending a great deal of time within an organization can result in functional staff becoming preoccupied with the companies' own products and personalities, and in the process losing sight of market opportunities.

AS A PART OF ITS GENERAL MANAGEMENT DEVELOPMENT PROGRAMME A LEADING INDUSTRIAL COMPANY ENSURES THAT ALL ITS HIGH FLYERS ARE GIVEN SOME OPPORTUNITIES TO 'RUN A BUSINESS'. A NUMBER OF PROFITABLE – BUT IN TURNOVER TERMS VERY SMALL – SUBSIDIARIES ARE KEPT MAINLY AS 'TRAINING GROUNDS'.

Question 58:   In each of the following cases of a recent acquisition, discuss the likely problems faced by the acquiring company management in integrating the new venture into their existing organization:

- (*a*)   a fish and chip shop acquired by an up-market steakhouse chain
- (*b*)   a paperback publishing house acquired by a film production company
- (*c*)   a management consultancy acquired by a firm of professional accountants
- (*d*)   a small overseas factory acquired by a major domestic supplier with surplus domestic capacity
- (*e*)   an entrepreneurial growth company in a high technology field acquired by a nationalized industry.

EXAMINATION QUESTIONS

1. It has been suggested that brainstorming can be a valuable aid to innovation in marketing. Describe the methods involved, giving an example of a problem suitable for its application. How does the creative-thinking approach to a problem differ from the strictly analytical approach?

2. The 'right' organization is often thought to be the most important single factor in a successful programme of innovation. Comment on this view and describe more than one way in which the product development function could be organized in a company selling electronic products internationally to both the consumer and industrial markets.

3. The most senior member of the creative staff in an advertising agency is commonly called the Creative Director. Is this a contradiction in terms?

6. *Marketing communications*

There are many areas of communications that have a relevance for marketing. Advertising is clearly a crucial element. A salesman's visit is a form of communication, as is point-of-sale promotions, packaging, the organization's public relations activity, and dealing with customer complaints. Customer complaints provide important feedback and are an example of two-way communication.

6.1 MARKETING COMMUNICATIONS STRATEGY

The strategy underlying marketing communications could be long term or short term. A large organization's strategy will encompass long- and short-term objectives. There will be existing products to sell, market shares to increase, existing channels to service, together with new products to launch, new terms to introduce, and brand awareness and a corporate image to build.

A marketing-communications strategy must encompass the promotion mix. Few forms of communication succeed on their own. A lecture may need to be supported by written notes, an advertising campaign by point-of-sale material.

A 'push' strategy would aim at wholesalers, dealers, and retailers. These would be the primary publics, the object of communications being to encourage the stocking of products in retail outlets so that ultimate consumers are exposed to them, the goods concerned being pushed through the shops.

An alternative strategy, the 'pull' approach, would have the ultimate buying public as its primary target. The aim would be, by such means as heavy consumer advertising, to create a heavy demand for the product at retail level so that retailers and middlemen would place orders. The strategy then pulls goods through the shops from the consumer end.

In practice, a mix of strategies is generally used. Within a basically push campaign, for example, trade advertising might be used to reach trade buyers. Salesmen's visits particularly in industrial markets tend to be more effective when backed up by advertising. A combination of trade advertising and salesman's visit tends to be more cost effective than either on its own.

In many companies, a certain amount of communication will lie beyond the province of the marketing department. In such circumstances, marketing staff should press for a total organization approach to communications. For example, the labour force alienated by personnel department policies may be major purchasers of the company's products. Public relations may stress in a press release some aspect of company operations which the advertising department had decided to play down while writing copy.

Objectives should be co-ordinated. Messages should be compatible. An organization cannot afford to be perceived as speaking with a forked tongue. Many forms of promotional expenditures are investments in the sense that they create goodwill. Hence current promotional activity needs to be compatible with that which has gone before and that which is planned for the future.

A LARGE STORE BUILT ITS COMMUNICATIONS STRATEGY AROUND ITS POLICY OF NOT BEING 'KNOWINGLY UNDERSOLD'. THE STORE WOULD REDUCE ITS PRICES TO THE LOWEST AVAILABLE AT OTHER STORES. THIS SIMPLE MESSAGE WAS WIDELY COMMUNICATED. IN A STREET OF SIMILAR STORES, THE COMPANY 'STOOD OUT' AND BECAME QUICKLY IDENTIFIED IN THE MIND OF THE SHOPPING PUBLIC WITH ITS POLICY.

6.11 Factors Influencing Strategy

When formulating a strategy, one needs to ask what a market buys, why it buys, and how it buys. Effective marketing requires getting the product, price, promotion, and physical place of the product or service for sale right.

Durable and non-durable goods, physical goods and services, convenience and speciality goods are purchased to meet very different objectives. The reasons for a purchase must be understood if a communications strategy is to influence them.

Effective marketing requires precise market segmentation by such factors as geography, age, sex, objective of purchase, income, education, and social class. Markets can be segmented by benefits sought and received, frequency of purchase by individual product, or by combinations of product. If a marketing strategy is undifferentiated, there is little point in segmentation. To pursue a differentiated strategy of tailoring sales promotion to the characteristics of particular groups however it is necessary to segment markets.

Individuals vary in the extent to which they are dependable, compulsive, and ambitious. One person can be content, another restless for further promotion. Some are introverts, others extroverts. People can be naturally authoritarian or democratic. A person can be a leader or a follower. The nature of people should be reflected in the way in which they are approached.

Reference groups influence purchase behaviour and the response to advertising. Among face-to-face groups, family and work groups can be particularly influential. These groups change over time, at work as one gains promotion, in the family as children are born, grow up and leave, and one moves from rented flat to a house and then retirement bungalow. Marketing strategy should reflect this.

It is important to realise that awareness does not necessarily automatically lead to understanding or comprehension and comprehension does not in turn lead inevitably towards favourable attitudes, an intention to purchase, and actual purchase. Within the communication programme, mix elements may be necessary that are tailored at each of these 'levels'.

There might be widespread awareness of the existence of a product but this might be associated with largely neutral attitudes. In such a case, the emphasis of a communications programme might focus upon establishing the product in question as desirable.

In some cases, a communication which has a positive impact at one 'level' may have a 'negative' impact at another. Sex in advertising may achieve attention but confuse understanding. Where negative impacts exist, they might be overcome by effort elsewhere. The harm that is done by one item in the communications mix might be outweighed by the good that it does elsewhere.

Advertising is but one element of a company's total communications policy with its markets. The kind of communications a company develops will depend very much upon marketing objectives. Specific communication decisions will need to be taken within the framework of both objectives and an overall communications budget.

The communications budget will encompass such wide-ranging activities as promotion, packaging, advertising, and possibly public relations. An initial analysis of a business situation, the setting of communications objectives might suggest channels and messages. On other occasions it may be necessary to first establish communications goals and then devise messages and channels to meet these goals.

The key to success lies in the initial analysis of the communication problem. If the 'problem' is wrongly defined, all subsequent activity will be largely wasted. The initial 'problem' could be a lack of awareness, misunderstanding, or a failure to reinforce. Until one has decided which groups need to be communicated with and has carefully defined their interests and needs, messages and channels cannot be selected.

Those responsible for divisional promotion should check for the existence of company-wide guidelines. An awareness of the promotional activity of other divisions can prevent treading on toes. Divisions may disagree upon what company-wide communications policy ought to be. Agreement upon priorities, upon what ought to be stressed and what glossed over might be the outcome of protracted negotiations.

A MAJOR INTERNATIONAL OIL COMPANY DEVELOPED AN EXTENSIVE PROGRAMME TO ENCOURAGE THE FORMATION OF NEW BUSINESSES. A COMPETITION WAS ARRANGED IN CONJUNCTION WITH A REGIONAL BUSINESS SCHOOL. EXTREMELY SMALL SUMS, FROM THE COMPANY'S POINT OF VIEW, WERE SET ASIDE TO ENCOURAGE INDIVIDUALS TO SET UP BUSINESSES OF THEIR OWN. A MANAGING DIRECTOR OF ONE OF THE COMPANY'S MOST IMPORTANT SUBSIDIARIES JUSTIFIED THIS ACTIVITY BY POINTING OUT THAT HIS PARENT COMPANY, ONE OF THE WORLD'S LARGEST MULTINATIONAL COMPANIES, ITSELF BEGAN AS ONE MAN SHARING A DESK AND THAT THE CONTINUED EXISTENCE OF LARGE BUSINESSES DEPENDED UPON A HEALTHY SMALL FIRM SECTOR.

Question 59: Describe the factors you imagine would be of special importance in the development of marketing-communication strategies in the following businesses:

(*a*) commercial television
(*b*) industrial chemicals
(*c*) marketing education
(*d*) tinned vegetables.

6.2 IMAGE

The image of an organization and of its products will be affected by its marketing-communications strategy which in turn should reflect these images. A programme may be directed at strengthening an image or at changing an image which is regarded as undesirable. The importance of image is highlighted in the next chapter on customer attitudes and behaviour.

6.21 Organizational Image

An organization's image will depend upon its current and past communications. An image is an overall impression which might be favourable or unfavourable. When an organization with a reputation for quality changes hands, it may be valued above its net asset value on account of goodwill.

An image will be a result of a whole battery of communications. It is generally important that messages are consistent. There may be a weak link in the communications chain that is undermining efforts elsewhere.

The image of a product or company may or may not accord with reality. It may be favourable or unfortunate. Communications from a company will affect its image for good or bad. It is well to be aware of this, as communication to achieve short-term advantage can lead to long-term harm.

A brand that is technically excellent may fail as a result of having the wrong image. Imagery can be important for industrial-good sales. One company's compressor may just look more modern and efficient than another.

A marketor should understand the symbolic qualities of what is being offered and the extent to which these are compatible with the imagery of consumers.

Chapters 1 and 2 examined a number of concepts such as authority, value, and status. These are of great importance in marketing communications. An authoritative, high-status source has great credibility. Too much exposure however can devalue a source as can certain treatments. The style of an advertisement can communicate authority and class. Status may be an important quality of a product being sold, as with a Rolls Royce or anything in a Harrod's bag.

A NUMBER OF LANGUAGE AND SECRETARIAL SCHOOLS HAVE ESTABLISHED THEMSELVES IN OXFORD AND CAMBRIDGE. THESE SCHOOLS FEATURE THE WORDS OXFORD OR CAMBRIDGE PROMINENTLY IN THEIR NAMES. THEIR FOUNDERS HOPE THAT THE HALO EFFECT OF BEING LOCATED NEAR TO WORLD FAMOUS COLLEGES MANY OF WHICH DATE BACK TO THE MIDDLE AGES, WILL ENCOURAGE STUDENTS TO THEM AND IN PARTICULAR INFLUENCE THE PARENTS OF POTENTIAL OVERSEAS STUDENTS.

Question 60:   Describe the images conjured up by the following words:

   (*a*)   Stanley Gibbons
   (*b*)   Hoover
   (*c*)   Mars
   (*d*)   Wedgwood
   (*e*)   Swinging-sixties.

6.22   Product Image

Buyers sometimes attribute qualities to products on the basis of their image. A product with a more 'manly' image may be perceived as stronger than its competitors. A soap that is advertised in luxurious surroundings may appear to be expensive, a quality product that the housewife otherwise penny-pinching might 'dare' to purchase.

When changing an image, it is important to remember that as new perceived attributes are created, so long-established ones may wane. The additional consumers attracted may have to be balanced against existing ones lost.

Words as well as images can be misunderstood. Where, for example, large advertising budgets are at stake, copy testing is advisable. Single words may bore or clash with others. A paragraph may contain two slightly conflicting ideas. Redrafting may make a message more persuasive or remove a source of alienation to a minority. Copy must do its job economically.

A test must be realistic and relevant, and from a technical sampling point of view, reliable and valid. Large audiences, group sessions and 24-hour recall panels may be used according to whether or not one wants interaction between respondents. Some copy may be implicit rather than explicit and this must be borne in mind when testing.

The total-evaluation approach examines all aspects of an advertisement's effectiveness. The weight attached to evaluation techniques should reflect their inherent reliability and validity. Levels of confidence should be examined in conjunction with test findings.

An advertisement could aim at the immediate needs of consumers or at their longer-term goals. Other things being equal, a consumer may prefer a product which can be identified with an ultimate desired state to which the consumer aspires.

A marketor may find that his product ranks favourably vis-à-vis competitors' products on a quality or characteristic which customers do not rank all that highly. One possible strategy in such a case is to attempt to change what the consumer considers to be important. A campaign might stress that arriving on time is preferable to travelling in comfort, making use of an executive with whom target groups are likely to identify and who is short of time due to tight deadlines. Being in a hurry might be seen as a sign of importance.

A more direct approach in the last example would be to attempt to alter the consumer's perception of the product in question and its competitors.

A NUMBER OF LEGAL DISPUTES HAVE RELATED TO THE USE OF INDIVIDUAL BRAND NAMES AS GENERIC PRODUCT NAMES. ASPIRIN AND SELLOTAPE ARE BRAND NAMES. IN A DISPUTE WHICH ATTRACTED PUBLIC ATTENTION A COURT WAS ASKED TO RULE ON WHETHER A COMPANY COULD CALL ITS DRINK COGNAC ALTHOUGH ITS OPERATION WAS SOME DISTANCE FROM THE AREA IN WHICH THE DRINK ORIGINATED.

Question 61: You are the marketing director of a retail chain which specializes in goods for children below the age of five. Your company's baby products are household names. You would like to introduce a fashion range of ladies clothing into your shops. What do you do about your image?

6.3 PERSUASION

The question of persuasion and what persuades involves a number of considerations. Values considered in Chapter 2, attitudes examined in Chapters 7 and 8, and the credibility of a message highlighted in Chapters 1 and 16 will all influence the extent to which a stimulus leads to action.

There are several levels of response to a stimulus. An unconscious reaction can occur. Emotions and attitudes can be stirred. Exposure to a stimulus can result in learning. Over a longer period and repeated exposure, behaviour can change. A message can appeal on all these levels, and it can be designed to appeal particularly to one of them.

A communicator must have clear objectives and draw up a concise brief before a message is produced. It is possible to appeal strongly to emotion, for example producing great amusement without effecting any significant change in purchasing behaviour.

A stimulus can irritate and annoy, becoming counter-productive. It can be seen as irrelevant. It can manipulate emotion.

Advertising, for example, may work on a number of levels. It can influence attitudes and challenge beliefs. It may also act on purchasing behaviour directly by the power of suggestion in addition to acting on it indirectly through attitudes. Behaviour suggested by advertising may be imitated. In laboratory experiments children for example have been found to imitate certain forms of behaviour exhibited by adults on television programmes.

Consumers receive so many messages from such a variety of sources that obtaining attention can be very difficult. Position, style, colour, design, all act as stimuli to the eye faced with competing messages.

A great deal of what is absorbed by the senses is quickly forgotten: retention is of crucial importance in advertising. Some advertisements have confused, and even been counter-productive as a result of selective absorption — the 'wrong' image being retained. A message, in order to motivate, may have to challenge its target's viewpoint, but not to such an extent as to lead to its rejection.

A target need not like a message to be influenced by it, but should be interested by it. When identification with an advertisement is achieved its effectiveness greatly increases. Some advertisements present so much information that targets are no longer motivated to try for themselves. Recall tests with panels are often worth staging prior to the full release of an advertisement.

Messages that are congruent, fitting in with existing beliefs, tend to be more effective than those which challenge existing beliefs. Individuals resist messages that challenge their view of the world and prefer those that reinforce their existing beliefs and attitudes, and confirm and rationalize their past behaviour. Messages, to be effective, should therefore work with rather than confront target groups. If not repeated often enough, a message will be forgotten.

A frequently-understressed aspect of advertising is the length of time the target is exposed to it. A television advertisement might reach a captive audience for 15 seconds, a newspaper advertisement its target for a split second as a page is turned. A poster on a hoarding may be glimpsed for half a second by a speeding motorist, a tube train advertisement, by contrast, may be re-read from beginning to end several times during a twenty-minute commuter journey.

Buying habits are conformed to with varying degrees of rigidity. The more often one consumes a brand the more often its consumption is likely to continue. People tend to rationalize their behaviour and having made a choice tend to play up the advantages of what is selected and to play down the advantages of competing products that were rejected.

Successful advertising reinforces existing habits. Many consumers strive to achieve consistency in their purchasing behaviour. An advertisement can lead to a conflict and the need to make a choice between the potentially superior qualities of an advertised product and the habit of purchasing another brand.

A customer may feel that changing represents an acknowledgment that the right product was not bought in the first place, and may resist the change. The advertisement may have to help the customer 'bridge' the required change in behaviour perhaps implying that it is now time for a change or that due to an altered business environment the old ways may not necessarily be the best.

THE GOVERNMENT PARTY IN AN AFRICAN COUNTRY FOUND THAT MANY OF ITS VOTERS WERE ILLITERATE AND THUS COULD NOT READ THE PARTY NAMES ON BALLOT SLIPS. A GENERAL ELECTION WAS APPROACHING. THE GOVERNMENT DECIDED TO MAKE USE OF SYMBOLS RATHER THAN NAMES TO IDENTIFY THE PARTIES ON THE BALLOT PAPERS. AGAINST STRONG PROTESTS FROM ITS OPPONENTS THE GOVERNMENT IDENTIFIED ITS MAIN RIVAL, THE OPPOSITION, WITH THE SYMBOL OF A SNAKE.

Question 62: Examine how persuasive you find the following communications to be:

- (*a*) an appeal from the Chancellor of the Exchequer to 'tighten your belt'
- (*b*) a public health campaign appeal to stop smoking
- (*c*) a television commercial urging you to take your next year's holiday in Spain
- (*d*) an advertisement complete with starving dog asking you to donate to charity
- (*e*) a radio commercial suggesting you 'go to work on an egg'.

7. *Buyer Behaviour and Motivation*

Ultimately the customer, existing or potential, is the *raison d'être* of all marketing communication activity. Customers are perhaps the key public with whom one needs to communicate. This chapter examines aspects of customer behaviour and how it might be understood.

7.1 CONSUMER BEHAVIOUR

How do buyers arrive at their purchasing decisions? Social-science theory provides some clues, and empirical research has suggested some tentative conclusions.

Purchasing behaviour varies so much that generalization is difficult. One purchase may be spontaneous, another the culmination of a detailed investigation lasting several months. The former category of sale may rely heavily upon point-of-sale promotion, the latter upon the provision of technical manuals.

Models of consumer behaviour have separated out such stages as awareness of need, search for alternatives, and final selection. A consumer may be modelled as rationally matching needs and requirements to product attributes in an industrial market situation, and responding primarily to advertising stimuli in the case of a consumer market. Consumers may employ such strategies as imitation, gambling, satisfying, even procrastination or the purposeful avoidance of the taking of decisions.

The challenge to modelling is that the consumer may be active or passive. Learning and experience may vary in importance from one purchase decision to another. One individual is subject to a battery of promotional stimuli, vast quantities of information. When evaluating hypotheses of consumer behaviour the *ceteris paribus* or other things being equal requirement is difficult to meet. When testing one variable, other variables are often, in practice, difficult to control.

Question 63: Contrast and compare the likely reasons for buying a particular kind of:

(*a*)   china ornament
(*b*)   cat food
(*c*)   suède shoes
(*d*)   foreign holiday
(*e*)   lavatory paper.

7.11   Consumer Attitudes

Assessment of attitudes sometimes gives an advance warning of consumer behaviour. Performance may be evaluated in attitude terms on the grounds that today's attitudes may be tomorrow's purchasing pattern. Attitudes represent clues to necessary corrective action and can reveal the achilles heels of competitors' brands.

Some researchers have found little correlation between attitudes and behaviour while others have concluded that a significant link exists. How research in this area is to be interpreted depends largely upon how broadly attitudes are defined.

A distinction needs to be drawn between beliefs that motivate action and descriptive beliefs which do not. The beliefs or attitudes under investigation must be relevant to the behaviour in question.

Evaluative rather than descriptive beliefs do provide clues to buying intention. Buying behaviour follows intention but with a varying time lag and degree of drop out. It is important to remember that pre-purchase attitudes will to some extent be modified by post-purchase experience, and between stating intention and actually buying many things can happen including the introduction of competing products.

A marketing manager should not regard behavioural research as an esoteric ivory-tower activity but as a source of insight. While researchers themselves may lack experience of practical marketing situations, their work can be suggestive of promotional activity.

Psychology is providing further understanding of how the world is perceived and how, through actions, expectations are adjusted to meet what is possible. Much more is now known about the learning process and this is reflected in marketing practice.

Periodic advertising campaigns are frequently based upon the reinforcement concept. Learning and conditioning are related. While the response of animals to stimuli in laboratory situations can be evaluated and predicted human beings are much more difficult to test as a result of the variety of stimulus responses they bring to a laboratory situation.

A PUBLIC LIBRARIAN SPEAKING AT A LUNCHEON PRAISED THE ATTITUDE OF THE LOCAL COMMUNITY TOWARDS ITS OWN HISTORY AS EVIDENCED BY THE REGULAR FULL OCCUPATION OF WORK STATIONS IN THE LOCAL HISTORY WING OF THE CITY

LIBRARY. THE WING HOUSED AN EXTENSIVE COLLECTION AND WAS THE LIBRARY'S MAIN CLAIM TO FAME.

A SURVEY OF READER ATTITUDES COMMISSIONED BY THE LOCAL AUTHORITY OVERTHREW THE 'CONVENTIONAL WISDOM'. A MAJORITY OF THOSE USING THE LIBRARY WERE FOUND TO BE OVERSEAS STUDENTS PREPARING FOR PROFESSIONAL EXAMINATIONS. MOST OF THEM STAYED IN 'LOCAL BED SIT' LODGINGS AND DID THEIR ACADEMIC WORK AT THE LIBRARY.

Question 64: Explain and discuss what aspects of consumer attitudes you would bear in mind when considering the following marketing actions:

(a) introduction of a new strawberry-cream chocolate bar
(b) changing the company's name
(c) elimination of 'lounge bars' from pubs in order to introduce 'one-armed bandits'
(d) mass production of wooden-framed houses in place of conventional designs
(e) promotion of ciné-camera insurance.

7.12 Consumer Types

Conservative buyers can be slow to act and fiercely loyal to brands they have already purchased. Cautious customers may need a great deal of information and persuasion before taking the plunge. Some customers look for 'quality', others for 'quantity'.

One customer may make up his own mind and put a high value upon independence; another may follow trends and be easily led. Impulsive buyers act on the spur of the moment. Time may be of no object to a retired customer and non-existent for the rushed executive with an ulcer. A consumer may opt for variety for the sake of it.

Sales staff should be compatible with the type of customer they serve. A salesman who is continually fidgeting after five minutes with any one customer and eager to drive to the next would not be appropriate for customers who like to 'examine all the angles' carefully before making a decision.

A RETAILER OF CAMERA EQUIPMENT DIVIDED HIS CUSTOMERS INTO THE INFORMED AND UNINFORMED. THOSE WHO REGULARLY KNEW ABOUT THE AVAILABILITY OF NEW ITEMS OF EQUIPMENT WERE THE HEAVIEST PURCHASERS. THEY WERE NOT NECESSARILY THOSE WITH THE MOST MONEY TO SPEND OR THOSE WHO TOOK THE GREATEST NUMBER OF PHOTOGRAPHS. UP-TO-DATE INFORMATION WAS THE KEY STIMULUS TO PURCHASE.

THE RETAILER ESTABLISHED A CAMERA CLUB, PRODUCING A MAGAZINE GIVING UP-TO-DATE INFORMATION ON NEW DEVELOP-MENTS WHICH WAS POSTED MONTHLY TO MEMBERS. MAIL-ORDER SALES BOOMED. SOON THE RETAILER'S PREMISES WERE LARGELY GIVEN OVER TO THE MANAGEMENT OF THE CAMERA CLUB AND THE RELATED MAIL-ORDER SALES.

7.2 CONSUMER PREFERENCES

How important are such factors as economy, convenience, choice, personal service, and delivery to consumers? The answer will depend upon the product in question and according to the group of consumers one is considering. The retired, for example, will have more time available for shopping than the working young housewife. The couple struggling with a young family will probably be mc economy conscious than the middle-aged. Convenience is more important to those without motor cars as is delivery. The elderly may have particular need of delivery services.

Marketing managers need to know how much disposable income their consumers have, how mobile they are, and how frequently they shop. Many people establish a shopping routine.

Products made by nationally-known firms tend to be preferred to shop brands. Consumers tend to feel that a national organization has a reputation to keep up. Thus in certain markets it is very difficult to challenge an established supplier. Shop brands of chains with the quality image of a Sainsbury or a Marks and Spencer are acceptable to consumers.

Role perceptions are very important in purchasing situations. Many consumers select products not so much for their intrinsic characteristics but because of what they 'say' about those who buy them. In the case of a prestige and class conscious customer, where a product is bought may be more important than its technical properties. The label on the dress may assume much more significance than its style or colour.

A CLOTHING RETAILER WAS STRUCK BY THE GREAT DIVERSITY OF CUSTOMERS WITHIN HER SHOP. THEY RANGED FROM THE ECONOMY CONSCIOUS TO THE 'IMAGE SEEKER'. SHE WONDERED HOW SHE COULD ACCOMMODATE SUCH A VARIETY OF CUSTOMER TYPES.

THE ANSWER LAY IN CREATING SHOPS WITHIN A SHOP. A 'BARGAIN BASEMENT' DREW THOSE SEEKING ECONOMY, AN UP-MARKET BOUTIQUE THOSE WHO WERE MORE INTERESTED IN 'STYLE'. CERTAIN TYPES OF SHOPPER WERE FOUND TO BE ATTRACTED BY PARTICULAR 'ATMOSPHERES' THUS CREATED

WITHIN THE OVERALL SHOP RATHER THAN BY PRODUCTS. MANY
MORE CUSTOMERS BEGAN TO COME INTO THE SHOP.

Question 65: Contrast and compare the importance of consumer preferences in
the following product-modification decisions:

(a) replacing expensive perfume bottles with plastic containers
(b) replacing wooden hammer handles with plastic handles
(c) introducing plastic flowers onto the tables in a restaurant
(d) putting 5% more carrot into a tinned vegetable soup
(e) replacing the Secretary of State with a junior minister as a guest
speaker at a political association's annual dinner.

7.21 Preference Problems and Issues

Consumers may prefer individual brands, select from a number of equally acceptable brands or not have a brand preference. Purchasing a particular brand can
become a habit, easing the problem of choice. Branding then can simplify the
shopper's problem of selection. In the case of long production run brands lower
unit costs may be possible. Brand loyalty is strongest when brands concerned are
perceived as having quality advantages over competing brands.

Price cuts and special deals are more acceptable when relating to nationally-
known brands. Customers tend to be suspicious of the price cuts of lesser-known
brands. The inference is sometimes drawn that the product in question must be
'cheap' and of lower quality. In the case of products with national reputation
price cuts tend to be seen as bargains.

Deals are sometimes counter-productive. Consumers may resent the inference
that the producer feels they will 'fall' for the deal. When gifts are given away,
customers sometimes feel that the product in question is over-priced.

Price cutting may be seen by customers as an alternative to the offer of free
gifts. A free sample tends to be accepted by customers if a product is new, though
suspicions are sometimes aroused in respect of free samples of existing products.
Competitions can create an interest in a product but many consumers find them
tiresome. Trading stamps can complicate the task of consumption as consumers
strive to compare prices with and without stamps. It also can take a long time
to accumulate sufficient stamps to obtain a really worthwhile gift.

THE SECOND LARGEST RENT-A-CAR FIRM IN THE US NEEDED
A WAY OF DISTINGUISHING ITSELF FROM THE DOMINANT FIRM IN
THE BUSINESS. THE 'PRODUCT' OFFERED BY BOTH COMPANIES
WAS ALMOST IDENTICAL. THE SLOGAN WAS COINED 'WE'RE
NUMBER TWO, WE TRY HARDER'.

Question 66: Assess the value of the following promotional devices in competitive
markets:

(*a*)   a plastic 'Smurf' given away at petrol stations
(*b*)   a 'spot the ball' competition on a cereal packet
(*c*)   a 'buy one toilet roll and get one free' campaign.

7.22   Consumer Values

Values attached to products, consciously or not attributed by a producer, will attract some consumers and repel others. One consumer may be seeking something modern, exciting and expensive, another may prefer a conservative product, that is safe and value for money. A producer of a beverage may seek to associate it with hot or cold weather according to where the largest market is thought to lie. A product can be promoted as masculine or feminine, for the mature or the young and trendy.

A car might be valued for its sleek appearance, its economy, its speed, its carrying capacity, how popular or exclusive it is, for the fact that it stands out in a crowd, or because it is not too obtrusive. Noise may be a problem to the family man but desired by the young man eager to impress a girlfriend. Products have values associated with them. A producer is often in a position to determine by such means as packaging and advertising the image of a product.

Some people shop for economy, others for durability or even prestige. An economic shopper seeks value for money and tends to compare prices. A fancy extra may be regarded as less important than whether a basic product will do the job for which it is intended.

To some shoppers the personal factor will be more important than price. The friendly neighbourhood shop may be preferred to the cheaper but impersonal supermarket. Personalized shoppers build up relationships with sales staff that can be important to them.

A number of shoppers may consider such ethical questions as whether a supplier has investments in South Africa, whether a container is plastic and might pollute the environment and whether the High Street should be patronized to prevent the shops from being wiped out by the newly-opened hypermarket. Of course some shoppers will be concerned with convenience above all. Many executives and housewives value time highly, more highly than the small sums shopping around, which is expensive in time, might save.

A housewife with a strong sense of the 'proper' role of a wife may serve products that appear to bolster this role. She might reject a convenience product in favour of one that enables her to feel that she is doing more for her family. Traditional values may be important and products selected that will match self-image and husband expectations. These will in some areas be strongly conditioned by social class. Middle-class housewives might be more concerned with convenience, working-class housewives with economy. In purchasing food, health considerations may be uppermost in the minds of some shoppers while others are barely aware of them.

IN THE UK THE SMALL BAKER WAS ALL BUT WIPED OUT BY THE LARGE BAKERY MASS PRODUCING STEAM-BAKED, WHITE-SLICED WRAPPED BREAD. THE 'NEW BRAND' WAS AVAILABLE IN SUPER-MARKETS EVERYWHERE AT A RELATIVELY LOW PRICE.

ONE OR TWO SMALL PRODUCERS DETECTED A CHANGE OF MOOD. CONSUMERS BEGAN TO COMPLAIN ABOUT MASS-PRO-DUCED, STEAM-BASKED BREAD. MANY TALKED OF THE 'GOOD OLD DAYS'. QUEUES BEGAN TO DEVELOP AT THE DOORS OF SMALL BAKERS OFFERING 'OVEN FRESH' BREAD. LARGE SUPER-MARKETS WERE FORCED TO COUNTER THEIR LOSS OF BREAD SALES BY INSTALLING SMALL ELECTRIC OVENS IN THEIR STORES IN PROMINENT POSITIONS SO THAT THEIR CUSTOMERS WOULD SEE THAT THEIR BREAD WAS BAKED ON THE PREMISES.

Question 67:   Contrast and compare the consumer values of a person at the following stages in life:

(a)   teenage courtship
(b)   newly wed
(c)   young family
(d)   middle age
(e)   single elderly survivor.

7.3   ASSESSING PREFERENCES

Consumer panel data can enable brand sales and market penetration to be predicted. The key to future sales is the rate of purchase and repurchase. Once a repurchase rate has settled down, a good base exists for the prediction of future sales. Such predictions may assume adequate distribution, steady promotional expenditure, and relatively constant market conditions.

Share prediction analyses have had mixed success. Low repeat purchase rates sometimes leads to brand withdrawal. A management is put on guard if early analysis reveals that a breakeven point of sales will not be reached unless corrective action is taken. More sophisticated models assume that there will be different repurchase rates at various stages of a product's life-cycle.

Certain combinations of result can be highly revealing. A product may have a low initial take-up rate but high repeat-purchase rate or a high take-up rate but low repeat-purchase rate. The former case is *prima facie* more satisfactory in the long run as an initial take-up rate may be boosted by an initially greater promotional expenditure. Measuring the performance of brands in test market conditions can significantly reduce the risk of national launch failure and allow the testing of such marketing strategies as low initial price or the use of free gifts.

Market share models can and do work. They can yield valuable clues as to how long a brand will take to reach a stable market share and as to how consumers react to new brands and to consumer loyalty.

Sophisticated tests are devised by manufacturers of consumer durables to determine consumer preferences. Attitude surveys may involve putting checklists of alternatives ranked on a scale to panels of consumers. For example respondents may be asked to position on a scale of five or ten units between say mass-produced or handmade where their ideal product would lie.

Maps of consumer preferences can be prepared upon which can be superimposed the locations of existing products to determine 'gaps in the markets', a niche that can be exploited. Factor analysis is an example of a technique which has been devised to determine the relative importance to consumers of the various attributes of a product. To form the basis of a successful product a group of attributes should be identifiable, measurable, be appropriate to market needs, and be feasible, capable of being achieved.

A number of behavioural techniques have been employed to determine what motivates purchasers. These range from in-depth interviews, observation of store behaviour, tests of word association, sentence completion, picture interpretation and completion, caption and story completion to quite sophisticated aural and written tests. Some advertisers work close to the boundary of knowledge in some areas of the behavioural sciences and contribute to their development.

The use of predictive analysis can be of particular value in new launch situations. Usually the sooner a project is killed, the lower crawl-out costs will be. Using a trial period, a model could be used to predict time to breakeven point and ultimate sales levels.

THE SKATEBOARD WAS INTRODUCED AS A HIGH-PRICED PRODUCT IT WAS ASSUMED WOULD SELL IN SMALL QUANTITIES AS WAS TRANSFER LETTERING. IN BOTH CASES HIGH-VOLUME SALES WERE ACHIEVED AT THE 'PREMIUM' PRICES. THE SKATEBOARD CRAZE PEAKED BUT THE DEMAND FOR TRANSFER LETTERING HAS REMAINED HIGH.

Question 68: Explain how you would go about estimating likely demand for the following new products:

- (*a*) bar of soap
- (*b*) combat aircraft
- (*c*) children's toy
- (*d*) felt-tipped pen.

7.4 DEMAND MANAGEMENT

Marketing management can be seen as demand management. The demand for a company's goods and services could be managed in quantity, quality mix, and timing to meet the organization's productive capacity. There is little point boosting sales if the resources are not available to meet orders. Marketing then is the process of matching actual to desired demands.

Demands can be existing or latent, deficient or excessive, irregular or steady, uncertain or predictable. During a product's life-cycle it may pass through a variety of demand states. Latent demand for the product may for example be converted into actual demand by a launch promotional campaign which if overdone can result in the rapid exhaustion of stocks, i.e. excessive demand. Demand for the sake of it may not be as important as the regulation of demand.

A demand may not exist and may have to be created. An alert company is always on the look out for latent demand, a shared need for a product that does not yet exist. Latent demands are product opportunities. Not all latent demands are the basis of profitable products.

Demand cannot be taken for granted. Where it exists, there is no guarantee that it will continue. Demand may falter and need to be revived and extended by the introduction of new features. In the case of a seasonal demand some activity to stimulate off-peak consumption may be needed. The urban transport and electricity industries would readily accept the importance of demand management with their off-peak travel and electricity usage programmes.

Excess demand presents many problems. When extending an order book, should some priority be given to old and regular customers or to new ones? Failure to increase capacity can lead to the introduction of competing products. If this is inevitable then perhaps the strategy of choking off demand by raising the price should be adopted, a strategy of making hay while the sun is shining. In the case of a loss-making product or one whose sales have fallen below the profitability break-even point, pulling out of the market may present a host of problems.

Some campaigns are directed at the prevention of certain activities. The marketor may consciously set out to reduce demand. Public campaigns to reduce the level of drinking and cigarette smoking could be said to fall in the category of social marketing. The promotion of a birth control programme may draw upon marketing skill of the highest order.

ICE-CREAM SALES REGULARLY SLUMPED DURING THE WINTER MONTHS AND ROSE TO A PEAK OVER THE SUMMER PERIOD. THE INDUSTRY THROUGHOUT THE YEAR CARRIED THE OVERHEAD NECESSARY TO MEET PEAK DEMAND. HITHERTO ICE CREAM HAD BEEN SOLD FOR IMMEDIATE CONSUMPTION. THE SPREAD OF SUPERMARKETS AND THE EXPANDING OWNERSHIP OF HOME FREEZERS LED TO THE IDEA OF FAMILY PACKS. ICE CREAM

COMPANIES NOW ACHIEVE LARGE SALES THROUGHOUT THE YEAR OF FAMILY DRUMS OF ICE CREAM OF MANY FLAVOURS BOUGHT AT LOCAL SUPERMARKET AND GROCERY STORES.

7.5 THE INDUSTRIAL MARKET

Any market consists of the individuals and organizations who are actual or potential customers for a product or service. Knowledge of a market consists of an awareness of what is in fact being bought, why it is bought, by whom and by what means.

Markets can be subdivided in various ways. Consumer goods for example can be divided into services, and durable or non-durable goods, or into convenience goods bought on the spur of the moment, shopping goods purchased after comparison with other similar goods and speciality goods that may be acquired after a great deal of effort.

Many industrial purchases are rather like durables and speciality goods. They may take a long time to acquire and may yield a flow of services over a long period of time.

7.51 Industrial Goods

Industrial goods, unlike consumer goods, are not used by individuals but by organizations to contribute to an ultimate objective such as the maximization of profit or return on capital employed. This contribution is frequently based upon the flow of services an industrial good such as an item of plant or machinery can provide. The industrial good is distinguished by the reason for its purchase. The objectives of many organizational purchases in the public sector will not be profit but the provision of a service. The industrial good will be bought not for consumption as an end product but for the part it will play in the production of another end product or service.

An industrial purchaser may be less concerned with price than the purchaser of a consumer good. Whether or not a product will do the required job and whether it can be delivered on time may be of greater importance. What is of the greatest significance is the price of the ultimate end product. It is the demand for this that will set the demand for intermediate industrial goods.

The industrial purchaser then acquires goods for use in the production of other goods and services. Industrial purchasers tend to be concentrated in certain areas. Some industries are specific to particular locations. The motor industry in the UK is geographically concentrated in the Midlands.

Industrial goods include raw materials, components, semi-manufactured goods, plant and equipment, buildings, office equipment and supplies generally. Certain maintenance, utility, and advisory services could be termed industrial. Some industrial goods are bought infrequently at high cost while others which are relatively inexpensive may be consumed continuously.

Whereas consumer goods are bought to satisfy human needs, industrial goods are acquired to meet the needs of production situations. The demand for such goods is derived rather than primary. Personal preferences are generally secondary to the needs of the production context.

Industrial goods can be complex. A purchaser may select on the basis of a package that embraces a family of complementary products and a range of after-sales services. What is being sold may well be a relationship rather than a specific good or service. This would be the case with the 'purchase' of the services of a computer bureau offering particular hardware and software facilities. Vast sums of money can be at stake in an industrial sale. A consortium of firms might be involved. The sale itself may involve negotiations spread over months, even years, and teams of people with varied skills and professional backgrounds and result in several points of contact between buying and selling organizations.

A MANUFACTURER OF FILM PROJECTION EQUIPMENT SOLD ITS PRODUCTS TO A SMALL NUMBER OF BUYERS WHO PURCHASED ON BEHALF OF THE MAJOR CINEMA CHAINS. THEN THE 'HOME MOVIE' BOOM BEGAN. PEOPLE STARTED TO SHOW FILMS IN THEIR LIVING ROOMS AND DEMAND RELATIVELY INEXPENSIVE PORTABLE PRO-JECTION EQUIPMENT. THE COMPANY FOUND ITSELF IN A CON-SUMER DURABLE AS WELL AS AN INDUSTRIAL MARKET. BY THE TIME IT HAD ADJUSTED TO THE CHANGE MOST OF THE VOLUME HOME MOVIE MARKET WAS BEING SUPPLIED BY ANOTHER PRODUCER.

Question 69:　Does the British Steel Corporation buy any consumer goods?

7.6　THE INDUSTRIAL PURCHASER

A team of people rather than one person may be involved in an industrial purchase. Each sale may need to be tailored. Each product package may be unique, the sales approach reflecting the needs and nature of each individual customer.

Among industrial purchasers will be those who buy and resell. Agents, ware-houses, stockists, distributors, stores will all buy industrial goods. Such purchasers may have a 'buying committee' who examine proposals put up by individual buyers who are in direct contact with suppliers. The buying committee may seek technical advice when offered a new good and could call in a specialist to examine whether better terms could be obtained on existing goods.

Government and public sector bodies are major industrial purchasers. They generally buy whatever is needed to provide certain services. Priorities may change when new governments come into office.

Some public bodies have their own buying departments while others pool purchasing resources. In the UK one body has been responsible for the property 'purchases' of a number of departments and other agencies.

Question 70: Your company sells paint and other supplies to both construction and decorating companies and 'do-it-yourself' home decorators. Compare and contrast what each category of customer is looking for in your products.

7.61 Industrial Purchaser Motivation

Industrial buyers differ from consumer buyers in a number of important respects. The fact that they may not be price-sensitive has already been referred to. They may also be secretive, less willing to discuss their requirements with other consumers. In contrast, they often prefer a more open relationship with those selling to them. Industrial customers are more interested in obtaining a solution to their particular problems and are less likely to follow fashion than is the case with consumer purchases.

The trade press is generally regarded as an important source of information on new products by industrial purchasers. Trade fairs are also much frequented by those in the market for new industrial products. Brand image can still be important to many engaged in technical work. Among one's peers, prestige may be based upon employing an item of equipment supplied by a manufacturer with a reputation.

The purchaser of a consumption good is concerned with the satisfaction of individual or family needs. The industrial good consumer may aim to satisfy both industrial needs and the needs of the employing organization. A marketor in aiming to satisfy the latter should not forget the former. An employee will prefer a product or service that will enhance his own knowledge or promote his or her own reputation within an organization or possibly a profession.

Delivery reliability is often a major factor in influencing industrial purchases. The availability of testing facilities and back up and replacement services are also important. An industrial purchase is normally designed to create a facility which will yield a flow of benefits over time.

Where a product is likely to be replaced by a similar item, then at the moment of initial purchase a company may be about to enter into an arrangement that is likely to last for some years. An example would be the purchase of a piece of office equipment from manufacturer A rather than manufacturer B when expansion and upgrading is planned, for the purchaser may feel constrained to buy accessories and upgrading facilities as well as replacements in due course from A. The discounted value of cash flows over this period may exceed the value of an initial outlay.

A MANUFACTURER OF TYPEWRITER SPOOLS COMPLETELY RE-DESIGNED ITS MAJOR PRODUCT LINE, BOUGHT IN NEW MACHINERY AND REARRANGED ITS WORK FLOW TO ACHIEVE LONGER PRO-DUCTION RUNS IN ORDER TO HOLD DOWN THE UNIT COST OF ITS SPOOLS. AT A TRADE FAIR AN IMPORTANT CUSTOMER TOLD THE MANUFACTURER THAT HIS SPOOLS WERE BOUGHT PRIMARILY BECAUSE OF THE UNUSUAL ACCURACY OF THEIR MACHINING. AS THEY WERE SUCH A SMALL ITEM IN THE TOTAL COST OF A TYPE-WRITER THEY WOULD STILL BE BOUGHT AT TWICE OR THREE TIMES THEIR CURRENT PRICE.

Question 71: Explain in what ways a purchaser could satisfy personal goals in the purchase of the following industrial goods:

(*a*) milling machine
(*b*) executive jet
(*c*) office furniture
(*d*) nuts and bolts
(*e*) maintenance services.

7.62 Industrial Good Packages

Some suppliers have recognized that the industrial buyer may regard one item as merely an individual component of a total system. The performance of the whole system may be important not that of an individual element of it.

A total system could comprise a range of products and associated services. A specialized company might aim to sell such a total package. The company's value added could stem from experience in assembling the components manufactured by other producers. The products themselves may not count as individual products. They may be of little value in themselves. The way in which they are combined may make the difference between a successful and a struggling operation.

Computer, aviation, transport, and construction companies frequently sell a complete package. Teams of salesmen, perhaps from several companies in a consortium, can be brought together to draw up a tender. The team will need to be managed. The management job may be regarded as unattractive, as a tender is a naturally speculative activity, or alternatively it could be much sought as a source of contacts and particular experience.

AN ENTREPRENEURIAL COMPANY ACHIEVED A RAPID GROWTH RATE PUTTING TOGETHER PORTABLE TELEVISION STUDIO PACK-AGES. THE COMPANY DID NOT MANUFACTURE ANY PRODUCTS ITSELF BUT DEVISED METHODS OF FITTING SUNDRY PIECES OF TELEVISION EQUIPMENT INTO STANDARD AIR TRANSPORTABLE

CONTAINERS. THE OPERATION RESULTED IN A VERY HIGH PROFIT MARGIN AND LARGE SALES TO THIRD WORLD COUNTRIES.

7.63 Products and Services

In the marketing of industrial goods, a related service may be as important in the buying decision as the product. In some cases it may be difficult to separate service and product.

A service can reduce a buyer's workload, leading to a reduction of permanent overhead. A service such as a guarantee can reduce risk from the buyer's point of view. A repair service might increase the useful life of a product. Not only can a service be an integral part of a 'product' but services can greatly increase the appeal of a product to a potential purchaser.

Technical advice, help with installation, cleaning and routine maintenance, a replacement guarantee, delivery insurance and a training programme to familiarize staff with a new piece of equipment all represent services which can lead to the preference of one industrial product over another which is otherwise equal in technical quality. Other things being equal, a buyer may have a strong preference for a product whose associated services significantly reduce the risks of the purchase.

Question 72: Explain and compare the relative importance of the service element in each of the following product—service pairs:

   (*a*)   guided missile—operator training
   (*b*)   computer frame—programmer
   (*c*)   motor car—garage services
   (*d*)   paint—test laboratory of producer
   (*e*)   telephone—telephone engineer service.

EXAMINATION QUESTION

How do you account for the fact that some companies appear to display an excessive concern with their 'corporate image' and others none at all?

8. *The Purchase Decision*

An impulse purchase might be made by a single individual. Several members of a family might influence the purchase of a consumer durable. Children could be a significant influence upon the purchase of breakfast cereal. In the case of an organizational purchase, a much larger number of people might be involved and the purchase process itself might be spread over a much longer period of time. A marketor might have, at different times, to communicate with a number of individuals in various departments. This chapter examines the industrial buying process, drawing upon some of the lessons drawn from models of organizational buying behaviour.

8.1 INFORMATION

Before an industrial purchase occurs, the buying process passes through a number of stages. A need must first be identified and defined. This may be far from easy and in the case of a major purchase may have consequences for company strategy, finance, and organization.

The number of items required and their characteristics must be determined. There may be conflicting views within an organization upon what is required. Such divergences may have political origins.

Potential suppliers need to be identified and evaluated. Tenders may be called for and the submissions analysed and compared. The selection process may be protracted and involve difficult trade-offs.

With a new purchase there may not be any prior experience to fall back on. An ordering procedure may need to be devised along with post-purchase monitoring and servicing. Subsequent performance can be an important influence upon future purchasing.

An industrial purchaser needs to be aware of sources of supply, be equipped to compare and make investment decisions and have the ability to negotiate a 'good deal'.

Techniques such as value analysis and the buy grid may be used to determine what is required. Industrial purchasers tend to think of themselves as rational people. With a buy grid, for example, attributes of competing products are objectively compared and matched with requirements. Industrial buyers, nevertheless, to some extent in their purchasing are likely to aim to satisfy personal as well as organizational objectives.

Industrial buyers get their information on new products and services and on changes to existing ones from a variety of sources. Salesmen pay visits to buyers and buyers visit trade shows, demonstrations, and exhibitions. Buyers are reached individually by direct mail shots, advertisements, and press releases. Many are members of professional organizations and attend professional conferences, technical courses and pick up ideas and information when mixing with their peer group. While some of this information may be actively sought, in other situations the buyer may be an unexpected recipient of a message. More interest is likely to be shown in the former than latter case.

IN 1974 BRITAIN ORGANIZED ITS LARGEST TRADE FAIR EVER TO BE HELD OVERSEAS IN SAO PAULO, BRAZIL. ON THE THIRD DAY STAFF ON ONE OF THE STANDS WERE SEEN TO WITHDRAW THEIR BROCHURES AND PLACE THEIR INFORMATION SHEETS BENEATH THEIR COUNTER. WHEN CHALLENGED BY AN ENGLISH VISITOR ONE OF THE STAND MINDERS REPLIED 'ONE OR TWO OF THESE BRAZILIANS LOOK AS THOUGH THEY ARE ABOUT TO BUY SOMETHING AND I DON'T WANT TO COME DOWN HERE AGAIN'.

Qestion 73: A plan is afoot to hire an aircraft carrier, fill its hangar with your country's goods and sail it to New York where it would be opened as a trade fair. Describe what promotional material you would assemble if you were a manager responsible for the following products:

- (*a*) turret lathe
- (*b*) steel cable
- (*c*) production management consultancy
- (*d*) oil tanks for hire.

8.2 BEHAVIOURAL FACTORS AND INFLUENCES

A great many factors determine an industrial purchase, individual attitudes, needs and preferences, the relative strengths of personalities in group situations, formal organizational objectives, and informal practices and external factors such as the availability of finance and industrial trends.

Some influencing factors will be objective and rational, others will be judgmental and irrational. The objective factors such as the job to be performed by the required product tend to be relatively more important than is the case with consumer purchases.

A very important influence in any purchase decision will be the gatherer of information and still more a person drawing up a shortlist or preparing a purchase brief. Such a person who controls and sifts information is known as a gatekeeper. A gatekeeper may be more important in terms of the purchase decision than other executives who are nominally more senior in the organization chart.

A purchasing manager can act as a gatekeeper, purposefully discouraging a sales-man from talking directly with engineer and technical personnel and with staff in user departments. A purchasing department can act as a screen, sifting out possible suppliers and passing on information on shortlisted companies which consciously or not may be biassed.

Purchasing staff and engineering personnel stem from different professional backgrounds and may well have differing perceptions about what is important in a particular purchase decision. Motives and expectations can vary between those in a purchasing team.

A disagreement on questions of fact can usually be resolved by obtaining further information. Disagreements over values, over what is important, will need to be resolved by discussion, negotiation, and persuasion.

Information received is frequently distorted. A buyer may have biasses due to background experience, satisfaction with previous purchases, and the views and expectations of others. The individuals training role, life-style, position, and the demands of the buying situation can all result in the selective screening of information received.

The buying decision may be influenced by financial or time constraints. The purchase may be risky or potentially risky from the point of view of the buyer and the buying organization. The organization itself may delegate varying degrees of dicretion to a buying manager. A manager may have individual authority or may have to work with a team. The company may have prior links with the potential suppliers or with other suppliers.

A strong buyer with a decided preference may employ a variety of ploys such as the production of biassed reports and persuasion and bargaining to convince colleagues of the merits of the desired course of action.

Some industrial purchases will be repeat purchases. The terms of a purchase may be covered by a previous contract. A product may be required for an existing or new use. Perhaps an entirely new industrial product has to be developed to meet an industrial requirement. Re-orders may be according to a re-order cycle. A one-off purchase may be geared to a critical path requirement.

A major influence on a purchase could be the possibility of reciprocal trad-ing. In international trade negotiations, products such as oil and grain are bartered for other goods such as steel. Major companies may have great scope for reciprocal trading when analyses reveal they already buy and sell many of each others' products.

It frequently occurs within organizations that particular pairs of individuals are incompatible. A manager who gets on well with most people in the organization may just not be compatible with a subordinate or superior.

Rivalries within a buying organization pose particular problems for suppliers. These may stem from distrust, sheer lack of time, differing attitudes or result from a history of competition between groups such as departments or points of view within an organization. An attempt is sometimes made by an internal faction to seek the support of an external supplier. Needless to say, it is preferable to back winners.

A BUYER SWITCHED HIS MAJOR SOURCE OF SUPPLY TO THE SOUTH COAST. THE NEW SUPPLIER WHILE TECHNICALLY WELL-QUALIFIED AND PRODUCING EXCELLENT PARTS WAS PUTTING PRESSURE ON THE TRANSPORT MANAGER'S BUDGET IN VIEW OF ITS DISTANT LOCATION. WHEN HIS EXPENSES CLAIMS WERE EXAMINED THE BUYER APPEARED TO BE FREQUENTLY VISITING THE SUPPLIER. ON INVESTIGATION IT WAS FOUND THAT THE BUYER HAD BEEN 'FORCED' BY HIS WIFE TO BUY A HOLIDAY HOME ON THE SOUTH COAST AND THAT HE USED HIS TRIPS SOUTH TO CARRY OUT REPAIR WORK ON IT.

8.3   THE PURCHASERS

Those responsible for purchasing can be divided into initiators, those who influence decisions, those who make decisions, those who implement purchase decisions, and users. There may be a number of conflicting influences involved in an industrial purchase. The relative importance of those associated with purchasing can change from one purchase decision to the next.

A major industrial purchase can involve many departments within a buying organization and lead to the generation of considerable quantities of paperwork. Memos may pass to and from branch, divisional, and head offices. Accounts and engineering departments will be involved. There may be tenders to consider or even a performance competition. Some companies, for internal control purposes, draw up extensive flow diagrams of their purchase procedures to ensure that unauthorized purchases do not take place.

More than one department may be involved in the buying process. Manufacturing, a laboratory and a testing department may all influence the buying decision, perhaps acting jointly. Major purchases are likely to involve management and financial accounting comment and perhaps discussion at board levels.

An organization must establish limits, amounts up to which each buyer can act before having to refer a decision upwards in the management hierarchy.

When competing products are very similar in their tangible attributes and more than one can 'do the job' there is a greater likelihood that intangible factors will sway a purchase decision. It may be that factors unrelated to a product such as the style and dress of a salesman could become important.

> A MAJOR MANUFACTURER SPENT A GREAT DEAL OF MONEY DEVELOPING A COMPANY-WIDE CORPORATE PLANNING MODEL. ON COMPLETION IT WAS FOUND THAT THE MODEL COULD NOT BE RUN IN MOST OF THE COMPANY'S DIVISIONS. EACH DIVISION HAD BOUGHT ITS OWN MINI-COMPUTERS AND MANY OF THESE WERE FOUND TO BE INCOMPATIBLE WITH THE PROGRAMMES DEVELOPED FOR THE HEAD OFFICE COMPUTER.

Question 74: Examine and compare the number of departments that might be involved in the following purchases:

(*a*) a laboratory stop-watch
(*b*) a telephone switchboard and system
(*c*) window boxes
(*d*) a factory extension.

8.4 HIGH RISK PURCHASES

The more risky a purchase decision, the more people likely to be involved in it. Uncertainty is a major source of risk and a team investigation may enable it to be reduced. A first purchase is more likely to involve a team of decision-makers than a repetitive purchase. Where time is short, a decision may have to be delegated to one individual.

A larger organization with an extensive buying department may include a number of people in purchasing decisions. Decentralization often leads to a larger number of people being involved in purchase decisions.

Where a purchase is a high-risk one, a customer may require a considerable amount of post-purchase reassurance. Frequently, just after a difficult purchase decision, doubts set in. This is particularly true where teething troubles are experienced. Reassurance can be the crucial factor in industrial purchase and repurchase situations.

In very technical fields, a buyer may have to lean heavily upon specialist advice. A buyer may resent this reliance upon external information as indeed buyers sometimes resent user-departments or technical departments defining their requirements so closely that the act of purchasing becomes little more than a clerical exercise.

A supplier needs to know the concerns and problems of his buyers. Effective buyers are those who are able to work closely with other executives in an organization. Buyers need to feel that they occupy an important role in the purchase process.

MANY PRINTERS SCATTERED AROUND THE COUNTRY MAKE USE OF PRINTERS' AGENTS LOCATED IN MAJOR CENTRES. ONE PRINTERS' AGENT IN LONDON ACTS FOR SOME FOURTEEN PRINTERS, VISITING THEIR CUSTOMERS IN LONDON ONCE A WEEK TO SEE THAT ALL IS WELL AND TACKLING EMERGENCIES AS AND WHEN THEY ARISE. A MESSENGER SERVICE IS MAINTAINED TO SPEED LAST-MINUTE PROOFS TO THEIR DESTINATIONS.

8.5 ANALYSING PURCHASERS

A systematic approach to analysing a buying decision is to identify all those with an influence upon it and to assign a weighting to each of these. The influencers may include the staff of specialist consultancies and these may form a public with whom one ought to be in continuous contact.

Joint decision-making involves the usual advantages and drawbacks of team work with the associated group dynamics. Within a buying team there may be conflicting personalities, a struggle for leadership in addition to varying judgements concerning the relative importance of such factors as delivery, accuracy, or running costs.

Industrial salesmen seek to identify allies in buying organizations, those who are sympathetic to the advantages of their products. Similarly, the priorities of buying organizations need to be covered. These may shift over time so that alert antennae are necessary.

The backgrounds of those making the purchase decision will be important. Some will have greater technical expertise than others. Some will be more familiar with a company's products than others.

Where an industrial good is purchased by a team, effective marketing requires the identification of who is really important in the buying decision. The person who is to use the industrial good may have little influence in its purchase. The buying department manager may fill in the forms but the purchase decision may lie elsewhere. It is sometimes possible to identify gatekeepers, individuals who sit at communication crossroads and decide what information is received by others.

In the case of a technical product the needs of an end user may ensure that the user is the key person in the purchase decision. In this case performance, the ability to do the job required may be the prime requirement, such questions as price being left to the purchasing or commercial department. In other cases, identifying who actually influences the purchase decision may be far from easy.

An engineering company purchase in a high-technology field is likely to be based mainly upon technical consideration and the options assessed by experts. Decision making in the smaller company, particularly the entrepreneurial enterprise is often in the hands of one individual.

> THE MANAGING DIRECTOR OF A LARGE SALVAGE COMPANY DELEGATED MOST OF HIS MAJOR PURCHASE DECISIONS TO HIS DEPARTMENTAL MANAGERS. BEING AN EX-SEAMAN HOWEVER HE INSISTED ON PERSONALLY SELECTING ALL WINCHES, COMPASSES AND OTHER SHIP-BORNE EQUIPMENT. HE USUALLY PURCHASED THE ITEMS REFERRED TO BY FELLOW MEMBERS OF HIS YACHT CLUB.

Question 75:   Compare the difficulties you would face in uncovering who is the most significant influence on purchases in the following organizations:

   (*a*)   a local garage
   (*b*)   a multi-national corporation
   (*c*)   a large family business
   (*d*)   a chain of depots.

8.6   THE   LARGE   PURCHASE

Major industrial purchases present special difficulties. Financing may need to be arranged. A large deal could be conditional upon reciprocal purchases or government blessing.

A large industrial purchase may have implications for a number of departments. The item being required may serve a slightly different function in each department and this can give rise to a difference of opinion over product or service specification. This may be resolved through informal bargaining or by a more formal process of arbitration, involving referal up the management hierarchy.

Disagreement itself is not as significant as the way in which and the ease with which it is resolved. A marketing manager should always be on the alert to distinguish between general disagreements over the merits of a case and disputes resulting from a clash of personalities.

A big buyer who purchases a significant proportion of a supplier's output is in a strong position to negotiate for special terms and advantageous conditions. Some producers become captive suppliers to certain consumers. The more that is sold to big buyers the stronger their hand becomes.

In some cases, the contribution earned on a marginal sale should be weighed against the increase in risk resulting from the additional sale. Some suppliers and buyers pursue a conscious policy of risk-spreading, spreading contacts in order not to have too many eggs in certain baskets. Alternatively, some firms integrate forwards and backwards to obtain control of customers and suppliers respectively.

More than one organization, perhaps a consortium or a company and its distributor, may be involved in a major purchase. A government department may need to be consulted on such matters as state financial aid, exchange control, import restriction or matters of security or national interest.

An agent or external consultant is sometimes brought in to assist with an industrial purchase decision. An engineering consultancy may specialize in a particular technology. A firm of management consultants might carry out financial appraisals of potential investments. Continuing sources of supply may be necessary and this requirement could lead to a joint investment in plant and infrastructure.

A giant company may enter into prolonged bargaining with a number of suppliers. A single supplier may be too small to satisfy its requirements. A major customer may consciously 'spread' orders around a number of suppliers. This could be done on a rotating basis or in such a way as to stimulate competition among suppliers.

The very large purchase could be frustrated by strikes, prices and incomes legislation, shortages, supply breakdowns, cold weather, mergers, and acquisitions. The default of the purchaser is not uncommon in certain overseas sales territories. Whenever large sums are involved, it is generally advisable to commission a detailed business and financial investigation of the contracting parties.

In some fields such as defence, government departments commission projects and products, paying for basic research and design, testing and development, and ultimate production. An extremely complex contract may be negotiated rather than subject to open tender. The main contractor in the case of a major defence contract could make use of the services of a large number of sub-contractors. In the case of open tenders involving secret bids, advertising and promotion becomes of little importance in the marketing mix.

LOCKHEED AIRCRAFT CORPORATION IN THE US RAN INTO FINANCIAL DIFFICULTIES WHICH AFFECTED SALES PROSPECTS OF ITS AIRBUS. THE AIRBUS WAS POWERED BY ROLLS ROYCE RB211 ENGINES. THE COMMERCIAL PRODUCTION OF THE ENGINE WAS DEPENDENT UPON AIRBUS SALES. THE DIFFICULTIES FACED BY LOCKHEED EXACERBATED ROLLS ROYCE CASHFLOW PROBLEMS AND HAD TO BE TAKEN OVER BY THE UK GOVERNMENT.

Question 76: Assess and compare the risks involved in entering the following marketing arrangements:

    (*a*)   prime contractor to the US Space Programme Agency NASA
    (*b*)   sub-contractor on a UK CEGB power station contract

(c)   contract to supply shop window units to a major chain store
(d)   contract to build a factory in South Africa.

8.7   THE INDUSTRIAL SELLER

Industrial good producers tend to be less market-oriented than producers of consumer goods.   Many firms invest heavily in plant and tools to produce new industrial goods without even attempting to examine their competitors.

With high barriers to entry and strong loyalty to suppliers, industrial markets can be almost impenetrable to a newcomer; an elementary market analysis would reveal this.   Market research can enable target users of industrial goods to be identified.   Sales estimates can be more accurate than is the case with high-volume consumer goods, the returns per pound spent on market research being correspondingly high.

The industrial-goods supplier is more likely than the consumer-goods supplier to be production-orientated and yet in the industrial-good field, market awareness can be equally as important.

One issue faced in industrial marketing is the trade off between corporate and product promotion.   A company which is not well known might by means of high-quality salesmen make inroads into an established market.

Creating a reputation can make the work of salesmen easier.   A buyer may find it easier to justify a purchase decision when the supplier has a reputation.   Technical personnel may of course give highest priority to product performance independent of corporate reputation.   Where a product requires some form of post-purchase servicing, reputation again becomes important.

Once a reputation is established it will need to be reinforced periodically or it will decline.   A company without a reputation has some advantage in that it need not spend as much on the maintenance of its reputation.

Personal influence is extremely important in industrial marketing.   This fact can come as a shock to those who transfer to industrial marketing from the impersonal world of consumer marketing.

While important, however, the personal element should not be allowed to dominate and drive out other marketing elements.   It is the integration of marketing elements which is often the key to marketing success rather than excellence in any one of them, albeit an important one.

In industrial marketing, integration of marketing effort may be more difficult in view of the number of buying-decisions-makers to be communicated with.   Buyers also can have different communications needs and channel preferences, at different stages of the communications process.

EXAMINATION QUESTION

'Industrial and consumer goods marketers are equally concerned to satisfy end user requirements.' Discuss.

9. *The Promotion Mix*

Prior to a consideration of individual marketing techniques in subsequent chapters, this chapter explains how complementary techniques are brought together to form an overall communication strategy.

9.1 THE PROMOTIONAL MIX

The promotional mix encompasses all activities whose purpose it is to inform or persuade. Promotion is of greatest importance when a number of similar products are on the market and when a product is new.

Promotional mixes change over time. Direct mail selling involves high promotional expenditure. As retailing switches from counter service to self-service, point-of-sale promotion becomes of greater relative importance.

The type of product one is selling is the prime determinant of the promotion mix. Thus as one moves from consumer to industrial goods, advertising may fall in relative importance while that of personal selling increases.

The promotional mix also changes during the course of a purchase decision. At the awareness stage, heavy promotional effort may be required on all fronts. Once awareness and understanding have been achieved publicity and advertising may become of less relative importance as potential purchasers resort to sales staff to obtain the more detailed information they require and to discuss their particular requirements.

A company with a good and extensive reputation may be able in favourable market circumstances, to spend relatively less on advertising than one which is not at all well known. In many, but by no means all, cases, the more mature the product the less important will advertising become.

The importance of the product, promotion, and strategy context should be borne in mind when new staff are recruited. An advertising manager with a successful track record in one field may be able to get to grips with a different situation. A new recruit may bring into an organization biasses and priorities

120

from another company employing a different promotional approach to the marketing of similar products.

> A RETAILER OF ICE PROMOTED HER PRODUCT IN A DIVERSITY OF MARKETS. BUTCHERS, FOR EXAMPLE, BOUGHT ICE TO HELP PRESERVE CARCASES OF MEAT. THEN THE HABIT OF PUTTING ICE IN DRINKS OCCURRED TO AN ICE SALESMAN. THIS HABIT BECAME THE FOCUS OF PROMOTION. DEMAND FOR ICE AND LATER FOR HOME ICE-CUBE MAKING MACHINES BOOMED.

Question 77: Explain to what extent you would expect the promotion mix to change over the manufacturing life-cycle of the following products:

(*a*)   a family motor car
(*b*)   a new type of pen
(*c*)   the mini-skirt
(*d*)   a convenience food.

9.2   PROMOTION MIX TESTING

Where test marketing is carried out in more than one region, then competitive performance testing may be possible. Different promotional mixes can be compared and their relative effectiveness evaluated prior to the development of a definitive campaign.

A large agency may have a media selection model which might be able to compare the effectiveness of different advertising solutions. A variety of used programming and marginal analysis models may be used to select optimum solutions. Other techniques such as simulation analysis can be used to evaluate probable outcomes.

A model is only as good as its basic assumptions and the quality of data fed into it. Models that allow the sensitivity of a solution to changes in various input values are particularly useful. The main defect of models in this area is that so many of the factors being modelled are interrelated in complex ways. Given lack of knowledge of how certain key variables interrelate, simulation models have some value in helping marketors to understand better the system they are seeking to model.

The 'ratchet' effect sometimes appears to operate in marketing. On a trial or test basis, new methods of promotion are tried and existing one extended but there is at times a great reluctance to cut expenditure on a long-established item for fear of the consequences. Thus for year after year, a company might carry advertisements in journals and directories, mount exhibitions and publish catalogues. That the expenditure in question is small might be given as a reason for its continuance.

The fact that costs are indivisible is often the reason why marketing resources are not always allocated in proportion to effectiveness. While it might be possible to adjust the number of catalogues printed or the number of people reached by a direct mail shot, the mounting of an exhibition, the equipping and fitting out of a stand might represent a high fixed cost. There might be a threshold of minimum effectiveness to cross.

A HOBBIES MAGAZINE WAS TEST MARKETED IN AN AREA OF THE INDUSTRIAL MIDLANDS. THE MAGAZINE PERFORMED SATIS-FACTORILY AND ITS LAUNCH WAS EXTENDED TO THE REST OF THE COUNTRY. A YEAR LATER THE MAGAZINE DISAPPEARED FROM THE BOOKSHELVES. SUBSEQUENT EVALUATION REVEALED THAT NOT ONLY DID THE TEST MARKET AREA HAVE AN ABOVE AVERAGE NUMBER OF NEWSAGENT OUTLETS BUT ALSO AN ABOVE AVERAGE NUMBER OF ENTHUSIASTS FOR THE HOBBIES COVERED IN THE MAGAZINE.

9.3   PACKAGING

Packaging is at times an underrated component of promotion mix. A product's container, the way a service is packaged, is an element of communication.

Packaging serves a variety of functions. It must attract, arrest, interest, impart information, engender glamour and excitement perhaps, but certainly encourage purchase. Packaging should highlight those factors most likely to encourage consumption.

Packaging must often meet the needs of a variety of communication channels. It may have to attract attention in both television commercials and point-of-sale display cards.

Consumers are attracted to certain sizes, shapes, and colours and become attach-ed to packaging. In the case of Coca-Cola, the package shape, its bottle, came to represent for many people a major part of the product and to symbolize it.

Packaging can communicate an image. The same cosmetic could be packaged in square economy packets for the low price mass market and in slim elegant bottles for a high price more select market.

A MILK DISTRIBUTOR REPLACED ITS GLASS BOTTLES WITH DISPOSABLE PLASTIC CONTAINERS. IT WAS FELT THAT THE NEW CONTAINERS WOULD BE MORE CONVENIENT. THEY WERE WITH-DRAWN FOLLOWING A HOWL OF PROTEST FROM ENVIRONMENTAL GROUPS.

Question 78:   Contrast and compare what you feel to be the relative importance of packaging in respect of the following products:

(*a*)   a wedding anniversary card

(*b*)   a breakfast cereal

(*c*)   a 'girlie' magazine

(*d*)   chocolate-coated nuts and raisins

(*e*)   an electric hedge clipper.

9.4   ADVERTISING

Advertising is an aspect of marketing communication and should be viewed as such rather than as a separate activity to be carried on by a distinct group of professionals independently of other marketing activity. Advertising decisions should be in the context of an organization's overall communications mix. There may, for example, be a direct trade-off between expenditure on advertising and for example salesmen's visits. This is worth stating at the outset as too often advertising programmes develop a life of their own, unrelated to other marketing activity.

An organization must have or be able to obtain some understanding of how advertising works and how it complements other aspects of the marketing mix. Criteria and means need to be established for setting the advertising budget and, within this, putting together a package of messages and channels to reach target audiences.

Budget and performance are interrelated as one channel reaching more of a target audience than expected can allow other channels to be deleted from a programme and cost savings achieved. Alternatively, advertising objectives could be made more ambitious within an existing budget. Clearly the ability to take such management decisions depends upon the continuing and accurate monitoring and evaluating of advertising effectiveness.

One organizational and behavioural problem often faced in the advertising area is the consequence of the difficulty in measuring the effectiveness of some advertising. A campaign may need to run for some time before the benefits are apparent. This can result in pressures to sacrifice a programme likely to bring in large long-term benefits in the interests of smaller but shorter run returns.

There may be certain campaigns that promote both product and company or division. Different parts of the organization may have varying preferences for where the priority should lie, whether the emphasis should be placed upon product or organization. Brand managers typically look for means of maximizing returns from the point of view of their own particular brands. Over a period of time, such priorities practised company-wide can result in a company having a relatively unknown corporate image. Some emphasis upon the company in brand advertising might spare a company an expensive corporate image campaign.

The effect of advertising is frequently difficult to distinguish from that of other aspects of the marketing mix. Much will also depend upon the effectiveness of competing communications received by target audiences. The relative importance of advertising within the marketing mix will depend upon such factors as overall strategy and the life-cycle stages of products.

While highly visible, advertising is but one component of the marketing mix. On average, it is about 10% of marketing expenditure although it may be much higher for confectionery and tobacco and significantly lower for capital goods. Where there is competitive advertising to neutralize, the proportion will go up.

Purchase decisions are normally based upon the total effect of the marketing mix. Consumers will vary in the weight they attach to such factors as price, quality, and availability. There are a great many purposes and objectives of marketing from which the advertising manager must abstract priorities.

Industrial and consumer advertising differ as does standardized product and custom-built product advertising. A service, an intangible, may be more difficult to communicate than a product. The advantages of some products and services are more immediately apparent than others. With a seasonal industry a campaign may need to build to a peak.

A new product clearly needs greater promotion in the early and take-off phases of its life-cycle than a mature established product. Current advertising will depend upon the quantity and quality of past advertising.

Given a customer and a product, the allocation and extent of advertising can still depend greatly upon overall strategy. One publisher for example may sell management books by 35% retail margins and relatively heavy advertising in management and professional journals, while a rival mounts an in-house direct sale mailing operation, cutting out general advertising and retail distribution.

There are many forms of advertising. Packaging advertises products on shelf display. Some advertisements are aimed at ultimate consumers, others at inter-mediate industrial buyers. In one campaign, initial take-up may be important; in another, repeat purpose may be the main priority.

One school of thought stresses the need for an advertisement to stress the unique selling point of a product, where it has the greatest comparative advantage *vis-à-vis* the competition. Such a proposition must be clearly understood by sales staff and be put, clearly, concisely, and in an appealing way, to the target group.

Another view is that consumers are not as rational as the unique selling-point approach assumes. Rather than seeking to maximize, customers may aim to satisfy, achieiving a comfortable balance or compromise between a variety of factors they consider to be to some extent important.

Question 79:   Assess the relative importance of advertising in the promotional mixes of the following organizations:

    (*a*)   a football pool
    (*b*)   an exclusive club
    (*c*)   a mail-order house
    (*d*)   a motor-cycle spares shop
    (*e*)   an ethnic restaurant.

EXAMINATION QUESTIONS

1. How have the great changes in (*a*) technology and (*b*) communications over the past 30 years affected the organization problems of industry?

2. Explain how a product's packaging can contribute to the effectiveness of its total communications plan/task.

3. Assess the usefulness (*a*) to the marketor, and (*b*) to the media planner, of research data which links media exposure to buying behaviour.

10. *Sales Management*

As has already been pointed out in Chapter 1, interpersonal communication tends
to be the most effective means of communication when a message is relatively
complex and a recipient is relatively uninformed and hesitant. While a salesman's
message may be delivered to a group, most sales situations will consist of the
interaction of two individuals. This chapter considers salesmanship and sales
management, by which means sales staff are put as cost-effectively as possible
into sales situations.

10.1 SALESMANSHIP

In an interpersonal relationship, once a rapport has been achieved, the prospects
of a sale increase. A rapport tends to be easier to achieve when parties are similar
and perceive each other to be 'birds of a feather'. People tend to prefer people they
perceive as reflecting themselves. A sales situation needs to be structured if there
is a potential for rapport to ensure that it is achieved. With a large salesforce,
results might repay the effort of carefully matching sales staff to prospects.

In Chapter 1 the importance of credibility was stressed to the responsiveness of
a target or subject to a message. We will return to the question of credibility in
respect of media in Chapter 16. A salesman who is regarded as credible is likely
to be more persuasive and effective. Credibility could depend upon a number of
perceived attributes such as appearance, confidence, integrity, experience, knowledge, prestige, and patience. When such characteristics are 'overplayed' and a
salesman seeks to 'talk down' or 'pressurize', then credibility can be lost.

With a cynical prospect, credibility may be difficult to achieve. More than one
visit may be needed to 'win' a difficult prospect over and the individual salesman
must use judgement as to whether a future visit will be worth the time. A doubter
may be convinced on the grounds of performance or a single factor such as technical expertise. On occasions, stubborn persistence has its admirers.

126

A sales-situation interaction should not be one-sided. The subject should be allowed to put questions or a point of view. The effective salesman is a good listener. One of the functions of a salesman should be to bring back market information.

Many subjects will put a great store upon initial impressions. A prospect should be approached in favourable circumstances such as a convenient time. A salesman should endeavour if possible to make his sales pitch an enjoyable occasion for the prospect.

10.11 Sales Messages

An effective salesman's message is that which is interesting and holds attention, is simple and easily understood, compatible with a subject's existing attitudes and values, and well structured so that main points are stressed, preferably at the beginning and at the end when attention will be highest. A prospect could be involved in a pitch perhaps by participating in a demonstration. A visual aid could assist in the making of a difficult point. An unusual aspect might be remembered. A better-informed and initially-unsympathetic subject might be more impressed with a message that dealt with both the drawbacks and the advantages of a product or service. Where a customer is unfamiliar with a product, it might be advisable to first create an awareness of need.

In the case of a consumer durable purchase, both a husband and wife might be involved. The salesman should seek to appeal to both targets and should be ready to 'stand back' on occasions and allow one of the prospects to become an 'ally' by helping to persuade the other.

Some husbands resent too direct an appeal to their wives while some wives may be sensitive to any suggestion by a salesman's manner or approach that a decision is the husband's rather than a joint decision. Although sexist, it is often effective to direct practical and technical points to a husband while referring such attributes of the product as design, colour, and perhaps compatibility with an existing decor, to a wife. A clinching point could be a reference to an influential or respected family in the area who have already purchased the product.

A salesman should tailor a message to what is known about the individual subject. An effective approach is often to get the target to talk about his or her problems before suggesting a solution. An experienced salesman develops a feel for the sort of person he is dealing with, whether or not the prospect will be impressed by a 'name', is anxious or dogmatic, or likely to be reached by appeals to logic, emotion, or prestige. A sale can be easier where a prospect has already been 'softened up' by advertising.

Question 80: Explain how you would tailor a sales message concerning a deep-freeze, family-food store to each of the following prospects:

(*a*)   a young punk rocker about to leave with a boy-friend for the disco
(*b*)   a weatherbeaten farmer propping up a gate
(*c*)   a romantic pair of newly-weds
(*d*)   a company director polishing his Rolls Royce in the drive
(*e*)   Bert and Ethel, the occupants of a terraced back-to-back house.

10.2   SALES FUNCTION AND ORGANIZATION

A salesman can pass on information, deliver a product as with milk, take orders passively or actively in the company's establishments or out among buyers, build goodwill, maintain contact and deal with problems, or act as an influencer. There is a great variety of buyer—seller relationships. Most salesmen, however, perform a mix of selling, servicing, and information-gathering work.

The objectives set for salesmen, including communication objectives, must ensure that all important aspects of work are encouraged. The nature of the objectives and tasks to be performed will establish how many salesmen are required. The exact number could be calculated by grossing up some indices of sales-staff productivity or by building up workload units, putting together work packages, by grouping customers by size and type and establishing call frequencies.

The form of organization structure adopted: whether product- or market-centred, may determine whether the salesforce is structured upon a territorial or a product basis. The territorial system tends to be used when products are more or less homogenous. When products are complex and diverse, the product-centred system tends to be used. In order to build up expertise about customer-needs, sales staff could be allocated to certain customer types or distribution channels.

As a company's product range changes and new customer targets emerge, salesforce organization may need to be adapted to ensure that relevant communication skills are brought to bear upon evolving communication problems. No method of organizing a salesforce is perfect. If a customer basis is used or a product basis, this can lead to long journeys and may be much more expensive of time than the territorial basis. In practice, a variety of methods might be employed. As effective communication becomes more important, there may be more emphasis upon the characteristics of likely recipients of messages.

10.21   Sales Territories

The allocation of sales staff to sales territories can give rise to a host of behavioural problems. There is a basic question of whether territories should be allocated according to sales potential, workload, or type of customer encountered. The potential allocation may head off claims that one salesman has a 'better' territory than another. This can result, however, in territories of greatly differing size and one salesman may complain about having to travel so much further than others.

Where possible, communication skill should be matched to communication problems likely to be encountered. Inevitably, the grass will appear greener on the other side of the fence. The other salesman's territory will always seem more promising. Rumours may abound within the salesforce about small rich district territories in which sales are 'there for the asking', while in rural areas, staff work hard for the occasional sale.

Sales territories themselves can be of a variety of shapes. The travelling distance within territories of course depends upon the location of accounts. A number of computer programmes are in existence for the computation of optimum routes and optimum territory sizes and boundaries. Needless to say, as sales patterns change, territories and routes will need to be adjusted.

IN THE BRITISH GENERAL ELECTION WHICH BROUGHT MRS THATCHER TO POWER AS PRIME MINISTER THE CONSTITUENCY BOUNDARIES HAD NOT BEEN CHANGED FOR SOME TIME AND HENCE HAD NOT TAKEN ACCOUNT OF THE STEADY FLOW OF POPULATION FROM THE INNER CITY AREAS TO THE SUBURBS. THE POPULATION OF SOME RURAL CONSERVATIVE SEATS WAS THREE TIMES THAT OF SMALL INNER CITY LABOUR SEATS. HAD THE BOUNDARIES BEEN REDRAWN TO ACHIEVE A ROUGHLY EQUAL CONSTITUENCY SIZE, MRS THATCHER'S OVERALL MAJOR-ITY MIGHT HAVE RISEN BY SOME THIRTY SEATS.

From the point of view of effective salesmanship, there is a case for considering markets from the point of view of behavioural characteristics rather than physical territories. A behavioural territory allocated to a specific salesman could constitute the population of targets with whom the salesman is expected to communicate effectively. The salesman could have credibility because of the possession of some quality or characteristic thought by the group in question to be more important than would be the case with other groups. The manner and appearance of a salesman may be more likely to achieve acceptance with certain groups than with others.

10.22   The Location of Sales Staff

Sales staff can be located at the centre of a company's operations, in divisional or local offices, or work from their homes. Salesmen can be deskbound or largely 'on the road'. The location of the sales function and whether in-house or external staff are used will depend upon the nature of the product and the communication task, the type and location of customers, and the scheduling of the most economical call ratios and routes.

Where personal contact is important, sales staff may need to be located as close to the ultimate customer as possible. In some businesses — for example stockbroking, banking or advertising, typically service functions — the customers tend to 'call in' by telephone and small sales teams keeping an eye upon overall marketing strategy can be based at the centre.

A product that needs to be demonstrated will demand more grass-roots sales contacts than one, the merits of which are generally known. Where customers are grouped, say key industrial goods purchasers around a major industrial complex, then a local sales office may need to be established.

Cost-effective service to the customer should be the prime determinant of the location of the sales function. Customer-needs change. Locational decisions will need to be taken periodically, following regular reviews. The introduction of telephone, telex, and other communications devices such as remote terminals has in some industries greatly reduced the need for local sales contact.

A business can be based largely upon the question of the location of sales effort. Thus Avon developed the practice of the door-to-door selling of cosmetics with initially very encouraging results.

ONE ALARM MANUFACTURER, EXAMINING WHERE IT SHOULD LOCATE ITS ALARM SERVICING FUNCTION, PERCEIVED FOR THE FIRST TIME THAT IT WAS REALLY IN THREE BUSINESSES, THE MANUFACTURE OF ALARMS, THEIR INSTALLATION AND THEIR SERVICING. THE COMPANY DECIDED TO CONTINUE WITH THE MANUFACTURE AND INSTALLATION OF ALARMS BUT TO LEAVE THEIR SERVICING TO AN EXTERNAL AGENCY.

Effective salesmanship can require extensive two-way communication. Sales effort may need to be concentrated on environments that encourage interaction. Such interaction may need to occur at a number of different points in the sales process. The purchase decision may require human, technological, and organizational inputs, and a sales team may need to influence the behaviour of different individuals at a number of locations. The physical territory approach to sales organization and location can create unnecessary barriers.

Territory and location decisions should be designed to achieve compatibility between salesman and target. The immediate environment in which the sales pitch is made should encourage credibility and trust. Tight deadlines can result in a break-off from the prospect taking longer than expected to persuade. In some sales situations, ideal locations are those suitable for follow-up visits that build confidence and empathy.

10.23   Overseas Marketing

Overseas marketing communication raises special problems. In Chapter 12, the decision of whether to employ an agent or establish a local office is examined. The lessons of Chapters 12 and 13 are particularly relevant to the management of overseas sales staff.

The needs of the market should be the main determinant of how overseas marketing communication is organized. Where overseas purchases are small in value and infrequent, much of the sales work can be subcontracted. Distance, exchange rates, and differences of culture and nationality can present many difficulties. Local laws may present special problems. It is almost impossible to get information (and money!) out of some territories.

Full use should be made of local consular offices and official trade services. These can be of great value in developing market contacts.

Where a product message needs to be tailored to local conditions, then local nationals may be preferable as salesmen. Local nationals may be needed to identify elusive sales prospects and to weave a path through a local bureaucracy. In the case of an 'international' product, one whose merits are known locally and which is demanded by easily identifiable consumers then, provided there are no great language barriers, account servicing can be carried on by home-based staff or home-based staff on local tours of duty.

Such questions as currency and political risk should not be overlooked when selling overseas. A territory may suddenly introduce a 'national similars' or import-substitution policy. Local national firms may obtain preferential access to finance or to public sector finance. In these circumstances, one might need to explore the possibility of a joint venture arrangement.

The more rapidly-developing countries express a great interest in technology transfer. A company might need to develop a policy towards the transfer of its technology overseas by means of joint venture or licence arrangements.

When marketing overseas, the larger company should tap into the services of an experienced banker, a reputable local lawyer, and obtain access to one or more 'country experts' to advise on its 'exposure' in each of its major overseas markets.

Question 81: Outline, contrast, and compare the forms of marketing organization you consider would be most appropriate for supplying the middle-eastern market with the following products and services:

(a) a soft drink
(b) port design services
(c) a new steel plant
(d) Paris fashions
(e) advanced combat aircraft.

10.24 Marketing Technical Products

The technical product might require a very different form of sales organization from that demanded by the consumer good. The sales 'job' may be extended over a long period and involve a relatively large number of people. The product in question might be subjected to considerable testing and detailed evaluation.

The whole question of the marketing of industrial products is examined in Chapters 7 and 8. It is sufficient here to point out that selling technical products demands special skills. It demands the services of experts, specialists, and in this regard the lessons of the second section of Chapter 4 should be borne in mind.

The larger purchase might result in lengthy contract negotiations. As these proceed, it may be desirable to have access to both a lawyer and an accountant. The financial consequences of proposed changes in contract terms may need to be evaluated at very short notice.

Flexibility is a prime requirement of contract negotiation. The formal form of organization may have developed bureaucratic rules that prevent adjustment to the changing circumstances of a negotiation. This can result in lost sales. It should be pointed out, however, that at times excessive flexibility and conceding too much can result in the acceptance of contract terms that can only result in losses being made.

Many organizations have been pushed into bankruptcy as a result of entering into unfavourable contracts to which they have been bound in changing market and economic circumstances. Always introduce a margin for safety, some 'slack resource'.

AN AGENT OF AN AMERICAN LIGHT AIRCRAFT MANUFACTURER IN SOUTH AMERICA WAS LINKED BY 'HOT LINE' TO A MOBILE TEAM AT THE MANUFACTURER'S AIR BASE WHICH WAS PREPARED TO FLY A TEAM ANYWHERE IN THE WORLD TO NEGOTIATE BULK PURCHASE AND LOCAL LICENCE MANUFACTURE. A 'SPARE' PLANE REMAINED IN THE SALES TERRITORY AND WAS MADE AVAILABLE WHENEVER REQUIRED FOR TEST FLYING BY LOCAL PILOTS. IT WAS FOUND THAT IN BUYING AEROPLANES MOST ORGANIZATIONS RELIED HEAVILY UPON THE ADVICE OF THEIR PILOTS.

10.25 Contract Negotiations

Negotiation is an important element of salesmanship. A salesman should not always consider serving the customer to be inevitably at the expense of the company's interests. In reality in marketing, what is good for the customer is generally good for the supplying company. What is needed is high motivation to serve the company and the customer.

Both parties to a negotiation need to be realistic and to realise that there must be 'something in it' for each of them. It is not in the best interests of a negotiator to drive such a hard bargain that the other party is forced to default through subsequent inability to perform according to the requirements of the eventual contract.

It pays to speak with one voice in a negotiating situation. The other party can become confused when subjected to divergent points of view from the same side.

If differences exist in a negotiating team these should be thrashed out in private session among the team members concerned and not be allowed to surface around the negotiating table.

In a negotiating position, one should always put oneself in the shoes of the other party. The lessons of Chapter 13 on relationships with external agencies are instructive in this respect. Without an understanding of the pressures to which the other party is subjected, one might concede too much.

> IN ONE NEGOTIATION A DESIGN AGENCY PUT MUCH EFFORT INTO TRIMMING THE COST OF A SUBMISSION WHICH WAS EVENTU- ALLY ACCEPTED. THE ACCEPTOR FOUND THE SUBMISSION CON- CERNED TO BE ABOUT HALF THE COST OF RIVAL SUBMISSIONS AND INDEED HAD BUDGETED FOR TWICE THIS FIGURE PRIOR TO THE COMMENCEMENT OF NEGOTIATIONS.

Question 82: Describe a negotiation in which you have participated. Was the outcome successful from your point of view and what could you have done to make it more so?

10.3 MANAGING SALESMEN

Not all salesmen will require the same level of supervision. Those operating on a commission basis may be given much greater discretion than those who are on a straight salary.

A supervisor must ensure that sales staff allocate their time appropriately between the selling, servicing, and reporting functions. Central management can give guidance on the efficient use of time, perhaps, by publishing call norms and developing guidelines that can enable sales staff to evaluate new accounts.

Motivation will be a major concern of supervisors. A particular sales job may be unpleasant. The man in the field may need moral support and technical back-up. There will be human problems to deal with. Staff may 'fall out' within a team. A salesman might approach a supervisor with a personal problem.

A supervisor might be responsible for establishing quotas for sales staff. The quotas could be derived from a sales forecast. Quotas could be set at or in excess of sales forecasts. So long as they are perceived as capable of attainment, high quotas can motivate. Achieving quotas builds confidence.

Salesmen can be more highly motivated by a quota that is perceived as a challenge. Too easy a quota can lead to disappointing performance. An over-ambitious goal can cause salesmen to 'give up'. Having established quotas, managers should be motivated to see that they are obtained.

A marketing manager must decide how much discretion is to be given to sales staff. Should they be allowed to give discounts, offering goods on special terms?

Some companies give their salesforce considerable freedom, providing them with profitability data to allow them to allocate their time as they see fit. Such companies encourage their sales staff to think like managers. The efficient use of time can distinguish the experienced salesman from the raw recruit.

Care should be taken to ensure that sales staff equipped with profitability data do not pursue soft options. They may concentrate upon high volume purchasers of established products rather than push new products. This can lead to problems, as established products pass the peaks of their life-cycles.

The whole organization will assume a flavour from the sales staff's point of view. A company might consider its salesmen expendable fodder doing a routine job or as the company's prime source of new business, its ambassadors, its 'front end'. The latter approach is more likely to motivate sales staff.

A COMPANY ACQUIRED A WELL KNOWN SALESMAN FROM A PRESTIGIOUS ORGANIZATION TO SELL A NEW PRODUCT. A YEAR LATER THE SALESMAN LEFT THE COMPANY. HE HAD FAILED TO ACHIEVE RESULTS. HIS STRENGTH HAD LAIN IN SERVICING EXISTING CUSTOMERS RATHER THAN IN DEVELOPING NEW ONES.

Question 83: You have been appointed the marketing director of a company retailing office systems. You inherit sales staff who specialize in such diverse fields as pocket calculators and sophisticated computer systems. You wish to regroup your sales effort around key customers. What problems do you envisage?

10.31 Salesmen and Buyers

In a sales situation, when contact is face-to-face, the individual qualities of a salesman can be less important from the point of view of making a sale than the relationship which occurs between buyer and salesmen. One salesman may relate to a buyer while another who is equally qualified technically may not.

A sales manager must aim to select and train salesmen so as to achieve satisfactory customer—salesmen interactions. Compatibility can result from a combination of different factors. Personality, social status, physical characteristics, can all be important. There is some evidence that compatibility is highest between those of similar age, educational background, and social status.

Individual buyers will have various perceptions of the typical salesman and may have attitudes ranging from respect to hostility to their stereotyped image of a salesman. One buyer may prefer salesmen who are 'similar', another may expect salesmen to be 'different' and may undervalue one who, in fact, appears compatible on the grounds that someone who is selling a technical product ought to look scholarly or academic.

An effective marketing manager should build up personality profiles of major customers, and pair them with salesmen according to the characteristics of both. A watch should be kept on relationships between sales staff and their customers. Where these deteriorate then a shuffling of accounts or contacts may be needed.

The marketing manager must be aware of the behavioural component and seek to arrange compatible pairings. Sales staff should be selected and trained to meet the needs of customers. The more useful sales staff are those who can tailor their messages to the individuals receiving them and who are sensitive to 'feedback'.

> ONE MARKETING MANAGER WAS DISMAYED TO FIND THAT THE PERFORMANCE OF SALESMEN VARIED GREATLY FROM THE PREDICTIONS OF THE PERSONNEL MANAGER. THEN IT WAS REALIZED THAT THE PERSONNEL MANAGER WAS ASSESSING THE APPEARANCE OF SALES STAFF ACCORDING TO VALUES WHICH WERE VERY DIFFERENT FROM THOSE OF THE COMPANY'S LARGELY TEENAGE CUSTOMERS.

Question 84: Describe and compare the expectations you imagine typical potential customers of the following goods will have of the typical salesman selling them:

- (*a*) diamond-studded brooches
- (*b*) wet fish
- (*c*) bicycle chains
- (*d*) a new man-made fibre.

10.4 REPORTING AND INFORMATION

Effective communication requires prompt and objective feedback. If salesmen's efforts are to be channelled into the most profitable activities from the point of view of the company as a whole, sales staff must be given information on product and account profitability. Some companies keep such information secret. When this is done, sales staff are unaware of the extent of their contribution to overall performance. In some cases, activities which are unprofitable may be continued with.

There could be several reasons for failing to provide sales staff with account and product profitability data. The information might not be available. Margin data could be leaked inadvertently or purposely. A company may fear that disclosure of high profits might lead to claims for higher salaries. Many progressive companies link performance and profit contribution to salary levels, in order to reward effort and initiative.

Salesmen can make call reports in respect of all calls and, periodically, compile more extensive customer reports. Sales staff should be required to account for their expenses budgets, presenting receipts and other vouchers as required. One-off reports may be needed on new and lost accounts. Salesmen in distant territories may be requested to submit periodic background reports.

Regular reports may also be requested on salesmen themselves. In addition to covering performance, these may cover such factors as motivation, personality, knowledge of the company and its products, ability to accept responsibility, promptness of reporting, personal appearance, and willingness to progress.

When collecting information and reporting back, sales staff should be encouraged to collect details of competitor activity. Some companies have special competitor activity reports.

> ONE UK MARKETING MANAGER, LONG REGARDED AS A 'HARD-FACED GO-GETTER', TOLD SALES STAFF NOT TO WASTE TIME WITH TRIVIA AND ONLY TO REPORT WHEN THEY HAD MADE A SUB-STANTIAL SALE. THIS APPROACH TO SALES STAFF REPORTING WAS CHANGED WHEN A SALESMAN WHOSE EXISTENCE HAD BEEN FORGOTTEN BUT WHO HAD DRAWN HIS SALARY REGULARLY FOR TWO YEARS CALLED FROM THE SOUTH OF FRANCE TO ASK IF THE MANAGER WOULD LIKE TO TAKE A SEVENTH SHARE OF A YACHT.

Question 85:   List what you consider to be the main items of information that should be reported by salesmen of the following products/staff servicing the following accounts, and state how often you would expect such reports to be made:

- (*a*)   motor body wax—motorist customer
- (*b*)   motor body wax—major garage customer
- (*c*)   oil tankers—Greek shipping magnate
- (*d*)   chocolate bars—individual retailers
- (*e*)   chocolate bars—large wholesaler.

10.5 ASSESSING SALESMAN PERFORMANCE

Salesmen very in quality. In many companies, a minority of sales staff bring in the majority of sales. Salesmen are very expensive: a car, travel costs and an entertainment budget may be considered essential. Working on a 10% gross margin, a salesman would need to generate sales equal to ten times his total cost to break even.

It is difficult to generalize about what makes a good salesman. A need, a drive to succeed is an important ingredient. Energy, self-confidence, discipline, initiative, and an interest in financial success are desirable characteristics in sales staff. The ability to stand in another person's shoes is also important. Possession of these characteristics is suggestive of good performance, but this will not inevitably follow.

An individual company will attach weights to desirable characteristics according to the selling job that needs to be done. Persuasion may demand integrity. Where a product really 'sells itself', sheer energy may be the most important requirement.

One situation may require the establishment and building of long-term relationships, another the making of an instant impact. Paperwork may be more important in one situation than another.

Comparing salesmen can be misleading: it may be that all salesmen are wanting. The star performer may have had an 'easy' territory. These factors should be borne in mind when examining track records while recruiting.

Establishing the number and type of sales staff required could be handled by manpower planning. A personnel department might carry out job interviews. Where other departments are responsible for recruitment, the marketing manager must have some means of ensuring that he is getting what he wants. Where some formal rating and ranking procedure is employed, the marketing manager should be involved in establishing trade-offs and minimum levels of achievement. These will be necessary, as many applicants are likely to excel in some criteria and rank badly on others.

Comparing salesmen can set staff against each other. A certain amount of competition can be healthy, but excessive rivalry can be undesirable. If comparisons are to be fair then other things must be equal.

A widely-used method of performance evaluation is to compare the sales of one period with those of the previous period. This method has defects in the short term. Poor performance in one period can make it easy to do better in the next period. Changes in the demographic make up or the economic well-being of an area can also effect the ease with which sales are obtained. Overall market sales could be given a boost by the sudden removal of credit restrictions.

A more objective method of assessment is to compare actual sales with the potential of a territory. Ratios could be computed of sales expenses or time spent per call, or of profit or sales per account.

The total number of new and lost accounts can be revealing: numbers should not be taken at their face value. Accounts could be lost due to people moving. A high cost per account could reflect how widely-scattered accounts are in a rural area.

ONE CONSUMER GOODS COMPANY DEVELOPED AN ASSESSMENT FORM AND REQUESTED INDIVIDUAL SALES STAFF TO ASSESS THEMSELVES AND THOSE OF THEIR FELLOWS WITH WHOM THEY CAME INTO REGULAR FACE-TO-FACE CONTACT. THE ASSESSMENTS WERE THEN COMPARED. REWARD OR REMEDIAL HELP WAS CONCENTRATED UPON THOSE WHO WERE REVEALED AS HAVING THE MOST REALISTIC VIEW OF THEMSELVES.

Question 86: Consider what you feel would be the special problems that would be incurred in assessing the performance of sales staff in the following circumstances:

(a) new product
(b) products of a monopolist

(*c*)   failed product

(*d*)   an acquired company.

10.51   Training Sales Staff

There are a number of ways in which salesmen can be trained, although the diehard will claim that the good salesman is 'born'. A new salesman will need some understanding of his company, its products, and its customers. The company may have accumulated wisdom on how its products might best be sold, and there will be procedures to learn and personalities to identify and understand.

Introductions are important and should be carefully planned, as initial perceptions can be long-lasting. Trial assignments can enable new salesmen to be assessed and specific training laid on to deal with any deficiencies that might emerge.

ONE COMPANY TRAINS NEW MEMBERS OF ITS SALES FORCE BY REQUIRING THEM TO PAIR FOR A TRIAL PERIOD WITH EXPERIENCED SALESMEN.

Question 87:   Set out special training programmes for salesmen who are new to the following products:

(*a*)   an automatic rifle

(*b*)   a mink coat

(*c*)   an established dog food

(*d*)   a trading stamp

(*e*)   a beefburger bar franchise.

10.6   SALES STAFF REMUNERATION

Remuneration should attract, keep, and motivate. It should be fair, and seen to be and thought to be fair. Staff generally need a regular income; above-average performance should be rewarded.

A payment system should be simple to understand and economical to operate. Performance criteria should, so far as is possible, be unambiguous. Rates need not be excessive but an above-market rate may be necessary to attract 'premium' staff. The amount available for salesman remuneration could be fixed or tied to sales level or company cash flow.

Sales staff normally receive a fixed amount to cover regular living expenses, enabling some guaranteed regular earnings, a variable amount related to performance, an expense allowance, and a variety of 'perks' or fringe benefits. The performance-related element is designed primarily to motivate. 'Perks' can also be used to encourage above-average performance. In some cases, the nature of a perk, and its status can be more important than its monetary value.

The straight salary gives security and makes for easy budgeting. It does not, however, give the salesmen any incentive to excel unless a points system with prestigious awards and 'league tables' at conventions, using status to motivate, is used.

When fixed salaries are paid, it is difficult to 'cut' in an economic downturn. The benefits of simplicity, apparent at first sight, may not exist when increments have to be paid for qualifications, length of service, and experience. Regular cost-of-living adjustments will also need to be made in a period of inflation.

A straight commission method of remuneration can motivate. Income is directly related to performance and the cost of sales will fall as sales fall. By varying rates of commission, sales staff effort can be directed to products and markets management considers priorities. The disadvantage of this method of payment is that it can lead to short-term sales maximization. A host of routine servicing and reporting tasks may be ignored in the headlong rush for sales. Over-generous discounts may be given, or high credit risks taken in order to gain sales. Sales staff may feel extremely insecure under this method of remuneration.

A commission base could be gross or net income. There could be various definitions of 'net' income, according to what is deducted. The rates could be single or multiple, constant or stepped, changing as bands of sales levels are broken through. Commission could start at a zero or at a break-even level of sales. The starting point could be the sales of a previous period, less a 'decay' factor where repeat purchases occur. This prevents one salesman riding upon the back of an active predecessor. Where a sale results in an ongoing flow of income, as with the sale of an insurance policy, some method may need to be found to credit salesmen with a lump sum equivalent to their share of the income stream they have created discounted.

Where profit margins vary, indeed some products may be sold at a loss, it may be necessary to relate commission to profit or contribution, to prevent sales being pushed beyond the point of maximum profitability and possible productive capacity.

In practice, a combination of commission and straight salary deals with many of the defects of each of them alone. The commission element is often paid in the form of an annual bonus. Of course, not all marketing staff will be in a position to make 'sales'. Clerical staff and other desk-bound staff may resent the high salaries paid to front-line salesmen. With such staff, the market rate or job evaluation may act as the basis of remuneration decisions.

Question 88: You are in danger of losing your best sales staff to a competitor able to pay higher salaries and offering a range of attractive perks your company cannot afford. Set out and compare what you would say to your salesforce collectively and individually in an attempt to reduce the expected haemorrhage of staff.

10.7 SALESMAN STRESS

Industrial salesmen sometimes face role ambiguity. Salesmen can feel that the expectations and demands of different groups with whom they come into contact are incompatible.

The salesman operates between organizations, at the interface of company and customer, and naturally seeks to satisfy members of both organizations. Different accounts may impose varying demands. A salesman may come to some arrangement with a customer to find it countermanded back home. The more departments in the company and the more accounts with whom the salesman must deal, the greater will be the potential for role ambiguity.

The extent to which a salesman can adjust to the conflicting demands of a number of roles will depend upon how much discretion he has. Tight supervision can leave little room for manoeuvre. In such conditions, a salesman may feel he is facing unreasonable demands. Where supervision is personal rather than bureaucratic, joint discussion of problems can reduce the pressures arising from role ambiguity.

The experienced salesman can distinguish between the genuine crisis situation and the mere bluff. Over time, a person can become toughened, more sceptical and cynical, more resistant to pressure, less sensitive to stress.

Great frequency of contact with the company base can reduce salesman stress. Regular communication with managers can enable a salesman to settle problem areas and clarify the position in respect of conflicts of interests.

To satisfy a customer, a salesman may need to be flexible, imaginative, and innovative. This might be stifled by bureaucratic rules at head offices. Where useful and informative guidelines are offered, the formal procedures could assist the salesmen.

A SUBSCRIPTION SALES MANAGER OF A MAGAZINE REPORTED TO BOTH AN EDITOR AND A PUBLISHER WHO WERE AT EQUAL LEVELS IN THE ORGANIZATION HIERARCHY. THE VIEWS OF THE EDITOR AND PUBLISHER ABOUT HOW THE MAGAZINE OUGHT TO BE MARKETED DIFFERED, PUTTING THE SUBSCRIPTION SALES MANAGER IN A DILEMMA. THE SALES MANAGER WAS UNABLE TO DEVELOP A SATISFACTORY LONG-TERM SALES STRATEGY AND CONCENTRATED UPON SURVIVAL BY PLAYING OFF EACH OF THE TWO BOSSES AGAINST THE OTHER.

EXAMINATION QUESTIONS

1. What do you think is the ideal way in which to recruit and select salesmen?

2. How should a sales manager determine the size of his salesforce?

3. Can anything be done to improve the results of the sales manager's traditional attempts to spot winners when selecting salesmen?

11. *Brand/Product Management*

A one-product company may run a single comprehensive corporate marketing communication campaign. Such a campaign could incorporate elements such as corporate image advertising which sell the company more than a product. A company with products that have strong identities of their own may, in place of a single corporate campaign, run a number of separate brand or product campaigns. This chapter examines branding and some relevant aspects of brand management.

11.1 BRANDING

A product is more than a physical unit. In the mind of the buyer and potential purchaser it consists additionally of a number of intangible factors which encompass expectations concerning attributes and benefits. A brand name and image helps a consumer to distinguish between competing products that are offered. A brand will assist recognition, conjure up images of attributes and trigger expectations. A brand can be a mark of quality and consistency. The appeal of a brand may remain relatively constant even when a product's physical attributes may change. An existing brand may represent a considerable investment over a period of time in a 'name' and in goodwill.

Branding can be performed by an original manufacturer, a distributor, or by a retailer. With retailers and many distributors increasingly desiring to introduce their own label brands, a manufacturer has to decide whether the benefits of extra sales through such individual accounts will outweigh the loss of an overall market viability and standing. Similarly distributors and retailers are faced with a choice of trading upon a naturally-established brand reputation, or seeking to introduce a private distributors or retailer brand in order to distinguish themselves from competitors and build a reputation of their own.

Distributors and retailers own brand labels are more numerous in some business sectors than in others. There are also quite distinct policies which are pursued. One manufacturer may supply products in a variety of private labels, while another supplies only the manufacturer's own brand. One distributor may largely trade in private brands while another deals almost exclusively with manufacturer's national brands.

The incidence of private branding might reflect the general state of the market. A larger manufacturer in a relatively concentrated industry may feel more confident and willing to allow private branding than a smaller supplier in a more competitive market, eager to establish a reputation. To a large established company, a proliferation of brands could reduce the market share likely to be taken by a new entrant given a certain propensity to switch brands. Alternatively, where leading suppliers are reluctant to allow private branding, a willingness to supply a retailer with a product in the retailer's own label might be a means of securing entry to a new market.

Regardless of the source of branding, there is a tendency for a relatively few brands to predominate. A private brand is easier to establish when a total market is growing rather than contracting. With frequently-purchased goods, a high incidence of private branding may allow greater use of price differentials as a marketing tool.

Question 89:   Assess the relative suitability of the following products for branding, examining the merits and drawbacks of branding for producer, distributors, retailer, and customer:

    (*a*)   combat aircraft
    (*b*)   chocolate bar
    (*c*)   draught bitter
    (*d*)   children's clothing
    (*e*)   motor caravan.

11.11   Producer Brand Policy

A manufacturer when faced by a request must decide if, when, and on what conditions to allow private branding. The profit implications will vary according to the risks involved. When the company requesting a private brand is a major retail chain, it might be difficult both to 'say yes' and 'say no'. A conscious policy could be followed of only supplying the manufacturer's own brand, or of only supplying products as private brands or of supplying both private and the manufacturer's own brand.

The larger and more dominant a manufacturer is, the greater will be its ability to resist claims for private branding, should it wish to do so. There has been a tendency for more manufacturers to adopt mixed-brand strategies in response to demand. A retailer that is not supplied with a private brand might look elsewhere or, if of sufficient size, produce its own brand, perhaps by taking over a smaller supplier. Some distributors and retailers will wish to stock both private and manufacturer's brands in order to reap advantage of their own and a manufacturer's national promotion.

A private brand might differ only in packaging or be distinct in its physical attributes. Where private brand production runs are relatively small, they might be produced in slack periods in order to keep up a high utilization of plant. The success of a private brand that is physically a different product might yield clues about the extent to which and in what directions a manufacturer should modify its own national brands. The conditions imposed by a major distributor or retail, private-brand purchaser might tighten up general production standards.

Where private brands are produced they should, if possible, carry a fair share of overhead costs if a manufacturer's own brands are not to suffer a competitive cost disadvantage. Because of the larger size of individual purchase contract quantities, the manufacture of private brands can lead to lower margins. The more strongly a private brand is established in the marketplace, the greater will be the pressure upon a manufacturer's margins.

When a private brand supply arrangement is negotiated, a manufacturer might insist upon a minimum-order quantity. The committed mixed-brand supply might also offer promotional assistance. A periodic review of an arrangement might also be desirable: a distributor or retailer in a relatively strong market position might seek access to cost information and play one manufacturer off against another by ordering from more than one supplier at a time.

The supply of a private brand direct to a retailer could damage a relationship with a distributor seeking to promote the manufacturer's national brand. Not only may a middleman lose sales, but there may be fears of less commitment by a manufacturer to national-brand promotion.

11.12 Private Brand Policy

Before a retailer or distributor can establish a private brand, there must usually be some expectation of a reasonable volume of sales. The threshold volume would clearly be less in the case of frequently-purchased, low-unit value items where branding might involve only a label change than with consumer durables where branding could involve capital costs. Where entry to a private brand market is easy, an opportunistic strategy may be employed. Where promotion is likely to be heavy, supply contracts difficult to negotiate, or there may be some after-sales service to supply, a decision may need greater consideration.

Profit potential will depend upon the relative strength of existing brands and the willingness of customers to switch brands. A store with experience of private brands and an existing family-brand identity and reputation will be in a stronger position than a store which does not. A private-brand promotion may be able to 'ride on the back' of a general store promotion which is in the pipeline. A private brand must generate sufficient additional profits to cover negotiation and handling costs.

In order to establish a private brand, a promotion and advertising campaign may be needed. In the case of a non-standardized product, initial re-design or retooling may raise unit costs. With more complex goods, a brand service facility may need to be provided and long-term contracts entered into. Against the additional costs, private branding can result in image and publicity advantages. A greater element of control, a stronger store identity, the extension of a brand family, and an improved bargaining position *vis-à-vis* suppliers can result.

Question 90: Assess the advantages and disadvantages to both manufacturer and retailer of allowing a private brand in the following product categories:

(*a*) chocolate bar
(*b*) household detergent
(*c*) portable electronic calculator
(*d*) book
(*e*) hamburger
(*f*) bracket clock.

11.2 THE PRODUCT MANAGER

The product manager is responsible for developing marketing plans for a product or group of products. The responsibility could include pricing, sales promotion, advertising, packaging, distribution, and product modification.

In discharging their responsibilities, product managers will work with other specialists. Accountants will help on analyses of performance and possibly on the establishment of prices. Production specialists may need to be consulted on product modifications.

Product management thrives in multi-product companies whose individual-product sales are significant but not such that the sales of one or two products determine the overall financial performance of the enterprise. The multi-product company may feel that insufficient attention is likely to be given to each product unless individual managers are given responsibility for particular products or for a group of products with similar characteristics.

Low volume items may not generate sufficient revenue to justify the sole allocation of staff. A major seller by contrast might be so crucial to the success of a company as a whole as to justify the direct involvement of senior staff. The advantages of brand management will be lost if a manager is given too many brands to look after.

11.21 Evolution of the Concept

Brand management originated in the 1920's, but only in the 1950's did its use become widespread as, due to brand proliferation, it became increasingly difficult for executives to watch the performance of a number of brands. Beyond a certain number of brands, marketers organized on a functional basis can find themselves jumping so often from one product to another as to be unable to build up a detailed knowledge of any one product.

Product managers assumed responsibility for such objectives as sales or market share or profits, calling upon the services of functional managers as and when required. Thus at least one marketing executive is, on a fulltime basis, conversant with the needs and progress of each product.

In many organizations, the advertising function has been shifted from a single functional department to individual brands. Brand managers have assumed responsibility for advertising. Individual brand managers within many organizations maintain contacts with a variety of advertising agencies. Each brand manager is able to devise the advertising and promotional package that is the optimum from the point of view of his or her particular brand.

Product managers may in future play a more significant role in the day to day management of their brands. Activities in which product managers play a major role are likely to include planning, budgeting, scheduling, drawing up procedures, managing and motivating staff, reporting and representing. The active participation of a brand manager in the setting of objectives is usually desirable. Product managers having the greatest discretion may be rewarded in part on a performance basis.

11.22   Product Responsibilities

Product management allows the profitability of brands to be planned and managed on a continuing basis. No two organizations are likely to agree on what the role of a product manager should be. A number of patterns may be employed within a single company.

A static brand may require few major decisions. It might be administered by a brand manager with wide discretion. Another brand might be about to enter the take-off phase of its life-cycle, a period in which it is thought that major decisions will need to be taken. The manager of such a brand could be given far less discretion.

Many companies are reluctant to delegate decisions which could be termed 'marketing decisions' to brand managers. While a brand manager might be involved in questions of product, package, price, advertising, research, and promotion changes, the involvement of more senior managers may be needed before salesforce instructions are given on policy matters. The brand manager may have little say in the overall size of a salesforce or over the 'hiring and firing' of agents and distributors.

A product manager may have greater discretion in respect of external marketing services. Similar services located within the organization might be under the control of another manager. Changing the promotion mix can alter a product manager's role. One who is unfamiliar with a new element of the promotion mix may have to yield discretion to another specialist manager.

A distinction can be drawn between managers who play a major role or a minor role in decision taking, between those who are consulted and whose opinions are sought, and those who are merely given a *fait accompli*. The authority and responsibility of a brand manager is likely to depend upon the number of management layers involved in the decision-making process. When there are several layers, the product manager is likely to be a watchdog, keeping an eye on a product's progress and making recommendations for changes which will be passed upwards through the management hierarchy. Such a product manager is an initiator. Decisions may be taken in such an organization at a level remote from direct daily contact with a brand's problems.

Brand proliferation and the growing autonomy of product management has led to the requirement for intermediate supervisory levels of management in the larger organizations. Co-ordinating managers may have watching briefs over groups of brands.

The desire for autonomy and resistance to bigness has led some large organizations to push devolution to the point at which brand managers become general managers. Some organizations have gone too far in this direction, giving brand managers profit responsibility but not the matching independence and authority. In such cases conflicts can arise between brand managers and senior staff in functional departments.

A BRAND MANAGER DID NOT 'GET ON' WITH A SENIOR MEMBER OF STAFF IN THE ACCOUNTS DEPARTMENT. THE ACCOUNTANT, JEALOUS OF THE BRAND MANAGER'S STATUS AND INCOME, CONTINUALLY PROBED PETTY CASH EXPENDITURE, QUERYING VERY SMALL AMOUNTS AND SPREADING RUMOURS THAT THE BRAND MANAGER WAS 'ON THE FIDDLE'. THE MANAGER'S FINANCIAL APPRAISALS WERE ALWAYS PUT AT THE BOTTOM OF THE FILE.

AT THE ACCOUNTING YEAR END THE MANAGER WAS FORCED TO WAIT FOR A MONTH FOR A CASH FLOW FORECAST WITHOUT WHICH APPROVAL FOR A NEW LAUNCH WAS NOT OBTAINED. THE BRAND MANAGER'S IMMEDIATE SUPERIOR REFUSED TO HELP. THE BRAND MANAGER DEVELOPED AN ULCER AND WAS EVENTUALLY MOVED TO A LESS SIGNIFICANT APPOINTMENT.

Question 91: Contrast and compare the responsibilities you imagine would be given to product managers in the detergent, confectionery, and aircraft construction industries. Would you envisage significant changes in the extent of these responsibilities during the course of the life cycles of the products concerned?

11.3 BRAND AND FUNCTIONAL MANAGEMENT

Where a company has few brands and one is predominant, then there are some advantages in a functional form of organization. An over-enthusiastic brand manager might put product before organization. Some organizations with well-known brands have found themselves in the shadow of their products and have launched large corporate advertising campaigns.

A brand manager coming new to a one-product situation can be over-protective. Having previously left the details of advertising to those in functional departments or to an agency, the new product manager may examine every line of advertising copy. This can delay decision-making.

In some cases companies have allocated major decisions to functional specialists and detailed implementations to brand managers. Unless such a divison of responsibilities is clearly drawn, both brand and functional personnel will be continually on the look out for ways and means of enlarging their areas of activity at each others' expense.

An organization must achieve balance between the needs of brand and functional management. The brand manager clearly needs some authority if the benefits of co-ordination are to be achieved, but grant excessive authority and the central functional departments may be weakened. The contentious areas can embrace market research, advertising, testing, pricing, sales, legal matters, and even production.

Individual brand managers will, of course, vary in expertise and maturity. Responsibility which whets the appetite of one brand manager may submerge another. One manager may slip easily into a co-ordinating role while another might strive for fuller entrepreneurial duties. The more entrepreneurial the responsibilities, the greater the authority that will be required.

An organization may not establish a standard pattern of brand management but rather tailor the management of each product to the individual task and the people concerned.

Question 92: What conflicts of viewpoint and values would you imagine developing over time between brand manager and senior staff in the accounts, production, finance, and research functions respectively, and how might these be monitored, assessed, and resolved?

11.4 MANAGING BRAND MANAGERS

In developing brand management, a practical approach is to build upon strengths and take action to deal with weaknesses. The key area of brand management is often seen as communications, dealing with information. A brand manager must collect and assess a variety of information about a brand and its market position, and evaluate the extent to which marketing objectives are being achieved. This role, a purely communications one, can be of great value even in the absence of profit or sales responsibilities.

An alert brand manager, while monitoring progress and developments, identifies both problem and opportunity areas. Putting a finger upon a decision that needs to be made is a valuable skill. Knowledge of a product-market situation should allow the brand manager to pick out the single cloud in the sky which might be the following day's thunderstorm.

The allocation of marketing resources must match the needs of the organization as a whole. This raises the 'judgement' issue. A brand manager is closer than a central department to the marketplace, and may be in the best position to assess the prospects of a particular brand.

While brand managers are quite forward in demanding additional resources as brand sales increase, many are reluctant to see their resources slimmed as sales slump. When products are beyond the peaks of their life-cycles it is particularly important that senior managers obtain realistic information. Brand managers should be encouraged to make frank and honest reports. Exaggerated and misleading reports can lead to a misallocation of resources to the detriment of high-performing brands which might be starved of the resources they need.

An organization must decide for how long managers should occupy brand manager positions. To encourage talent into brand manager posts, it may be necessary to demonstrate prospects of career advancement. At the same time, some experience of a product-market position is often a necessary precondition of a satisfactory long-term strategy and performance.

The product manager's role must be carefully defined. It cannot be left vague. The role should generally be an initiating one.

A reporting and control system needs to be devised to assess product manager performance. How this is done should be understood by and acceptable to the product managers themselves.

Where generalist product managers are dealing with specialists, their respective roles and authority *vis-à-vis* each other should be formally laid down, along with some procedure for resolving disputes. Conflicts of interest should be identified and resolved as soon as possible after they arise.

TWO BRAND MANAGERS IN A COMPANY DEVELOPED AN INTENSE RIVALRY. EACH CLOSELY MONITORED HOW MUCH ADVERTISING AND MARKETING SUPPORT WAS BEING DEVOTED TO THE OTHER. THEY FREQUENTLY ARGUED PUBLICLY ABOUT THEIR RESPECTIVE ALLOCATIONS AND ON ONE OCCASION CAME TO BLOWS. BOTH MANAGERS WERE REPLACED BY A SINGLE MANAGER RESPONSIBLE FOR BOTH PRODUCTS. SHE FOUND THEM TO BE COMPLEMENTARY. BY SPLITTING A SINGLE MARKET-

CENTRED ORGANIZATION INTO TWO PRODUCT UNITS THE TWO
MANAGERS HAD BEEN PLACED IN AN INHERENTLY DIFFICULT
POSITION.

Question 93: What use could be made of a tired brand manager with some ten
years to retirement within the marketing area of a medium-sized company? What
special skills is the manager likely to have acquired as a result of twenty years of
brand-management experience and what deficiencies is the manager likely to have,
particularly in respect of future contact with functional specialists?

11.41 Brand Manager Problems

One product manager could be given authority for the timing of promotions while
another might need to settle such questions in conjunction with senior management. More freedom can be given in larger organizations though brand turnover is
not directly related to brand manager discretion. It is precisely because a brand's
turnover is high and large sums of money are involved that senior management may
feel justified in retaining some power of veto.

A common complaint of brand managers is the attitude of specialists within the
organization whose services are required and who, because they report elsewhere,
are not subject to the brand manager's authority. A specialist may develop an off-
hand manner with brand managers. In such situations, the position of the brand
manager can be strengthened by instituting a service change, an internal user-charge.
The brand manager will then only use those services thought to be worthwhile and
the specialist is likely to become more concerned with the interests of the 'client'.

One of the most common complaints of brand managers is the imbalance
between responsibility and authority. A brand manager may have responsibility
for the profitability of a brand and yet no line authority over specialist managers
whose work might be crucial to brand performance.

A brand manager who cannot 'order' must develop other methods of influence.
The influence of a brand manager could stem from enlightened specialists self-
interest, the political clout of those with whom he associates, respect given to
specialist expertise or just personal compatibility. Even though without authority
over a specialist, a brand manager may have a 'hold' as a result of being able to
'put in a good word', allocate funds or interesting work. Progress within a specialist
department may depend upon a reputation for serving well brand managers.

Without authority, a product manager must rely heavily upon persuasion. The
product manager may worry about being tied too long to one brand, obtaining
extensive knowledge relating to one product but not experience in any one of the
specialist functional fields.

A product manager may be deficient in one particular skill which is badly
required by the product in question. The brand's major problem could be its

advertisement image. An advertising specialist might spot this, a generalist brand manager might not.

Product management can add to overhead costs as brand managers recruit assistants and other staff to help them in their co-ordinating role. Some product managers attempt to accumulate functional specialists, building up mini-departments. This process can lead to extra levels in the management hierarchy which slow down decision making.

> ONE BRAND MANAGER CULTIVATED A BOHEMIAN IMAGE. WORD SPREAD AROUND THE COMPANY THAT THE BRAND WAS 'GOOD TO WORK FOR'. THE BETTER SPECIALISTS SOUGHT OPPOR- TUNITIES TO WORK ON THE BRAND CONCERNED. A CENTRE OF EXCELLENCE DEVELOPED AROUND WHAT WAS OTHERWISE A VERY ORDINARY PRODUCT.

Question 94: List and assess the potency of the various means a brand manager might employ to persuade staff within an organization who do not directly work for him to support his brand.

11.42 Brand Manager Advantages

A brand manager can gain status as a result of regular reporting contact with top management. A specialist may need an allocation of funds and act with deference towards a brand manager thought to be influential at board level, or to have unspent funds in a budget.

A brand manager's authority can rest upon a virtual monopoly of incoming market information. The manager may claim, with varying degrees of justice, to be the only one able to see the complete picture. Specialist staff may feel that whatever their technical expertise the brand manager, being close to the market, is in the best position to judge.

Over a period of time, a brand manager can build up relationships with staff specialists. In the past there may have been an exchange of favours or joint work on interesting projects. Such contact can lead to informal activity, the giving of advice over lunch which does not appear on a time sheet.

A successful relationship tends to be built upon mutual respect. It is difficult to have other than a working relationship with those who stand on their position and who seek to manipulate by alternate use of the stick and the carrot.

> ONE COMPANY IN SELECTING CANDIDATES FOR MIDDLE MANAGEMENT COURSES GIVES TOP PRIORITY TO BRAND MANA- GERS. NOT ONLY HAVE THEY BEEN FOUND TO BE RECEPTIVE TO 'INPUTS' FROM A VARIETY OF DISCIPLINES BUT ON COMPLETION

OF THEIR COURSES THEY ARE BETTER EQUIPPED TO HAVE DIA-
LOGUES WITH FUNCTIONAL SPECIALISTS AFTER HAVING
OBTAINED A BASIC UNDERSTANDING OF THE 'LANGUAGES' THE
SPECIALISTS SPEAK.

11.43   Product Accounting

Product managers need an understanding of fixed and variable costs, and the contributions of the products for which they are responsible. The structure of costs can
vary over the life-cycle of a product and, in decision making, incremental costs and
revenues count.   'Sunk' costs, those sums already spent and irrecoverable, are
irrelevant.

A knowledge of costing can lead to cost-reduction programmes. Profits can be
increased by cutting costs as well as by raising revenue.

A product manager must recognize that a product will have a life cycle and be
prepared to alter the emphasis of promotion even the entire marketing strategy as
a product passes through successive stages of its life cycle. The cash recovery of
an investment will normally lag behind the rate of sales growth. Positive cash
flows may exist well beyond the sales peak and continue as sales decline. With
some products, for example, a film, success will depend upon the recovery of the
tail-end revenues.

A product manager may come into conflict with accountants aiming to appor-
tion overhead costs upon some arbitrary basis. The apportionment of overhead
costs may, in fact, be beyond the product manager's control. As any such allocation will be arbitrary, product managers should be on their guard and, if
decisions are made, should certainly attempt to resist any imposition of sunk costs.
Where joint facilities are provided, the product manager may get into similar arguments over the allocation of common costs.

When drawing up budgets the product manager who, after all, will be largely
responsible for implementation, should be involved. In order to control performance, a product manager will require regular reports of actual performance compared with budget. If conditions are rapidly changing, then short-term forecasting
may be necessary.

Question 95:   What accounting information would you require and how often if
you were the brand manager of a bar of soap? In what ways would your information needs vary from those of a product manager responsible for a type of electric
drill, and to what extent would each set of needs change as the products concerned
progressed along their life cycles?

11.5   BRAND ISSUES AND STRATEGY

A brand manager needs to understand the product concept, the attributes of the product, where it is positioned in the market and its position on the product life-cycle. Product policy decisions will depend greatly upon life-cycle position.

A manager responsible for a group of products may develop a line of closely-related products or a mix of products. The width of product mix is the number of different lines produced, the depth of the mix being the number of items offered within each line. There should be some consistency, possibly resulting from production requirements or distribution arrangements, if a grouping of products is to be satisfactory from the product management point of view.

A strong brand can be used to launch other products by capitalizing upon a 'name'. Alternatively, a firm could pursue a multi-brand strategy, developing a number of brands that compete with each other. A company may have to decide at what point modifications in terms of quality improvement, the addition of extra features or a new look, constitutes such a change to an existing brand as to justify promotion as a new brand.

There might be a choice between the promotion of the overall image of a product in order to increase overall market size, and promotion which aims to increase a single brand's market share within the context of a largely static market. The former campaign will concentrate upon non-buyers while the latter will aim to encourage existing buyers to switch brands.

A market leader might be more willing to promote overall market sales than a company with a very small market share. In some situations where no company is prepared actively to promote consumption of a product by extending its total market, the product concerned and all the firms that produce it may lose ground to a substitute product and the firms that produce it. A trade association or a public sector body might find it easier to mount a market-increasing advertising programme.

> A LEADING MOTOR MANUFACTURER IN THE UNITED KINGDOM WISHED TO ADOPT A NEW NAME THAT WAS MORE ASSOCIATED WITH EXCELLENCE IN MOTOR CAR DESIGN. TALBOT WAS SELECTED AS A COMPANY WIDE NAME IN VIEW OF ITS STRONG LINKS WITH THE PIONEER AGE OF MOTORING AND THE HIGH QUALITY OF FORMER TALBOT CARS. THE COMPANY WANTED A NAME THAT WAS ASSOCIATED WITH TRADITIONAL ENGINEERING VALUES AND WHICH WAS MORE LIKELY TO LAST THAN A MORE 'TRENDY' NAME.

Question 96:   What would be the implications of a movement from a product-centred to a market-centred form of organization from the point of view of brand strategy?

11.51   Brand Attributes

Products have various attributes.   A marketing manager needs to identify that attribute or those attributes of greatest importance to customers. How important is time, or inflight food compared with the number of stops and the size of the aeroplane?

While consumers may choose on the basis of many criteria, there may also be minimum standards. Should one attribute fail to reach a minimum standard, then the product or service may be rejected even though other attributes may lead the field.

Conjoint measurement is a technique that breaks down a customer's overall judgement into its component parts so as to enable new combinations of attributes to be tested. Separating an attribute in this way can give some clues as to the sensitivity of market sales to changes in the attribute in question. Conjoint measurement information can enable existing products to be modified and new product defined.

Brand names serve a variety of purposes, identifying, providing legal protection, informing, donating quality, associating with an image. Producers can establish their own brands or provide products to distributors for branding. Some retail chains insist upon putting their brands upon the products they sell. Names can be individual to a product or can cover an entire family of products, perhaps all the products a company produces. The brand name could incorporate the company name in some way.

The importance of a brand name can be tested using conjoint measurement, as can the value of packaging or a service guarantee. Some features may be identified which can be deleted. Other features which cost little may be found to have a disproportionately high contribution to the overall appeal of a product.

The value of conjoint measurement falls as the number of attributes to be examined increases. As more attributes are added to the analysis, the potential for interaction between them increases. The appeal or essence of some products may not be susceptible to disaggregation, the whole being greater than the sum of the parts. What, for example, is 'star quality'?

Different combinations of factors making up a brand can be tested by means of panel testing, background research, prediction of market changes, and consumer attitude surveys. Gap analyses and product evaluation can be made more systematic by means of checklists.

A COMPANY MANUFACTURING A CIDER THAT WAS THOUGHT TO BE 'WEAK' AND A 'LADY'S DRINK' LAUNCHED A 'MANLY' PROMO-TIONAL CAMPAIGN ASSOCIATING THE DRINK WITH MACHO OUT-DOOR PURSUITS. LATER TESTS OF CONSUMER RESPONSE REVEAL-ED THAT, FOLLOWING THE CAMPAIGN, THE DRINK'S MAIN ATTRI-BUTE WAS SEEN AS ITS ABILITY TO 'SATISFY' A STRONG THIRST

RATHER THAN ITS BEING SOMETHING 'SAFE' FOR THE WIFE TO DRINK.

Question 97:   Contrast and compare what you consider might be, from the consumer's point of view, the most significant attributes of the following products:

(a)   a garden fork
(b)   a mink coat
(c)   a hamburger or hot dog and chips
(d)   a central city flat
(e)   a machine tool.

11.6   BRAND PERFORMANCE

Why is it that some brands are so much more successful than others? Being first in the market sometimes gives an advantage that lasts. Long-term performance is strengthened by unique qualities, product attributes that are not duplicated by other products. Some brand names become identified with the product in question, such as OXO, Kit-e-Kat, Andrex, Heinz Baked Beans, Hoover machines or Kelloggs Cornflakes.

Successful new-brand introduction requires the identification of a bunch or cluster of unmet needs whether a ballpoint pen, paper clip, see-through umbrella, kitchen paper towels, or soft toilet paper. Brand names and images must appeal to reason, that is they must appear to satisfy a perceived need, but should also appeal to the emotions and the senses. Other things being equal, a brand may be chosen over competitor products because of its smell or its sophisticated image. A brand is a combination of physical product and associated feelings.

11.61   Brand Cash Flow

Brands vary in the cash flows they generate and consume. A problem brand may consume much of the cash it generates; a failing brand may consume more cash than it generates. Successful brands will need varying levels of cash input to generate a given level of cash output. Those with a high ratio of cash output to cash input clearly provide the bulk of the funds for new-product development.

There may be a trade-off between cash today and cash tomorrow. A market could be 'milked' in the early stages by charging a high skimming price. Alternatively, a lower market penetration price could be set for a new product which while reducing short-term cash flow would boost ultimate sales and cash flow. Likely cash-flow patterns at different prices could be discounted to yield net present values of the alternative strategies as a basis for choosing between them.

11.62   The Behavioural Implications of Brand Performance

The success of one brand and failure of another can have important behavioural implications within a marketing organization. An established reputation may be first challenged and then overtaken by a new 'wonder'. This can give rise to a host of behavioural complications creating resentments and rivalries. Allegiances may shift as staff try to hitch themselves to a 'rising star'.

Poor performance on the part of an existing brand can lead to a search for scapegoats for staff who are 'burnt up' or 'past it'. A new star may be regarded as a 'high flyer' or as just 'lucky', having 'been in the right place at the right time'.

There may be competition among service staff in advertising and market research departments for opportunities to work on brands on the way up. Being allocated to brands that are 'over the hill' on the product life-cycle may be variously interpreted as being 'put out to grass' or as an advance warning to those who are 'on the way out'.

A conflict can arise in a marketing department as a result of different staff being responsible for earning than for spending. An established and successful brand may generate large cash flows. Idle cash soon loses its value in a period of high inflation rates, and if a company is to survive should be spent upon the development of new products. In the early stages of a product, heavy capital expenditures may be necessary as a company invests in plant. Existing products can 'bankroll' new ones.

A brand manager of an established product may feel 'milked' by the need to 'subsidize' new ventures. The existing brand manager may feel the cash flow should be reinvested in improving existing products or used to improve the working and salary conditions of those employed on them. Instead, the successful product brand manager may face tight cash limits while managers of speculative products have large development budgets. This situation can breed resentment.

A large company in a field such as soap flakes or chocolate may manufacture a range of competing products each produced by independent brand groups. In such a situation, sub-optimization might arise.

Given a production constraint, the company's board might wish to alter the sales mix in favour of brands which yield the largest contribution per unit of the scarce resource used in their production. This might lead to additional advertising of one brand and a cut-back on the promotion of another.

A brand team might find it difficult to accept that it must cut back its sales and the revenue it earns, particularly when the operations of the group are profitable because of the opportunity cost of the resources it uses.

A DOCTOR EMPLOYED BY A MAJOR CONSUMER PRODUCTS FIRM
EXPRESSED THE VIEW THAT THE EMOTIONAL AND PHYSICAL
HEALTH AND THE FAMILY RELATIONSHIPS OF THE COMPANY'S
BRAND MANAGERS WERE CLOSELY ASSOCIATED WITH THE

FORTUNES OF THE BRAND MANAGERS' PRODUCTS. ANXIETY BEGAN TO APPEAR AS BRAND PERFORMANCE STARTED TO SLIDE. MANAGERS OF SUCCESSFUL AND LONG-RUNNING BRANDS TENDED TO BE MORE SELF-SATISFIED THAN AVERAGE AND TO HAVE DEVELOPED SUBSTANTIAL OUT-OF-WORK HOBBIES AND INTERESTS.

Question 98:   You have just learned that sales of the brand to which you have recently been allocated are steadily declining while a new recruit to the organization with much less experience than yourself has been given a similar position on another brand, sales of which are rapidly increasing. What do you do?

11.63   Selective Reporting

A marketing manager should beware of the tendency of staff to play up the value of their own contribution and to play down those of others. For example, when market share is declining a brand manager may seek to disguise this fact by redefining the market to make it smaller. While sales fall absolutely, they may actually increase as a proportion of a market that is shrinking, either because overall sales are falling or because a more narrow definition of the market has been adopted.

Exaggeration of performance can lead to reduced cash flows. If, for example, a product is diagnosed as about to enter the decline stage of its natural life-cycle, cutting off future investments in production and advertising and reducing staff and servicing to a minimum level can maximize tail of life-cycle return.

Self-deception is widespread. A product manager may be most reluctant to accept that his or her product is weak. Time devoted to it might be charged to other accounts. Extra effort may be put in to promote it then starving other products of much-needed support. When this is done, a weak product that is allowed to continue can harm the image of other more successful products.

In order to prevent weak products from lingering on, all products whose performance fall below a cut-off point should be periodically subjected to objective review. Such independent reviews should cover the product's future, whether it could be modified or promoted in new and better ways and what benefits could be obtained from alternative uses of the resources devoted to it. There will also be costs and benefits attached to abandonment, both penalty clauses and assets which can be realised.

A MANAGER OF A NEW BRAND OVERSTATED THE PERFORMANCE OF THE BRAND BY CHARGING ITEMS OF COST TO OTHER CENTRAL ACTIVITIES. SUBSTANTIAL AMOUNTS HAD BEEN SAVED BY MOVING THE MANAGER'S OPERATION IN-HOUSE AHEAD OF OTHER ACTIVITIES WHICH BADLY NEEDED THE SPACE THUS TAKEN.

A NEW ACCOUNTANT PERSUADED THE DIVISIONAL DIRECTOR TO INTRODUCE CHARGES FOR CENTRAL SERVICES PROVIDED AND A NOTIONAL RENT FOR THE SPACE TAKEN. IT QUICKLY BECAME APPARENT THAT THE BRAND HAD BEEN FAILING FOR SOME TIME AND THAT PERCEIVED IMPROVEMENTS IN ITS PERFORMANCE HAD BEEN DUE TO THE DIVERSION OF EXPENDITURE TO OTHER HEADINGS.

11.64   The Management of Failure

Some companies get sentimental about long-running products. One might hold on and hope for better times. The fault may be thought to lie other than with the product. A 'lost leader' argument may be put up.

Pride may prevent a manager of a sickly brand from seeking help. A manager may fear redundancy and endangered career prospects as a market share begins to falter. A sales decline can occur for a variety of reasons in spite of the best efforts of the most able of marketing managers. In such situations staff should be encouraged to be open and frank.

Failing products can sometimes be brought together in such a way as to economize in support costs. This can raise questions of staff pride, already alluded to. Who is to lead the new group?

Another option with weaker products is outright sale or licence to another company. A small company adopting a 'niche' strategy may, with lower overheads, be able to make money out of a product which is no longer of interest to a large company. The larger company wishing to sell may find the staff associated with the product in question unwilling to move.

The consequences of failure may be less traumatic than expected. What is most feared will often not occur. A declining market share will not inevitably lead to cutbacks. It could, for example, lead to the takeover of a competitor in order to boost market share or to a relaunch of the product in question.

A COMPANY 'WINDING UP' ONE OF ITS OPERATIONS DISCOVERED A SPARE PARTS MARKET. THE MANAGER OF THE DISCONTINUED PRODUCT DEVELOPED A LUCRATIVE NEW BUSINESS SUPPLYING SPARE PARTS AND MACHINING 'ONE OFFS' TO ENTHUSIASTS OPERATING MODELS OF THE PRODUCT AND OF SIMILAR PRODUCTS WHICH WERE NO LONGER BEING MANUFACTURED.

Question 99: Two able members of staff for whom you have envisaged and planned a bright future in the organization have applied for outside jobs due to the continued fall in sales of the brand for which they are responsible. Little investment is tied up in the brand concerned but skilled management at this stage could bring in useful revenue the organization badly needs. What do you say to your two managers?

11.65 Killing Brands

Success does not always breed success. A brand that yields a highly positive cash flow could be at the end of the plateau phase of its life-cycle. Heavy investment in new productive equipment at this point could result in over-capacity and raise eventual costs of closure or withdrawal.

A brand manager must know when to cut a product. The kill decision should not be postponed for too long. What may appear a temporary hiccup could be the start of a long-run cycle of decline. The faltering product may soldier on, tying-up resources that might be employed more profitably elsewhere. A disproportionate share of management time may be devoted to the solution of its problems.

Killing a brand can create enormous behavioural problems. A brand manager may become as wedded to a brand as a captain to a ship. The withdrawal of a brand might effectively be the end of a career. If a 'ship is seen to be sinking' the more able and ambitious may 'want out', thus leaving those who remain without certain skills required in the rather difficult area of brand rundown.

In seeking to motivate staff, the advantages of running down a brand should be stressed, the fact that money will be saved and resources released for more rewarding projects. Pulling out of an area can represent a considerable management challenge. Contracts and agreements may have to be re-negotiated, and one-off problems such as the sale of stocks organized. In the case of durable products, some residual responsibility for servicing may remain after production has ceased.

11.66 Learning from Failure

A company should learn from its failures. When brands fail, an investigation should be commissioned to determine why.

The reasons for failure tend to be specific. Often the seeds of failure lie in early potential product-market estimates. At other times, the reasons for failure can be as varied as a price being higher than a competitor, or the establishment of an import barrier.

Failure can result from a combination of factors, disappointing sales, squeezed profit margins, excessive development costs and higher-than-anticipated initial investments. Where these general reasons for failure occur, one should always probe into why each happened, uncovering the underlying specific cause. The 'it's water under the bridge' approach can deny an organization the opportunity to identify a failure of communication or performance that might be improved by changing the design of an organization.

Low sales can result from competitor activity, excessive early-sales estimates, an error in pricing, poorly-directed marketing effort or from technical product defects. These failings cannot be remedied if they are not first identified. Some reasons for failure will be controllable; others will lie outside of the particular organization.

EXAMINATION QUESTION

'The brand or product manager's bluff has been called and he is now being consigned, on the whole, to well-merited oblivion.' Do you agree?

12. *Distribution*

This chapter focuses particularly upon the relationships between a business organization and its distributors.

12.1 THE DISTRIBUTION OUTPUT

We have considered in Chapters 7 and 8 how a demand for goods and services can arise. The demand that is created should be profitably supplied. We now consider, in this chapter, the outwards flow of goods and services: the distribution output. In many respects distributors can be regarded as an extension of a marketing organization. Often, not only will customers be supplied through middlemen — they may be initially contacted by middlemen.

12.11 Distribution Policy

The aim of a company's distribution policy is to ensure that goods arrive at the right place, when required, and at the lowest possible cost. There may be a number of alternative ways of distributing goods and, for each option, there will be choices between doing it in-house or making use of an external organization.

A marketing manager coming new to a market should begin by asking first-principle questions: are there existing arrangements the company could utilize? There may well be a choice of selling direct or through middlemen and, in the latter case, there will probably be a choice of middlemen. Perhaps the company could integrate forward, or franchise or begin a joint-venture negotiation. The distribution could be general, the policy being to maximize the number of out-lets, or alternatively one might aim at exclusivity by appointing a sole distributor. Channels need to be set up, assessed, motivated, rewarded and, periodically, reviewed.

There are location decisions to consider: where should the company's plants and stores be located? Management techniques such as the transportation method of linear programming are available to tackle this sort of problem. Goods can be shipped direct to customers or to warehouses. Local assembly or manufacture may be a possibility. If this option is selected, the company might be able to ship abroad components and materials, rather than completed units.

Establishing a distribution policy also requires answers to a series of technical questions. Given a sales and reorder pattern, a level of service, appropriate inventory levels and reorder quantities will need to be established. For a particular operation, there will be a break-even level of sales at which the appropriate costs are covered. Different arrangements will have varying degrees of flexibility. Criteria should be established for assessing the effectiveness of distribution policy, and for evaluating both modifications and fundamental changes.

One of the major reasons why the motor industry initially employed distributors was to reduce the large amount of capital tied up in stock in order to invest in greater production capacities.

Question 100:   Map out the distribution system of an organization with which you are familiar, clearly identifying the external relationships. How compatible are these with the organization's distribution policy, and how flexible are they?

12.12   Why Use Middlemen?

Middlemen are the most numerous form of external organization with which the marketing manager has to deal.

There are a number of traditional reasons why they are used. A manufacturer may lack the financial resources to hold large volumes of stock. The middlemen can accumulate specialist expertise. There may be economies of specialization and concentration. From the point of view of profitability, a company may find that its expertise and comparative advantage lie in manufacturing.

Working through a middleman greatly reduced the number of external contacts a company must maintain and service. Middlemen may break bulk, combine, even assemble and perform other operations to bring goods closer to the requirements of ultimate customers. In doing this, they perform the vital function of matching supply with demand.

In view of the existence of distribution economies of scale, there has been a tendency towards concentration and integration, and away from loose channels composed of independent units. Larger companies have integrated forwards, perhaps achieving single ownership of all stages in the marketing chain or, as a result of their market power, co-ordination by domination.

The advantages of economies of scale can be obtained by independent units coming together and purchasing as a group, or forming retail co-operatives or by franchising. These arrangements exist to increase market power *vis-à-vis* some other group. In the soft-drink industry, the wholesalers obtain a licence to bottle in certain areas. In the case of service franchises such as motels and car-hire, the organizer of the franchise can have enormous bargaining power, as a result being able to influence the purchase of thousands of cars or chairs. In the motor car industry, the franchise is manufacturer-sponsored, the producers giving dealers licences to sell their cars in particular markets.

In addition to this vertical approach to the distribution sub-system of the marketing system, horizontal arrangements are also possible. One's own distribution system could be used to handle other people's products: a joint arrangement might be possible. A warehouse or an overseas facility might be shared, the costs being apportioned on a usage or some other basis.

The middlemen system will not work if its members are not motivated. Over-remuneration of middlemen can lead to reduced profitability, while under-remuneration can lead to a loss of middlemen interest in the company's products. Performance levels should be agreed between company and middlemen, and subsequently monitored. As sales territories vary, it is wise not to compare performance with averages but with quotas set, taking particular local circumstances into account. Disappointing performance should be discussed with the middlemen concerned.

MANY CONFECTIONERY PRODUCERS WHO SOLD SMALL AMOUNTS OF CONFECTIONERY TO A LARGE NUMBER OF RETAILERS FOUND THEIR LOCAL DISTRIBUTION COSTS TO BE SO HIGH THAT THEY BEGAN TO OPERATE THROUGH WHOLESALERS. SPECIALIST CONFECTIONERY WHOLESALERS AROSE WHO VISITED RETAIL POINTS WITH VAN-LOADS OF CONFECTIONERY. THEN THE MANUFACTURERS REALISED THAT THEY WERE ALL 'IN THE SAME BOAT' SO FAR AS DISTRIBUTION WAS CONCERNED. WHILE COMPETING FIERCELY IN NATIONAL ADVERTISING IN THE UK, TWO MAJOR PRODUCERS ESTABLISHED A JOINT DISTRIBUTION ARRANGEMENT.

Question 101: List the middlemen with which the organization you are most familiar with deals, in each case describing the function the middleman performs, their strengths and weaknesses, how they are motivated, their effectiveness as communicators, how they were selected, and how their performance is assessed.

12.13 Middlemen and the Marketing System

The great majority of companies use middlemen of some form. An entire marketing strategy can be influenced by whether or not a middleman is used. They come in many forms: agents, wholesalers, brokers, co-operatives, dealers, distributors, agencies, jobbers, and voluntary groups. Arrangements with middlemen should not be entered into lightly, as they can result in long-term commitments with outside organizations that may constrain an entire marketing strategy.

The set of intermediaries or middlemen chosen by a firm becomes its marketing channel. A few companies sell direct to ultimate customers. More common, however, are one- and two-stage channels that involve one and two intermediaries respectively, perhaps just a retailer in the former case and a retailer and wholesaler in the latter case.

Middlemen form an important part of the marketing system. Physical goods and promotional material flows from the company, through the middlemen to the ultimate customers, while payment flows from the customers through the middlemen back into the company. The information flows both ways, or should flow both ways; a marketing manager should watch out for any predominance of the information flow in one direction. This might suggest one party is not pulling its weight.

Some managers, who are reasonably happy with the physical flow of their goods, overlook the communications aspects of the middleman function. These should always be borne in mind and made explicit before distribution arrangements are entered into. Being closer to the ultimate consumer, a middleman can become its supplier's eyes and ears. It should not become an important part of the supplier's market-intelligence system without being aware of this.

When specific market information is required or a new product is being launched, the question of how promotional expenditure is to be allocated between company and middleman, may crop up. Many middlemen actively promote their suppliers' goods. When negotiating, it is worth pointing out the value in motivational terms of both parties being risk-takers. If a new product looks as though it might be a winner, the middleman may be justified in investing in promotion. On other occasions, when the rewards are less certain, given that the middleman needs to make a living and may service other suppliers, it may be necessary to offer to pay for work done.

A PUBLISHER HIGHLY SKILLED IN WORKING WITH AUTHORS BEGAN TO RELY INCREASINGLY HEAVILY UPON EXTERNAL RETAILERS, STOCKISTS, PRINTERS, AND DESIGN CONSULTANTS. ONE DAY THE PUBLISHER REALIZED THAT SO MUCH HAD BEEN DELEGATED TO EXTERNAL ORGANIZATIONS THAT THE NATURE OF THE BUSINESS HAD FUNDAMENTALLY CHANGED. HE FORMED AN ARRANGEMENT WITH A LEADING PUBLISHER AND BECAME A PROMINENT LITERARY AGENT, CONCENTRATING UPON THE AREA IN WHICH HE HAD THE GREATEST COMPARATIVE ADVANTAGE.

Question 102: Take a selection of the middlemen with which your company deals and list the product lines each handles. How important to each of them is your company's business? If you were in each middleman's shoes, how would you want these relationships with your company to develop? Draw up a questionnaire you would use to assess the value of continuing these relationships.

12.2 CHANNEL SELECTION

The selection of the most appropriate distribution channel will depend upon a number of factors. Certain fundamental considerations exist, such as whether the company is selling to an ultimate customer, a retailer, or to a wholesaler. There are questions of which channel can be used and should be used. One must be sure, before making changes, that extra benefits to be obtained are greater than any additional costs to be incurred. That is, in the accountant's jargon, incremental revenue must be greater than incremental costs.

The market is, of course, the major constraint in channel selection. The type, number, and distribution of customers, their purchasing patterns and how susceptible they are to different channels is crucial, as is the absolute level of sales. As sales increase, it may make sense to progress steadily from agent, through local warehouse to local manufacture.

The nature of the product itself will be important. Purchases may be infrequent, even one-off, or frequent and repeat. Products range from the mass-produced to the custom-built. There may be particular storage and distribution problems or local legal restrictions, and, possibly, government regulations.

Some companies pursue a policy of selective distribution. That is, the company is prepared to enter into a variety of contracts with a number of middlemen, the arrangements varying according to the market context. The various jobs to be done include physical transportation and storage of goods, advertising, setting prices, seeking out customers, and agreeing the terms of sale, and the ability of a middleman to carry out these tasks will probably vary from territory to territory. Eggs should not always be put in one basket.

Within a selected channel there are likely to be a number of sources of potential conflict. These must be taken into account when recruiting channel members, and subsequently. The objectives of the various vertical stages may not coincide. Middlemen at a particular stage may be in conflict over, say, the position of a dealer boundary and at the same time be co-operating as a group with a view to obtaining better terms from suppliers.

Some middlemen may become jealous of special terms offered to others, or feel that a supplier is creaming the market by its direct selling effort. Flexibility is important: the avoidance of long-term contracts can increase adaptability and reduce legal conflicts. A policy should be established concerning how much middlemen should be told about each other, and how the company should communicate with them, not only as individuals, but also as a group.

A MANUFACTURER OF A CRAFT-BUILT MODEL DECIDED TO ENTER SERIES PRODUCTION. A SMALL NUMBER OF DISTRIBUTORS WAS SELECTED UPON THE BASIS OF THEIR 'LOVE' FOR THE PRODUCT; IT WAS A SUCCESSFUL SELECTION STRATEGY. THE POTENTIAL MARKET FOR THE MODELS WAS LIMITED TO ENTHUSIASTS

AND COLLECTORS: THOSE WHO 'LOVED' THE PRODUCT WERE MORE LIKELY, THROUGH FOLLOWING THEIR RATHER SPECIAL ENTHUSIASM, TO MEET POTENTIAL CUSTOMERS.

12.21 Channel Management

How a channel relationship is managed will depend in part upon its position and role in the marketing chain and upon marketing policy. The company may wish to pitch its promotional effort at customers in the hope of pulling its products through middlemen or, alternatively, it may concentrate its promotional effort on middlemen in an attempt to push its products through them.

An optimum solution from the point of view of the company might not be possible. A distribution policy should be realistic. Middlemen and retailers must be prepared to handle the product on the terms and at the remuneration offered. The policy will also depend upon the company's own financial resources, its past distribution policy and those of its competitors, and the degree of control desired and allowed.

Distributors are frequently faced with a bewildering variety of products to handle. The company must not only try to understand the problems of the distributor, but should ensure that the distributor is aware that his problems are understood.

It is always a valuable exercise to put oneself in the shoes of a retailer faced with the problem of finding shelf-space for yet another product. In many consumer goods areas, a level of turnover which is considered satisfactory by a producing company may represent, from the point of view of retailers, average retail sales of only a few units per outlet.

On occasions, a supplier may go behind the back of a distributor and deal with a customer direct. The better accounts may be taken from the distributor and handled in-house. Distributors in such circumstances can feel robbed of the fruits or relationships that have taken some time to build up. A customer might also, in these circumstances, end up confused about who he is really dealing with. It often pays to be frank and to send copies of direct correspondence with customers to distributors. If this is not done, false rumours may spread.

Further problems can arise when a supplier decides to develop new products and services, and new markets. The distributor might have a different view about how relationships with customers ought to be built up. The appointment of new distributors can lead to problems with existing ones. These problems can only be solved by discussion and mutual understanding. It is worth remembering that distributors are unlikely to be naive, and will not expect a relationship which is not to the advantage of a supplier to last.

A BREWERY BOOSTED SALES OF ITS BEER BY SLASHING CONSUMER ADVERTISING AND INTRODUCING A SERIES OF PERKS AND

COMPETITIONS FOR LANDLORDS AND THEIR FAMILIES. MANY OF THE PUBLIC HOUSES TO WHICH THE COMPANY SOLD ITS BEER WERE FOUND TO BE LOCAL MONOPOLIES. CUSTOMERS LARGELY DRANK WHAT WAS AVAILABLE. IN EFFECT, IN THE BREWERY'S MARKETING STRATEGY, THE DISTRIBUTOR HAD BECOME THE CUSTOMER.

12.22 Industrial Distributors

Industrial distributors perform a variety of distribution functions including stockholding, marketing, delivery, and financing. They may handle capital goods or consumables, carry a wide range of industrial products or a limited number of items. Some sell direct to retailers and ultimate consumers as well as to industrial customers.

By using an industrial distributor, a company can avoid the fixed costs of local operations. The distributor in turn can spread costs across the products of many suppliers. Effective use of such a distributor requires mutual understanding, a common commitment and, usually, roughly-equivalent bargaining power.

The increasing complexity and cost of industrial equipment has led to distributor concentration. Industrial distributors are becoming larger and many of them employ a variety of modern techniques such as computerized stock control. The increased costs of stock holding, greater product standardization which has eroded brand loyalty, the concentration of purchasing, and the willingness of distributors to do extra work, perhaps sub-assembly or even maufacturing, to meet customer requirements have all strengthened their position. The larger size of distributors has also brought some benefits of specialization.

The different roles performed by supplier and industrial distributor can easily give rise to communications problems. A supplier tends to view a distributor as a link in his distribution chain, and may become concerned about the degree of commitment shown towards his products. Suppliers also tend to complain about the lack of market information passed on by their industrial distributors.

The distributors in question probably have a very different view. They will consider themselves independent businessmen and will probably be proud of their independence and standing in local communities. They may be customer-, rather than supplier-orientated, considering each of their individual suppliers to be just one of many.

Distributors in many consumer markets are more likely than their supplier organizations to be power cultures, dominated by founder entrepreneurs. They may not employ the management techniques, and checks and balances found in the supplier organizations. This is particularly likely to be true when a supplier organization is much larger and older than its distributors.

To build effective partnerships, such distributors may need to compromise some independence and take help from the supplier. A distributor may in turn, as a result of being more entrepreneurial, want a greater freedom to deal with each customer, as the situation demands. In some cases, there can be considerable competition between the supplier and distributor for control of the relationship with the customer.

> THE LOCAL DISTRIBUTORS OF AN AIRCRAFT MANUFACTURER WERE REQUIRED TO DEMONSTRATE ANNUALLY THEIR ABILITY TO OVERHAUL AN AIRCRAFT ENGINE IN ORDER TO RETAIN THEIR DISTRIBUTORSHIPS, WHICH WERE AWARDED ON TWO-YEARLY CONTRACTS. IN ONE TERRITORY, A LOCAL MOTOR CAR DEALER WAS FOUND TO BE ABLE TO ADEQUATELY SERVICE AN AIRCRAFT ENGINE, AND WAS ACCORDINGLY AWARDED THE DISTRIBUTOR-SHIP.

Question 103:   Explain how you would set about identifying potential regional distributors of the following products:

    (*a*)   paint
    (*b*)   small tools
    (*c*)   motor cycles
    (*d*)   large lathes.

12.23   Selecting Middlemen

The key question to consider when selecting middlemen is the extent to which the possibilities are motivated to push one's goods. This will depend upon their resources and capacity, and whether or not they handle competing lines. A middleman will tend to push those items which yield the largest return per unit of sales effort. The other products currently and likely to be handled by a potential middleman thus assume some importance. Examining the product lists of potential distributors is therefore essential.

A potential distributor should also have, or be willing to acquire, the expertise to handle the goods or services in question. It is worth looking for a willingness to keep this expertise up-to-date. However well-managed and connected a distributor may be, this cannot compensate for an obvious lack of interest in one's product. In such a case, forming an arrangement can be equivalent to tying one's hands behind one's back: it rules out opportunities for other more satisfactory agreements.

It sometimes pays to wait. Many companies have burned their fingers as a result of rushing too quickly into distribution arrangements: an initial trial period may be desirable. Avoid signing agreements covering large areas: a distributor that dominates one market may be weak in another. Signing up distributors is often a question of finding horses for courses.

To ensure that important factors are not overlooked and that distributor selection decisions are objective, a questionnaire should be drawn up. The same questions should be asked of each potential distributor, and points awarded according to the extent to which requirements are met. Remember, when devising a questionnaire, that market information and promotion are distributor functions as well as the physical handling of goods.

Always carry out periodic credit checks on potential and existing middlemen. Obtain sets of accounts from Companies House and work out financial ratios. Read press reports and trade publications. Follow senior staff changes. Periodically examine the calibre of a distributor's management team and of its salesforce. There is little point selecting as a distributor an organization that is about to collapse: this can lose one vital time, perhaps a year or more.

Question 104: Why do people buy the goods your company produces? List the sources of the information upon which your answer is based and assess how up-to-date they are.

12.3 CHANNEL EVALUATION TECHNIQUES

A marketing manager cannot be expected to be *au fait* with every available management technique. Detailed knowledge of techniques can, in fact, be dangerous when it is assumed such skills can be applied rather like patent medicines for the remainder of a working life. In a changing world, techniques become outdated and replaced by others. A willingness and an active desire to keep up-to-date is a prime requirement of effective management.

What really is important in marketing management is an ability to identify areas in which change is needed and where techniques can be applied. Knowledge of the existence and practical applicability of techniques can be more valuable than a detailed understanding of their theoretical working. In bringing techniques to bear upon his problems, the marketing manager should make full use of both the internal and external resources available to the company.

Question 105: List the channel evaluation techniques with which you are familiar and describe instances of their use and whether or not their use was justified, or identify distribution problems susceptible to the use of each technique.

12.31 Channel Changes

A marketing manager should continually monitor channel performance and carry out periodic channel reviews. These reviews should pose questions at a number of levels. There may be individual middlemen who need to be dropped. A particular channel may no longer be the most effective way of reaching a certain market.

Perhaps the whole distribution system of the company needs to be changed.

When deciding whether or not to drop an individual middleman, the problem should be approached from a number of points of view. There is an economic question of costs and benefits, and also a legal question dependent upon contract terms. What is not always so apparent but nevertheless does require consideration, is the possible impact of the decision upon other aspects of the distribution system.

Channel changes can be triggered by shifts in purchaser behaviour and by the action of a competitor in, say, offering direct sale discounts. Again, before making a change, it is wise to pause and examine the possible repercussions upon the total system.

A COMPANY FIRED ITS DISTRIBUTOR IN AN OVERSEAS TERRI-TORY FOLLOWING AN APPROACH FROM A TECHNICALLY BETTER QUALIFIED AGENCY. THE DISGRUNTLED FORMER DISTRIBUTOR FAILED TO HAND OVER PAPERS RELATING TO THE DISTRIBUTOR-SHIP AND EVENTUALLY BURNT THEM.

THE FORMER DISTRIBUTOR HAD PLAYED A GATEKEEPER ROLE. THE COMPANY HAD LOST CONTACT WITH MANY OF ITS CUSTOM-ERS AND HAD NO KNOWLEDGE OF THE IDENTITY OR STATUS OF LOCAL ACCOUNTS. A SENIOR MARKETOR CONSIDERED THE CHANGE HAD SET BACK THE COMPANY'S PROGRESS IN THE MARKET BY SOME FIVE YEARS.

12.32 Monitoring the Buyer Sub-system

An adaptive organization is constantly examining changes in the business environment that might have an impact upon buyer behaviour. For example, industrial concentration and customer's organizational changes can alter the location and level of the purchasing decision. These changes may require a restructuring of one's salesforce, perhaps on a key-account rather than on a regional basis.

The buying decision itself may increase in complexity as ever more departments in customer organizations become involved. To effectively sell, a salesforce may need to have a variety of contacts with key individuals from diverse departments, each of whom has some say in the final purchase decision. As organizations evolve from power- to role-cultures, buying decisions may cease to be individual and may become a group activity.

As part of one's external monitoring process, a careful watch must be kept upon who is actually important in the buying process within customer organizations. Individuals come and go. Power positions change. It is important to keep up to date. For a really big purchase decision, external consultants might be called in. Perhaps a substantial part of the selling effort should be directed at these influential advisers.

Research into customer requirements might reveal a need, not for one item of equipment, but for a whole package of associated products and services. To satisfy this need, a joint venture might be formed with other supplies. When such an opportunity is missed, rather than grumble and search for scapegoats, one should act to prevent a recurrence of a failure of market intelligence. The aggressiveness with which channel members seek out new buyer requirements will depend largely upon their level and method of remuneration and whether or not this motivates them.

12.33 Salesmen's Role Changes

In many markets, the notion of one salesman influencing one buyer is no longer applicable. Instead, a variety of people within supplying organizations will be seeking to influence their diverse equivalents within customer organizations. The suppliers' engineers, design, and marketing staff will all be seeking appropriate points of contact that enable them to influence those who play a part in the purchase decision process. Whole project teams may be involved in the marketing of a complex technical product.

Marketing staff in the 'many to many' situation will be playing an overall management rather than an individual selling role. They may act as team leaders. They will need to be able to examine customers' organizations and communications systems to determine where power and influence lies, total customer requirements, and what contacts should be forged when and by whom within the organization. It will also be necessary to build a promotion team and to manage the variety of contacts created.

The resulting marketing organization is more likely to be customer-centred. Sales effort will be concentrated upon total customer requirements. Individual technical expertise relating to specific products will become of lesser importance, as such expertise is likely to be found within a balanced sales team. The sales staff themselves will require management and particularly team- and project-management training.

A multi-functional sales team can throw up some of the organizational problems of the matrix organization. Some staff will be responsible to both functional heads and to those overseeing accounts with particular customers. Other functional staff will require sales training. Some special form of remuneration may be required for those who have played a key role in a particular sale.

IN A DEVELOPING COUNTRY A BREED OF ELDERLY ENTRE-PRENTEURIAL OWNER MANAGERS WHO HAD TOGETHER CREATED A MINI-BOOM BEGAN TO GIVE UP CONTROL OF THEIR ORGANIZA-TIONS TO US EDUCATED BUSINESS GRADUATES. A COMPANY'S LOCAL SALES EFFORT HAD BEEN GEARED TO PERSONAL CONTACT WITH THE FORMER OWNER MANAGERS. THE LOCAL MARKETING

OPERATION WAS FOUND TO BE UNABLE TO COMMUNICATE WITH THE YOUNGER GENERATION OF MANAGERS WHO PURCHASED ON THE BASIS OF THE OUTCOME OF FINANCIAL APPRAISALS RATHER THAN LENGTH OF PERSONAL ACQUAINTANCE.

12.4 THE PRODUCTIVITY OF DISTRIBUTION

Distribution is a service function and a labour-intensive one. Typically 60% of distribution costs are labour costs. Traditionally it has been thought that there are fewer opportunities for increasing productivity in the service sector than in the manufacturing sector. This view is now being challenged. There is scope in most organizations for considerably increasing distribution productivity, but this usually requires careful analysis.

A marketing manager seeking productivity improvements must first identify the areas of weakness and opportunity. The accountant should be called in and asked to work out the rate of turnover of assets achieved in the various distribution areas and the associated rates of return on capital employed. This can, for a start, identify those units which are performing less well than others.

The operational researcher should certainly be called in to examine the possibility of introducing improved stock control and vehicle scheduling systems and techniques such as simulation might be considered to assist in the calculation of optimum stock levels. Mixing, perhaps at lunchtime, with management services staff, can create for the marketing manager opportunities for discussing his problems and identifying techniques that might assist in solving them.

It is worth stressing again that while one may not be familiar with a technique, this does not mean that it cannot be used. The marketing manager should learn to make use of expertise that lies elsewhere in the organization, to identify areas where other functional specialists can employ their skills. To do this, of course, first requires an awareness of the expertise that is available throughout an organization.

There may be considerable scope for warehouse economies. For example, moving to lower cost locations, stacking goods higher, bringing in more efficient, less labour-intensive handling techniques or pushing warehousing functions back onto suppliers or forward onto retailers can reduce costs. Direct marketing, franchising or a co-operative venture might be possible. A marketing manager should draw up a check list of possible areas of economy and employ this as the basis of a periodic distribution audit.

Question 106: Identify areas in which you consider the productivity of a distribution system with which you are familiar could be improved. List any management techniques you would employ when carrying out improvements, giving in each case reasons for their use. Why do you think the techniques you have listed have not been employed and what do you think the reactions of staff to their employment would be?

12.41   Evaluating Particular Channel Alternatives

There are a number of economic tools available to the marketing manager facing channel decisions. For example, the choice between opening a branch in a particular territory and employing a local sales agency could be resolved by break-even analysis.

The fixed costs (FB) of a branch are considerably higher than those (FA) of contracting an agency, but thereafter the costs per unit sales are less. Beyond the break-even point (BP) in the figure it pays to open a branch rather than employ an agent.

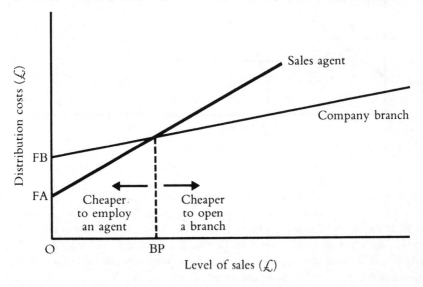

Figure 12.1   The branch or agent decision

Most manufacturing companies have a single plant supplying a single market. When a company has a single plant or multiple plants and multiple markets, it faces a choice between direct supply, local assembly or local manufacture. The break-even analysis approach can be employed to choose between the alternatives and between leasing or buying a plant or warehouse.

An important additional variable in such analyses can be delivery time. The longer the delivery time, the lower the transport costs as consignments can be consolidated, but the higher the costs of lost sales. The optimum delivery time (OT) can be obtained by drawing the cost curves as shown in Figure 12.3.

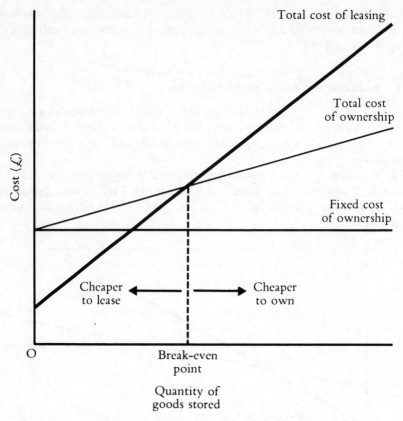

Figure 12.2   To lease or own a warehouse

A similar form of analysis can be used to determine the optimum size OS of a plant.   As plant size increases unit production costs will fall but, as the larger output will be sold over a great area, unit transportation costs will rise. Combining the cost curves reveals the optimum plant size.

12.42   The Total-Cost Approach to Distribution

Before the costs of distribution can be controlled, total cost must first be identified.   The total-cost approach can avoid many of the pitfalls of *ad hoc* cost cutting.   Very often, if one aspect of distribution is examined in isolation, costs cuts achieved can be more than counterbalanced by increases in costs elsewhere.

Distribution costs tend to be inter-related. In total, they can amount to between a third and a half of the sales price of a product. They are likely to be spread across departments: frequently, no one executive is responsible for the whole of the distribution function. Major reductions, across the board, in distribution costs are

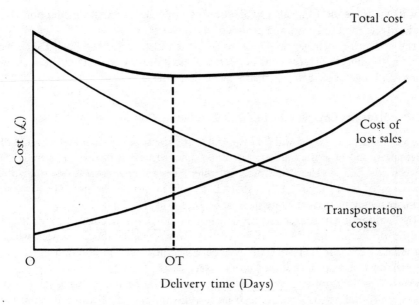

Figure 12.3   Determining the optimum delivery time

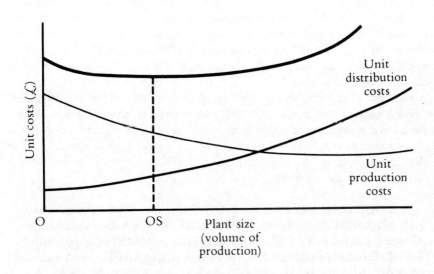

Figure 12.4   Determining optimum plant size

only likely to result from an examination of how the distribution function as a whole affects the total costs and profits of the business.

The marketing manager may need to seek the assistance of the Chief Executive in order to achieve greater control of total distribution costs. Only he may be able to pull together the departmental heads concerned.

12.43 Managers Contributing to Total Distribution Cost

The warehousing manager will be responsible for the type, number and location of warehouses, and how they are operated and manned. He is involved in a trade-off between cost and service. The stock controller faces a similar cost/service trade-off. The policy of each will affect the other. Both will, in turn, be influenced by overall company policy on, say, the rate of obsolescence of its products.

The production manager has an impact on distribution costs through plant location decisions, and decisions concerning which plants should service which customers. The production team will be concerned with production costs and materials costs but not necessarily with delivery costs.

One-off deals negotiated with particular customers, while increasing sales, may depress profitability by causing distribution disruption. The whole distribution function will be influenced by sales strategy and vice versa. The purchasing strategy may suddenly change due to alterations in relative costs and this may require the opening of new storage facilities.

Changes in the type, number, and location of warehouses will have important consequences for the transportation manager. A consolidation of storage facilities that reduces warehousing costs can substantially increase trucking costs. Similarly, alterations in storage and transportation policy can have a significant effect upon the policy of the accounts and data-processing departments. In some companies storage, manufacturing, sales, accounts and other departments may be competing for the same office space.

Ultimately, a marketing manager is concerned with sales and their profitability. He must be aware that changes in stockholding and warehousing policy, while it leads to costs savings, can, through stock-outs, longer delivery times, and generally lower customer service, result in a loss of sales and a more than proportional fall in profit. In such cases, the marketing manager must become an advocate of his departmental view and represent it at the highest policy-making level.

A MAJOR COMPANY HAD BEEN WORRIED FOR SOME TIME ABOUT THE APPARENT RELATIVELY HIGH COST OF ITS RAW MATERIALS. AS A RESULT OF A COST EXERCISE THE COMPANY FOUND THAT THE OVERHEAD COST OF ITS TRANSPORT OPERATION WAS BEING WHOLLY CHARGED TO 'GOODS INWARDS' WHILE IN PRACTICE SOME TWO-THIRDS OF TRANSPORT JOURNEYS WERE DEVOTED TO THE DISTRIBUTION OF FINISHED PRODUCTS. AS A CONSEQUENCE

A PROPORTION OF THE COSTS ALLOCATED ULTIMATELY TO RAW
MATERIALS WAS TRANSFERRED TO THE MARKETING DEPART-
MENT WHICH HAD INITIATED THE COST EXERCISE IN ORDER TO
EXPLORE WAYS OF CUTTING MARKETING COST!

12.44 Implementing the Total Cost Approach

The total cost approach to distribution involves taking each aspect of the business
in turn and calculating which of its costs are influenced by distribution policies and
to what degree. In each case the impact of the distribution alternatives should be
calculated. At this point the individual area costs can be added up to obtain a
total cost for each of the distribution alternatives.

Achieving a total distribution cost is, in practice, far from easy. In some areas
the costs are hidden, they may not be available, let alone reported. Such a programme is, however, worth undertaking as a number of companies have, as a result
of such an exercise, achieved significant economies.

A total cost analysis can have great significance for individual decisions. The
optimum number of warehouses, for example, might be one from the point of view
of storage and building costs, ten from the point of view of transport costs, 15 from
the point of view of customer-service costs, 3 from the point of view of finance
function costs, and 8 from the point of view of stock control costs. There are
clearly a variety of solutions, depending upon one's departmental perspective.
From the viewpoint of each department costs will fall until the optimum number
of warehouses is reached and will then rise again. Only by adding all these cost
curves together will the total cost curve for the whole organization be obtained.
This may yield an answer that, from the point of view of the whole organization,
the optimum number of warehouses is six.

Individual managers should be encouraged to look beyond the boundaries of
their own departments when making distribution decisions and to ask the question,
how will this affect the total distribution costs of the organization? This approach
will, of course, mean extra work, but this is the cost of moving closer to the
optimum distribution system.

A LOCAL AUTHORITY FOUND THAT ITS PARKS DEPARTMENT
VEHICLES TRAVELLED FULL TO A REFUSE DUMP AND RETURNED
EMPTY WHILE VEHICLES FROM THE ENGINEER'S DEPARTMENT
TRAVELLED EMPTY TO THE REFUSE DUMP AND RETURNED WITH
SEPARATED METAL MATERIAL FOR COMPRESSION AT A CENTRAL
SITE CLOSE TO THE PARKS DEPARTMENT DEPOT. AS A RESULT OF
AN ORGANIZATION AND METHODS EXERCISE CERTAIN OF THE
VEHICLES OF BOTH DEPARTMENTS WERE POOLED AND COST
SAVINGS RESULTED FROM THE VEHICLES BEING FULL ON BOTH
OUTWARD AND RETURN JOURNEYS.

Question 107:   Draw up an action programme for implementing the total-cost approach to distribution in an organization with which you are familiar and assess the chances of its proving effective.

12.45   Implementation and Modelling

When examining whether or not there are distribution alternatives, one should always begin with the existing and potential customers. The customer analysis should cover the number, type, and location of customers and their particular requirements. Having identified destinations, one can work back through routes and storage points to the best supplier. Plant costs should include all costs the company incurs in equiping the plant and in supplying it with raw materials.

Computer-based modelling techniques are now available that can handle this sort of distribution problem. A physical distribution model might print out cost curves for each plant, showing how total-plant cost varies with the size of order or calculate an optimum route given load, transport, and congestion costs. This information, once accumulated for each plant, would assist in the decision of which plant should supply a particular order to a certain customer.

By using a computer-based model, it is possible to feed in alternative assumptions and to examine different options. This might reveal that changing load sizes, moving equipment from one warehouse to another, changing from rail to road transport, or opening a new depot would improve profitability. The same model might print out the rates of return upon any initial investments these changes would require.

12.46   Implementation and Behavioural Problems

The problems encountered in employing the total-cost approach tend to be behavioural rather than technical. The full support of top management is essential: a senior executive should be given responsibility for the assignment. He should, in the large organization, be backed up by a team of specialists in such disciplines as production, operational research, computing, transportation, warehousing, and stock control. A smaller organization, unable to put together such a team, might consider the employment of external consultants.

Recommendations for change should list the changes proposed together with their expected benefits. The value of the information obtained during the exercise and of any mathematical models constructed will be ongoing. As the company adapts to changes in its market environment and to its own evolution the distribution system will need to be continually monitored, assessed and altered. Continued top management support will be required to overcome departmental inertia and to deal with disagreements between the staff distribution specialists and the departmental line managers.

EXAMINATION QUESTION

What do you consider would be your priority considerations with regards to dealer policy if you were taking over a board appointment marketing motor cars in the UK manufactured by your employers in Japan?

13. *Relationships with External Organizations*

As was made clear by Chapter 12 not all marketing service functions will be internal, performed within the organization. Many will be external, use being made of specific external services on the basis of comparative advantage. In Chapters 15 and 17 on advertising, it will be seen that a satisfactory partnership between internal and external resources can be vital if marketing communication is to be effective.

The external organizations with which a company may wish to associate in its marketing communications activity will need to be selected, briefed, and evaluated.

This chapter examines an organization's information system and how organizations manage their relationships with external service agencies.

13.1 ALLIES AND ASSOCIATES

Few companies can entirely satisfy their customers without calling upon other organizations to provide specialist services. Serving customers is a matter of getting the product, promotion, price, and place right. The company that can, unaided, produce a good product at a competitive price might still need outside specialized help to get the product in the right place and to help promote it. Once outside help is sought, one becomes involved in relationships with external organizations.

In this chapter we examine these relationships with external organizations and the problems they can create. This requires placing the company within the context of its marketing system, and examining how it works with various outside specialists in order to satisfy its customers.

Our focus in this book is communication. The relationships of the company with outside organizations will be examined from the point of view of the organizational and communications problems which typically arise. Some attention will be given to the crucial question of how one selects external partners, works with them, and assesses their individual and joint performance. While the monitoring and control of advertising will be discussed in this chapter, the advertising function itself will be considered in Chapters 15 and 17.

Question 108: List the external organizations with which your company has a lasting working relationship. Why do you think each of these relationships was entered into, and what benefits do they now provide for the parties involved?

13.11 The Marketing System

The whole process of buying and selling, exchanging money for goods and services in a society, constitutes a marketing system. This embraces both the company and external organizations. An individual company is interested in that part of this system which affects its relationships with its markets. Mapping these relationships between organizations can provide useful clues to how a company operates from the marketing point of view.

The simplest way of looking at the marketing system is in terms of the company and its markets. The company gives the market information about its product and supplies it with goods and services, receiving in turn information and money for sales made. Of course the company is not alone in the market: there will be competitors. It may reach its final customers through middlemen, while the whole market may be subject to government policy and social and technology changes.

In response to the business environment, the company will develop objectives and marketing strategies that take account of its, and its competitors', strengths and weaknesses. The strategy will lead to product, price, promotion sales, and distribution policies.

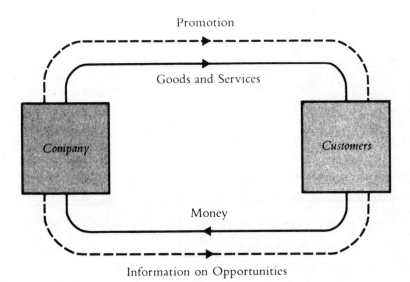

Figure 13.1 Market environment

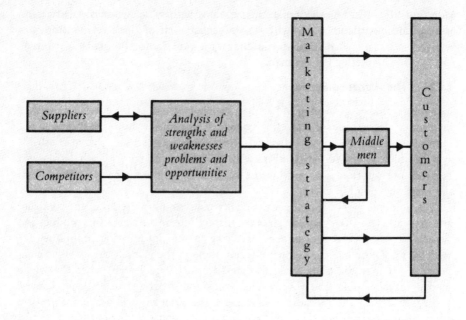

Figure 13.2   Relationships in the System

Question 109:   Take the organization with which you are most familiar and sketch its marketing system, indicating clearly the external relationships and the flows of both information and of goods and services.

It is sometimes useful to examine particular components or sub-systems of the marketing system. Each component receives some form of input and generates an output. The buyer, for example, receives information from the company which generates sales. Another important sub-system is the distribution system. This was examined in some detail in Chapter 12.

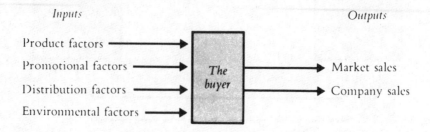

Figure 13.3   The Buyer Sub-system

Question 110:   Outline the marketing system in respect of the market for green-houses, paying particular attention to the buyer sub-system.

13.12   The Marketing Environment

Mapping out a marketing system can allow one to weigh the various factors that influence sales such as environmental, customer, competitor, and company influence, whether one's marketing mix outputs match inputs and whether one's marketing effort is correctly allocated amongst its products, customer segments, and sales territories. The diagram or analysis might reveal an input for which the company has yet to generate an output. It may reveal a marketing strategy that differs from those of competitors or a below-average response of sales to different levels, allocations, and mixes of marketing effort.

The external environment, composed of individuals and organizations, poses both threats and opportunities. The reactive firms may move too late to survive when external changes occur. The adaptive firms will survive, while the creative firms might actually contribute to and influence the external changes.

The marketing environment can be seen diagramatically as a set of squares, one inside of the other, rather like a set of Chinese boxes. This is illustrated in Figure 13.4. At the heart is the individual product, which exists within one's own organization. The company in turn exists within a market consisting of existing and potential customers with their needs, wants, and buying habits, together with competitors, each with strengths and weaknesses and a market share.

The market itself exists within a wider macro-environment composed of forces, practices, and institutions that create a framework within which the company carries on business with its customers. This wider environment consists of cultural factors, social forces, the economic situation, the state of technology, and public policy.

One organization's gain can be another's loss. A strong UK balance of payments position as a result largely of North Sea Oil and a Government policy of switching taxation from direct to indirect taxation created overnight, an initially hostile environment from the point of view of the tourist and hotel industries. The high value of the pound and the higher rate of value added tax acted together as a considerable deterrent to potential overseas tourists. The following year was the first for some time in which the number of overseas visitors to the UK actually fell.

Question 111:   List the factors in the external environment likely to be of particular importance to organizations in the following markets:

   (*a*)   oil
   (*b*)   television
   (*c*)   ice-cream
   (*d*)   washing machines
   (*e*)   package tours.

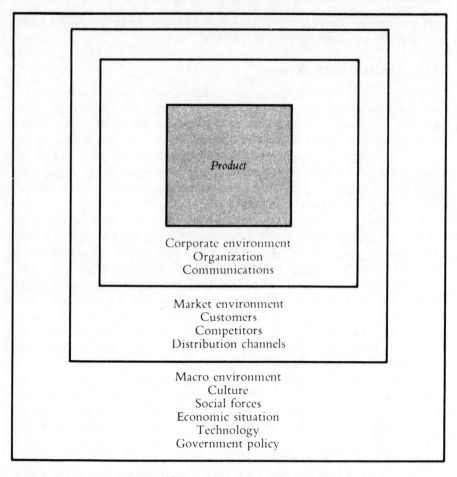

Product

Corporate environment
Organization
Communications

Market environment
Customers
Competitors
Distribution channels

Macro environment
Culture
Social forces
Economic situation
Technology
Government policy

Figure 13.4   The Marketing Environment

13.2   EXTERNAL COMMUNICATIONS

Communication between organizations presents special problems. Communicating organizations can have different values: they will not always agree on what is important and upon what should have been passed on. Each time a message is passed on there is scope for loss and distortion. Information will progress through successive filters that will screen out according to interest, prejudices, and past experiences. Information arriving at the end of the chain may be a pale reflection of the original.

A marketing manager should be prepared to carry out an information audit. This requires examining the total information system in two stages. First, each component should be examined as an independent entity to determine how receptive it is to incoming information, how it assesses what is important, and how regularly and with what accuracy it passes on significant information. The second stage, by means of case studies, examines the whole system to assess how well the components fit together and to identify weak links in the chain.

This 'depth checking' is achieved by first identifying a number of significant events. Some of these may be found in trade magazines and may not have been reported through one's marketing system. The focus could be a couple of sensational orders. They may have gone to a competitor. Perhaps the retailer informed the wholesaler, but the message was then relayed too late, or perhaps to the wrong person or department, or even not at all. Once a message starts along the chain, if it does not arrive and should have arrived, then someone is at fault.

The failure could be mechanical or institutional: no-one may have been briefed to act on a particular file. In this case a fault will have been found in a procedure. In another case, the error might be judgemental. Perhaps the file was consulted but the manager concerned did not feel its contents were of sufficient importance to justify passing them on. Corrective action could be disciplinary, training, or a change of staff.

Question 112: What are the main differences between internal and external communication? Need you be concerned about them?

13.21 The External Dimension

Once external organizations or third parties, are involved in an information chain, communication problems multiply. One's own staff will not have any executive authority *vis-à-vis* staff employed by these other bodies. Goodwill is required for communication to occur at all: it takes two to communicatate. This goodwill may not exist in sufficient measure to allow an information audit to take place.

It would be naïve to think that organizations are always willing to co-operate and communicate. There may be economic or political reasons for burying or distorting information. A middleman serving many masters must decide what to tell each of them and may even play one off against another. Coping with this type of situation may require political perception and cunning rather than experience of information techniques.

Information is rarely neutral: the contents of a message are likely to benefit some more than others. A message can harm. An organization may consider it has grounds for delaying or refusing to transmit. Another party may disagree; this can lead to bargaining. When one is dealing with an external body it is no use calling in a chief executive, a higher authority. The parties to the negotiation may be equal. If the information concerned is valuable one may have to pay to obtain it.

When negotiating, it is beneficial to know one's adversary. A forward-looking organization carries out organizational and communications analyses of the external organizations that form part of its marketing system. Not only can the results allow one to understand more fully what has occurred and is happening, but they can assist prediction. If an external organization is about to regress to a power culture, one might expect at some point in the future to negotiate at a higher level. If an external organization is devolving and diversifying, one may have to switch points of contact from its head office to its divisions.

Chapter 1 was devoted to the theory of communications, and most of it is applicable to communications with external organizations. In pointing out the special problems of external communication, one should not exaggerate them. What is advertising if it is not external communications? Separate divisions, even departments, within one company may have differing cultures and technologies, distinct lines of authority, conflicting values and objectives, and communications between them can be unsatisfactory and exhibit a tendency to negotiation and bargaining.

Question 113: Name an 'external' organization with which you have difficulty in communicating, and explain why this is so. Is there anything you could do to improve the situation?

13.22 Managing Diverse Relationships

When a company makes use of a variety of external services, the marketing manager is faced with the difficult job of managing an extremely diverse set of relationships. Managing diversity is an art: while recognising individual differences, the unique properties of each unit, the whole must be put together in such a way as to achieve 'synergy', i.e. the whole must be more effective than the sum of the parts.

Before fitting the jigsaw pieces together, one must first identify their individual characters. Each unit must be examined to determine the business it is in, its competitive position and strategy, how stable it is, and how it is controlled. It is most important that one's company and the external organizations that service it have common goals in the areas of co-operation.

A definition of the businesses service agencies are in and an examination of their strengths and weaknesses can help one to decide whether or not one is really making use of what each agency can do best. Do we really understand what they are about? Their behaviour will also be conditioned by their maturity. If they are new firms they may be chasing new accounts. A mature organization will be more stable; an ageing organization may be losing clients. These changes will have implications for external relationships.

A COMPANY MANAGER RECEIVED A DISTURBING REPORT ABOUT AN EXTERNAL ORGANIZATION WITH WHOM THE FIRM HAD A SERVICE AGREEMENT. IT WAS LATER FOUND THAT THE SOURCE OF THE 'RUMOUR' WAS THE DIRECTOR OF A RIVAL COMPANY

WHICH HAD SUBMITTED A COMPETITIVE BID AT THE TIME THE CONTRACT HAD FIRST BEEN AWARDED TO THE EXTERNAL ORGANIZATION WITH WHOM THE MANAGER'S COMPANY WAS DEALING.

Question 114: Describe an instance drawn from your own experience of information having been consciously distorted or hidden. Why was this done and what were the consequences? How could this action have been prevented?

13.23 Evaluating Service Agencies

An examination of the competitive position of service agencies is a useful exercise. It helps to confirm whether or not the right choice of agency has been made, and may shed some light on agency behaviour. The behaviour of an agency will be easier to understand after an examination of its strategy.

If a relationship is being entered into, the more one knows about the other party, and is realistic in incorporating this in assessments of areas of co-operation, the more successful the relationship is likely to be.

The management styles of the people in the external agencies with which a company deals are of particular importance. They should be matched by arranging 'pairings' with similar types within one's own organization if compatibility is to be achieved. Experts should be matched with experts.

The maturity of the service organization can provide vital clues to its management style. If it is a new organization, watch out for the entrepreneur, with a large degree of freedom, operating few rules, reluctant to commit to paper, informal, deciding on the basis of gut-feel, and expecting payment by results. In an older, larger organization there will probably be more rules, some reporting, longer delays before decisions are reached, fixed salaries, and greater formality. The mature organization may be run by administrators with their paperwork, formal and detailed reporting and analysis, and perhaps it will have a functional form of organization.

Putting together objective profiles of service agencies can throw a great deal of light on the reasons for their behaviour. It can identify common interests, possible areas of conflict, and potential personality clashes. It can provide the information necessary for the effective management of a relationship. The outcome might be proposals for a change of direction, or for a new strategy, or for different personnel servicing an agency, or even a change of the agency itself.

Large companies can maintain multi-disciplinary teams able to carry out objective profiles of the external organizations with which they deal. In the smaller organization, this work sometimes just does not get done. The result can be misunderstanding between in-house and external staff.

The marketing manager should be able to put together one-page profiles of the organizations with which he deals. This is why he needs some knowledge of organizations and of communications. The marketing manager should be prepared to tackle unique situations, to stand in someone else's shoes, and to try to understand why they behave the way they do.

Question 115:   You read in a trade magazine that your advertising agency has lost one of its major accounts. What do you do in respect of your own organization and what, if anything, would you say to your contact in the agency?

13.3   ESTABLISHING AND MANAGING SERVICE RELATIONSHIPS

It is vital that external providers of services understand the appropriate goals of the company. The company must, for example, have a clear idea of what it wants from its advertising before approaching an agency. It should also have some idea of what it can afford, established on the basis of 'how much is in the kitty', or a rough rule of thumb such as percentage of sales or matching a competitor. A more sophisticated approach is to calculate the costs of achieving one's goals in some detail.

An external brief should be sufficiently tight to ensure the firm concerned understands what one is trying to achieve. It should not, however, be so tight as to inhibit suggestion and comment. Perhaps one's goals need to be sharpened or a switch in emphasis might be more cost-effective. Where an external creative input is required, it is advisable not to interfere in the early stages of the creative process.

A list should be made at the outset of decisions in which the client company would like to participate. A company appointing an advertising agency, for example, will wish to vet a media schedule before the agency went ahead to produce artwork for every newspaper or journal on the list. It might also wish to apply some control criteria such as dropping items on the schedule which involved a 'cost-per-thousand' above a control limit.

It must be made clear at the outset which party is to bear the costs of certain categories of incidental expenses. Some design contracts, for example, do not make it clear who is to pay for artwork. Arguments about who should pay a certain bill halfway through a relationship are not conducive to harmonious working.

A CONTRACT BETWEEN A LEADING MANAGEMENT JOURNAL AND A PRINTER FOUNDERED ON THE QUESTION OF WHAT AUTHORS' CORRECTIONS WERE REASONABLE. THE PRINTER HAD CHARGED FOR AUTHOR'S CORRECTIONS WHICH WERE CONSIDERED 'EXCESSIVE'. THE PUBLISHER OF THE JOURNAL REFUSED TO PAY. IN A SUBSEQUENT CONTRACT WITH A NEW PRINTER THE SAME PHRASE 'REASONABLE AUTHOR'S CORRECTIONS' APPEARED AND SIMILAR DIFFICULTIES AROSE.

Question 116: Draw up a profile of a service agency with which you have had to deal. Give reasons why you used the agency and why you would use it again. Compile a brief for the commissioning of further work.

Question 117: A contract with a designer failed to specify who is to pay for artwork. Excluding artwork costs the agreed fee is within your budget, but if artwork costs are included, your budget is exceeded. Explore the options open to you.

13.31 Servicing the Distributor

Many distributors are order-takers rather than aggressive sellers of new products and chasers of additional accounts. In these cases, detailed written briefs should be prepared and contracts entered into on a restricted basis, and for a trial period only. It pays to be cautious: one should avoid loose and open-ended commitments.

A supplier should give distributors proper support that reflects their independence. The function of the distributor should be examined, formally set out, and understood by both parties. The company's sales force should be encouraged to concentrate upon distributor relationships, and the distributors in turn should be encouraged to seek their advice as and when required.

A programme could be established to improve the management skills of distributors by means of seminars and course, factory visits, technical briefings, and sales literature. An interchange of staff on a temporary basis might be appropriate. Training programmes should concentrate upon such areas as stock control and account-profitability analysis, the techniques that can help the distributor to manage his business more effectively.

One way of motivating distributors is to carry out a local advertising or direct mail campaign to support them in the field. The provision of market research details can also enable distributors to more effectively optimize the allocation of their sales effort.

IN A PERIOD OF FALLING DEMAND A MANUFACTURER OF CON- SUMER DURABLES FOUND ITSELF RUNNING SHORT OF STORAGE SPACE AND REQUESTED ITS DISTRIBUTORS TO HOLD HIGHER STOCKS TO RELIEVE THE PRESSURE AT THE POINT OF PRODUC- TION.

MOST OF THE DISTRIBUTORS REFUSED TO CARRY HIGHER STOCKS, ARGUING THAT DUE TO THE LOWER RATES OF SALE THEY COULD OBTAIN A GREATER RETURN BY DEVOTING THEIR STORAGE SPACE TO ALTERNATIVE AND FASTER SELLING LINES AND THAT THE PRODUCING COMPANY OUGHT TO REDUCE ITS RATE OF PRODUCTION. THE COMPANY STOPPED PRODUCTION OF ITS OLDER MODELS AND BOUGHT BACK STOCKS OF THESE FROM

DISTRIBUTORS IN RETURN FOR PROMISES OF ADDITIONAL POINT
OF SALE PROMOTION OF THE NEWER MODELS.

Question 118:   Examine the parties to an external relationship with which you
are familiar and identify instances of behaviour having been influenced by particular characteristics of the parties involved. Are their cultures, values, and goals
compatible? Does the bargaining or negotiating process favour one party rather
than another?

13.32   Marketing Control

The marketing manager should not forget the monitoring and control function, the
taking of corrective action to bring actual performance closer to the objectives that
have been set regarding desired performance. As a company grows and passes
through different stages of organizational development, and as the rate of change
in its market environment or technology speeds up, the control problem can
become acute.

Control is a senior management responsibility, and it is the job of the marketing
manager to ensure that the control problems of the marketing system are understood at board level. In the case of marketing, the control problem is complicated
by the impact of other departments such as production, warehousing, and transportation upon marketing performance, the position in the distribution chain of
external organizations and the variety and possible geographical dispersion of
marketing staff.

Marketing performance is far from under the control of one's own staff. Results
can be swayed off course by the unexpected behaviour of customers, competitors,
and government. The range of activities within a marketing department can run
from the general to the specific. Measuring the effectiveness of some activities may
be extremely difficult, while other projects might be tightly controlled by techniques such as network analysis.

In view of these difficulties it is suggested that control be considered separately
from the points of view of the efficient utilization of resources, the achievement
of budget performance, and of whether the marketing system as a whole is contributing effectively to the achievement of the company's long-run goals.

Efficiency control is a matter of determining whether each activity is cost-
effective, whether the same could be achieved at lower cost, or more achieved for
the same cost. This involves examining the size of the sales force and their use of
time, the priorities on the media schedule, and whether distribution costs should
be shared.

The annual budgeting process should incorporate the setting of standards, the
measurement of performance, the reporting of variances and the analysis of their
causes, and the taking of corrective action where deviations from standard are due
to factors one can control. Performance itself can be measured by means of devi-
ation and statistical control charts and ratio analysis.

An examination of the causes of unacceptable deviations from standards should draw a clear distinction between controllable and uncontrollable factors. Corrective action can involve one's own staff through pressure, manpower cuts or greater incentives, one's external agents through discount policy or the selling of warehouses, and even competitors if a price-cutting programme is started.

Question 119: Outline what corrective action you could take and would take in respect of falling sales in the following areas:

- (*a*) children's buckets and spades sold in seaside resorts
- (*b*) attendances at West End cinemas
- (*c*) sales of lottery tickets in newsagents.

13.33 Marketing Audit

Some companies carry out periodic reviews of their whole marketing systems, examining not only performance within the policies established, but also the policies themselves. Such an audit could examine all the components of the marketing system and how they fit together, and in addition encompass in-depth analyses of particular components. It involves three steps, determining how something is being done, examining its value, and then recommending what ought to be done.

The audit should commence with the marketing objectives. They may have become out-of-date in a changing world and may no longer reflect the threats and opportunities the company faces or its strengths and weaknesses. The marketing programme should then be examined, the resources committed to it, their allocation to particular components, and the efficiency of their use. This should lead to an examination of the details of each aspect of the programme: the examination should concentrate first upon areas of greatest weakness.

The audit should, of course, examine the organizational aspects, the distribution of authority and responsibility both formal and informal, the structures and the qualities of the staff and whether they match the tasks to be performed, and the demands of the company's technology and its strategy. It should also cover the communications system, focussing particularly upon the areas of potential weakness.

The audit could be implemented in a number of ways. Staff could be asked to examine their own activities or those of their subordinates. Outsiders could be commissioned in the interests of objectivity. These could be staff from other departments or even from outside of the organization. Some companies maintain in-house internal audit departments; external auditors can offer advantages of objectivity, speed, and specialist audit expertise.

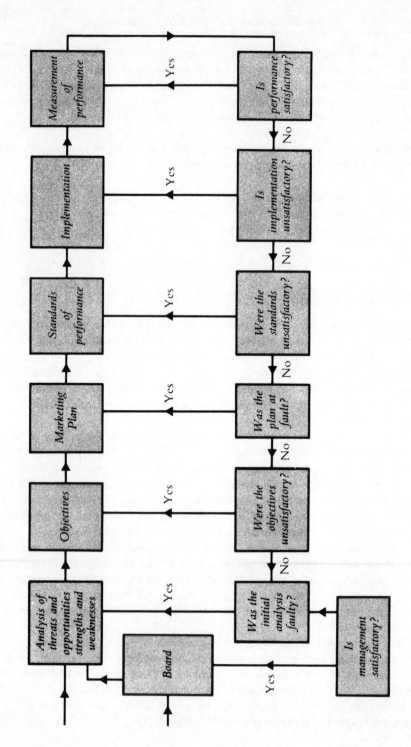

Figure 13.5

13.4 THE MARKETING CONTROL SYSTEM

This chapter begins and ends with the systems approach. A control system can be set up that is automatic or 'closed loop'. Rules could be established for comparing actual and desired performance and the automatic adjustment of whatever activity is being undertaken to bring actual and desired performance closer together. In an 'open loop' system, company staff make individual comparisons between what has happened and standards, and use their discretion in deciding whether or not corrective action needs to be taken and, if so, of what kind.

Figure 13.5 illustrates a control system that involves the assessment of each stage of the planning process. Changes that are made at particular points in the system work their way through and in time can lead to further changes. At each stage one needs to ask the question: does the fault lie with the system itself or with the responsible staff who operate it?

Question 120: Select an external relationship with which you are familiar. Sketch the marketing system, drawing in the specifically control aspects. Describe how it is serviced by each of the parties involved, the degree of commitment each demonstrates, and how each monitors and seeks to control the relationship.

EXAMINATION QUESTIONS

1. What are the integrated characteristics of the new 'total systems' approach used in the creation and modern management of an organization? How do they compare with 'classical management theory?

2. Taking an organization of your choice, examine the different major environments in which it operates.

3. What social constraints are likely to affect the National Coal Board's ability quickly to exploit newly-discovered coal deposits in mainland Britain?

14. *Public Relations*

The credibility of a marketing message can be enhanced by good publicity. Public relations can improve the image and reputation of both a company and its products. This chapter examines how good public relations can help to build understanding between a company and a number of publics with whom the marketor is communicating or may wish to communicate.

14.1 PUBLIC RELATIONS FUNCTION

Public relations practice is defined by the Institute of Public Relations as 'the deliberate, planned and sustained effort to establish and maintain mutual understanding between an organization and its public'. Public relations communication is two-way communication: effective public relations communication tends to be that which is highly selective, the tailoring of messages to the specific needs and interests of carefully-defined audiences. Ideally, each recipient of a public-relations message would receive an individually-tailored communication.

An organization is likely to be simultaneously communicating with a variety of internal and external groups. Specific public relations specialisms such as public affairs, shareholder relations, employee relations, financial public relations, corporate image relations, and press relations have emerged. Public relations might be organized as a separate function within an organization or, alternatively, each functional area such as marketing could retain its own public relations experts. In some companies, those with public relations skills call themselves business communicators.

To some extent, public relations can be used as an alternative to other marketing communication techniques such as advertising. It is however distinct: advertising can be highly selective and tailored but in many companies tends to be concerned with reaching the maximum number of people at the lowest cost with a persuasive message by means of a one-way flow of a message along a channel of communication. Public relations can be used to persuade, and advertising is used as a technique when appropriate by public relations practitioners. More usually, practitioners. More usually, however, public relations is concerned with two-way communication, using a variety of channels with the purpose of achieving mutual understanding.

14.11   Public Relations Resources

Where public relations is organized as a separate function, the marketing specialist should be aware of the organization's internal and external public relations skills and resources. It should be remembered that public relations specialists will have many publics to communicate with, other than those of prime concern of the marketor such as customers and distributors. The marketing specialist should make the public relations expert fully aware of the marketing opportunities in, for example, shareholder or local-community communication. Some companies enclose product information with annual reports and accounts. It should be remembered that, given the many objectives set for and commitments of a public relations department, only so much time will be available for specifically marketing-communication activity.

The effectiveness of an organization's employee-relations practice can have a strong influence upon employee satisfaction. When particular problems emerge in this area, for example communication with salesmen, it may well be that public relations specialists will be able to help.

14.2   MARKETING AND PUBLICITY

Publicity can be free but need not be favourable. It is difficult to control, and it is usually easier to influence good publicity than bad publicity. Good publicity can spread a company or a product name, and make recipient groups more favourably disposed towards an organization and the purchase of its products. Having a 'name' can itself be regarded as an indication of standing and quality.

Public relations activity can encourage good publicity and seek to minimize the damage done by bad publicity. It is not true that 'all publicity is good publicity'. The chances of failing to react to bad publicity and of missing opportunities for good publicity can be reduced by planned public relations activity. An organization can control to some extent the 'news' it itself puts out, and in the absence of an organization's own message an alternative message, possibly inaccurate and misleading, may be taken up.

Publicity does require good stories. News is expensive to obtain and can be scarce. Good publicity is not going to be easily achieved by an organization that is both inactive and has little of interest to say. Publicity can however, when it occurs, be dramatic and reach large audiences. Greater consumer awareness, dealer interest, and requests for information can follow a news item. Consistent publicity on a particular issue can do a great deal to build or to harm an image or a reputation.

The 'Fit for Work' advertisement campaign of the Manpower Services Commission employed a series of full-page newspaper advertisements featuring such personalities from the past as Nelson, Beethoven, Julius Caesar, Milton, Leonardo da Vinci, Sarah Bernhardt, and Franklin Roosevelt with the question: 'Did you know all these people were disabled?' The simple and effective message of the advertisements was that many disabled people who are not employed may well have considerable skills, which if used would more than compensate for their disability.

Question 121: Has your company examined the extent to which good public relations would enhance its marketing effort and bad public relations would harm it?

Question 122: What specific skills in your organization's public-relations department are relevant to the solution of its marketing communication problems?

14.3 PUBLIC RELATIONS RESPONSIBILITIES

The public relations department could have a great many tasks. An organization's strengths and weaknesses should be regularly analysed, the public relations area being specifically concerned with communication threats and opportunities. Problems will need to be identified which are susceptible to solution by public relations action.

At board level, directors and below them managers, need to be aware of internal and external developments that are likely to affect the reputation of the company. A public relations department might have a watching brief over the public relations implications of marketing area activity. The public relations department itself should be a repository of expertise upon all aspects of internal and external communication, maintaining expertise in techniques, and the facilities and contacts to enable them where appropriate to be used.

Contact should be made with important external decision-makers, opinion formers, and sources of information. Public relations staff should be the eyes and ears of a company. A public affairs specialist in contact with a politician could alert a marketing manager to a proposal to establish tighter product licensing controls, which could have traumatic consequences in a particular market.

Information should flow to selected publics and all parties with an interest in the organization by means of all appropriate channels of communication; specific research projects may be undertaken to remedy information gaps. Management will require regular reports on the evaluation of public relations problems and resulting activity.

A range of specific tasks can be delegated to a public relations department, such as the design of Annual Reports and Accounts, the organization of an event, or the running of a house organ. Such public relations skills as writing, publishing, speaking, audio-visual presentation and production, interviewing, press liaison, and monitoring could be made available to other departments as and when required.

Certain marketing activity will have public relations consequences. On occasions, a corporate reputation can be easily harmed: the public relations department should establish a system for dealing quickly and effectively with crisis occurrences.

Not all the skills an organization requires will be found within the public relations area external advice can be sought and obtained. The public relations practitioner should arrange the mix of internal and external resources most appropriate to the needs of an organization.

14.4 SYSTEMATIC PUBLIC RELATIONS

The effective public relations practitioner is sensitive to the needs of others. While there can be no substitute for drive, flair and personality, it generally pays to be systematic when tackling public relations or communications problems. The indiscriminate plying of drink and the mass mailing of standard press releases which end up in wastepaper bins gave rise to the 'gin and tonic' image of the public relations person. Today's more skilled practitioner tends to adopt a more considered and logical approach.

In some situations, emergency 'off the cuff' reaction will be required but even the disaster can be anticipated with practised crisis procedures. More usually, it is advisable to reflect, to think before acting. Firstly, the situation should be carefully analysed to find out what the problem really is. It may not be what first appearances might suggest; it is important to get to the bottom of a marketing communication problem and not to confuse symptoms with underlying causes.

Once a problem has been identified, objectives according to resources and priorities should be defined. Time and money are less likely to be wasted by those who think carefully about what they are trying to achieve. Target groups or publics should then be identified, those with whom the organization is or ought to be communicating in respect of the problem concerned. Publics should be subdivided wherever possible, in order to identify particular characteristics, needs, and interests.

Suitable messages need next to be drawn up which are appropriate to the problem, the organization's objectives, and the peculiarities of the publics to be communicated with. Having identified publics and drawn up messages, channels can be selected which appear to be most suitable for putting the messages to the priority publics. As resources are generally finite, a programme should be drawn up and carefully costed of which messages should be communicated to which publics with what channels, when, where and why, in order to achieve the objectives which have been established.

Once a programme is in the process of implementation, at intervals it should be evaluated in order to determine the extent to which objectives are being achieved. Such an evaluation enables the programme to be modified if need be, according to what has been learned from an assessment of feedback. Public relations activity should be carefully planned, and where significant in terms of money and/or time cost, reporting procedures should be established to enable it to be carefully monitored and controlled.

Question 123:   Outline a specific public relations procedure for handling product-liability problems.

14.5   PUBLICS

Publics should be identified and carefully classified. Major publics can be subdivided into smaller groups with common interests and needs. Not all of these groups will need to be communicated with. Bottlenecks, gaps, and gatekeepers might be identified. Where resources are limited some groups will have a higher priority than others.

A detailed analysis of publics can enable more tailored messages to be prepared and more suitable channels identified. Given time, it might be advisable to tailor communication to particular individuals who are known to be influential within target publics. Certain omnibus channels reach more than one public, and on occasion should be used with caution.

Question 124:   How tailored are your company's marketing communication messages to the needs and interests of its various customer publics?

The public relations practitioner is aware of the factors to be considered when messages are drawn up and channels selected. The tone and structure of a message must be appropriate to the recipient and the context. The public relations specialist is also likely to be familiar with a number of communication channels such as the press release, the facility visit, or the speech which may be rarely used by a marketor and which have particular message requirements.

14.51   Marketing Publics

Customers come in many forms and should be segmented into publics, and sales messages should be compatible with the needs and interests of the customer groups at which they are directed. Thus, convenience is more important to those without cars and to those who work and hence have less time to shop. Corporate image public relations activity can encourage potential customers to be favourable towards a well-known organization which it is thought has a reputation to keep up.

Messages that reinforce existing beliefs tend to be more successful than those which challenge them. A wide range of public relations activity can enhance an organization's profile and credibility. A careful analysis of marketing publics can result in more relevant messages being sent only to those likely to be interested in receiving them.

A marketor concerned about the state of communication with particular customer publics could order a communication audit from a public relations practitioner, with a view to the identification of barriers to effective communication.

To an extent, reputation is indivisable. Publics will overlap and messages can reach those for whom they are not intended. A marketing communication can have implications for other areas of activity. Some channels such as news agencies can be used as a clearing house for reaching a number of publics. With printed and audio-visual material, the context in which the information is viewed and discussed cannot always be controlled.

A SHOP MANAGER REFLECTED ON THE VARIETY OF HER CUS-TOMERS. THEY APPEARED A FAR FROM HOMOGENOUS PUBLIC WITH DIFFERENT GROUPS GETTING IN EACH OTHERS' WAY AND EXPECTING QUITE DIFFERENT FORMS OF SERVICE. SOCIALLY THE SURROUNDING RESIDENTIAL AREA WAS VERY MIXED. THE MANAGER DIVIDED HER CUSTOMERS INTO GROUPS AND LISTED THEIR SEPARATE REQUIREMENTS. EACH CATEGORY OF CUS-TOMER EMERGED AS BEING ONLY INTERESTED IN A SMALL PROPORTION OF THE RANGE OF GOODS OFFERED FOR SALE.

THE MANAGER DECIDED TO CREATE SUB-UNITS, SHOPS WITHIN A SHOP, TO APPEAL TO TWO IMPORTANT MINORITY PUBLICS, A CHIC UP-MARKET 'BOUTIQUE' FOR THE TRENDLY INTERESTED IN STYLE, AND IN THE BASEMENT AN ECONOMY AREA OFFERING CUT-PRICE GOODS. GROUPS OF CUSTOMERS WERE ATTRACTED BY THE SEPARATE ATMOSPHERES THUS CREATED AND NEW CUS-TOMERS WERE ATTRACTED TO THE STORE. IN TIME THE SHOP OWNER NEGOTIATED A DEAL CREATING SEPARATE BOUTIQUES IN THE STORES OF OTHER COMPANIES.

Question 125: Is your organization's marketing-communication activity co-ordinated with and consistent with the promotion of its overall image?

14.52 Interests in a Company

There are a number of publics with an interest in a company and able to harm a company in cases of inadequate communication. Shareholders, if not satisfied, can sell their shares and fail to subscribe to new issues. Employees who are unsettled will not give of their best. A creditor may in the absence of adequate information, call in a loan. A local community that is hostile can prevent the expansion of a local plant. A company can be hard hit by the implementation of legislation introduced by an unsympathetic government. Rumours of a product defect can lead purchasers to take their custom elsewhere.

The board of a company has to arbitrate between a number of legitimate and competing interests. Each interest represents a key public with whom a company must communicate, and which must be satisfied.

A MARKETING AND PUBLIC RELATIONS MANAGER MET OVER LUNCH IN THE COMPANY CANTEEN AND DISCUSSED THE COMPANY'S FALLING SALES. THE PUBLIC RELATIONS MANAGER MENTIONED THAT IN TWO MONTHS TIME THERE WOULD BE MASS MAILINGS OF ACCOUNTS TO BOTH SHAREHOLDERS AND EMPLOYEES. THE MARKETING MANAGER HAD A THOUGHT. PRODUCT BROCHURES AND SPECIAL OFFER VOUCHERS WERE ENCLOSED WITH BOTH MAILINGS OF ACCOUNTS AND A SIGNIFICANT INCREASE OF SALES OCCURRED.

14.53 Shareholder Relations

Marketing activity can be a prime determinant of a company's financial performance. Financial publics such as existing and potential shareholders, financial analysts, and financial journalists may seek periodic market and product information. Potential investors might be particularly concerned with the prospects for tomorrow's products.

While financial communication will be the prime responsibility of the company secretary, the financial director and the board, a marketing contribution will be made to the content of certain channel's messages. In takeover and new-issue situations, product and market information will be sought by a number of parties.

The marketing department could make a contribution at an Annual General Meeting. A presentation could be made of progress with a major project, a display arranged in a foyer, or product brochures placed on seats. The AGM itself and the results of an AGM could be marketed to shareholders.

A Chairman's statement could contain references to marketing activity, and personnel. Product and geographic analyses of turnover could be presented in an Annual Report and Accounts, along with product photographs and information. Financial publics interested in such information could include creditors, bankers, the media, the Stock Exchange, statistical services, financial analysts, employees, investment managers, treasurers, fund trustees, public bodies, key customers and suppliers, business partners, and opinion formers.

THE ARMITAGE SHANKS GROUP LTD HAS INCORPORATED A GLOSSY BROCHURE OF THE COMPANY'S BATHROOM PRODUCTS WITH ITS REPORT AND ACCOUNTS. THIS EXPLAINED HOW THE

RECIPIENT COULD PLAN AND EQUIP A BATHROOM WITH ARMITAGE SHANKS PRODUCTS. GEO. G. SANDEMAN SONS & CO. LTD HAVE ENCLOSED AN ACTUAL ORDER FORM WITH A SET OF INTERIM ACCOUNTS.

Question 126: Evaluate the value of a marketing contribution to an information package sent with a 'welcome' letter to new shareholders.

Question 127: Does your organization make full use in its marketing effort of its Annual Report and Accounts?

14.54 Employee Communication

A large organization can find its employees a significant marketing public. Employees have families, and outside of office hours move in many circles. Unlike many other publics, they are also likely to be well disposed towards the organization and a number of channels exist which could be used to make sure that they are also well informed.

The employee public will not be homogenous. Different groups will have distinct needs and interests. Employee communication may also have to take place against an unfavourable background of bitter wage negotiation or anticipated redundancy. There will also be office politics and minority issues to contend with. Some employees may consequently be relatively hostile while others are strong allies. Communication will be most effective where there is mutual confidence.

Employee reports and house journals can be consciously used to circulate marketing information to employees and to incentivate employees to marketing effort. In the case of an international organization, local-language versions of such documents may need to be produced. International publics can be very diverse and great care may need to be taken to avoid triggering local legal, moral, and political sensitivities.

14.55 Minorities

Racial and ethnic bias can creep into marketing communication and if picked up can lead to boycotts and a significant drop in sales. An international company can on occasions find itself having to maintain a difficult balance and having to calculate trade-offs between say trade with South Africa or Israel and that with Black Africa or the Arab World. An unnecessarily qualified description in a communication can reinforce a stereotype. The mentioning of minorities is best avoided.

In marketing copy, certain words with colour connotations should be avoided. A minority in one context can be a majority elsewhere. Adjectives and labels should be selected with caution. A terrorist to A can be regarded as a freedom fighter by B. A term such as non-white can be taken to imply that a standard exists.

Marketing communication should avoid patronising and token approaches. Members of minorities should not be hidden or drawn attention to in advertisements in an exaggerated way. An honest and open approach that seeks to avoid stereotypes and emotive terms should be employed.

The handicapped and women can be particularly sensitive to the use of certain terms. Words such as manpower, founding fathers, manmade, and gentlemen's agreement have non-sexist substitutes such as workforce, forebears, synthetic, and informal contract. A noun such as 'lady' can imply a male norm. In visual images, care needs to be taken to avoid sexist labels and sexist assumptions concerning roles. What is acceptable in one context can cause problems in another. The term salesman used in this book could be regarded as sexist.

A press release on the first black or woman to be appointed to a certain position can backfire when taken as evidence of how little progress is being made or how behind competitors a company is. An organization operating internationally may find the relative prominence given to nationals and expatriates a sensitive issue. A management may have to bend over backwards in its communications to portray itself as a national rather than a foreign company. Certain forms of discrimination may be illegal and the marketing area may have to conform to a company-wide anti-discrimination policy.

Question 128:   What steps does your organization take to ensure that racism and sexism does not creep into its marketing communications?

14.56   Public Affairs

The impact of the activities of government upon an organization can be considerable. A change of credit policy or the lifting or imposition of import restrictions can greatly affect a company's sales. Action to bring down the rate of inflation can reduce business activity for a long period.

Many government departments are substantial purchasers. For many companies the government is a major customer. Cutbacks in public spending in such circumstances can have a traumatic effect. Similarly the removal of a state monopoly power can, at a stroke, open up exciting new market opportunities.

The government purchasing system can be complex and hidden. Alert intelligence is needed to pick up changes of personnel and to determine the relative weights of the various influences contributing to the purchase decision. There may be a bevy of rules and regulations to contend with at a national and regional level. Local authorities will have standing orders. Tender arrangements, pricing arrangements, profit formulae, review procedures, and payment terms may all be formally set down in manuals.

The public affairs function will have responsibility for monitoring changes likely to have a significant influence upon a company's business. Changes in laws must be complied with; influence may have to be brought to bear in the case of proposed changes in the pipeline. Within the public sector the location of power can be hidden. Access may have to be obtained to an influence network: a company will have to decide whether to act alone or to leave lobbying in respect of a particular issue to trade or representative bodies. In the case of the latter, a viewpoint may have to be fed into appropriate trade associations.

Representation requires tact and caution. A great deal of effort can be expended to little effect. Political publics can be sympathetic to a reasonable case but crude lobbying can alienate. To influence a local authority, it helps to know the objectives of a committee or council and to be supportive, perhaps by suggesting a joint venture package that will meet the aims of both council and company.

So far as central government is concerned, on matters of technical detail it is often advisable to approach Whitehall rather than Westminster. Civil servants represent a continuing pool of experience while elected Ministers come and go. The civil servant often acts as a 'gatekeeper', in a position to control the information-flow to a Minister. Considerable powers can be delegated in legislation to the executive branch on matters of detail, and in the implementation and the drawing up of regulations, civil servants at times welcome external informed advice.

Politicians themselves are a difficult public to cultivate. They are frequently distracted by the demands of constituents, their political machine, and their official duties. There is often insufficient time to examine anything in depth.

When negotiating with both civil servants and politicians, it is important to be aware of the constraints under which the other party is operating. Discretion and time will be limited. Many senior figures do welcome the opportunity of an informed and objective briefing. Too much store should not be placed in contacts built up, as out of office and on the backbenches a politician can have little influence.

Most MPs will have particular interests. These can be identified through reference books and with the help of specialist Parliamentary consultants. An MP may be willing to act as a spokesman or consultant with or without a fee. A satisfactory relationship can result in opportunities for the putting of appropriate Parliamentary questions.

Effective lobbying is that which is co-ordinated, timely and systematic. There will be competing and hostile lobbies to contend with; credibility in the long run depends upon integrity.

IN 1979 SHELL OIL ESTIMATED THAT ITS COMPANIES IN THE US SPENT IN EXCESS OF 500 EMPLOYEE-YEARS OF WORK AT A COST OF SOME $25 MILLION DEALING WITH US FEDERAL REGULATORY AGENCIES.

Question 129: Has your organization ever surveyed the total impact upon it of government activity?

Question 130: Who are the most influential individuals and what are their prioities and attitudes towards your organization in the government departments and regulatory agencies with which your organization deals, and where it has problems what would be the most cost-effective means of exerting influence?

14.6 PUBLIC-RELATIONS CHANNELS

A company can obtain considerable media coverage of product developments by means of effective press releases, press conferences, and individual journalist contact. Editorial comment that is largely 'free' tends to be considered as more objective than paid for advertising.

14.61 Press Releases

The public-relations specialist should have a system for the cost-effective dissemination of press releases. Press release mailing lists should be kept up-to-date and used selectively. Releases should be tailored to the specific needs and interests of each recipient, crisp and concise with the 'story' summarized in the first paragraph, and preferably only issued on those occasions when the company has something interesting and useful to say. There should be a conscious strategy behind each issue of a press release.

Most organizations issue releases on distinct press-release stationery. There is also usually an authorization procedure that should be adhered to. Those with responsibility for the issuing of releases should ensure that adequate stocks of people and product photographs are available to accompany releases when required, and that background information such as product sheets and *curricula vitae* are filed. Journalists tend to become annoyed when they have to wait some time for a photograph of a newly-launched product to be taken, developed, and delivered.

Question 131: Is marketing activity in your company fully integrated into its press-release strategy and machinery? Are your organization's press mailing lists kept up to date?

The timing of the issue of a press release can be crucial. Messenger services can be used to hand-deliver releases in a large urban area such as London, where the media is concentrated. It is important to make sure that well-briefed staff are available in and out of office hours to provide further information on the telephone to those calling as a result of having received a release.

It is best to use press releases sparingly. Unless an item is 'hot', an embargo should not be used as some journalists find·one off-putting. Names, addresses and contact telephone numbers should also be put at the foot of a release.

14.62   Press Contacts

The press release is by no means the only method of obtaining press coverage. Relevant and interested journalists can be kept informed of product developments by means of individual contact, press conferences and briefings, visits and stands at press shows. The marketing manager should be aware of the relevant trade press and should be prepared to use the resources of a public relations department to effect suitable introductions. In some cases, a story might be 'seeded' or a contribution to a forthcoming special report suggested.

'Letters to the Editor' should not be overlooked as a channel of communication. A short letter to a local newspaper on a matter of some concern can reach many local opinion formers such as councillors checking to see which of their colleagues have achieved a 'mention'. There may be an ongoing debate upon which a company can piggy-back. In such cases, a prompt response is desirable. Where a press date is imminent it might be a good idea to telephone an editor to provide some advance notice that a letter is on the way.

Question 132:   What editorial needs of major external publics are not being met by your organization? Is feedback encouraged?

14.63   Internal Channels

A marketor should not forget a company's own internal journalists and the opportunities for obtaining news coverage in house journals. It is surprising how often in many large companies staff in one division are unaware of marketing activity in other divisions. A house-journal editor might be delighted to give editorial space to the launch of a new product or the winning of a large order. The achievement of a certain level of sales such as the 1000th delivery or an anniversary of the first introduction of a product can be the occasion for coverage in the trade, local, and house press.

Communication of marketing news and information to employees can also be achieved at internal conferences and meetings, by display stands in foyers, notices on boards and by the internal circulation of information sheets.

Question 133:   Are the internal communication relationships between the public relations, marketing, advertising, and production departments in your company satisfactory and how satisfactory are the relationships between these departments and external middlemen and suppliers?

14.64   Printed Material

Leaflets, handbills, and booklets can be used to put a message across to a great many publics. The marketing manager should check with a public-relations department for opportunities for the wider distribution of product information leaflets. In some companies, the public relations area will be able to advise on or take responsibility for leaflet copywriting, design, and production.

Many companies issue information booklets about themselves which analyse sales, set out a group structure, provide a guide to key people, products and facilities, provide a summary history and the address of registrars, a financial calendar, and details of directors and professional advisers. Such a booklet or brochure together with .product information and a published Report and Accounts can be put into a folder to provide a usual information pack to a potential major customer or joint venture partner. Many people like to know something of the past history, performance, size, and standing of companies with whom they are proposing to do business.

14.65   Broadcast Media

In the event of major orders, perhaps for the export market and won in the face of stiff competition there might be scope for radio and television coverage. While national coverage might be limited to a mention, an interview could be possible, together with a visit to the works, on local radio and television. The broadcast media can be a minefield for the unwary and the unprepared. The public relations department should be able to advise on the initiation of ideas for programmes and upon interview techniques.

Independent local radio tends to be overlooked. Advantage can be taken of phone-in opportunities, while a tape can be prepared. Producers of radio programmes are looking for two-minute tapes and such tapes can reach an audience of millions for a relatively small initial cost. Programme schedules should be monitored to identify opportunities.

14.66   Interview Techniques

Prior to live appearances and recordings, it is always wise to draw up a list of the main points to be made. While programme producers tend to look for a senior representative, preferably the chief executive, there is some advantage in putting forward a representative skilled in interview techniques. Interview training courses are available.

If contacts are made and kept with broadcast journalists interested in the company's area of operation, programme ideas can be initiated. On other occasions, a broadcast appearance will be a reaction to some event, perhaps a crisis of some kind.

Dress for television interviews should avoid check patterns and that which is likely to distract. Combing one's hair and a last-minute shave can also be advisable. Before accepting an invitation to be interviewed, it is generally advisable to note the subject, expected interview length, who else is to appear, and whether the programme is to be live or recorded, and to reflect for a couple of minutes before giving a definitive answer.

As time will be limited, it is best to concentrate upon putting over just a few main points. An early arrival to the studio and a last-minute visit to the lavatory can be advisable. A late drink should be avoided.

While an interview is in progress, the camera should be ignored and eye-ball to eye-ball contact maintained with the interviewer. Television exaggerates eye movements. A robust approach to tricky questions makes for good viewing, but almost regardless of what is asked the main points should be put across. Once a point has been made it is wise to stop. An interviewer will on occasion allow a subject to ramble in the hope of a controversial comment emerging. A complex idea can best be put across by means of a story.

On television, the image that comes across is very important. Thus if a product part is being produced more cheaply in order to economize, it is wise not to have the Chairman's Rolls Royce in the background.

In a large company context, it should be remembered that closed-circuit television facilities might be available. If used, a programme should be carefully planned and produced to high professional standards. A programme that allows for two-way communication tends to be more credible to an audience.

Question 134: Examine how systematically your organization makes contact with local radio and television stations. Are media spokesmen selected on the basis of their seniority or their competence as communicators?

14.67 Visits

In the marketing area, there may be occasions when the organization has something new or interesting it wishes to show to a group of visitors. The opening of a new plant or the introduction of a new model or service can be the occasion for inviting along customers, distributors, journalists, and opinion-formers.

If a visit concerns a news item and journalists are invited at short notice, communication facilities should be made available so that news reports can be fed back to base. On other occasions when a long period of notice is available, guests likely to have busy diaries should be given a couple of months' warning.

Guest lists should be carefully drawn up to ensure that relevant people are invited. A visit can backfire if at the end of the day guests feel they have been misled and have wasted their time. The purpose of an event must be clear and the venue and date planned with both access and availability in mind. Transportation and catering arrangements will need to be made.

A certain proportion of invitations will be rejected and a proportion of those accepting will not be able to turn up on the day for a variety of reasons. Thus invitations should be attractive and informative. Those not replying can be diplomatically followed up by telephone call.

On the day of a visit a reception area will need to cater for arriving guests. There may at this point be information to hand out. On certain occasions name badges, perhaps in different colours to distinguish publics, may be desirable. Press packs should not be too voluminous if they are to be read. There is usually no need to cater excessively: no amount of food and drink can compensate for a lack of intrinsic interest in an event.

Where speeches are to be made, a rehearsal may be desirable. If guests are not likely to know each other prior to arrival and latecomers are expected, it may be a good idea to start off with a drinks reception. An excessively long introduction can be avoided by sending an event programme along with a route map and other details sent shortly before an event is held.

Informality while desirable is often difficult to achieve. Careful structuring may be necessary if an occasion is to appear informal without seeming unco-ordinated and confused.

With events of all kinds, some follow-up is usually desirable. There may be new contacts to be kept alive. Where interest has been shown, names can be added to mailing lists. Promises made at events should, where possible, be kept. Thank-you letters should be sent to all those who have contributed to the success of an event.

Question 135:   Does your organization automatically carry out post-mortem type examinations of events and visits it stages, and are suggestions for future modifications and improvements recorded and subsequently made where appropriate?

14.68   Channel Review

Channels of communication need to be kept up-to-date. A notice board can become cluttered and should be managed by one person. Exclusion from a mailing list can cause resentment. An audio-visual production that looks amateurish can be counter-productive. Printed material can soon become out of date. Timing can be crucial: communication that is too late can be an ineffective ritual. Too much detail can be self-defeating. Periodically, the effectiveness of each major channel of communication used should be reviewed.

14.7   PUBLIC RELATIONS PLANNING

The public relations plan will aim to close a perceived gap between the state of communication between an organization and its publics, and how management would like it to be. The plan could begin with an assessment of the current state, for example, a company's image. Because of the need to react to crisis occurrences, public relations planning and budgeting should provide for some slack in the system.

There will be communications implications of activities likely to be undertaken as part of a wider company plan.

The public relations input to corporate planning would include identification and assessment of the likely reactions of various publics to proposed changes and the forecasting of major social, economic, political, and technological changes. In some cases, public relations and marketing objectives could be in conflict. A business proposal while profitable might be thought to compromise a company's image.

A twelve-month communication plan would incorporate more detailed costings, estimates of time allocation, and short-term objectives ranked in priority along with the required internal and external resources. Costs to be budgeted for would include telephone, telex, printing, stationery and audio-visual and other equipment, leaflets, handbills, booklets, tapes and films, conferences, visits, AGM's, conventions, and press briefings.

A PUBLISHER IDENTIFIED A GAP IN A MARKET FOR A NEW PERIODICAL. CONTACT WITH POTENTIAL ADVERTISERS AND FORECASTS OF SUBSCRIPTION LEVELS LIKELY TO BE ACHIEVED SUGGESTED THAT AN EXTREMELY PROFITABLE PUBLICATION COULD BE INTRODUCED. BEING A START-UP SITUATION, AN INITIAL INVESTMENT WAS NEEDED WHICH REQUIRED BOARD APPROVAL. THE BOARD REJECTED THE PROPOSAL. WHILE IT PROMISED ATTRACTIVE COMMERCIAL RETURNS IT WAS THOUGHT THAT A 'TRADE' PAPER WOULD NOT BE COMPATIBLE WITH THE COMPANY'S IMAGE AS A PUBLISHER OF LEARNED AND PROFESSIONAL PERIODICALS.

Question 136: List the public relations activities undertaken in your organization. Are there gaps and is the allocation of resources adequate?

14.8 EVALUATION

The measurement of the effectiveness of public relations activity can be achieved by routine monitoring of press cuttings and broadcast transcripts, letters in the press, the tone of comments, complaints received, sales and market reports, reports of speeches, and by special studies such as shareholder surveys, attitude surveys and image studies. Statements of the impact of an organization's communications on certain key publics can be compiled and communication audits undertaken.

A number of companies have undertaken social responsibility audits. Others have commissioned detailed corporate image studies. Opinion research findings can be sought. Feedback can be obtained via employee communication channels. From time to time, there could be detailed external comments in digests, reviews, yearbooks, stockbroker, and analysts reports.

Dealer and consumer surveys and an analysis of stock movements can yield clues about marketing communication effectiveness. In the case of programmes designed to change opinions or attitudes, surveys should be undertaken both before and after planned activity. Share price movements and trading levels, and the size and nature of the response to new issues can yield evidence on the relative success of financial public relations programmes.

Evaluation should be objective and honest. Often trade associations and consumer organizations undertake comparative surveys.

Question 137: Does your organization set objectives for and budget its public relations activity? Is performance systematically and adequately monitored and controlled, with programmes modified accordingly?

14.9 CORPORATE IDENTITY

An organization's marketing effectiveness can be strongly affected by its overall image. The identity of an organization can derive from its tasks, technology, history, or the people within it. A founder entrepreneur can personify a company, as did Colonel Saunders of Kentucky Fried Chicken.

The image or identity of an organization need not be taken for granted: it can be consciously built and modified. An identity focus can be shifted. The identity may be product-based: Marks and Spencer has a quality image based upon its efforts to achieve high standards in the products it sells. The reputation of Rolls Royce derives from technological excellence and has not been significantly affected by commercial failure and a split of motor car and aerospace operations. In the case of a financial intermediary such as a bank, building society, or insurance company or an oil or transportation company, considerable effort may be needed to distinguish an individual company's identity from the industry of which it is a part.

A favourable identity can be of commercial value. A muddled identity can be a source of confusion and misunderstanding. A major customer, a distributor, suppliers, and sub-contractors may all attach considerable weight to an organization's 'name'.

> PEPSI-COLA INTRODUCED A NEW 'COME ALIVE WITH PEPSI' SLOGAN FOR INTERNATIONAL USE. IN TAIWAN THE SLOGAN WAS TRANSLATED AND INITIALLY PROMOTED AS 'PEPSI BRINGS YOUR ANCESTORS BACK FROM THE DEAD'.

14.91 Corporate Image Promotion

A corporate image advertising campaign can help to make an organization better known. In the case of a company producing products with strong brand names, the company itself may be little known. A campaign in such circumstances might involve introducing a company name at an appropriate point in brand advertisements in addition to a separate programme of company name advertisements.

A corporate advertising campaign can reach a variety of influential publics. An overseas government may be more willing to license a joint-venture agreement with a company that has a 'name'. Where a company is under attack from say a consumer or an environmental lobby, a corporate campaign can help to put an organization's message across.

The credit granted by a financial institution or by suppliers, the eagerness of shareholders to take up a new issue or the willingness of a buyer to put an organization upon a tender list can all depend upon reputation. Potential employees or potential takers-up of a new product can also be attracted by a good name. Awareness can be crucial to reputation. Many organizations find that key publics are not aware of the full range of their activities.

A desired corporate image must be credible and realistic. A campaign may need to tackle a negative image. The returns to such a campaign can appear intangible but could be measured by means of before-and-after opinion surveys. The initial examination should be entirely objective, and returns should not be expected too quickly. Paradoxically, when times are hard and advertising budgets are cut, it is often the time when a boost to a flagging image is most needed.

The marketing manager may become closely involved in a company-wide corporate image campaign. Such campaigns have been headed up by brand managers. A name can be an important part of an identity and an organization may have to choose between product group names more than one group of its products may have a well-known name. A marketing manager may object to the promotion of a company name at the expense of an established product group name. Using the halo effect, the marketor should be alert to the possibility of spreading a well-established name over a wider group of products.

A logo or symbol can act as an identifier. The Shell symbol has become recognized internationally as a badge of identity. A consistent image across a wide range of operations can be difficult to achieve and costly if a whole new range of printed material incorporating a new logo and house style has to be produced. A corporate image campaign can present the marketing area with both problems and opportunities.

IN 1978 PILKINGTON, THE UK GLASS MANUFACTURER, COMMISSIONED A MORI OPINION SURVEY WHICH FOUND THAT OF 1,952 PEOPLE INTERVIEWED, WHILE 15% FELT THEY KNEW PILKINGTON 'FAIRLY WELL', 44% HAD HEARD OF IT BUT KNEW LITTLE OF ITS ACTIVITIES AND 41% HAD NEVER HEARD OF THE COMPANY. AS A CONSEQUENCE, PILKINGTON RAN A 'HOW'S THAT FOR ENTERPRISE?' CORPORATE ADVERTISING CAMPAIGN. THE CAMPAIGN WAS ESTIMATED TO HAVE REACHED OVER TEN MILLION ADULTS AND LATER IN THE YEAR A FOLLOW-UP OPINION SURVEY

WAS UNDERTAKEN. THIS REVEALED THAT SOME 73% OF ALL RESPONDENTS HAD HEARD OF THE COMPANY WHILE 43% REGARDED IT 'VERY FAVOURABLY' OR 'MAINLY FAVOURABLY' COMPARED WITH 28–32% FOR OTHER COMPANIES WITH SIMILAR FAMILIARITY RATINGS.

Question 138: How satisfactory and consistent is your organization's overall image? Examine changes that would make your image more satisfactory from the point-of-view of communication with certain publics and how such changes might be achieved.

14.10 CRISIS COMMUNICATION

Public relations activity can be particularly important in crisis situations. Many managers have difficulty in dealing with the unexpected. The response to a failure such as an unfavourable judgement in a product-liability suit is often to cut channels of communication just when they are most needed. The gap between perception and reality can be a wide one in emergency situations. In the absence of communication, rumours can abound; sometimes it is necessary to grasp the nettle.

A closed organization with rigid procedures can find itself unable to cope with a sudden shock. Unfavourable occurrences should be anticipated, risks assessed, and wherever possible contingency arrangements made. A company has often to face up to bad news rather than hope it will go away. An organization can be regarded as condemned by its silence. This is not to say that one should fire from the hip in an emergency. A decision not to react should be a positive and considered one, and not the result of inactivity or fear.

When crises occur, the media in particular are likely to be in search of information. The spread of bad news can damage a company: news of the loss of an order can depress a share price. News of future redundancy can unsettle a labour force. Whether or not to disclose and how much to disclose can be difficult decisions.

In some cases, ignorance can fuel a fire. Bad news can be heavily discounted in advance. Procedures should be established for coping with the peak demand for information in a crisis situation if rumours are to be scotched. The truth tends to leak out in time. It is often advisable to take the initiative in the communication of bad news.

Public relations staff should be quickly on the 'spot': in a crisis, priority should be given to the establishment of a communication centre able to provide accurate reports and informed comment. A response a day later may be buried when other stories have claimed the headlines. Informed comment should if possible be based upon an organization's own objective assessment of what has happened. It is dangerous to put too much reliance upon media reports.

IN NEW YORK, BELL TELEPHONE FOUND ITSELF WITH A FIRE THAT APPEARED TO BE OUT OF CONTROL. THE DECISION WAS TAKEN TO ESTABLISH A MOBILE VAN COMMUNICATION HEAD-QUARTERS IN ORDER TO FEED MEDIA REPRESENTATIVES ON THE SPOT WITH ACCURATE INFORMATION. THE FIRE EVENTUALLY BURNED FOR 22 HOURS. THE ON-THE-SPOT PRESENCE HELPED TO PREVENT THE SPREADING OF RUMOURS.

Question 139: List the crises your organization could face. Is there a satisfactory contingency plan for dealing with each of these and are the plans regularly reviewed?

15. *Advertising*

Advertising is a major marketing communication tool. Advertising is persuasive and public: it tends to simplify and dramatise. As a channel of communication it is relatively impersonal. It can perform a variety of functions such as informing, entertaining, persuading, reminding, reassuring, complementing, reinforcing, and can actually add value to a product by changing attitudes towards it. A premium price may be based upon an image of quality or exclusivity fostered by selective advertising. Advertising has a number of positive purposes and yet it has drawn criticism.

Advertising was introduced in Chapter 9 as an element of the promotional mix. This chapter examines the nature of advertising and the organizational and behavioural aspects of its use as a means of communicating with target groups. Advertising can be defined as any paid form of non-personal presentation and promotion, which informs or persuades (ideas, goods or services), so long as it is undertaken by an identified sponsor. Advertising is both controlled and identifiable and, being non-personal, by definition, is by some means of mass communications media. As advertising is paid for directly its sponsor is identified. Presentation that is non-personal can be directed at individuals but is not made in person by the seller in the presence of the prospect.

15.1 TYPES OF ADVERTISING

Advertising is a major communications tool. It ranges from TV commercials through handbills to outdoor advertising. It can have a variety of purposes; it is highly public and can be repeated.

To some extent, all advertising is general and impersonal. Unlike with direct personal contact, the recipient of an advertising message is not under any obligation to respond.

Publicity and public relations work can lead to 'free' advertising. News stories have very high credibility and generally reach captive audiences, and are designed

214

to highlight what is thought to be of greatest interest to these audiences. Unlike advertising, however, the public relations 'message' is not within one's control.

Advertising can have a variety of aims: it can appeal to emotion or reason, be directed at a number of audiences at more than one level. Advertisements vary greatly in content. They can be sponsored by producers, middlemen, or retailers and aimed at local, regional, national, or overseas audiences. Opinions differ on how advertising works and over how effective it is.

An advertisement can inform, suggest a good idea to potential consumers, jog memories, and reinforce the attitudes and behaviour of existing consumers. In planned advertising, what is important is that a company fully understands the levels upon which its advertisements are operating, the degree to which they are successful, and why they are successful. Without this knowledge, it is difficult if not impossible to modify campaigns in the light of experience and understanding.

People and situations change: one form of advertising might be appropriate at one moment, another the next. Consumers are in a continual state of flux. Even the most selective target group is omnibus in that it is likely to contain consumers with very different attitudes to a product in question. Some may have already tried the product in question; others will not have heard of it. Existing purchasers will experience varying degrees of satisfaction.

A PROMINENT LOCAL COUNCILLOR HAD NOT RECEIVED AN INVITATION TO A PRESTIGIOUS DANCE. HE ADVERTISED IN A LOCAL NEWSPAPER FOR A TICKET BUT FAILED TO GET A RESPONSE. HE WROTE TO THE EDITOR OF THE NEWSPAPER EXPLAINING HIS PLIGHT. A REPORTER AND A CAMERAMAN WERE DESPATCHED AT ONCE. THE COUNCILLOR BECAME FRONT PAGE NEWS COMPLETE WITH PHOTOGRAPH OF THE POOR MAN IN DESPAIR SITTING ON THE STEPS OF HIS HOUSE ALL DRESSED UP IN TOP HAT AND TAILS BUT WITH NOWHERE TO GO. THE 'MOVING HUMAN STORY' LED TO SEVERAL 'OFFERS' FROM LOCAL LADIES NEEDING AN ESCORT TO THE DANCE.

Question 140: Assess and compare the effectiveness of the following channels:

- (*a*) a company's newspaper advertisement
- (*b*) the huge sign on the wall of its factory
- (*c*) the labels on the packaging of its products
- (*d*) its direct-mail promotional literature
- (*e*) its 'open day' demonstrations.

15.2 ECONOMICS AND ADVERTISING

Advertising is commonly most extensive in industries which are oligopolies, that is which are dominated by a small number of suppliers. A heavily-promoted brand may be perceived by consumers to be so different from others as to confer virtual monopoly power upon its producer. In an oligopoly situation, the firms in the market may be reluctant to reduce advertising for fear of losing ground to competitors, and may additionally be tempted to increase advertising to gain a competitive edge. A ratchet effect comes into operation. Advertising tends to drift upwards and is rarely reduced, if at all. This can lead to high advertising expenditures that cancel each other out. In the tobacco and washing powder industries, this effect with an oligopolistic market may have led to an even stronger dominance by a small number of companies.

Advertising tends also to be high in certain industries where it is not easy for consumers to evaluate the relative advantages of products. This is true of much medical and pharmaceutical advertising.

Advertising informs the public about existing and new products: a market thrives on information and this role is very important. An advertiser needs to be aware, however, of the most frequently made criticisms of advertising. Many academics feel that advertising artificially stimulates demand, the process of 'want creation', and fails to give consumers sufficient information to really make an informed choice between products.

Few believe that advertising lowers costs, although by increasing sales and allowing longer production runs advertising can reduce unit costs. Very few people indeed link advertising with employment or with support of the media. Commercial television, for example, has advertising as its lifeblood.

Those disapproving of advertising consider it pushes prices up. It is thought to be misleading, unnecessary, a waste of time, repetitive, and boring if not deceptive, luring the unwary consumer into purchasing goods and services they do not really want. One common school of thought is that if a product really is good it should not need to be advertised. There is some evidence that advertising which is thought to be excessive can bring all advertising into disrepute.

Advertising, it could be argued, encourages innovation by reducing the risk of introducing new products. Such a hypothesis is difficult to prove. Even with frequently-high advertising backup, the majority of new products fail. The Edsel failed even when promoted by Ford, one of the motor industry giants. Many industries such as tobacco that have historically high rates of advertising expenditure do not appear outstandingly above average in terms of innovation.

The argument that advertising subsidizes the media is a dubious one. If newspapers would be prohibitively expensive in the absence of advertising, one could argue that the consuming public at large is subsidizing readers of newspapers, people who would not continue their habit of newspaper reading if faced with the true economic cost. Advertising might well result in a significant transfer of resources and benefits from some sections of society to others.

MEDICAL PRACTITIONERS HAVE TRADITIONALLY BEEN INUNDATED WITH DIRECT MAIL SHOT AND ADVERTISING PROMOTION

OF DRUGS. THERE HAS BEEN MUCH CRITICISM OF THE WHOLE QUESTION OF DRUG PROMOTION AND PRICING. DRUG COMPANIES ARGUE THAT HIGH PRICES ARE NEEDED IN ORDER THAT COM-MERCIALIZED DRUGS CAN PAY FOR THE MASSIVE RESEARCH AND DEVELOPMENT EXPENDITURE BEING IN THE INDUSTRY INVOLVES. NEVERTHELESS, THE PROMOTION WHICH WAS THOUGHT TO BE 'EXCESSIVE' LED THE GOVERNMENT TO CALL FOR AN ENQUIRY INTO THE ECONOMICS OF THE INDUSTRY.

15.3 HOW ADVERTISING WORKS

There has been a long debate about how advertising works, whether it actually converts or primarily reinforces existing attitudes. Advertising can have a variety of influences, supplying information, reminding consumers of past sources of satis-faction and affecting attitudes. It also can call for varying responses from target groups. A direct response in the form of purchasing behaviour might be required, or telephone number given and coupons provided for clipping, the required response being the seeking of further information.

Whether or not advertisement aims at a direct response or the seeking of further information, will depend very much upon the media used and the target group. Some advertising aims directly at a need, hoping that target groups will identify with some condition portrayed and welcome the suggestion given as to how this might be dealt with. Such advertising can link a product to a particular occasion — for example, after-dinner mints or a bedtime drink. One disadvantage of this approach is that the products in question may no longer be consumed on other occasions.

Where repeat consumption is required, an advertisement can be used to jog memories about past consumption. In competitive consumer fields when a variety of similar goods are available, advertising can encourage consumers to stick with existing brands rather than to switch. Success then results not from conversions but from the prevention of conversions taking place.

Given the uncertainty regarding how and why advertising works, various members of an advertising department are likely to develop their own 'pet' theories. This can lead to disagreement and conflict. At times, a manager may be faced with the problem of having to resolve a disagreement without being able to fully understand the arguments deployed by the protagonists.

Judgements will inevitably differ over many aspects of advertising even within a small team. One member of the creative staff may swear blind that the best advertisement for a new piece of office equipment is one that shows a shapely and scantily clad girl standing next to it, while another may feel that such an advertise-ment communicates the girl only and is likely to be less effective in putting across the merits of the particular machine that an advertisement without the girl, featur-ing a blown-up diagram of the equipment.

A TELEVISION SAFE DRIVING CAMPAIGN HAD BEEN BASED PRIMARILY UPON THE USE OF CARTOON CHARACTERS. AUDIENCE TESTS REVEALED THAT THE CARTOONS WERE VIEWED AS 'CUTE' AND AS ENTERTAINING BUT THAT THEY DID NOT MOTIVATE VIEWERS TO TAKE ACTION ON SUCH QUESTIONS AS THE PURCHASE OF SEAT BELTS.

A MORE DRAMATIC APPROACH WAS CALLED FOR: A NEW CAM-PAIGN WAS LAUNCHED PORTRAYING PEOPLE WITH HORRIBLE WOUNDS WHO HAD BEEN CRIPPLED BY ACCIDENTS, AND INCOR-PORATING SLOW-MOTION FOOTAGE OF BODIES CRASHING THROUGH WINDSCREENS, IN ORDER TO SHOCK THE PUBLIC INTO ACTION.

Question 141:   Contrast and compare the ways in which the following advertisements 'work':

  (*a*)   a notice of an increase in social security benefits
  (*b*)   a dashing young man scaling a one-thousand foot cliff in order to take a box of chocolates to the one he loves
  (*c*)   a group of apes taking tea
  (*d*)   a party political broadcast
  (*e*)   a statement of how a particular company is at the boundaries of technology in most that it does.

15.31   Signs and Meaning

An advertisement is a set of symbols and signs. Signs can take verbal and non-verbal forms. Meaning tends to be subjective and is the responses and attitudes which are consciously and subconsciously aroused in reaction to a sign. To a large degree meaning is learned. Thus, one's attitudes and responses will be shaped by the context and environment within which one has grown up. Individuals can be socialized into certain roles.

The association of words with certain objects gives rise to sign—object relationships or denotative meaning. Other words are more personal and subjective, for example 'good' and 'bad'. While denotative meaning tends to be relatively objective due to widespread agreement, a connotative meaning or the relationship between a sign, an object, and a person can cause more problems in communication due to the possibility of a variety of interpretations.

A particular sequence of signs such as a group of words can give rise to structural meaning, the relationship between a sign and other signs. A sign may mean different things according to the context in which it is used. There is a further form of meaning, contextual meaning.

When measuring the effectiveness of communication, it should be remembered that people can generally recognize more easily than they can recall. Thus a questionnaire can test recall whereas the impact of point-of-sale displays will depend upon recognition.

Question 142: Explain why the same sign could mean different things to different people, and explore the implications of this for marketors.

15.32 Learning

When responses to a stimulus change over time, or behaviour is modified as a consequenc, of external factors in ways which are not due to innate reflexive reactions derived from basic human needs such as food and shelter or the avoidance of danger, then learning can be said to have occurred. Certain media will be consciously instructive in that their express purpose will be to encourage learning.

A periodical that is designed to spread the results of research between the members of a certain field would be considered a learned journal. The purpose of a trade journal or a professional magazine may be to update practitioners about what is happening in a certain field. To some extent, consumers of news media and the purchasers of hobby or interest magazines will have learning as well as entertainment and relaxation objectives.

Learning can be instrumental and conditioned. Instrumental learning occurs when a person receives a reward for what is perceived as a correct or desired response. Acceptable responses can be reinforced over a period of time. Sanctions may be applied in the case of incorrect or undesired responses. Conditioned learning occurs when one stimulus comes to be associated with another. Thus the motorist becomes conditioned to act in a certain way when confronted by a red light.

Behaviour can be reinforced and instrumental learning encouraged by a marketing department. The purchaser of a new camera may be automatically sent a letter containing an invitation to join a camera club and a voucher offering a discount on future purchases of attachments offered by the company. Thus brand loyalty can be encouraged. Friendly service can act as a reward and via instrumental learning can lead to repeat purchases.

Associative learning can be achieved by means of symbols and images. Thus, advertisements of Martini feature attractive young people enjoying themselves in exotic surroundings in the hope that potential customers will identify and seek to associate with what is perceived as an attractive lifestyle. Advertisements aimed at potential recruits to the armed forces featured the desirable aspects of service life such as the opportunities that were presented to travel abroad.

Learning tends to be faster in certain situations than in others. Necessity is the mother of invention. When a need is strong and time is short, rapid learning can occur. The more frequently a reward is given, the more quickly will learning occur. Messages should be repeated. When the reward is automatic, learning occurs the quickest.

A greater reward is more effective than a lesser reward. Thus, the product which offers extra benefits, provides additional features, will tend to be the more successful.

IN THE SUMMER OF 1981 FOLLOWING HEAVY PRESS REPORTING OF THE PLANNED DISPOSAL OF A NUMBER OF ELDERLY SHIPS THE ROYAL NAVY (OFFICER ENTRY SECTION) ISSUED A FULL PAGE FACTUAL ADVERTISEMENT IN THE QUALITY NATIONAL SUNDAY PRESS. HEADED 'ROYAL NAVY CUTS. AFTER THE BALLYHOO, ARE YOU READY FOR THE FACTS?' THE ADVERTISEMENT POINTED OUT THAT THE SHIPS TO BE DISPOSED OF 'MAINLY FIFTEEN TO TWENTY YEAR OLD FRIGATES' WERE TO BE REPLACED BY 'NEW, HIGHLY COST-EFFECTIVE WARSHIPS'. THE ADVERTISEMENT POINTED OUT THE SIGNIFICANT ROLE THE NEW NAVY WOULD PLAY AND THE CAREER CHALLENGES IT OFFERED OFFICERS.

The less the delay between stimulus and reward, the smaller the effort required to achieve the 'correct' response, the earlier in a sequence or the closer to the end of a sequence a stimulus occurs, the fewer people that are involved and the fewer competing stimuli that are present, the more rapidly will learning occur. A stimulus that is familiar will be more effective than one which is unfamiliar. Imitation can therefore be an attractive marketing strategy for a new entrant.

The professional educator is aware of the value of involvement and participation in the learning process. Learning can be speeded up by trial offers, test drives, and sending out products on approval. The educator is also skilled at breaking down complex messages into components or units which are easier to group. Some preliminary work may have to be done with building blocks. A marketor cannot spend too long preparing the ground, and people are less willing to accept messages they do not perceive as relevant.

Question 143:   Draw up a list of advertisements taken from the media and distinguish between those that rely upon instrumental learning and those that rely upon conditioned learning.

15.33   Advertising and Learning

An effective advertising message is that which builds upon and reinforces prior learning experience. An advertising campaign should aim to be cumulative. As some groups will be more interested and motivated than others and able to learn more quickly, advertisements should be tailored to the specific target groups at which they are directed. Once a message has been learned it can be kept 'alive' by much less frequent periodic reinforcement.

A message should be couched in terms that are understood. Learning is quicker where there is understanding and also where there is interest. Demonstration and repetition can assist the learning of technical points. Attention is likely to be highest at the beginning and at the end of a message. An effective advertisement stands out from other advertisements and clearly presents rewards.

The returns from varying a message as opposed to straight repetition are often not cost-effective. Over a long period of time however a message may bore and diminishing returns can set in, so some variation may be necessary. Repetition itself will not succeed if benefits or rewards are not perceived and accepted.

Emotional involvement can assist learning. In advertising, a message based upon a strong emotional appeal can be very effective.

The most rapid loss of what has been learned occurs soon after the subject has been exposed to a stimulus. Thus, promotional activity should be highest when a brand is first launched. Initially, it may be desirable to plan a burst and integrated campaign of advertisement and public-relations activity, couponing, point-of-sale display and special events in order to encourage an early use of the product. Once the habit of purchase has been acquired, a much less intensive and lower-key reminder promotion programme can be introduced.

In the case of brands of equal strength in the marketplace, because of ensuing effects the older brand will probably, other things being equal, require less promotional effort to maintain a market share than the newer brand. The longer a purchase habit has been established, the less likely it will be to stop.

Question 144:   Assess the relative value of different approaches to the encouragement of learning in respect of the promotion of:

- (*a*)   a new type of apple
- (*b*)   a cassette recorder
- (*c*)   axle grease.

15.4   ADVERTISING OBJECTIVES

Goals, objectives should be set for advertising as for other areas of management activity. Advertising is a form of communication, and can be assessed by communications criteria such as awarness, comprehension, agreement, and action. Recall and retention rates are clearly important, but the crucial factor is the extent to which these lead to increased sales.

Advertising, as was pointed out in Chapter 14, complements other activities and cannot be judged in isolation from these. Effective advertising can increase sales-force productivity, and advertising expenditure can be regarded as an alternative to some extent to salesmen's salaries.

The objectives of advertising could be to create awareness, build preferences, differentiate, encourage purchase now rather than later, consolidate an existing reputation, encourage a response or request for further information, correct misleading claims of others, build up morale within the organization, transmit information, or to encourage understanding.

Advertising can be aimed at creating awareness, understanding, conviction, or action or at a number of stages simultaneously. When aimed at more than one stage, then multiple effectiveness criteria may be necessary.

An advertisement can be aimed at changing an existing attitude or prejudice. The impact of such a campaign can be quite long-term and this form of advertising tends to be carried out by large long-established companies that are aiming to increase the total market for a product.

Advertising designed to reinforce existing attitudes may be particularly crucial at a time when existing patterns of consumption are under threat due perhaps to innovation and the introduction of new products. Such advertising is frequently carried out by brand leaders eager to hang on to existing market shares. Most consumers will know what soup is or cigarettes, or chocolates, or a Polo mint, but manufacturers of such products may need to reinforce attitudes or risk loss of market share. Loyalty may be the key to long-term success in competitive consumer markets.

A MAJOR INTERNATIONAL OIL COMPANY BOOKED A SERIES OF WHOLE PAGE ADVERTISEMENTS IN THE UK 'QUALITY' NEWS-PAPERS. EACH ADVERTISEMENT WAS DEVOTED TO THE PRESENTATION OF BACKGROUND FACTS RELATING TO SOME ASPECT OF THE 'OIL CRISIS'. THE FINAL ADVERTISEMENT IN THE SERIES WAS DEVOTED TO THE COMPANY'S WORK IN THE DEVELOP-MENT OF NEW SOURCES OF ENERGY.

Question 145:   State what you imagine the purposes of the following advertisements to be:

    (*a*)   a poster explaining the facilities at a local tennis club which already has a long waiting list for membership

    (*b*)   a full-page advertisement in a popular newspaper setting out the case of a group of major employers in an industrial dispute

    (*c*)   an advertisement in a trade magazine showing off the impressive offices a professional firm has newly acquired

    (*d*)   a product's name painted on a fence on the edge of the field at the ground of Manchester United Football Club

    (*e*)   a sailor eating fish fingers surrounded by cheering children.

15.5 A G E N C I E S

Few major organizations design their own advertisements. Most rely upon the services of an agency. The services provided by agencies normally include message development, advertising copy writing, advertisement design, and make-up to artwork stage and media scheduling.

On being told how much a client is prepared to pay, an agency will develop a media schedule giving details of which media should be used and why, how many insertions of what length should be made and so forth. In the case of a major campaign, an agency is likely to draw up a proposal which will set out campaign objectives and show how these can be furthered by sending certain messages along selected channels to priority identified target groups. A breakdown of the budget may also be given showing how much is spent on creative development and on buying space and air time.

A proposal should include benchmarks — points at which effectiveness can be assessed so that a campaign can be modified if need be. The second or subsequent stage of a campaign might depend upon the satisfactory completion of an earlier stage.

A good agency is particularly valuable as a source of suggestions on which media should be used. Many agencies present their clients with media 'shopping lists' ranking channels in order of priority and giving the cost of each, together with the cumulative cost thus far. The client can then establish a cut-off point.

The natural uncertainty of the advertising world, the lack of fixed points of reference in a changing landscape, can cause problems for those with a low tolerance for ambiguity. Within an organization, suitable creative staff may be difficult to find. Creative talent can congregate in a good agency.

An agency will be remunerated by a mixture of fee and commission on advertisement placed. The media offer a commission to those placing advertisements with them. In many cases, an agency will be remunerated entirely by commission; in other cases a campaign budget might include a management fee.

AN AGENCY WAS DELIGHTED TO FIND ONE OF ITS TELEVISION ADVERTISEMENTS WINNING A PRIZE AT A LEADING FILM FESTIVAL. THE RESULTING PLAQUE WAS GIVEN PRIDE OF PLACE IN THE COMPANY'S BOARDROOM. A FEW MONTHS LATER THE CLIENT INFORMED THE AGENCY THAT THE COMMERCIAL WAS TO BE DROPPED AS IT WAS NOT THOUGHT TO BE COST-EFFECTIVE.

15.51   Agency Selection

An agency should be selected upon the basis of its ability to generate creative and cost-effective solutions to an organization's communications problems. To a company of standing and reputation, technical excellence, responsibility and an understanding of its image will be important.

A selected advertising agency should possess a realistic, and satisfactory understanding of a company's business, its problems, strengths, and weaknesses. The agency should know the qualities of the key people within the organization with whom it will be working.

The agency should preferably have experience of similar types of work. Sympathy and understanding is important along with an ability to work with what is, rather than with what ought to be.

A company should beware of an agency that seeks to sell it a package. No two businesses are alike. An 'off-the-shelf' approach may be evidence of a reluctance to get down to detail, and of an intention to 'milk' an account by servicing it with a package, the development cost of which has already been recovered.

Unlike a relationship between a company and its auditors, stockbrokers, or legal advisers, those with agencies change more frequently. Agency staff change as creative groups break away to establish new 'shops'. Movement up and down the rankings of the top fifty or a hundred agencies can be rapid. Outstanding creative success is difficult to repeat and sustain. A company moving into new areas may seek new agencies with more relevant expertise. An 'out of town' company based say in Birmingham or Manchester might move an account from a London to a local regional agency.

Those working on a creative account can, after a time, become stale. The larger consumer accounts tend over a period of time to appear to be shuffled rather like a pack of cards between agencies in search of new insights, new inspiration. The agency world itself thrives on the movement of accounts. So long as business changes hands, there are opprotunities for new 'shops' to acquire accounts.

Advertising can, on the creative side, be an intense business. There are, in many agencies, relatively few 'managerial' positions, so those who 'burn out' creatively must move into new fields. Thus high salaries often need to be earned by the young while a track record should be viewed with caution.

From time to time, a number of agencies may be asked to 'pitch' for an existing or a new account. In such circumstances, the company buying agency services should think carefully about what it is seeking, the relative weight to be put on creativity, management, or production expertise. The 'young' agency may have the enthusiasm, the larger established agency the back-up in such areas as a research department.

Selecting a new agency may be something of a gamble, but it should be borne in mind that while a 'big name' agency will have a reputation to keep, the newer agency staff will be working hard to establish one. A final decision might come down to the question of compatibility with the individuals performing the work and sensitivity to what one is trying to achieve.

A check should be made concerning which agency staff will actually handle an account. An agency may display a number of awards in its foyer but the creative work that led to them might have been performed by staff who have left the company or who are to be working on other accounts.

In the negotiation of terms, it may be found that one agency is in greater need of work than another. An arrangement if it is to work must be to the benefit of both parties. On occasions it may be worthwhile to pay a little more to achieve creative solutions that are in tune with what one is trying to achieve.

An established company and an existing brand may both have a widely recog-·nized image. Certain aspects of such an image might be regarded as satisfactory. Caution should be exercised in dealing with a prospective agency partner unwilling to work within the constraints of an existing image. An alternative creative solution or advertising concept might be superior from an aesthetic and a technical point of view but there are advantages in building cumulatively upon an existing reputation. This is not to say that an organization should not be open-minded about alternative approaches. Ultimately, for the company the objective is to sell, not to win creative awards.

Work needs not only to be done, but within the time available. Massive back-up resources and extensive technical expertise are of little value if they cannot be swiftly and with precision brought to bear upon a problem in hand.

Question 146: Explain what weight you would attach to the following circumstances in an agency selection situation:

(*a*)   a legal action has resulted from the publication of a technically outstanding advertisement designed by agency A

(*b*)   it is rumoured that two directors of agency B are about to leave to set up their own agency

(*c*)   a newspaper strike is supposed to be severely affecting the fortunes of agency C which was hitherto one of the fastest-growing agencies in the business

(*d*)   agency D has existed for three generations

(*e*)   agency E is reputed to pay the highest salaries of any agency.

15.52   Managing Agency Relationships

When managing a client—agency relationship, a company manager needs to make a frank assessment of work done and who on the ground handles particular accounts. An agency may be strong in one area and weak in another. One prize certificate on a wall does not mean that all an agency's designers are creative.

Often in practice with non-specialist staff unsure of their creative judgement the nature of the product combined with the sizes of the advertising budget will largely decide media selection. Where remuneration depends in part upon commission income, an agency is likely to advocate spending more rather than less.

Because an agency is likely to obtain a significant proportion of its remuneration in the form of commission from the media in which it plans advertisements on behalf of its clients, it is likely to be tempted to place advertisements so as to maximize commission income while minimizing costs. Thus, while a company may prefer a media selection package that is extensive and tailored to a number of defined publics via small circulation media, an agency might prefer to deal with a single broadcast media offering a substantially higher commission. The more obscure and the more specialized media, particularly those not so experienced at dealing with agencies, can find it extremely difficult to obtain a place on media schedules.

Agencies have traditionally booked space or time, acting as a principle in law and have taken a commission of about 15% from the media concerned. Today, following an Office of Fair Trading view that a standard 15% commission represents a restrictive practice, there is greater competition among agencies. With fee and/or commission arrangements offering below the equivalent of 15% an agency may have to offer less than the full range of services especially to clients with smaller budgets.

Other things being equal, the more profitable work on a media commission basis is, from an agency viewpoint, that with one advertisement in one media as compared with campaigns that require, say, tailored advertisements in a great many different magazines. To reduce cross-subsidization there has been greater use of cost-plus arrangements with percentage mark-ups on charges sent in by suppliers and on staff time as allocated by time sheet, the client in effect being charged for measurable work done.

The dependency of an agency upon media commission income can result, in a national economic recession, in an agency facing a severe cash flow squeeze. Ultimately, the client pays the media bills and when business as a whole cuts back on its advertisement expenditure, both the media and agencies find that while their overhead costs, in the case of an agency relatively expensive staff costs, remain fixed, their income may fall significantly. In such circumstances, a client might find an agency seeking alternative methods of remuneration, the result being a squeeze upon an already-diminished advertising budget.

In some agencies, frequency of insertion is a criterion rather than frequency of exposure. An agency may exhibit a bias towards certain media and may not fully appreciate, or may pretend not to appreciate, the extent to which advertising can be traded off against other forms of marketing expenditure.

A LEADING INTERNATIONAL AGENCY TOOK ON A NEW CLIENT. AN EXISTING CLIENT IN ANOTHER TERRITORY CONTACTED THE AGENCY HEAD OFFICE AND STATED THAT IT OBJECTED TO THE AGENCY HANDLING ANOTHER ACCOUNT IN THE SAME BUSINESS. THE LONG-ESTABLISHED CLIENT ARGUED THAT, IN PRINCIPLE, AN AGENCY SHOULD NOT HANDLE MORE THAN ONE ACCOUNT IN THE SAME BUSINESS AND, BESIDES IT WAS LARGER THAN THE NEW CLIENT. THE AGENCY 'DROPPED' THE LONG-ESTABLISHED CLIENT.

15.6   ADVERTISING   RESEARCH

The cost of major advertising campaigns is such that advertising decisions need to be systematic. A number of techniques have emerged which attempt to quantify variables and to attach probabilities to outcomes that are uncertain. The use of such techniques can help to narrow the range of expected outcomes and hence reduce risk.

Advertising research can aim at measuring the impact of advertising upon attitudes and knowledge as with communication-effect research or the impact upon sales as with sales-effect research. Which technique is used and the likely effectiveness of measurement will vary from business to business. Some operations such as direct-mail marketing are particularly suited to effectiveness measurement.

The influence of the creativity of advertising is difficult to measure. Quality is statistically more difficult than quantity to handle. Where there are significant differences between the advertising creativity of companies in a market, a model that does not cope with quality may well produce a significant 'unexplained' residual component.

Question 147:   Assess the relative ease with which it is likely that advertising effectiveness research could be used in respect of the following products:

- (*a*)   airport radar installations
- (*b*)   direct mail garden tools
- (*c*)   milk
- (*d*)   a video-recorder.

Effectiveness measurement is easier where goals are specific, such as the creation of an x% preference for product y among a defined category and number of customers within a given period. Precise objectives such as the establishment of quantified minimum levels of performance can allow variance reports to highlight programmes that require management action.

15.61   Measuring Cognitive Effects

Communication-effect tests can measure recall and/or comprehension. A consumer jury or panel may be used. The design of tests and the validity of test results will depend upon the extent to which recall is in fact a measure of advertising effectiveness. Story-board tests and laboratory tests such as psychogalvanometer, eye camera, or tachistoscope tests can be used but may have doubtful validity due to the artificiality of a laboratory setting. The cost of comprehension measurement tests such as individual interviews and group discussions tends to be high, and relatively small samples tend to be used with consequent effects upon validity.

Measuring communication effectiveness requires the comparison of post-advertising or post-test findings with pre-advertising or pre-test findings. Opinion research asks subjects to state their opinions. Individual subjects or groups of subjects can be questioned. A cross-section sample or panel may be assembled for use with repeated tests. This can reduce the costs of sample selection, but a learning and familiarization effect can introduce sources of bias.

The measurement of attention-getting, and the length of an impact or retention can be measured by means of memory tests. A sample may be repeatedly questioned over intervals of time about aspects of a message they are able to recall. Simple recognition testing can be achieved using actual media and asking subjects which media they have encountered before. A random sample of subjects can be important in such testing in order to minimize systematic bias.

Recall tests can be aided and unaided. In the aided tests, advertisements are named while in the open-ended unaided tests, subjects are asked without prompting to name and describe advertisements they remember. Such tests can allow companies to compare responses to their own advertisements with those of competitors.

Within laboratory settings, psychological and physiological reactions to media stimuli can be tested. A question must remain in such cases of the extent to which the laboratory context, compared to the contexts in which subjects are normally exposed to stimuli, distorts findings.

Question 148:   Assess the relative value of various cognitive effect tests in relation to typical advertisements for the following types of products:

- (a)   ice-cream
- (b)   diesel trucks
- (c)   caravans
- (d)   toys
- (e)   cigars.

A problem with many testing techniques is the *ceteris paribus* or other things being equal assumption. Subjects can be exposed to relevant influences other than the advertisement stimulus in question such as habit, the impact of price and product changes, and word of mouth influences.

Caution is particularly needed when measuring the direct effect of advertising upon sales. The sales-effect approach is of greater value when advertising is the dominant element of the promotion mix and other elements are relatively constant. Where other elements and factors are also changing, then sophisticated multivariate statistical analysis may be necessary. The carry-over effects of previous promotional efforts also needs to be taken into account. Some allowance may need to be made for the fact that some promotional elements will have a quicker and more measurable impact upon sales levels than others.

Experimental data can be less subject to non-model influences than historical data. With historical data, a great many influences may have accounted for observed changes independent of the changes being assessed.

The ideal test compares two randomly selected groups: an experimental group and a control group. A sample population is randomly selected and tested. Members of the sample group are then randomly allocated between the experimental and control groups. The experimental group receives the stimulus, the effectiveness of which is being tested while the other group does not. Thus, theoretically, the only difference between the two groups is that which is being tested. Both groups are then given a post-test and the outcomes compared. Such a research design is relatively high in reliability and validity, but even so there is the possibility of a Hawthorne effect in that the circumstances in which one group is exposed to a stimulus while the other group is consciously denied the stimulus could itself introduce a source of bias.

Prior to devising a message, one needs to understand the state of a buying group's mind in order to identify those appeals which are likely to be the most persuasive. Chapter 20 on market research examines techniques that can be used to determine rewards that potential buyers might be seeking to satisfy. Some rewards will be rational and related to the tasks the product will perform while others may be sensory and social or related to the ego. Effective performance resources are those that relate to values and rewards which are important in the purchase decision.

15.62 Measurement

The measurement of intention and the prediction of purchase behaviour is particularly difficult. Certain techniques such as projective techniques including word association or thematic perception and depth interviewing can be used. Great skill, however, needs to be exercised in interpretation, as respondents frequently record responses they consider acceptable or likely to be sought after and consciously avoid responses they feel will be less desired or which may be taken to reflect adversely upon themselves. Samples of subjects in such tests should also be carefully chosen in order to ensure that, so far as is possible, they are representative of the wider target groups that are the object of study.

15.63 Sales-effect Measurement

Data on sales levels achieved at different levels of advertising can be used with the aid of standard computer packages to determine sales/advertising curves. A sales response and decay model may allow an optimum level of advertising to be determined. In some situations the sales/advertising curve may be S-shaped, a 'threshold' level of advertising being required to make an initial sales impact, while beyond a 'plateau' level, as the more promising targets have purchased, diminishing returns may set in.

A relatively sophisticated model must take account of different response rates at different levels and mixes of advertising, the existence in some cases of saturation levels beyond which expenditure leads to 'over-kill', while there will be delay effects of advertising that occurred in previous time periods to be accommodated.

A simple model could accommodate just two variables, price and advertising:

$$
\begin{array}{c}
\text{Change in} \\
\text{rate} \\
\text{of} \\
\text{sales}
\end{array}
=
\begin{array}{c}
\text{Sales} \\
\text{generated} \\
\text{per pound} \\
\text{spent}
\end{array}
\times
\begin{array}{c}
\text{Level} \\
\text{of} \\
\text{advertis-} \\
\text{ing}
\end{array}
\times
\frac{
\begin{array}{c}
\text{Saturation} \quad \text{Actual} \\
\text{level} \quad\; \text{—} \quad \text{level} \\
\text{of} \qquad\quad \text{of} \\
\text{sales} \qquad\;\; \text{sales}
\end{array}
}{
\begin{array}{c}
\text{Saturation} \\
\text{level of} \\
\text{sales}
\end{array}
}
-
\begin{array}{c}
\text{Sales decay} \\
\text{factor —} \\
\text{i.e.: rate} \\
\text{at which} \\
\text{sales fall} \\
\text{when} \\
\text{advertising} \\
\text{is zero}
\end{array}
\times
\begin{array}{c}
\text{Actual} \\
\text{level} \\
\text{of} \\
\text{sales}
\end{array}
$$

Such a model could be used to estimate the consequences of different levels of advertising to determine the minimum level of advertising necessary to hold an existing level of sales.

A more complex model could take account of brand loyalty among past customers, the level of competitor advertising effort and sales performance, overall market growth, and the relative importance of other marketing communication factors such as salesman effort and relative price changes.

The techniques a company uses must follow from the chosen model of the advertising process. Thus, intermediate variables will be included in a model that follows the communication process with estimates made of the level of awareness, the degree of understanding, and the relationship between message exposure and trial following the intermediate steps of awareness and understanding, a progressively smaller share of the original target group remaining as one progresses from stage to stage along the communication process. Assumptions need to be made and subsequently tested on such questions as the number of those who try to go on to purchase, and subsequently the level of repeat purchases.

The responsiveness of sales to advertising can be measured by spending more and less than average in a small number of typical markets in order to test whether perhaps in the subsequent period the average level of advertising should be raised to the higher or dropped to the lower figure. Such an approach allows a model to be continually adapted to changing market conditions.

The competitive element can be built into a model by means of game theory. Such an approach can be particularly valuable where it is felt that rival suppliers are neutralizing each other's efforts through wasteful competitive advertising.

In the long run, when products are similar and rival suppliers adopt a similar approach to advertising, a company's market share may tend towards its share of total advertising expenditure within the market.

Question 149: Assess aspects of sales-effect measurement which may be particularly difficult in respect of advertisements relating to the following subject areas:

(*a*)   classified job advertisement
(*b*)   corporate image advertisement
(*c*)   chocolate bar coupon advertisement
(*d*)   tableware advertisement
(*e*)   cigarette advertisement.

In the following example two companies A and B can each promote two products a_1 and a_2 and b_1 and b_2 respectively. If A advertises a_1 and B advertises b_1 then B will gain 5 sales and A will lose 5 sales. The game is zero sum in that the loss of A is the gain of B. If A advertises a_2 while B advertises b_1, then A's loss and B's gain will be limited to 3. The best outcome for A would be to promote a_2 while B promoted b_2 in which case B would lose 4 sales and A would gain 4. In the game (illustrated below) A has more to gain by promoting a_2 while B by promoting b_1 rather than b_2 will take less of a risk of loss and will impose a loss upon competitor A.

		A	
		a_1	a_2
B	b_1	5	3
	b_2	6	-4

This game is zero sum because it assumes that customers have only so much to spend and a purchase with one company will automatically mean the loss of a purchase by the other company. With a positive sum game both players might gain from certain strategies. Multi-player games with several parties can lead to quite involved matrices.

A brand-switching model can be expressed in the form of a matrix as below. There are three brands A, B and C and the table expresses proportions of the customers of each brand who repeat purchase in a subsequent time period, and the proportions for each brand which switch to each of the other brands. Each row adds up to 1.

Of those who bought brand A in the previous period, 80 per cent will continue to purchase while 15 per cent will buy B and 5 per cent C. B obtains three times as many of A's customers who switch than C, and hence represents a greater competitive threat. A obtains 20 per cent of the customers lost by B since the previous period, compared with only 10 per cent of those lost by C.

From	To		
	A	*B*	*C*
A	0.8	0.15	0.05
B	0.2	0.1	0.7
C	0.1	0.3	0.6

The matrix above presents both repeat-purchase and switching-in and switching-out rates and, given the use of techniques to handle matrix manipulation over various numbers of time periods, such data can yield sales and market-share forecasts where switching rates in certain time periods are changed to reflect advertising programmes.

15.64 Optimizing Media Models

The basis elements of media planning are advertising exposure, audience coverage or reach, penetration, frequency of exposure, and continuity. When building a model, judgement will be required to attach weights to the relative perceived values of different target populations. Weights may be attached to the appropriateness of media where such factors as prestige, association, or credibility are regarded as significant. Weighting could reflect editorial integrity, the presence of neutralizing or reinforcing advertisements, likely receptivity, probably exposure, or estimated perception.

Given the amount of judgement required and the assumptions that will need to be made to build a media model, it is desirable that media objectives are not crudely stated. Considerable thought should be given to the specification of precise objectives such as the optimization of the combination of reach and frequency in relation to stated brand objectives, and the nature of the advertisement itself. Separate response functions may need to be established for each brand.

Media models cannot be a substitute for the marketing judgement that is required to determine underlying relationships. Models can, however, because of their ability to allow the rapid handling of large amounts of data, enable the impact of alternative media mixes to be rapidly determined and thus allow more alternatives to be considered.

The highly-structured optimizing model aims to reduce available media data to a limited number of parameters and simplifying assumptions. This is the formula approach, the use of an alogorithm to produce 'best' results. The more detailed and sophisticated individual or tailored model may be more sensitive to a particular product market context but unable to present an optimal solution.

Simple differential calculus can be used to determine which combination of promotion mix inputs will maximize outputs. Then if sales (S) are related to price (P) and advertising (A) and coefficients are known, if a relationship can be expressed in such a form as:

$$S = a - bP^2 - cP + dA^2 + eA$$

where a, b, c, d and e are constants then an optimum price/advertising combination can be determined.

Linear programming is particularly suited to situations in which constraints are present and relationships are linear. In media selection, there are such obvious constraints as media availability and budget size. The determination of an optimum mix requires the specification of an effectiveness criterion such as the number of effective exposures to members of a defined target group. Thus, given the exposure value of different media and knowledge of media costs, the specification of a budget constraint would allow the optimum mix to be determined, i.e. the media mix that maximized exposures.

The linear programming approach has a number of drawbacks. Relationships that are important in advertisement-effectiveness measurement are not linear. Thus, repeat exposures do not have a constant marginal effect. Also costs are not necessarily linear in that space and time discounts may be available. Certain media will also result in audience duplication, while the timing of an advertisement can be crucial.

Linear programming is most suitable when limited resources are allocated to competing ends to achieve an objective such as exposure maximization. In the example below, the number of advertisements in medium a (x) times the unit cost 10 plus the total number of advertisements in medium b (y) times the unit cost of 15 must be less than or equal to the budget of £100. The maximum number of advertisements that can be placed in media a and b are 12 and 4 respectively, while the number of exposures for media a and b are 500 and 800 respectively.

It is assumed that the exposures of the two media a and b in regions 1 and 2 are 200, 300 and 600, 200 respectively. If at least 2,000 exposures must be achieved in each region, then the table of information provided and the formulation of the problem for solution by linear programming is as below:

Information

	Medium a	Medium b
Cost per unit	10	15
Maximum number of units	12	4
Total number of exposures per unit	500	800
Number of exposures in region 1	200	600
Number of exposures in region 2	300	200

Mathematical Statement of Problem

Maximize $500x + 800y$
Subject to: $10x + 15y \leqslant 100$ budget constraint
                   $x \qquad \leqslant 12$)
                   $y \leqslant 4$)   medium constraints
                   $200x + 600y \geqslant 2{,}000$)
                   $300x + 200y \geqslant 2{,}000$)   regional constraints

The problem of audience overlap can be handled by a sequential model. This determines the best initial media choice and then examines subsequent choices, taking account of audience overlap or duplication, and the availability of potential discounts. Subsequent options are compared with existing exposure and subsequent media added so long as in each case exposure is increased within the budget limit. Such sequential or iteration models are still imperfect in that they do not allow for timing or previous advertising.

All optimization models rely upon the media planner modifying reality to meet mathematical constraints.

Non-linear programming can be used where either some of the constraints or the effectiveness criterion, or both, are non-linear, but it cannot produce a standardized technique capable of application to a wide range of problems. Dynamic programming can be used where a series of consecutive interdependent decisions have to be made, and it attempts to allow for carry-over effects but usually with only a limited number of variables, and even big models cannot produce schedules with mixes of media.

15.65   Non-Optimizing Media Models

Simulation is of limited use in the determination of optimum media mixes, but can allow the rapid estimation of the number of exposures resulting from certain media plans. A simulation can store probabilities of the media choices of a large number of media users that collectively make up a fair cross-section of a target group, and when a particular schedule passes through the model, the number and type of user reached is accumulated to produce an audience profile. Subsequent runs can be attempted with changes in the mix made to determine whether or not and to what extent the audience profile could be improved. Simulation does not of itself determine the optimum schedule, and its value depends upon how representative of the target group the models users are.

Probability analysis attaches 'weights' between 0 and 1 to certain events occurring, the sum of the probabilities of all possible consequences being 1. Multiplication of probabilities by expected returns yields expected monetary values. In the example below, the expected monetary value (EMU) of the consequence of advertising expenditures of £1,000 and £2,000 are compared. The figures in brackets represent the probabilities of the three estimates of sales contribution occurring.

	Advertising level £	Sales contributions (i) £		(ii) £		(iii) £	
(a)	1,000	(0.2)	500	(0.5)	1,500	(0.3)	2,000
(b)	2,000	(0.4)	1,400	(0.4)	2,000	(0.2)	3,000

The expected monetary value (EMV) of outcomes (a) and (b) are calculated as follows:

$$\text{EMV } (a) \quad = 0.2 \times 500 + 0.5 \times 1{,}500 + 0.3 \times 2{,}000$$
$$= 100 + 750 + 600$$
$$= £1{,}450 \text{ or } £450 \text{ in excess of advertising cost.}$$

$$\text{EMV } (b) \quad = 0.4 \times 1{,}400 + 0.4 \times 2{,}000 + 0.2 \times 3{,}000$$
$$= 560 + 800 + 600$$
$$= £1{,}960 \text{ or } £50 \text{ less than the cost of advertising.}$$

The EMV comparison shows that while the higher level of advertising offers the prospect of a higher sales contribution, when probabilities are taken into account, a lower level of advertising would be more cost-effective. When there are a great many variables, some of which are probabilities while other relationships are taken as exact, simulation techniques can be used to test alternative strategies by allowing distribution curves showing the most likely outcomes to be compared.

The timing of advertisements should take into account leads and lags. Simulation can allow alternative timing strategies to be compared. Such a model can take account of seasonal influences upon demand. The key factors to be estimated in such a model are the carry-over effects at different levels of advertising and repeat purchasing behaviour.

Simulation models allow for a fuller and more realistic statement of a media problem than optimizing models, but they do not produce a 'best' schedule. Simulation models are essentially descriptive. The earliest simulation model attempted to identify major steps in the communication process and to assign numerical values to each of the stages. The outcome produced was a single number as the measure of the 'effectiveness' of a given media schedule. Other models simulate reach and frequency for an individual in a target population. Like optimizing models, they have difficulty in handling media discounts or carry-over effects.

Question 150: How important would lags and carry-over effects be in the case of advertisements for the following products?

    (*a*)   toilet rolls
    (*b*)   bread
    (*c*)   motor car
    (*d*)   summer holiday.

15.66   Scheduling Over Time

The timing of an advertisement or its scheduling can have a major influence upon its impact. An advertiser faces a macro-scheduling problem of deciding how to spread a total advertising budget across a year by month and a micro-scheduling problem of allocation of advertisements within months by day or even time of day.

When taking account of seasonal factors in macro-scheduling, the delayed effect of advertising must be borne in mind. Where lags can be specific between advertisement and awareness and sales, a simulation model could be used to examine alternative timing patterns. For a consumer product, the carry-over effect will need to be separated from the repeat purchase habit effect. A carry-over effect of 0.4 indicates that 40 per cent of the effect of the last or previous month's advertising will be felt in the current month or month being considered. A repeat purchase rate of 0.6 indicates that 60 per cent of purchasers will repeat their purchase of the product in question, independent of any external marketing stimulus. Normally, seasonal variations in advertising will precede expected variations in sales.

Given audience measurement data such as that provided by broadcast media, simple models can be used to compare exposures of different micro-schedules. When micro-scheduling in connection with the broadcast media, the advertiser will take account of what is known about different audiences for various programmes throughout the day. Choices remain to be made between individual messages transmitted at a regular frequency, or groups of messages that are concentrated in bursts with a rising or falling frequency.

A message that strongly motivates recipients may only need to be exposed once per target so an appropriate micro-schedule would aim to maximize reach with a relatively low level of repetition. If the objective is to create awareness and a learning effect, then a smaller target group might be selected and subjected to more frequent and reinforcing exposures. A company with a production constraint might use intermittent advertising in order to stimulate a relatively stable level of orders.

Over-repetition can not only be wasteful but can bore and alienate. Laboratory research on message retention can be used to establish the relation between repetition and learning in order to determine the most cost-effective level of repetition, and the most desirable length of time between reinforcement bursts. There is some evidence that retention increases initially with repetition, and that a burst of exposures that leads to quick learning can result in greater retention than is the case with intermittent advertising that results in slower learning. The existence of overlapping audiences complicates such researching findings.

Question 151:   Assess the importance of seasonal factors in respect of measurement of the effectiveness of advertisements for the following products:

  (*a*)   fireworks
  (*b*)   Wellington boots
  (*c*)   fashion clothes
  (*d*)   pastries
  (*e*)   convenience foods.

EXAMINATION QUESTIONS

1. To what extent can companies' attempts to discriminate between real or imagined market segments be reflected in cost-effective media choices?

2. Why do you think manufacturers of:

  (*a*)   cosmetics
  (*b*)   razor blades
  (*c*)   baby powder
  (*d*)   records

continue to advertise on television in the evenings, when they are interested in reaching only minority groups within the total audience?

3. Ignoring seasonal factors, how would you try to demonstrate the value of one pattern of advertising expenditure as against another for an established product in an established market?

4. Say to what extent you would wish to minimize the size of the organizational gap between the advertising decision-makers in a company and the creative staff in its advertising agency and why.

16. *Media*

Chapter 15 introduced the communication and economic functions of advertising and the work of advertising agencies. A company's agency will be an expert adviser on media. Advertisements are carried by the media; without the media there would be very limited opportunity to advertise. The advertising business can be conceived of as a tripartite relationship between clients, agencies, and media.

This chapter introduces the major media. In many cases, advertisements will be the major source of a media's income. A medium may go out of its way to attract advertising and a major purpose of editorial and programming plans and viewer building, circulation and readership development plans will be to increase the attractiveness of a medium to potential advertisers.

A medium itself will be involved in extensive relationships with agencies. The agency world could be a medium's major public, and a mix of promotional devices will be used to encourage agencies to place advertisements with the medium in question rather than with competing media.

16.1 MASS COMMUNICATION

Compared with interpersonal communication, mass communication is indirect, impersonal, and does not allow immediate feedback. The sender of a message and the recipient will be removed from each other by time (in the case of a film screened in a cinema) or by space (in the case of a television announcer and a 'live' programme). The message will be directed at a group of people rather than at a particular individual.

Mass communication tends to be one-way communication. Although the 'phone-in' programme does allow a relatively quick response from a listener or viewer, the feedback is not immediate. There is a time-lag which means that the communicator delivering a message is not able to adjust it to the situation while it is being presented.

The main difference between interpersonal and mass communication is the technical method of transmission, the physical properties of the channel whether the printed page or the electronic signal. The audience can be involved with mass communication as with interpersonal communication in an emotional sense.

IT IS ESTIMATED THAT ON THE 29TH JULY 1981 SOME 700 MILLION TELEVISION VIEWERS WORLDWIDE WATCHED LIVE COVERAGE OF THE WEDDING IN ST. PAUL'S CATHEDRAL OF HRH THE PRINCE OF WALES AND LADY DIANA SPENCER.

16.2 MEDIA CHARACTERISTICS

Media are channels of communication. Different media will have relative strengths and weaknesses in respect of particular messages. Thus, the broadcast or oral media tend to be more effective than the print media at putting simple messages across to the less educated and less intelligent. Access can be achieved more quickly with the broadcast media, which tend to have priority in crisis communication.

Print media tend to be more effective when a complex message has to be put to audiences of varying abilities and knowledge. Print media can be more selective: print messages are relatively easy to store, can be accessed relatively easily without expense and cumbersome equipment, and can be read at a speed acceptable to the reader. While audio-visual storage and playback facilities are becoming available to more people, and cable and satellite broadcasting can greatly increase channel choice, the print medium is likely to remain an effective competitor for some time.

Broadcast media can reach and assemble vast audiences. At certain times of the week, close to entire populations may be reached. Broadcast media also appear as realistic. Film perhaps the most realistic of the visual media in view of the relatively high quality of the photographic as compared with the electronic image, is subject to a variety of conventions which result in the portrayal of a particular, and approaching a universal view, of reality. Print media are to a much greater extent symbolic.

Media have a number of characteristics in common. Each will have a particular status and credibility. Audience attention in most cases will be self-selective: people to a degree choose what television channels to watch or what newspapers to read, although there will be some habitual viewers of whatever is on a television or whatever magazine is to hand.

There will be considerable variation in the credibility of individual media and in the extent of media choice. In some areas, a particular medium may not be available; in others there may be only one television channel. A distinction may be made between official and unofficial media. Certain media may be banned: media expressing a particular viewpoint, for example an opposition newspaper, may be closed down.

To a large extent, the media reinforce rather than change attitudes. Inter-personal communication tends to be more persuasive than mass communication. In the case of a complex product the mass media may never provide an alternative to the salesman's visit and the trial demonstration.

Question 152: Imagine your region has been devastated by a climatic disaster. The Government wishes to communicate information to those resident in the area on what to do. Assess the relative merits of and possible uses of the following media:

(*a*)   radio broadcasts
(*b*)   sirens
(*c*)   television cards
(*d*)   loudspeaker vans
(*e*)   policeman door-to-door calls.

16.3   PRINT MEDIA

Print media can be read at various times and in various places. A reader can jump from one point of interest to another and skip columns of text that are not rele-vant. The reader can be highly selective of what is read and of what is stored. With print media a reader is given the greatest opportunity to pursue a topic at the speed and to the depth an individual may desire, and such an enquiry can usually be pursued in isolation, without involving or interfering with other readers. In con-trast with the broadcast media, the recipient must either reject or accept a particu-lar package that is offered. When there is only one television set the whole family is often forced to watch the same programme, usually with varying degrees of enthusiasm.

Complex material can be presented diagrammatically in print and considered at leisure. Print can be tailored to the individual requirements of a single recipient or a small group of recipients, as with a memorandum or photo-copied report. Print can be re-examined as often as required without the need for playback equipment. Because of the existence of a relatively developed book library system, material that is out of print can usually be traced. Unlike audio-visual media, in the case of print media there is a developed international copyright system. Copies of all books published should be deposited with copyright libraries.

The specialist nature of certain print media and their ability to reach select audiences has resulted in certain publications, for example the leading academic and current affairs journals, having great prestige. In public-relations work, the print media are of particular value in enabling messages to be tailored to quite specific publics.

DURING THE FIRST WORLD WAR, ON OCCASIONS, MAJOR BELLIGERENTS ON EACH SIDE OF THE CONFLICT, DROPPED, INSTEAD OF BOMBS, PRINTED BULLETINS CARRYING A 'MESSAGE' BEHIND THE ENEMY LINES. THIS WAS A LITERAL EXAMPLE OF THE PEN BEING MIGHTIER THAN THE 'SWORD'.

16.31 Newspapers

Newspapers are a varied media. There are quality and popular papers, morning and evening papers, daily, weekly and Sunday papers, broadsheet and tabloid papers, national, regional and local papers, subscription, and giveaway or controlled circulation and free distribution papers. Overall, newspaper readership is high and, while spread across all groups in society, tends to be particularly high at the upper socio-economic level.

The development of the local press has meant that newspapers are geographically a very flexible form of marketing communication. An advertisement can be placed in papers circulated in particular towns in order to test a market. Such advertisements can be tailored to quite specific local interests.

Whereas a consumer may only occasionally visit a cinema or perhaps only watch television for any length of time at the weekend, a daily newspaper may be read every morning without fail on a commuter journey. Newspaper reading tends to be a habitual and a thorough activity. A newspaper reader will tend to at least glance at every page.

Newspapers can be read in public and in crowded situations. The tabloid format is particularly easy to handle. The eye is able to take in at a glance most of the material presented as the pages are turned. A display advertisement can have a very high probability of being noticed by the average reader, if not actually read.

FROM TIME TO TIME GROUPS OF READERS BAND TOGETHER TO BUY ADVERTISING SPACE IN 'THE TIMES' TO PRESENT THEIR VIEWS ON A SUBJECT THEY FEEL STRONGLY ABOUT. ON ONE OCCASION, A JAPANESE BUSINESSMAN EXPENDED A CONSIDERABLE SUM PURCHASING A FOUR PAGE SUPPLEMENT IN ORDER TO PRESENT HIS PERSONAL PHILOSOPHY OF LIFE.

The newspaper reader is still presented with a relatively extensive choice of papers. In a large city, foreign newspapers will be found on news stands while significant urban groupings of ethnic minorities may support ethnic language papers. To a much greater extent than with, say, television, a newspaper is selected by the reader. Having the discretion, furthermore, to select which stories are read, the reader of a paper tends to become relatively involved with what is read.

For many groups, what has been read in a newspaper on a journey to work in the morning can become a subject of conversation. In the case of the local newspaper, readers can actually read about themselves. Journalists tend to mention as many local people as possible in reports of local events, as people tend to buy such newspapers in the expectation of coming across a 'mention'.

Feedback is easier with newspapers than with other media. The editor of a local paper may positively encourage correspondence on a particular subject. In other papers, there will be crossword puzzles to fill in which will attract a loyal following.

Newspapers can encourage a variety of actions. In addition to stimulating debate and crossword puzzle filling-in, a newspaper can present information in such a way that it may be cut out and kept for reference. Thus, form cards or tables of currencies or stocks and shares may be retained for consultation during the day.

Many newspapers run special reports which tend to be clipped and filed in press libraries. Many public-relations departments, while finding the monitoring of broadcasts and the obtaining of transcripts too expensive to be cost-effective, will clip and paste-up selected articles from the newspapers and circulate to interested managers. Competitions may be run to stimulate involvement.

Newspapers complement a number of other media: film and theatre reviews will be regularly published; each issue will contain a guide to television viewing and radio listening; editorial copy and advertisements will inform readers of local papers of what is on in their immediate area. While the popular tabloid may serialize the latest pot-boiling pulp novel, the quality daily or weekly, in addition to an extensive book review section, will be more likely to serialize a statesman's memoirs.

Newspapers have a regular and fixed press date. Editorial copy can be placed within minutes of the presses rolling. Newspapers can often accept advertisements within twenty-four hours of the closing of an issue, a much quicker access time than is the case with television. This relatively short deadline can allow a marketing manager to respond quickly to take advantage of a local situation.

Comprehension of a complex message presented in a newspaper can be relatively high. In the case of news messages, many more individual stories can be presented than is the case with broadcast media devoting more of their time to entertainment and less of their resources to information. Retention of a newspaper message tends to be higher. The newspaper may be dipped into a number of times during a day.

A number of newspapers feature regular shopping guides. These could focus upon a particular category of good or service, or upon an individual shopping centre. A motoring correspondent might examine a different car each week. Readers may regularly consult their newspapers to find out which special offers are running during the week in local supermarkets. The advertiser may not have to motivate readers to look for a particular advertisement or fight to attract attention, but may instead, in a local paper, present goods available and their prices.

The quality of the visual image is relatively poor in newspapers which tend to be printed on the cheapest of paper, basic newsprint. In special issues and in supplements, colour printing of reasonable quality may be available. For most of the week, however, the advertiser may have to make do with advertisements of poor reproduction quality. They may also contain the occasional error as proof reading will not be possible to the standards available to other print media with much longer lead times.

In some areas, a promotional package that can guarantee 100 per cent coverage of households can be obtained by means of an insert or advertisement in a free distribution or 'giveaway' newspaper. In some cases, an arrangement can be agreed whereby the free distribution paper is only delivered to households who do not receive a paid daily paper into which an insert could be placed.

Question 153: Assess the relative value as an advertising medium to a company with which you are familiar, of the following newspaper media:

(*a*) *The Financial Times*
(*b*) *The Sun*
(*c*) *The Sunday Telegraph*
(*d*) *The Eltham Times*
(*e*) *The Edinburgh Evening Advertiser*
(*f*) *The Economist*
(*g*) *The Birmingham Post.*

16.32 Magazines

Periodicals such as journals and magazines can have a significantly longer life than newspapers. They may also have a considerably higher pass-on readership: the business magazine may be circulated to a number of managers within an office; the glossy magazine may be read by many people while it lies on the reception or waiting area table. The majority of magazines will have a readership that is a multiple of circulation.

While a number of general-interest magazines have failed, interest, hobby, trade, and other specialist titles have multiplied. There appears to be a trend towards more specialized publishing, as readers become more aware of their particular requirements and conscious of a choice, and advertisers become more specific and define more closely the target publics they are aiming to reach.

The magazine like the newspaper can be read and re-read at an individual's speed. Only the bits that interest can be studied. Magazines are generally easy to carry about and can be read on many occasions when it would be difficult to do much else. Magazines thus tend to be retained and re-read while waiting for an appointment or while on a train journey.

Given the greater range of titles available, magazines are even more selective than the newspaper as a channel. There are magazines to cater for almost every kind of work and leisure interest. A magazine advertiser can reach predominantly male or female readers, a specific age-group, a particular category of purchasers, or consumers of a particular income group. A marketing manager may find a group of hobby, trade, or product magazines which closely match a company's media requirements. Many occupational and geographic groups can be reached by specific magazines.

There is a growing list of titles in the consumer-durable area. Then there are motor car, yacht and boating, caravan and holiday, house, stereo, cooking, and freezer magazines. Not only are there specific geographic magazines such as county journals but many national publications have regional notes, special features or even regional editions. Geographically, however, newspapers tend to be more flexible.

Many magazines are published in coated papers of some quality. Most are a considerable improvement on basic newsprint. The glossy magazines may offer the potential advertiser colour printing of some quality. Where the magazine is retained, the advertisement can have a longer life than a newspaper advertisement. The partwork magazine when bound can be kept longer than many books; a number of hobbies ranging from cooking to military history have been served with partworks.

Particular magazines may be extremely authoritative. Some will be considered to be 'the' standard journal and in such cases a halo effect may spill over onto advertisements. Magazines may be very selective in terms of the type and number of advertisements they will accept.

Magazines that tend to be bought over the counter in newsagents require an eye-catching design. While coupons can be printed and leaflets can be stitched into such journals, the magazine that is posted to subscribers on either a paid-for or a controlled-circulation basis can offer greater promotional possibilities. A variety of insert material from leaflets to floppy records and sample products can be enclosed in an envelope. Scratch and sniff microfragrance advertisements have been placed in some 'women's' magazines.

With magazine media, the possibility of a message spilling over to non-target publics can be much reduced. Thus, few atheists will read a church magazine. An advertisement could be placed in a boxing magazine without alienating those who feel that 'violent' sports such as boxing should not be shown on television.

16.33   Categories of Journal

The potential business-magazine advertiser will be faced with a choice between paid-for and controlled-circulation journals and 'horizontal' and 'vertical' journals. Having paid for a subscription, a consumer may be more inclined to read a bought magazine than one which arrives unsolicited through the letterbox. Against this, controlled circulation can offer the advertiser greater reader information and the possibility of reaching a high percentage of a carefully defined group. Magazines with a relatively high news-stand purchase rate find it more difficult to define their readership.

Horizontal journals are those that reach a certain kind of reader across a wide range of industries. Many professional magazines are of this kind, being read by functional specialists in accounting, engineering, marketing, buying, personnel, advertising, or public relations across a great many business sectors. A number of such journals may be received automatically by virtue of membership of certain professional bodies.

Vertical journals circulate to a range of reader types within a particular business sector; trade magazines are largely of this type. The focus will be a particular industry such as motor car production or oil, or a sector such as electronics or energy. Some magazines are more difficult to categorize as a result of having both a horizontal and a vertical readership. Thus, a computer magazine may be read by computer specialists across a number of industries and by a wider range of reader-groups within the computer hardware and software industry itself.

Horizontal and vertical journals can reach an interested readership. The professional journal can promote a self-image and thus reaches a sympathetic reader. An Institute journal, however, may have a relatively low pass-on readership where a copy is regarded as personal to the recipient. Trade journals can attract a motivated readership eager to discover contacts and new ideas and keep an eye on competitors: trade publications can achieve high pass-on readerships.

WHILE PRESIDENT OF THE UNITED STATES, JIMMY CARTER FOUND HIS STANDING IN THE OPINION POLLS FALLING FOLLOWING WIDESPREAD BROADCAST AND NEWSPAPER REPORTS OF CERTAIN STATEMENTS ABOUT HIS INNER FEELINGS MADE DURING THE COURSE OF AN INTERVIEW WITH PLAYBOY MAGAZINE.

Question 154:   Compare and contrast the value to a consumer-good producer and an industrial-service supplier respectively of advertisements placed in the following publications:

> (*a*)   a learned quarterly medical journal
> (*b*)   a controlled-circulation accounting tabloid
> (*c*)   a news-stand purchased fishing magazine
> (*d*)   a local parish or church magazine
> (*e*)   the motor industry's monthly journal
> (*f*)   a professional Institute's journal
> (*g*)   a company house magazine.

16.34   Directories

Reference publications such as yearbooks and directories can be referred to a great many times during the course of a year. Many offer advertisers opportunities to reach specific audiences. A number of professions and trade groups support authoritative yearbooks and directories.

The Yellow Pages, a commercial telephone directory available to all telephone subscribers both personal and business, is a regularly referred to source of information on companies offering a wide range of products and services. Regional editions are available. A potential consumer will tend to consult Yellow Pages once a need has been recognized and the possibility of purchase to meet it has been considered. Being close to the purchase decision, such consumer readers represent an attractive target group to advertisers.

Compared with the daily newspaper and the weekly or monthly magazine, yearbook and directory copy is less flexible. Should a company change its address or telephone number or introduce a new product or service, it will have to wait up to a year or more before its advertisement copy can be modified.

Question 155: List the reference publications in which an organization with which you are familiar might appear. Where there are gaps and you think an entry would be desirable, explain how the organization would achieve it and when the subsequent entry would appear, accounting for the delay.

16.4 ELECTRONIC INFORMATION

Even the most specialized of journals will contain redundant material for most readers. Physically, print media must be delivered to the consumer, often to the individual doorsteps of each reader. The more specialized the print message, usually, the longer the reader has to wait for it. Some information is so detailed as to be published once a year in a yearbook or directory.

Print media have mushroomed. Many scholars find it difficult to keep up to date with even the names of new journals in their fields. Subscribing to a range of publications can be expensive and not cost-effective when individual copies of certain titles may only be consulted occasionally, if at all.

There is a trend towards electronic or database publishing. Using disc and other storage devices large quantities of information can be stored and up-dated relatively cost-effectively. Once stored it can also be reproduced in a number of ways. Thus individual, company, subject, and geographic versions of a research index could, given adequate coding, be reproduced at the touch of a button.

Material stored on a data base can be continuously updated. Access can be instantaneous via a telephone terminal link or a video display screen. Consumers can obtain rapid access to just the material they are interested in, and could theoretically just be charged for the material consulted as and when it is consulted.

As energy costs rise relative to the cost of living and communication costs fall, patterns of work and leisure may change as it becomes cheaper to take work to people than people to work. Information can be sent to executives working at home via modified television screens. As the quality of the electronic image improves, quite complex visual images may be presented without the need for much of today's printed material.

There are still problems of copyright and of establishing methods of charging for the use of electronic information. The new media represent both problems and opportunities for advertisers. Users may wish to exclude extraneous information and go straight for the information they need, cutting out the gloss of unnecessary advertising. On the other hand, compared with the short one-day shelf life of the daily newspaper, electronically-stored information is both longer-lasting and more easily updated. Consumers may actively consult buyers' guides information files on specific goods and services. The comprehensive nature of the information provided may make it easier, once the habit of file-system consultation is established, for a company to reach the target consumer. The trend may also lead to a much greater tailoring of what is offered to the particular requirements of individual consumers.

Question 156: List the various data bases which you could make use of in the course of a typical day. If they all existed, how many of them would you actually make use of?

16.5 OUTDOOR ADVERTISING

At election times and, in the UK, on royal occasions, the general public tends to become aware of the potential of outdoor advertising. Poster advertising can be relatively expensive; a large billboard can present an eye-catching message. The major audience of such messages however, either on foot or travelling in cars, buses or trains, tends to be on the move. A glimpse of a poster may be fleeting and hence a poster message should be designed to catch attention and quickly present its message.

A major hoarding at the approach to an airport or station, or a collection of neon-light signs at a city centre junction or interchange can become a familiar landmark. A message in such circumstances can be taken for granted but may still be at work subconsciously. The dramatic poster site will be more expensive and may well justify some individual design treatment.

Outdoor advertising can be specifically local; impact can be relatively dramatic. A message can be so placed as to reach shoppers en route to purchase decisions. An available space can be individually painted or covered by a standard poster. In some situations, a three-dimensional image or model may be appropriate. At night, portions of a message can be illuminated; mechanical or electronic 'movement' could be provided.

Smaller posters can be placed at points where travellers congregate, as at above-ground and underground railway stations, bus stops, or in airport lounges.

Particular income groups can thus be reached. A small poster could be presented as a handbill or incorporated on a brochure, ticket, or wrapping material. A message could be placed adjacent to notices and signs that are frequently read or below the dial of a parking meter.

Certain companies offer the potential advertiser a range of outdoor advertising sites. A large company will itself own outdoor display possibilities such as factory walls, chimneys, lorries, and delivery vans. The company logo or symbol could be displayed at a number of points. The obtaining of planning permission should not, however, be taken for granted: local planning regulations and procedures can be quite strict and time-consuming, hence the value of access to an already-existing chain of sites.

Outdoor advertising need not be fixed. Small posters can be put up inside of tube trains to reach a captive audience. Vans, buses, and in some countries trains and taxi cabs can be used to carry advertising messages. Such advertising possibilities tend to attract producers of consumption goods and leisure services. Transit advertising is relatively inexpensive: a travelling audience may be frequently exposed to a tube or train advertisement.

More imaginative forms of outdoor advertising include neon-signs on airships, messages on balloons, banners across streets and towed from aeroplanes, and vapour-trail skywriting.

Question 157: A circus is coming to town. List all the outdoor advertising sites in your immediate neighbourhood which could be used to promote the forthcoming attraction. Bearing in mind the need for the circus to make a profit on its visit, which of the sites would you use and why?

16.6 BROADCAST MEDIA

The broadcast media tend to be controlled by the state to a greater degree than other media. In the UK, certain television and radio channels obtain their income in the form of a licence fee and do not accept advertising. They employ strict controls to prevent the broadcasting of a message that could be construed as advertising. In light-entertainment programmes, care is taken to avoid using the names of particular companies and products.

The 'commercial' channels in contrast seek to attract advertising and hence aim to build large audiences *vis-à-vis* their licence-funded competitors. They are however limited in the volume of advertisements, the grouping and frequency of advertisements, and the type of advertisements which they can accept.

16.61 Television

Television combines a relatively realistic image with sound to form a particularly persuasive medium. Coverage of households is almost complete in developed societies. The television viewing habit is widespread, and a substantial proportion of leisure time is spent watching television. Significantly more time is spent, on average, watching television than in the consumption of all other media combined.

Where television advertising is allowed, a simple message can be put to a large audience and generally in their own homes at an economical cost per thousand recipients in an attractive way, using a moving and a coloured image. Instead of having to attract the recipient's attention to the site of a message, attention can be assumed. Frequently, there will not be competing messages to contend with at the moment a particular message is broadcast.

Television is a compelling medium, and viewers can become very involved in sports coverage and with the personalities of a series. It also has credibility in the UK and has been used for corporate image advertising. A programme of television advertisements can be a useful complement to other promotional activity. Employees are often delighted with a mention of their company on television; the very existence of a campaign can motivate dealers and encourage middlemen to stock a product.

Quite a lot is known about the television audience. Viewer surveys and audience-measurement techniques have been progressively refined. A potential advertiser can gain a rough idea of the social, age, and sex make-up of audiences at particular times in the day and for particular programmes. As the supply of advertisement time is generally fixed by law or voluntary agreement the cost of particular slots will reflect demand. Regional or local television now allows geographic selectivity.

In the case of an advertisement break within a programme the attention of a viewer tends to be held. The alternative of switching channels tends to be dampened by the inertia effect. Television tends to hold its audience while a magazine reader turns a page or a radio music-programme listener switches a channel to avoid advertisements.

Although television offers an economical cost per thousand viewers reached, the size of the television audience means that the absolute cost of television advertising on a national network is high. There is thus an economic barrier to entry and television advertising may not be feasible in the case of a good many marketing promotions.

The lead time with television can be relatively long, as many programmes and commercials take months to plan and produce. Because of the pressure of demand, the most attractive slots may be 'spoken for'. To get some 'prime time', an advertiser may have to accept some less-attractive insertions. With a new series or a one-off programme, an audience may take some time to build up, and its exact size and composition may be difficult to forecast.

As it is a technically sophisticated medium and the television image is fleeting, the actual cost of the advertisement itself as a product can be relatively high. Many television advertisements are in effect short films, and demand high standards of creativity and technical achievement, with the television audience holding high expectations concerning the aesthetic and technical quality of what appears on their screens.

The larger company should not overlook the possibility of television editorial coverage. With the growth of video-cassette recorder ownership, new opportunities are opening up as viewers are able to select from cassette shops programmes of personal interest to watch as an alternative to what is offered by the networks. Video-disc systems incorporating hi-fi sound, fibre or glass optic 'cable' systems which can allow access to a multitude of channels, and direct broadcasting by satellite offer challenges to the future of network broadcasting.

These developments will tend to reduce the sizes of mass audiences and the attraction of advertisements incorporated within programmes aimed at general consumption. Instead, individuals will be able to select, record or borrow from libraries, programmes according to their particular interests. Periodic summaries of professional, trade, legal, and product developments could be packaged by disc, cable, and cassette programme producers as an updating service. Access to the television medium will be opened both to minorities and to smaller companies with new products to present on new product programmes.

Question 158: Identify categories of advertiser who might be particularly attracted to advertising slots in a commercial break in the middle of the following programmes:

    (a)   a mid-afternoon children's programme
    (b)   the late-night news
    (c)   a Saturday-night feature film
    (d)   a midweek early-evening documentary
    (e)   a Saturday-afternoon sports broadcast
    (f)   a popular weekday comedy series
    (g)   a Sunday-evening carol service.

16.62   Radio

An extremely high proportion of households possess a radio. A growing proportion of cars have radios, although car radio listening might fall as cassette players are fitted in increasing quantities to cars. Radios are broadcast in many work situaations. Portable transistor radios are listened to by the mobile young. Many young mothers listen to the radio while doing their housework.

Radio tends to be a more selective medium than television: a greater number of channels is able to cater for a wider range of interests. Until the early evening, the radio audience can exceed that for television. As the number of independent local radio stations grows, and access time remains relatively short, compared with television, radio can offer greater time and geographical flexibility. Certain large towns and many cities have a radio station.

While radio can be an economical medium and a localized one with a lower economic barrier to entry than television, it is unable to offer the visual dimension of television, its message is fleeting and tends not to be recorded and played back, and for many listeners, it does not have the credibility of television.

Question 159:   Compare and contrast the value of independent local radio as an advertising medium to the following companies:

- (*a*)   secretarial job agency
- (*b*)   car hire firm
- (*c*)   industrial chemicals supplier
- (*d*)   soft drink manufacturer
- (*e*)   local furniture retailer.

16.7   F I L M

Film is largely a minority interest, as for the greater part of the population the cinema-going habit has been lost. The great bulk of the cinema-going audience is now made up of young people, and cinema advertising may be cost-effective for advertisers seeking this particular public.

Cinema advertisements tend to be a mixture of the national, short films shown in a wide range of cinemas promoting a national brand consumer product and the local. A short 'card' advertisement can be used to advertise, in one cinema only, a restaurant that might still be open when the film that is being screened has finished.

16.8   T E L E P H O N E   S E L L I N G

The telephone can allow direct selective and interpersonal communication. The telephone selling message can be modified according to the feedback received. Being an aerial medium, a product cannot be usually demonstrated on the telephone. Instead, the telephone can be used to make an initial contact to be followed up by a salesman's visit or the putting of a brochure or other direct mail item in the post.

Telephone selling has been used by a variety of social and political groups and lobbies to attract support. The interaction allowed by this form of communication allows an individual's concerns to emerge, and questions can be answered on the spot.

Question 160:   How receptive do you consider typical members of the following publics might be to a telephone sales call:

(*a*)   an elderly spinster living alone
(*b*)   a teenage rock-music enthusiast
(*c*)   a local councillor
(*d*)   a chartered accountant
(*e*)   a housewife with the mumps.

16.9   MEDIA CREDIBILITY

The credibility of media will vary greatly. Some journals will be regarded as more trustworthy than others. To those 'in the know', one journalist may have a reputation for greater expertise than another. A journal with a smaller circulation may have a higher status and greater prestige than a competitor, and be regarded as more authoritative.

A message's credibility will reflect the credibility of the media that carries it. An editorial mention may be regarded with greater cynicism in a controlled-circulation journal, especially when opposite a paid advertisement, than an identical message in another journal which is funded entirely by subscription income from a paid circulation.

A change of ownership can lead to questions concerning a newspaper's future credibility. Not only journalists but a government may seek assurances regarding editorial freedom when influential media change hands.

16.91   Media and Messages

A message can appear 'out of place' in a particular context. When seeking to place messages in the media, it may be a question of horses for courses. Where publics have strong expectations and attitudes towards certain media, these may have to be carefully assessed. The placing of an advertisement, for example, in a party-political journal could be taken by many readers as evidence of political support.

A publication that is associated with an established 'stable' may appear more authoritative than a similar one established as a one-off venture. An editor or a broadcaster may lend prestige to a particular paper or programme; many potential contributors will ask for a copy of a publication before agreeing to put pen to paper. Similarly some VIP's have a policy of not appearing on certain shows.

The credibility of media will change over time. Over a period a low-credibility source, such as a new journalist, often tends to gain authority while readers may become more resistant to another journalist of initially higher credibility in a rival paper.

Assessments of the media need to be kept up to date. One television channel may gain on a rival following the introduction of a new series. One Sunday newspaper may gain in circulation *vis-à-vis* others by introducing a colour magazine. Over time, it is likely that successful innovation will be imitated.

Communicators and those at whom their communications are directed influence each other: a producer will be swayed by viewer surveys and movements in audience size; an editor may find it difficult to resist a one-sided post-bag or pressure from a major advertiser when advertisement revenues are difficult to come by. Viewers and readers may also over a period of time come to reflect media views. A communicator who expresses support for an audience's viewpoint tends to find it easier to persuade than one who initially expresses opposition. A newspaper putting across a political viewpoint on a particular subject can be a potent force where its position is accepted by the majority of its readers.

Audiences and readers tend to identify with their favoured media. The more credible sources tend to be those which reflect self-identity. Where the identity is close, perhaps consciously forged, a following can be extremely loyal. In the magazine world, a publication with a smaller and loyal circulation may outlast another with a circulation which is larger but more fickle when new titles are introduced to the market.

Messages can colour views of their sources. The decision of a journalist to run an unusual, perhaps controversial, series of articles can result in readers re-examining their image of what a newspaper stands for. A biased or incorrect report can do great harm to an authoritative reputation.

Successful media in the long run tend to be those that respect their audiences: talking down to an audience can alienate. Confident and respected media are able to take an occasional objective and critical look at themselves. Mistakes can be acknowledged and critical feedback broadcast or published. A policy of whitewash and suspicion of censorship can rapidly discredit a medium. Technical excellence can be no substitute for editorial integrity.

Question 161: List the media to which you are exposed and assess their credibility. To what extent and in what ways are editorial policies of the media listed influenced by ownership and sources of financing.

16.10   MEDIA CONVENTIONS

A number of conventions and expectations have grown up concerning each of the mass media. Readers of quality dailies and popular tabloids each have distinct expectations concerning the relative priority given to different types of story, treatment, and presentation. In the broadcast media, a number of genre conventions have emerged. A producer and director will tend to set out consciously to make a 'western' or a 'gangster' film and will either feel bound to a particular set of conventions or will consciously set out to break them. Where a market is thought to exist, a film, play, or book may be produced to a formula in accordance with what is thought to be known about audience expectations.

Recipients of a message may be quite unaware of the extent to which the media is dominated by conventions. In the case of the broadcast media, the conventions can be international. To be commercially successful, a film must be made for the US/international market. A national cinema that is self-supporting can be difficult to establish.

Of course media conventions can be consciously broken. Alternative and underground cinemas have sought to involve audiences in the media by drawing attention to the ways in which meaning is conveyed. Thus, unusual camera movements aim to subvert realist and Hollywood aesthetics. Soundtracks can confront and subvert rather than complement and reinforce the visual image in order to force audiences to think about what is on the screen.

There are both narrative and structural conventions with which audiences can become so familiar as to uncritically accept. The conscious breaking of narrative conventions can give rise to such labels as radical. Visual conventions, in the case of film, lighting, set, camera angle, and composition conventions along with actor conventions can be challenged by a movement such as Italian neo-realism.

The extent to which the breaking of convention norms will be acceptable to an audience will depend upon the context in which a communication is received. An audience interested in stimulation may be more tolerant of the unusual and unexpected than one which wishes to be entertained. An audience wishing to be informed will give priority to narrative content and will probably wish to take form and structure for granted. On occasion, to achieve impact, to shock, an advertisement could consciously break a convention.

Question 162: Set out the narrative, visual, and casting conventions of the following genres:

(*a*)   James Bond film
(*b*)   the spaghetti western
(*c*)   the pulp-novel cover.

16.11   MEDIA CULTURE

Broadcast television is in many developed countries the dominant medium and a significant cultural influence. The ownership and control of the media and the values they represent are in a number of countries significant political issues. To those on the left, the mass media distract and de-politicize, postponing radical action while, to those on the right, the producers of the controversial documentary can be viewed as a subversive force.

In the UK, efforts have been made to make television non-political in a party-political sense. In West Germany in contrast, party-political debate on television has been encouraged, and there is no objection to the making of overtly political programmes so long as balance is maintained.

The mass media tend to portray a certain set of cultural, moral, and social values. Dominant values are manifest in news and current affairs programmes and underlie drama series. Access to the media is difficult for a great many minorities: on television, one or two minority slots can be consciously introduced. Some newspapers have been prepared to be more overtly party-political with a correspondingly lower possibility of access for those of different political views.

Citizens-band radio and emerging television technologies may allow more access to minorities. The media could then help minorities to retain and foster distinct identities and cultures. The dominant media culture has a subtle influence upon values, speech, dress, and habits.

Newspaper ownership in a number of countries is highly concentrated. Such a concentration can place great potential power to influence in a relatively few hands. Changes of newspaper ownership can attract government investigation.

To a degree, television as a medium is international. An international media culture has emerged based upon US editing practices, technical production expertise, and plot and narrative conventions. The domestic US television audience represents an attractive potential market: not only are many US television programmes and US films shown on European television but a significant proportion of European 'national' programmes are made with an 'eye' on the US market, and hence portray and reflect cultural norms acceptable to this market. This has given rise to charges of US-cultural imperialism.

16.12 THE MULTI-MEDIA APPROACH

Where a message is complex it may best be put across by a number of complementary media channels. The educator has long recognised the value of visual aids. Language teaching can employ a package of print, visual, and aural materials. A detailed image such as a map or a technical drawing is often easier to understand when accompanied by some form of oral explanation. Such an explanation can direct attention to particular parts of the whole; without such guidance a person confronted with a complex image may not know where to begin.

Multiple channels of communication are more difficult to ignore than single channels. In museums and exhibitions, visual displays that are accompanied by an oral explanation find it easier to attract and retain attention than those which are not. Audio-visual presentations employing both aural and visual channels tend to be more effective than single channels. A film screened in a darkened room has a further advantage of having less competition from rival stimuli.

An advertising agent will advise a client on which combination of media to use and in what ways to achieve the best results for a given budget and a given set of communication objectives. Inevitably, with media that are so different to spread a budget between, tradeoffs will have to be made. The most important consideration is to build an orchestrated campaign so that the whole is greater than the sum of the parts. Individual media decisions should not be taken in isolation.

17. *The Advertising Campaign*

Chapter 16 outlined some characteristics of the major media in which advertisements can be placed. This chapter concentrates upon establishing the strategy of planning, budgeting, and evaluating the effectiveness of an advertising campaign. A systematic approach should be adopted, preferably the successive analysis of the situation, problem definition, objective formulation, message generation, public identification, channel selection, programming planning, budgeting implementation, evaluation and subsequent control, and modification advocated in Chapter 14 in respect of public relations communication. This approach can equally well be applied to advertising communication, this chapter focusing upon some particular advertising considerations.

17.1 CAMPAIGN ELEMENTS

The elements of an advertising campaign will consist of objectives, messages, publics, channels, and assessment. The effective campaign will depend upon a successful client–agency–media partnership. While the client company must take the lead in defining the objectives, what it is seeking to achieve *vis-à-vis* identified publics of existing repeat-purchase or potential new customers, the agency may provide the main creative input into the translation of those product or service attributes the client wishes to stress into an effective selling message. The agency will also prepare an initial media selection package, suggested media channels for reaching the target publics, for client approval.

Many clients will be in a position themselves to assess the effectiveness of their advertising. Others will make use of the specialist services provided by their agency. The leading media, drawing a significant portion of their income from advertising will themselves have measures and estimates of exposure, viewer rating, circulation, and readership.

The exact division of work between a client and an agency will depend upon the extent of the relative experience and expertise of the parties. A new entrant to the fast-moving consumer-good field may rely heavily upon the advice of an experienced and successful agency in the field. The agency may be able to help with the identification of the most promising target publics, and may have a 'feel' for which product or service attributes might be most likely to appeal to each of the publics identified. Alternatively, an industrial-good supplier with experience of the market for its complex product may itself have a good idea of the message it would like to put across in terms of both treatment and content. It may know the publics and the best means of reaching them. An agency commission in such a case may be little more than a booking fee.

In the case of a television commercial, the advertisement itself may be produced by an agency. The agency may write a script, hire a director, and cost, pre-plan, hire studios and other facilities, arrange printing, editing and post production work, presenting a client with a final bill. Similarly, an agency may carry out the physical preparation of 'camera-ready artwork' in the case of an advertisement destined for an offset litho-printed magazine. In another case, the media itself might have a production department and may be able to prepare an advertisement 'in-house'. In practice the production of commercials is usually best done by a specialist supplier. The client may have to decide whether the 'polish' resulting from agency production is worth the extra fee.

17.2 ADVERTISING STRATEGY

Opinions differ on whether advertising should be continuous or concentrated into bursts. With some media, a burst approach may be needed to reach a threshold of effectiveness. The whole effect is frequently more than the sum of the parts and burst advertisements reinforce each other.

In the case of an established product, consumer loyalty and reputation may best be safeguarded by means of continuous advertising. A continuous strategy allows longer-term support to be given to retailers and distributors and allows some 'cash in the kitty' to meet unexpected competitor activity.

There are often conflicts between short- and long-run strategy. Having greater relative market strength *vis-à-vis* buyers, the supplier of a product that is almost unobtainable may, for example, be able to reap short-run windfall profits by charging what the market will bear. In the long run this could cause ill will and result in consumers switching to the products of other suppliers when the period of shortage is over. There may, alternatively, be for example, in order to favour certain customers, short-run advantages in breaking ongoing distribution arrangements. The extent to which the supplier must err upon the side of caution must depend upon how long the shortage is expected to last.

As well as boosting revenues, costs can be saved in the short term. Advertising expenditure could be cut for example to achieve short-term cost savings. In the longer term, however, a more satisfactory approach might be to run an advertising campaign explaining how responsible the company is and what it and customers are doing and can do in a period of crisis. Alternatively, advertising expenditure could be switched to the promotion of substitute products.

There may come a point at which a market is saturated. At this point, the returns from increased advertising expenditure may be negligible. Because of the time-lag between advertising expenditure and additional sales, as market saturation-point approaches it may be wise to cut advertising expenditure while sales are still on the increase. To those not directly involved it can appear that as soon as advertising actually began to work it was cut.

Advertising is, to some extent, seasonal. Many agencies avoid the Christmas and summer periods. Thursday and Fridays, preceding the weekend shopping spree, tend to be more heavily booked than Mondays and Tuesdays on which money may be tight.

A great many goods are bought for stock rather than for immediate consumption. A fresh purchase might not be made until existing stocks have run low. In the case of durables, a purchase might have to wait the accumulation of income or a suitable interval from a prior purchase. The payoffs from a durable advertising campaign often stretch way beyond one accounting time period. This can lead to cynicism among accounting staff and much questioning of the value of advertising activity. One of the most difficult tasks in marketing is often the marketing of marketing itself to management colleagues.

> A MAJOR MEDIA ADVERTISING CAMPAIGN HAD BEEN PLANNED TO COINCIDE WITH THE LAUNCH OF A NEW PART WORK. THE EARLY ISSUES HAD ALREADY BEEN PRINTED. THE PUBLISHER HEARD OF THE POSSIBILITY OF AN INDUSTRIAL DISPUTE WHICH MIGHT CLOSE THE MAJOR COMMERCIAL TELEVISION STATION TO BE USED BY THE CAMPAIGN. THE PUBLISHER DECIDED TO DELAY THE LAUNCH OF THE FIRST TWO ISSUES OF THE PART WORK BY SIX WEEKS UNTIL THE OUTCOME OF WAGE NEGOTIATIONS AT THE STATION WAS CLEAR.

Question 163:   Contrast and compare the advertising strategies for a consumer and an industrial good at each major stage of their life cycles.

17.3   THE ADVERTISING MESSAGE

An advertising message might contain a 'unique selling proposition'. It may be used for a period only or for a much longer time. It should be appropriate to the state people are likely to be in at the moment they receive the message. To achieve these, one needs to know something about the state of mind of the target group.

The message may be independent of others or designed to compete with or complement others. The classic competitive message is that of the Avis rent-a-car firm 'We're Number Two. We Try Harder!'.

The form of a message, its structure and content will reflect the group it is aimed at, its objective, and the channel that carries it. The message could be a sharp attention-getter, an explanation of attributes, a question or challenge, an examination of alternatives, or an exposition of how to go about buying. The message could be serious or humorous. A succession of messages can be related to a single theme — the parts refreshed by a beer that other beers do not reach.

A MOTOR MANUFACTURER WISHED TO DEMONSTRATE THE HIGH MANOEUVERABILITY OF ITS LONG SELLING SMALL CAR. IT DEVELOPED A TELEVISION COMMERCIAL SHOWING THE CAR DRIVING EFFORTLESSLY AROUND GIANT SIZED LETTERS OR ITS OWN NAME INCLUDING A TIGHT CIRCLE AROUND THE DOT ABOVE THE LETTER 'i'.

Question 164:   Set out what you understand by the following messages and what you believe their purposes to be:

   (*a*)   'graded grains make finer flour'
   (*b*)   'snap, crackle, pop'
   (*c*)   a white horse which can be taken anywhere
   (*d*)   a drink is consumed by those who hang-glide, drive speedboats, visit exotic locations, are glamorous, and have no visible means of support.

17.4   ADVERTISING EXPENDITURE

In theory, advertising expenditure should be pushed to the point at which the marginal unit of advertising adds just as much to costs as it does to revenue. Where a brand is a profit centre, advertising expenditure may in practice be conditioned by what the product can afford. In this case, one is caught in a chicken and egg dilemma. Advertising will increase product income but the product income needs to increase to pay for the advertising.

One criterion for advertising expenditure is the job which needs to be done — the message which must be put to selected publics for so long so often by such and such channels. This is the bottom-up approach rather than the top-down approach of how much can be afforded. A specified campaign can be costed with a reasonable degree of accuracy.

Some unsophisticated companies spend according to the expenditure of their competitors on advertising, in an attempt to match competitor spending absolutely, or per unit of sales, or per market share. This gives a rough guide to spending.

Individual companies will vary in their capacities to spend and may have wildly differing market shares. One may be intent on pushing up its market share, another content merely to hold on to an existing market share.

Advertising expenditure should be established upon the basis of cost-effective solutions to communication problems. Setting an arbitrary limit, perhaps as a result of the dictates of a group-wide budgeting system can result in a less than optimum performance. One may have to spend money to make money. Advertising should be continued so long as it adds more to revenues than to costs. A creative and entrepreneurial rather than a bureaucratic and administrative approach is needed.

Companies in practice, however, often establish their expenditure upon advertising by working out how much they can afford, setting a percentage of sales limit, matching the expenditure of competitors, or by calculating what is needed to do a particular job. Setting arbitrary limits can result in missed advertising opportunities but does control expenditure. If percentages are set, they should be flexible, varying by product and life-cycle stage. Sales percentage limits obscure the fact that sales in part stem from advertising and does not allow for 'investment' advertising.

When matching competitor advertising, one should bear in mind that competitors need not necessarily get it right. Also, a competitor's market and commercial position may be very different from that of the 'home' organization. Building up expenditure according to what is necessary to do the job can seem the most logical method, but can lead to battles with proponents of other claims on expenditure. Justifying advertising expenditure may require a comparison of estimated costs with hoped-for results.

When groups of companies seek to match each others' advertising expenditure this sometimes appears to outsiders as a form of market collusion.

Looking at what happened last year is a common way of setting an advertising budget. Figures might be raised to allow for inflation and special projects such as the promotion of a new product tagged on. In some companies, advertising expenditure appears to be conditioned more by the dictates of budgetary control than by the objective needs of the marketplace.

Simple rules of thumb such as allocating certain percentages of revenue to advertising face the drawback that sales growth point and point of advertising need do not always coincide. The point of maximum advertising is generally the point at which sales of a recently-introduced product begins to take off.

For many companies the chain of causation is from extra sales and resulting cash flow to additional advertising expenditure, rather than vice versa.

A CAMPAIGN WAS INTENDED TO INFORM THE PUBLIC ABOUT THE MERITS OF BUSINESS. A NATIONWIDE MEDIA CAMPAIGN WAS ENVISAGED. INITIALLY, MONEY WAS DONATED IN LARGE AMOUNTS BUT THEN THE RATE OF DONATIONS FELL BELOW WHAT

HAD BEEN HOPED FOR.

IT WAS DECIDED THAT THE PLANNED CAMPAIGN SHOULD NOT BE CUT AND THAT IT WOULD BE DELAYED UNTIL THE NECESSARY SUMS TO PAY FOR IT HAD BEEN RECEIVED. ALAS INFLATION PUT UP THE COST OF THE CAMPAIGN MORE QUICKLY THAN DONA-TIONS FLOWED IN. THERE WERE SOME MUTTERINGS THAT DUE TO THE DELAY THE PURPOSES OF THE CAMPAIGN HAD BEEN OVER-TAKEN BY EVENTS.

17.41   Setting the Advertising Budget

Establishing an advertising budget requires considerable judgement. A number of crude rules of thumb are current:

spending a fixed amount for each unit produced for sale;

spending a percentage of the preceding year's turnover by establishing a ratio of advertising expenditure to sales volume;

spending a percentage of turnover expected in the coming year;

spending above the level of advertising expenditure of the previous year by an agreed percentage;

spending a percentage of past or expected future profit;

spending whatever is necessary to achieve a particular advertising task, e.g. reaching a defined target group with a specified desired level of frequency;

spending to keep up (matching or exceeding) with competitors or to maintain a ratio of advertising expenditure to market share;

spending according to pre-established criteria such as a points system.

More sophisticated approaches replace these simple guidelines with theoretical methods such as the use of econometric or marketing models or empirical models that employ experimental feedback i.e. testing and learning, rather than historical data. In general, when using simple guidelines, a company tends to run with the pack instead of creatively seeking a competitive advantage. The main aim of advertising expenditure is to secure a profit advantage over competitors by spend-ing whatever is necessary to maximize current or long-run profits according to company strategy.

Subjective budgeting requires judgement. A number of factors may need to be weighed as advertising competes with other expenditures. Flexibility, being ready to adjust during the year to changing economic conditions, suggests some contin-gency or reserve fund within the budget. Market share, distribution pattern, customer and prospect characteristics, media costs, event times, the activity of competitors, expected returns, general market and economic data and the avail-ability of funds will need to be taken into account.

It may be felt that some products can afford more than others. The experience of previous years should not be ignored. Stage in a product life-cycle, the relative superiority of a product and the degree of product differentiation may be important.

There may be special considerations. With a television campaign, for example, there may be a minimum effectiveness threshold. Media costs may suddenly rise. A new product or dying brand may need particular analysis. Corporate advertising may be given a one-off budget sum. In the case of a mail order operation, where results are measurable, greater rationality may be possible. Creativity, timing, the extent to which performance can be controlled or reserve funds are available may be factors in budgeting.

Advertising may, along with promotion and selling, draw from a general marketing budget. It will in turn need to be broken down between products and product groups, between established and new products and geographically. Experience may yield clues relating to the responsiveness and profitability of advertising. Testing may be desirable by eliminating all variables except the weight of advertising employed.

Advertising should relate to market objectives, be realistic, affordable and able to do the job required. How long a company is prepared to wait for a return on advertising investment may be laid down in company policy. The company's marketing plan should be the basis of budget planning. Advertising should be focused on the solutions of particular communication problems, whether direct to customers, in support of sales activity or 'internal' advertising directed at employees. In some situations a number of different approaches may be desirable in order to build up a 'feel' for the level of advertising thought to be appropriate.

17.42   Advertising Budgeting Problems

Advertising is difficult to budget. Creativity is not easy to measure. Effects can be delayed and re-enforcement of other methods of communication effects can go undetected. Some managers do not find it easy to put a value upon an increase in awareness *per se*.

Advertising itself is subject to economies of scale. Doubling an advertising budget may lead to more than a doubling of effectiveness. Many advertisements are much more effective when reinforced: television, poster, and magazine advertisements can all reinforce one another. A limited advertising budget may lie below the threshold needed for success.

One drawback of the economies of scale argument in favour of advertising is that frequently the heaviest advertising occurs in sectors in which the economies of scale are not pronounced. In addition, the benefits of longer production runs may be taken in the form of increased profits rather than lower prices. By stimulating demand for a wider range of products, advertising might in fact lead to higher units costs.

One viewpoint is that advertising rather than enlarging the eventual sales of a new product acts mainly to speed up the rate of trial use and acceptance and thus brings forward the point of maximum sales. If advertising did nothing to increase sales and merely brought them forward this would alone, other things being equal, increase the rate of return of the capital invested in the production of the new product, and this benefit might outweigh the additional cost of production.

An advertising budget may be allocated regionally according to existing or potential sales, salesmen's reports, or agency data on advertising cost-effectiveness *vis-à-vis* selected target groups. An allocation may be modified to 'plug gaps' or to ease off in areas in which sales appear to have peaked.

Where a target group is specified in socio-economic terms, their areas of residence may condition a geographic allocation. A regional allocation must account for the minimum effectiveness threshold of each area and for the activities of competitors.

Question 165:   Explain how you might adjust your budget allocation to advertising in response to the following events:

(*a*)   a new firm is about to enter the market
(*b*)   your product sales are 13 per cent ahead of budget
(*c*)   your existing stocks are at a dangerously low level and your company has hit a production constraint
(*d*)   three people have just died of food poisoning as a result of consuming the contents of one of your high selling tins of food
(*e*)   restrictions upon radio advertising have just been removed.

17.43   Advertising as Investment

To some extent advertising can be considered as capital rather than revenue expenditure. Over a period of time advertising can build up considerable goodwill towards a company and its business. In the event of a sale of the business to another organization, the goodwill will attract a premium price. Cutting advertising to save revenue costs in one time period can lead to a much greater proportional fall in the 'stock' of advertising-generated goodwill.

Something that is spent in one period to yield a flow of benefits in future periods is an investment. Some advertising meets the criteria of an investment. It differs from other investments in that in many countries it is not regarded as a capital item for taxation purposes, it yields a variety of benefits, and these are especially difficult to evaluate.

If advertising is an investment, a company must find some means of evaluating returns from it in order to judge its productivity relative to that of other investments. To what extent does advertising increase the future worth of an organization? Answering this question may require the discounting of expected future incremental cash flows. As a capital item, advertising would compete with other items in the capital budget according to discounted cash-flow rate-of-return.

A MAJOR MANUFACTURER OF A CONSUMER PRODUCT SPON-
SORS AN AEROBATIC DISPLAY TEAM. THE TEAM GIVES DISPLAYS
AT AIR SHOWS THROUGHOUT THE SUMMER MONTHS, HIGHLIGHTS
OF ONE OR TWO OF WHICH HAVE BEEN SHOWN ON TELEVISION.
THE COMPANY HAS REVIEWED ITS SPONSORSHIPS POLICY. OTHER
LARGE COMPANIES HAVE SPONSORED CRICKET MATCHES AND
MOTOR RACING TEAMS.

17.5 MEDIA PLANNING

A purchase decision other than an impulse purchase may 'build up' over a period of
time during which a subject may be exposed to a variety of media influences. The
mass media are particularly effective at informing target groups of the existence of
product and services and in drawing attention to their main attributes. Potential
consumers can also be made aware of a need or a gap and, for those who 'follow
fashion', what others are doing. The media can re-enforce and remind. Media
channels are most appropriate to the early stages of the purchase process and
generally need to be supplemented in the case of consumer durables and industrial
goods by personal salesmanship at a later stage.

Media planning must take account of the media to which the desired subject is
likely to be exposed. Certain media will be more appropriate for marketing objectives than others. If informal decisions are to be taken then available media should
be systematically evaluated, perhaps by means of special procedures and forms.

Preferred media are those for whom the target group is a relatively high proportion of those reached, so that one is not paying for 'excess circulation'; those that
are reputable and credible and cost-effective. A particular medium may not be
felt to be appropriate to a company's corporate image.

Whereas some media are instantaneous others are kept and periodically referred
to, with the possibility of frequent exposure to a message. This reduces the cost
per exposure. The cost of using a medium will include the actual cost of production of the advertisement. In one case this may involve little more than type-
setting while in another expensive studio facilities may need to be hired.

A potential advertiser needs to take account of both the comparative costs of
different means of reaching each 1,000 targets, and absolute costs, the minimum-
cost threshold, that must be passed to gain access to a medium at all. A high
absolute cost beyond what is felt justified in a particular context might result in
the rejection of a medium offering a lower relative cost than one selected.

Comparative-cost figures should be interpreted with caution. The relative
quality of an image, the time of exposure, and the nature of any excess of wasted
audience or circulation should be taken into account. Some media will be more

flexible than others in allowing quick access or selective access to a particular geographic market. One medium may be more willing to accommodate a particular time of day requirement than another.

Media advertisements may be justified on indirect grounds because of their influence upon middlemen or opinion formers. The less selective the media the more extensive may be the spillover benefits.

The attribute that one is aiming to stress may suggest a particular medium. A glossy photograph can be studied and admired at leisure. Radio might be preferable to television in that it allows fine sound quality to be appreciated without the distraction of a visual image.

The editorial standing and bias of a medium and the existence of compulsory and voluntary restraints may have to be taken into account. Certain articles or programmes could create a favourable climate within which a message might be more acceptable. Special features may be planned with advertising support in mind, and in such cases it might be possible to 'help' with associated editorial text and illustration. Some presentations and treatments will have greater impact than others. An advertiser may wish to wait until a particular series is started or for the month in which a particular article will appear in a magazine.

Desired slots and positions will not always be available. Most informed purchasers of advertising space will endeavour to secure the best positions, and in such situations the potential advertiser should be prepared for some hard bargaining.

With a particular programme some considerations will be of greater importance than others. Weights could be attached to each selection criterion. By adding up points, one can ensure that due priority is given to the factors of greatest significance.

Question 166: Identify some media that have failed and give some reasons why you think they ceased.

Question 167: Assess the relative value to: (i) an industrial good seller and (ii) a fast-moving consumer-good seller of the following media:

- (*a*) public network television
- (*b*) independent local radio
- (*c*) a quality Sunday newspaper
- (*d*) a medical journal
- (*e*) a trade directory.

17.51 Media Scheduling

A target audience will have habits and media that reach it. Some media will be more suited to a product than others: where a product needs to be illustrated to be understood then media that do not allow pictures to be shown will clearly not be appropriate.

Selection among competing feasible media is usually according to some relatively-objective basis such as cost per thousand reader. Overlying such objective criteria can be the preferences of particular executives who, as a result of their experience, have a preference for this or that media.

Readership figures should be treated with caution. Advertisers are not so much interested in total numbers of readers or viewers as in numbers of potential customers among the larger figures. The readership among the target group is what is important.

Crude readership figures may also fail to reflect the difference in quality between two publications. One journal may have greater credibility than another.

The target group is likely to be exposed to a variety of media. Often more important than average cost per thousand readers is the marginal cost of reaching a group not accessible by other media. A small journal that gives access to additional members of a target group may be a better prospect than a magazine with a much larger circulation but whose readership is already exposed to one's message through other media. The selection of media can be handled by simulation, linear programme-based, and other models.

Media scheduling has become a complex business. Advertisements in journals among the target group adjusted for such factors as the extent of overlapping between media readership and the time of delivery to readers. Having established cost-effectiveness, there is the question of number of insertions and periods between them, not to mention the position of an advertisement. Prime positions will cost more, and one must decide whether the incremental sales likely to be achieved will exceed the incremental cost.

The scheduling problem becomes more difficult when advertising has both initial and delayed effects. Seasonal factors may also be present. Having scheduled media, one must still decide such questions as frequency of insertion, whether insertions are to be concentrated, continuous, or intermittent, whether they are to be steady, high initially and then tailing off, or rising to a climax. In the case of broadcast media, effectiveness and cost may vary widely according to the time of insertion.

Above a certain frequency of showing, an advertisement can cause irritation. This is particularly marked when the product concerned is irrelevant to the message recipient's needs. The negative effect of advertisements should be borne in mind when planning a campaign. Over-familiarity can breed contempt.

Advertisers of up-market goods should be aware that those with above-average education have an above-average dislike of advertising. Potential recipients may be far less gullible than those compiling a sales message imagine. Women shoppers have been shown to be more critical of advertising than their male counterparts.

There is some evidence in Europe and North America of the fragmentation of mass markets. While sale of many national newspapers and some general interest magazines steadily declines there has been a boom in several sectors of the local press, and trade and specialized publications. In future, messages may need to be far more closely tailored to the interests and needs of specific audiences. The omnibus channel may be on the way out.

A LARGE COMPANY SUSPECTED THAT THE NEW CRITERIA FOR THE PLACING OF ITS ADVERTISEMENTS WAS THE COMMISSION EARNED BY ITS AGENCY MODIFIED SLIGHTLY BY THE PERSONAL CONTACTS OF THE AGENCY MANAGING DIRECTOR. A NEW AGENCY WAS SELECTED. THE RESULTING MEDIA SCHEDULE WAS VERY DIFFERENT FROM THE LAST ONE DRAWN UP BY THE NEW AGENCY'S PREDECESSOR.

Question 168: Compare the media schedules you imagine might be drawn up to promote the following products:

(*a*)   glass-fibre fishing rods
(*b*)   disposable nappies
(*c*)   retirement homes
(*d*)   insulating material for steel pipes
(*e*)   coal.

17.52   Advertising Models

A model may be constructed to determine advertising expenditure into which ratios of advertising to sales revenue and likely trends in sales can be fed. Sophisticated models build in a link between advertising expenditure and the level of sales. Increases in advertising typically lead to a rise in sales until a 'saturation' point is reached at which the gains from marginal increases in advertising expenditure appear to tail off.

Special factors to include in an advertising model would be anticipated new product launches, problem product situations, allocated corporate or prestige advertising, and special campaigns such as direct mail shots for which there is a fairly typical relationship between advertising and sales. The model will need to be given a media mix and the duration and frequency of advertising. A few models can be programmed with such details as the rates for commercial television at different times of the day.

One form of advertising model aims to maximize profits by pushing advertising to the margin, the point at which any additional expenditure just equals the profit on the resulting sales. The main problems of this approach are that advertising coefficients are difficult to estimate and the ever-present time lag question. The marginal approach may not take account of the longer-term effects of advertising.

Advertising effectiveness may be discontinuous, perhaps in the form of a step function. An advertising campaign could steadily build up awareness of an interest in a product until a threshold point at which the consumer is motivated to purchase. Action then may depend upon repeated exposure to an advertisement over a period of time.

More sophisticated models build in coefficients for previous time periods so that sales becomes a function of various forms of sales activity including past advertising. A model might encompass saturation points, the sales response per unit of advertising, and to evaluate reduced and falling advertising expenditures the rate at which sales fall away in the absence of advertising or with less extensive and frequent advertising. The most sophisticated companywide model still faces problems in that predicting competitor activity may be well-nigh impossible.

Setting expenditure by model is as effective as the quality of the underlying model allows. Models need to take account of such factors as the tendency of sales to grow and decay, the fact that in oligopoly situations firms counter and match each others' expenditure, and that criteria for success need to be established as benchmarks. These could be set in absolute sales, market share, awareness, and trial or frequency of purchase terms. Sophisticated models take into account the interaction of competitors.

AN AGENCY HAD JUST PAID A LARGE SUM FOR THE CONSTRUCTION OF A COMPUTER BASED MODEL. THEN WITHIN THE SPACE OF MONTHS A NEW NATIONAL NEWSPAPER WAS LAUNCHED, PLANS WERE REVEALED FOR A NEWS MAGAZINE, TWO ENTRÉPRENEURS REVEALED THEIR INTENTION OF INTRODUCING SATURDAY NEWS-PAPERS TO THE NATION'S CAPITAL AND THE POSSIBILITY OF AN ADDITIONAL COMMERCIAL TELEVISION CHANNEL WAS ANNOUNC-ED. NATUR'ALLY NO FIGURES RELATING TO THE PROJECTED NEW MEDIA CHANNELS EXISTED. CLIENTS WERE EXPECTING SCHED-ULES FOR THE YEAR AHEAD.

17.6 EFFECTIVE ADVERTISEMENT

An effective advertisement is noticed, read, understood, believed, remembered, and acted upon. It provides not only information but must engender a favourable attitude, preferably a predisposition to purchase. Before buying a product, a customer must be aware of it, understand what it is and offers, feel the need for it, and be motivated to purchase. Effective advertising both creates awareness of need and how the need can be satisfied.

An advertisement that is unnoticed, does not attract attention, is uninteresting and uninformative, does not motivate or arouse desire is clearly a flop. A key factor to remember is that the purpose of an advertisement is to motivate purchase. An advertisement that is technically excellent and which is enjoyed but which does not encourage purchase may be an aesthetic success but is certainly a commercial failure.

Existing users of brands vary in their propensity to switch, as will the users of competitors' brands. Advertising can be effective when it prevents a decline in sales by reducing the propensity to switch to competing brands, even though this may not result in increased sales. Advertising can be defensive as well as offensive. Advertising is particularly effective when concentrated to coincide with an event such as a new product launch. On other occasions, advertising may be spread and clustered in difficult periods in order to help even out the demand for a product. Advertising peaks may have to coincide with particular periods when purchase decisions are taken. Summer holidays, for example, are often booked during the summer months.

The influence of advertising erodes over time. A television advertisement appears once before a vast audience. A billboard or a magazine advertisement may be seen many times. An advertisement in a journal may be seen many times, and may be seen long after publication. There is thus a delayed effect with some means of advertising while others are instantaneous.

A 'LOW KEY' BIRTH CONTROL CAMPAIGN HAD ADVERTISED IN A VARIETY OF MEDIA. THEN IT BEGAN TO MAKE A CONSIDERABLE 'IMPACT', WITH POSTERS OF A 'PREGNANT' MAN DISPLAYED ON FACTORY NOTICE BOARDS AND AT OTHER PLACES OF WORK.

Question 169: Describe and assess in relative terms the impacts made upon you by the following advertisements:

(*a*) Penguins advertising Penguin chocolate bars
(*b*) a long television commercial showing a foreign car to be entirely manufactured by machine
(*c*) classified advertisements in your local newspaper
(*d*) messages on the top of plastic tubs of margarine
(*e*) a political poster directed against the Labour Party showing a queue of supposedly unemployed people with the slogan 'Labour isn't working'/a political poster showing models of the leaders of a political party with the slogan 'Yesterday's Men'.

17.61 Measuring Advertising Effectiveness

Advertising varies enormously in effectiveness. Why is it that some advertising works so well? The answers are tentative; as there is a great deal of further behavioural work to be done on advertising effectiveness. Some factors are however clear: to be effective, an advertisement must be noticed, examined and read, understood, believed and remembered, and ultimately motivate or predispose to action.

Some awareness of the product and advertisement must be necessary. The simpler an advertisement is the more likely is its message to be understood. A copy writer needs to select carefully and ruthlessly a selling proposition that is likely to appeal to a target audience. An advertisement must be compatible with the target audience's view of themselves.

An advertisement may be read by past, present, and potential buyers. Its purpose could be to build up the loyalty of existing consumers by rationalizing their behaviour or to attract new consumers. Whichever orientation is chosen, the impact of an advertisement upon the non-target group cannot be ignored. The strategy may be conditioned by market performance. An established brand may adopt a protective 'build customer loyalty' strategy to ward off competition, while a new brand may have little choice but to seek to attract new customers.

The effectiveness of advertising is difficult to measure. Static sales may be evidence of effective advertising, when in its absence, sales would decline. Effective advertising normally builds upon existing attitudes and beliefs. There is an inter-action between attitudes and purchase and consumption.

An advertisement can sometimes be easily misunderstood. Retention can be more important than immediate impact; involvement can be more important than interest. Advertisements which encourage involvement and stimulate thinking have been found to be particularly effective.

When evaluating advertisements, it should be remembered that advertisements that are enjoyed and which are recalled by a high proportion of a test panel may actually have led to few sales. Advertising also needs to be evaluated in the context of total marketing activity. Effective advertising complements other promotional work.

The other-things-being-equal or *ceteris paribus* problem bedevils assessments of the effectiveness of advertising. Recognition and recall tests, the impact upon sales, all measure the impact of total promotion mix. Disaggregating the effect of advertising is often almost impossible.

THE UK CLEARING BANKS FEARED GOVERNMENT TAKEOVER. THEY DEVISED A MEANS OF PUTTING THEIR CASE TO THE PUBLIC. THEY ISSUED A SHORT SERIES OF WHOLE PAGE ADVERTISEMENTS EACH OF WHICH POSED A SMALL NUMBER OF QUESTIONS. THE ADVERTISEMENT ASKED READERS TO REGISTER THEIR VIEWS AND ANSWERS TO QUESTIONS ON A COUPON IN THE CORNER OF THE ADVERTISEMENTS, CUT THESE OUT AND SEND THEM TO THE CAMPAIGN HEADQUARTERS. THE NUMBER OF REPLIES RAN INTO TENS OF THOUSANDS. THE FINAL ONE PAGE ADVERTISEMENT IN THE SERIES WAS DEVOTED TO A SUMMARY OF THE PUBLIC'S RESPONSE, COMPLETE WITH SELECTED QUOTATIONS INCLUDING

REPRESENTATIVE OPINION OF THOSE OPPOSED TO THE OVER-
WHELMING MAJORITY VIEW WHICH WAS FOUND TO BE VERY
FAVOURABLE TO THE BANKS.

Question 170: Explain how you would propose to measure the effectiveness of
the following 'advertisements':

(*a*) a lady's girdle advertisement in a woman's magazine

(*b*) a bank's advertisement stating the loans it has recently placed
which appears in a journal read by businessmen

(*c*) an entry in the 'Yellow Pages' section of a telephone directory

(*d*) leaflets put through letter boxes with a giveaway broadsheet

(*e*) a notice in a house journal of a new pension scheme for long-
serving staff.

18. *Sales Promotion*

Chapter 6 explained how the various methods of marketing communication are brought together within an overall programme. Subsequent chapters have considered the contributions of sales staff, branding, middlemen, public relations, and advertising to such a programme. This chapter examines a number of other means of reaching customer publics which are normally considered under the general heading of sales promotion.

18.1 SALES PROMOTION

Personal selling, advertising, and the value of publicity or public-relations activity have been discussed. There are a number of other techniques which are designed to encourage quick sales and impulse purchases. Sales promotion can be particularly important in contexts in which interpersonal communications between a sales person and a potential customer is limited as is the case in many supermarkets and self-service stores.

Some sales promotion techniques such as special offers and coupons will be primarily directed at purchasers of consumer goods while others such as trade shows and exhibitions and conferences will be aimed primarily at the business customer. The common thread that links the various techniques available is the offer of an extra benefit, inducement or incentive, some additional factor which will not usually be present and which may thus, on the spur of the moment, 'tip the scales' and influence the target group.

18.2 SALES PROMOTION PUBLICS

Not all sales promotion techniques will be directed at customers. Some may be used to motivate middlemen, external agents, and dealers, while others may be directed at a company's own salesforce. Effective promotions have an urgent quality and may need to be dramatic to excite. If repeated too often, promotions may fail to be effective.

Some publics have become increasingly immune to certain forms of promotion. A customer may hold back purchases, waiting for a summer sale. A trade customer may buy while an offer lasts, and then revert to a previous buying pattern once an offer has closed. A promotion could encourage the habit of shopping around in the search for economy which could 'rebound' when competing promotions are staged.

A sales force attracted by a particular promotion may campaign for its continuance with the attendant risk of a choice between a price rise and a lower profit margin. A promotion could also affect the image and credibility of a product. The existence of a promotion could be taken as an indication of market failure, that stocks are building up and a company is anxious to sell, or that a particular batch is defective in quality, or a model is about to be replaced by a new version with more attractive features. Some publics may need reassurance.

Question 171:   Assess the relative importance that will be placed upon customer, middlemen, and sales-force promotion respectively by the following categories of company:

   (*a*)   a shipbuilder
   (*b*)   a beach café
   (*c*)   a cosmetics manufacturer
   (*d*)   a carpet manufacturer
   (*e*)   a hardware store
   (*f*)   a church
   (*g*)   a travel agency.

18.3   CONSUMER   PROMOTIONS

The special rewards or benefits offered to consumers can take many forms, samples, coupons, special offers such as discounts, trading stamps, or the opportunity to win prizes in a competition.

A sample allows a free trial of a product. Samples could be direct mailed, inserted, delivered by hand, or made available at a point-of-sale display. Where products are complementary or brand extension is desired, a company could attach a free sample of one of its new products to an existing product. It would thus only be available to purchasers of the second product. By this means, some consumers might be encouraged to try both products for the first time.

Coupons are relatively easy to distribute. A woman's magazine might contain several to be clipped out and taken along to a shop to claim a saving on the purchase of a particular product. Coupons can be direct mailed, hand delivered, inserted, or attached to or incorporated in the labelling or packaging of the product in question or other products. On occasion, retailers as well as manufacturers issue coupons. Couponing can be less expensive than sampling in the promotion of an existing product and can also be used more easily to promote a service. With a new product, sampling can be more effective in encouraging an initial trial.

Price reductions can be given in a number of ways and the marketor should be aware of legal restrictions relating to certain claims. A purchaser could be offered a return of all or part of the purchase price within a stated time, either automatically if so many labels are presented or in the event of not being completely satisfied with the purchase. An item could be simply reduced in price for a certain limited period, or extra quantity provided at the previous price or one or more products packaged and sold together at a reduced price.

A number of promotion techniques aim to give some benefit to quantity purchasers. This could take the form of a straight financial discount in the event of purchase within a stated time. A premium in the form of a small gift such as a plastic spoon or table mat could be attached to larger packs or to all packs. The product could be packaged in a special container which could have some value after the product has been used. Thus a glass jar might replace for an offer period the usual cardboard or plastic container.

Some gifts may be only supplied direct from the manufacturer on receipt of evidence of purchase. With the more substantial gift, a customer may have to save up a number of labels over a period of time. This is the principle behind the trading stamp offered by the retailer. The number and value of stamps given will depend directly upon the value of purchases. The stamps may be stored in books and redeemed for goods selected from a catalogue.

In some cases, a special price is offered to those who buy straight from the manufacturer or supplier. Such a promotion enables the provider to recoup the 'cost' of a price reduction out of a retail commission 'saved'. This principle is the basis of mail-order selling. When a product is supplied direct it can be accompanied by promotional material.

Competitions exist in many forms. Some offer a low probability of winning an attractive prize while others offer a more certain reward of lower value. The form of competition selected will depend upon what is known about the target group. With a sweepstake, a customer has only to enter the name or scratch to disclose the number on a card, while with a contest some form of entry will be required to be submitted and judged. A game involves giving a customer, perhaps a bingo card or a number to complete a sequence, or a letter to complete a company slogan each time a purchase is made, a prize being provided in the event of successful completion.

Point-of-sale promotions usually reinforce and remind when there may not be time to put across a new message. A point-of-sale technique can put a new message across which does not need to involve sales staff directly in the demonstration. A product's use or a process could however be demonstrated by sales staff and in some cases samples offered to those watching a demonstration.

An effective point of sale promotion can exert a strong influence upon a customer and can be used to back up other promotional techniques such as the use of coupons and premiums. A co-ordinated campaign will make use of complementary approaches which reinforce each other and build up as the point of purchase is approached. Thus, a banner or an external sign could attract the initial attention of the passing motorist who recognizes an image from a television advertising campaign. A prominent window display may then present some further information on the product in question and draw attention to the existence of some special offer. Entering the store to obtain further details, the physical route to the shelf location might be 'flagged' by arrows or coloured signs. The full extent of the temporary advantage of purchasing on the spot could be clearly presented on a counter card.

Question 172:   Identify and evaluate the relative cost-effectiveness of various sales-promotion techniques which might be particularly appropriate in respect of the following:

(*a*)   saloon car
(*b*)   coffee table books
(*c*)   frozen chicken
(*d*)   coin-operated laundrette
(*e*)   turret lathe.

18.31   Point-of-Sale Promotion

A customer at the point of making a purchase and confronted by a brand choice is a particularly important target public. In addition to packaging, display stands and cards, special baskets, and cardboard figures can be used to attract attention. Suppliers of series of booklets, toys, and post-cards will often provide stores with swivel display stands upon which their goods can be arranged.

In addition to in-store displays, point-of-sale promotion can also be used to attract customers into a store. Theatres and cinemas make bold use of external point-of-sale promotion. Balloons and banners can attract attention; troops of uniformed young ladies could be used for a special promotion.

Point-of-sale promotion can influence the impulse purchaser. On hot days, the majority of ice-cream lickers may be impulse purchasers attracted by the kiosk flag or the ice-cream van man's flag.

The way in which goods are displayed on a shelf or in a window can influence the rate of sales. A large window display may be professionally designed and periodically varied to retain interest among regular shoppers. Inside a shop, prominent signs and models may be used to attract attention to a counter display.

The form a counter display can take, the attractiveness of counter cards or display stands will not only influence customers but the willingness of the retailer to stock a brand. A point-of-sale promotion that is compatible with a store's image and décor can create interest and colour and attract customers to buy not only the good in question but other goods as well, once they have been attracted to a particular retail point.

Question 173:   Assess the relative value of point-of-sale promotion in respect of the following products:

- (*a*)   car tyres
- (*b*)   expensive jewellery
- (*c*)   take-away food
- (*d*)   industrial generators
- (*e*)   personal insurance.

18.32   Coupons

A coupon offers a certain reduction in price upon a specified product. Couponing can be used in isolation or in conjunction with other techniques such as sampling. Because a coupon usually has to be physically carried to the point of sale, as well as encouraging consumers to take advantage of a particular offer, it attracts customers into a store and can thus encourage a retailer to stock a brand in question. The retailer will not wish to disappoint a queue of eager shoppers with their coupons for redemption.

The coupon technique can be used to introduce shoppers to a new product or to give a boost to the sales of a long running product which is thought to be losing ground to a competitor. In the case of habitual users of a brand, additional consumption may not result, merely a temporary speeding up of stocking. Couponing is thus the least attractive when an established product is largely consumed by a loyal following and brand switching is minimal.

In the early stage of a product's life cycle, where the product is of a nature that once tried there is a high probability of repeat purchase and groups of consumers likely to use coupons can be identified and cost-effectively reached, couponing when used selectively can significantly increase trial usage. It is important that retailers are given advance warning of a coupon campaign. Much goodwill can be lost among both consumers and retailers if shop staff appear unaware of the existence of coupons or of what to do when they are presented. Retailers should not be taken by surprise by coupons or consumers faced with redemption problems.

CADBURY'S, THE CHOCOLATE MANUFACTURER, CONVINCED OF THE RELATIVE PULL OF ITS DAIRY MILK BRAND, ISSUED A ONE-PAGE COUPON ADVERTISEMENT IN THE DAILY MIRROR HEADED

'IT'S YOUR CHOICE'. THE ADVERTISEMENT INCORPORATED TWO COUPON POSSIBILITIES. THE PAGE COULD BE CUT TO PRODUCE A COUPON REDUCING THE PRICE OF ANY BAR OF CADBURY'S DAIRY MILK OR ALTERNATIVELY CUT TO YIELD A COUPON GIVING THE SAME PRICE REDUCTION ON A BAR OF 'ANY OLD CHOCOLATE'. THE CONSUMER WAS GIVEN THE CHOICE OF WHICH COUPON TO CUT BUT THE ADVERTISEMENT SUGGESTED – 'YOU'RE SURE TO CHOOSE CADBURY'S. BECAUSE – CADBURY'S IS CHOCOLATE. AND A HALF'.

18.33 Sampling

There will always be a group of potential consumers for whom seeing is believing. The promotional opportunities for showing how a product works includes demonstration to a group or putting a sample of the product into the hands of the consumer. The larger a sample is, the more expensive it will be to the producer but too small a sample may appear mean or not be regarded as a fair test. Sampling helps to encourage trial use of a new product and is most appropriate in the case of relatively cheap, easy-to-carry items which if adopted are likely to be frequently purchased.

Detergents, confectionery, toilet products, tobacco, and powdered drinks are suited to 'give-away' sample promotion. More expensive goods, such as consumer durables, could be provided on a 'trial' basis, to be returned if not purchased within so many days. Many books, particularly series, are promoted on this basis. Philatelists have traditionally circulated school-children with books of stamps on an 'approval' basis. Stamps not required are returned with a payment for those retained.

The cost of a sampling programme can be high, distribution can be complex, and the system is open to abuse. When used in conjunction with other promotional techniques, it can be cost-effective. Sampling can induce trial purchase, demonstrate an improvement or advantage that may not be apparent until a product is used, encourage stocking by middlemen, and reach those who tend to be cynical about a sales message not backed up by 'facts'.

18.34 Price Cuts and Premiums

A reduction in price on an item can be funded out of a reduction in profit margins or by giving up a part or the whole of a contribution towards overheads. A substantial reduction may still allow direct costs to be covered. Certain retailers may make a business of the sale of reduced-price items, covering the loss of margins by volume of throughput or by obtaining significant economy of bulk purchasing. A recession in the publishing industry can result in the opening of 'remaindered' book stores.

A premium that offers a substantial saving to the consumer can result in speeded up purchases and an additional quantity of purchase. A decision to introduce a premium will depend upon estimates of the long term total increase in purchases compared with the immediate revenue foregone. A number of purchases may be necessary before a consumer can take advantage of a reduced price offer or a free product or gift given. Such an approach may help to instil a purchase habit.

A form of premium that may be less attractive to the retailer is that which requires a number of labels, coupons, or tokens to be collected and mailed direct to the manufacturer. Requiring the collection of too many labels may fail to motivate or bore, if the expected return appears too remote. Where a free gift is offered, then sufficient stocks should be available to meet the expected demand. The customer will be alienated if a long delay is experienced. It is an advantage if an incentive offered is related in some way to the product concerned. A transportation company could offer a free journey.

BRITISH RAIL INTRODUCED A SPECIAL OFFER TO ANNUAL SEASON TICKET HOLDERS. A FREE CHEAP DAY RETURN TICKET TO ANY DESTINATION VOUCHER WAS OFFERED COVERING TWO ADULTS AND CHILDREN. THE VOUCHER COULD BE USED FOR STATED PERIODS DURING THE SUMMER WHEN CHILDREN WERE LIKELY TO BE ON HOLIDAY FROM SCHOOL. THE SCHEME INTRO-DUCED SOME OF THE BUSINESS TRAVELLERS TAKING IT UP TO THE POSSIBILITIES OF FAMILY LEISURE TRAVEL BY TRAIN.

18.35   Trading Stamps

The trading stamp is an example of a sales-promotion device that has gained and fallen in popularity on a cyclical basis. It is clearly an advantage to a retailer to join a scheme when it is expanding. Customers new to the trading stamp habit are likely to favour outlets offering their type of stamp and in an expansion period, the trading stamp company will be increasing the range of goods available for stamps redeemed and may well be running a media campaign to promote the stamp in question.

During the decline phase, the use of stamps becomes less attractive. Outlets wishing to drop them may fear alienating those customers 'close' to a good they have been saving stamps some time for. Competitors may be offering price reductions as an alternative that are attracting those who do not like 'licking and sticking' stamps. The novelty of stamps can wear off but the method of promotion tends to be more long-term than others, with greater attendant 'crawl out' problems.

When the majority of retail outlets used trading stamps, the competitive advantage to any individual store was lost while all stores were faced with the higher costs of running the trading stamp system. A manufacturer of a widely-used good of an oil company which provides a product which is regularly consumed could consider a company specific 'stamp'. The Co-op Movement has used coupon stamps to distribute a dividend to its customers who are, in effect, 'owners' of the business.

18.36 Give-aways

The purpose of a give-away is to remind and hence to reinforce a message. The ideal give-away is relatively cheap, frequently used and, if possible, seen by others. A pen, pencil, calendar, wall chart, or clock will be often used by the receiver. When mass-produced, the plastic pen and the calendar can be relatively cheap. A younger target public might be more willing to sport a tee shirt or to put a sticker upon a car or bicycle, thus introducing a message to others of their age group.

The give-away could present a brand or a company name. A give-away could be related to a product, for example, a can or bottle opener. The purchaser of a camera could be given a free film in the hope of effecting an introduction to a store's film processing service. There may have been a reaction against the plastic spacemen in the cereal packet but in other contexts an appropriate use of give-aways can promote repeat purchase and brand extension.

A give-away that is pitched at the right level can create goodwill. One that is perceived as too 'cheap' or as a 'bribe' can be counterproductive. A recipient is likely to be more pleased with a give-away that is promoted as selectively given to favoured friends and customers than to one which is automatically given away to all consumers or visitors. Once given regularly, a give-away can be taken for granted. The distributor can come to expect the glossy calendar.

AN AGENT PRESENTED A CLIENT WITH A LARGE BOTTLE OF WHISKEY FOR CHRISTMAS AND WAS SOMEWHAT SURPRISED TO RECEIVE AN UNFAVOURABLE REACTION. THE CLIENT WAS A TEE-TOTALLER AND HAD FELT THAT AFTER FIVE YEARS OF DOING BUSINESS TOGETHER THE AGENT DID NOT SEEM TO BE AWARE OF THIS FACT.

Question 174: Contrast and compare the value of the following sales promotion techniques in the encouragement of the purchase of an established fast-moving consumer good and a new consumer durable respectively:

- (*a*)   coupons
- (*b*)   samples
- (*c*)   special price offers
- (*d*)   trading stamps
- (*e*)   gifts.

18.4   TRADE   PROMOTIONS

A high proportion of sales may be achieved through middlemen. Trade promotions can encourage middlemen to stock and aggressively market certain products rather than others. Incentives available include price reduction, sale or return arrangements, assistance with advertising and other promotion, or contests of various kinds.

A special price may be offered to encourage stocking of a new product or the stocking up of an existing product in readiness for a producer's promotional campaign. The buying allowance must be sufficient an incentive to cover the one-off costs of introducing an additional line, and be available for long enough to enable a middleman to act. More notice and a longer take-up period may be needed than is the case with direct consumer promotion. The middleman has a choice of taking an allowance as an increased margin, spending it on promotion or offering a price reduction, passing on the benefit to a final consumer.

An allowance could be based upon a calculation of the rate of stock turn in order to encourage the stocking of faster-moving items. A manufacturer could offer to 'buy back' unsold stocks of an old product on condition that a certain number of new products or of an improved version are stocked in return. Volume allowances can be given to favour larger customers. These could take the form of reductions in the price of future purchases. Such allowances could be available on a percentage basis, the percentage rising as a series of thresholds are reached, thus giving high-purchase middlemen a relative advantage which can improve their competitive position *vis-à-vis* the ultimate customer.

Those who purchase a certain quantity of a good could be offered a free consignment of the same or another good. This could be done to secure stocking of a new good or to clear stocks of an old good. In the case of a good in the decline phase of its life cycle, or where competitors are offering an improved product, even a free consignment may be rejected when a middleman has relatively high storage and handling costs, and the prospects of significant sales are remote.

In return for stocking a good, a middleman might be offered physical or financial help in promoting the good. A manufacturer might pay an allowance for a 'mention' in local advertising or in a circulated catalogue. Display stands could be made available. The allowance could take the form of a percentage contribution to sums expended during an agreed period. The manufacturer's own advertising could carry the names and addresses of dealers and retailers who stock the good in question. Joint advertising might be possible on a cost-sharing basis. A motor car manufacturer may put a great deal of effort into dealer promotion.

A company may offer a middleman's salesforce a direct incentive in the form of a specified sum for every unit of a product sold within a stated time. While effective at motivating a salesforce, this technique may not be appreciated by the employing middlemen where, as a consequence, sales staff switch their efforts to the promotion of lines which, although more lucrative to themselves, offer the middleman a lower profit margin. A sales contest is in a similar position. The contest could be aimed either at middlemen or the middlemen's salesforces. To motivate, a reasonable chance of winning must be perceived.

The incentive could be given to a retailer in the form of a cash sum, a discount for quantity, a special gift, or help with point-of-sale promotion. Effective promotions are those which meet the retailer's needs of encouraging turnover and customer throughput, making a maximum return per unit of space, and contributing to an acceptable décor or ambiance.

An incentive in the form of a prize could be offered in conjunction with another company. Thus a prize to dealers of a holiday abroad could be promoted in such a way as to give publicity to a particular holiday or travel company and its services. Joint promotions allow complementary product producers to share costs.

A company whose products are handled by a large number of middlemen may employ direct mailings to inform them of new developments and new promotional schemes. A promotion will not work if it is not communicated to those it is intended to motivate.

Question 175: Develop a programme of promotions which might be particularly attractive to distributors and retailers respectively in the cases of the following categories of good:

- (*a*) motor cars
- (*b*) tins of paint
- (*c*) suites of sitting room furniture
- (*d*) 'fast food' hamburgers
- (*e*) confectionery
- (*f*) magazines.

18.41 Exhibitions

At a trade exhibition, a company will be competing for attention with other companies represented. A stand will need to be eye-catching to attract, and interesting to retain attention. A moving or dynamic or an audio-visual element will often cause one stand to penetrate through a confusing haze of competing messages.

Having attracted the attention of an informed potential purchaser or middleman, it is important that the desire for information that has been stimulated is satisfied. A stand should be manned by those knowledgeable about the product, and sufficient brochures and manuals should be available to meet an expected demand. It may be desirable not to have all the available information on display and to encourage those manning a stand to distinguish and discriminate between the 'professional' leaflet collector and the competitor's representative, and those genuinely interested in a potential purchase.

Some stands will be better positioned than others and will be correspondingly more expensive. The size and furnishings of a stand should match an organization's corporate image and the 'presence' it wishes to establish. There may be public relations as well as marketing objectives behind participation in an exhibition.

18.5 SALES-FORCE PROMOTIONS

A number of the problems of motivating a salesforce were examined in Chapter 10. Sales staff can be offered cash payments for the achievement of a certain level of sales. Their interest might be captured by a sales contest that fosters and appeals to the competitive spirit. Periodic conferences could be held to introduce new products, explain consumer feedback, discuss the relative effectiveness of different sales techniques, and generally motivate and raise morale.

A bonus scheme could be aimed at all sales staff or be designed to consciously discriminate in favour of above-average performance. A scheme needs to take account of the fact that some sales territories are more promising than others. An award on the basis of a percentage or relative increase might be more acceptable than one based on absolute sales.

Question 176: Identify promotion techniques which would be particularly well suited to the motivation of sellers of a fast-moving consumer good and an industrial good respectively.

18.6 PROMOTION OPPORTUNITIES

A number of media hold competitions of various kinds. Considerable promotional mileage might be obtained from the donation of a prize. On other occasions, an organization might be able itself to take the initiative and establish and sponsor a prize or award in conjunction with a programme or event.

An anniversary may be the occasion to stage a number of events. Promotions can be built upon the achievement of an honour or award, exhibitions or shows, new products, plants or orders, a joint venture or innovative plan, a position change in a league table ranking or the visit of a VIP. An organization may find advantages in some kind of formal association with one or more popular personalities.

Promotional material could be enclosed in a shareholder letter. Direct mail can allow a variety of publications such as house journals to be sent to a variety of publics. A house or dealer journal could stage competitions.

Gifts should be employed with caution. They should relate to a company's products, and should appear both reasonable and appropriate. A gift that is not pitched at the right level can be counterproductive. A gift may be more acceptable in certain contexts and at certain times than at others. A Christmas voucher can be acceptable while a calendar can put across a simple message for the duration of a year. Special discounts can be an incentive. Consumer-good companies with relatively cheap products which are frequently bought, generally find it easier to issue vouchers.

18.7 CHARACTER MERCHANDISING

Character merchandising aims to build upon an established image or reputation by means of the halo effect. Attributes or qualities associated with the image or reputation in question may be associated with or ascribed to the products or services to which it is symbolically attached. The technique is rather similar to brand extension, which spreads a good name across a family of products.

The subject of merchandising should be acceptable in terms of a corporate image, be quickly and easily recognized and understood, and arouse favourable and appropriate emotions. Care needs to be taken in setting up merchandising arrangements. Subjects aware of their 'pull' are likely to seek to negotiate high 'prices' in the form of fees and royalties.

Merchandising takes many forms. A family of products may be conceived at the outset or 'spin-offs' introduced later following initial success. A strong visual identity makes for easier merchandising. Micky Mouse for example is readily recognizable in many cultures. Some products are more easily subjected to merchandising than others. It is relatively easy to attach an image to a T-shirt or an ice-cream or ice-lolly wrapper. Merchandising can be used to associate sports wear and goods with a particular sporting personality. The sportsman or woman concerned might just allow a name to be used or go so far as to 'endorse' a product and actually actively promote it.

A successful film may give rise to a family of spin-off products. There will be the book of the film and the record of the film's music. An existing book may be brought out in a new edition, with a still from the film as a cover, in readiness for a film's opening. A particular style of clothing or a certain symbol could be used in clothes merchandising. A James Bond film could give rise to toy James Bond rocket-firing cars. A space adventure could give rise to a range of toy spaceships and plastic reproductions of film characters.

The possibility of merchandising income might be built into a project's budget and merchandising income actively sought. A major show or film production might involve positive approaches to manufacturers setting out the publicity and other spin-off advantages of having their name or products featured. A separate division or company may be established to market the merchandising exploitation of a popular cartoon character.

Swift action may be needed to take advantage of merchandising opportunities. The market for badges of a visiting pop star may be 'here today and gone tomorrow'. Fashion and entertainment are sources of opportunistic merchandising innovation.

Certain publics may be more susceptible to the merchandising approach than others. Merchandising can appeal particularly to the young and to groups with strong likes and dislikes. The child may find the same character type appearing on a cardboard cereal packet or a crisps packet, on an item of clothing, as a model in a toy shop, and as a character in a comic or cartoon strip. A visit to a summer fair may reveal adult-sized 'dressed up' characters.

Merchandising is particularly effective in out-of-doors and point-of-sale promotions. With durable goods, those involving time for reflection and perhaps the involvement of more than one person in the purchase decision process, the reaction to merchandising can be 'so what?'. Some characters are disliked as well as liked, so that merchandising can polarize. Some characters are 'longer lasting' than others; some will bore. In the case of widely-recognized characters, the general public may have prior expectations and attitudes which while appropriate to one product might not be to another. Thus, those holding merchandising copyrights may be reluctant to see an image, character, or name used in certain contexts.

A successful merchandising partnership can offer benefits for all parties. A major company investing in merchandising may not only gain from association with a particular character but may also do a great deal to promote the character. Being more widely-recognized and associated with a product that is favourably regarded may allow the copyright-holder to negotiate more lucrative future arrangements than would have been the case in the absence of a big company 'take up' of the character concerned.

IN THE EVENT OF THE VISIT OF THE POPE TO IRELAND THE CATHOLIC CHURCH ENTERED INTO A JOINT VENTURE ARRANGE-MENT WITH A PROFESSIONAL MERCHANDISING COMPANY IN ORDER TO PARTICIPATE IN THE PROFITS MADE OUT OF MER-CHANDISING OPPORTUNITIES ARISING FROM THE TRIP. THE JOINT VENTURE WHILE UNABLE TO PREVENT THE PRODUCTION OF 'PIRATE' SOUVENIRS WAS ABLE TO PRODUCE AN EXTENSIVE RANGE OF 'OFFICIAL' SOUVENIRS FOR THE VISIT.

Question 177:   Anticipate the problems that might arise in the cases of merchandising exploitation of the following subjects or properties:

      (*a*)   an emerging rock star
      (*b*)   an established television news reader
      (*c*)   a 'seaside' show comic
      (*d*)   a strip cartoon character
      (*e*)   a children's show puppet
      (*f*)   a supersonic aeroplane
      (*g*)   a style of clothing derived from a particular film

(*h*)   a mythical beast
(*i*)   a historical character/analogy.

18.8   SPONSORSHIP

Sponsorship can put a name across and promote an image. Large companies can sponsor a range of sports and arts activities; smaller companies and professional and other non-profit organizations can sponsor awards and lectures. One UK clearing bank supports 140 separate activities. Considerable sums of money are involved in sponsorship.

The most attractive activities from the point of view of the potential sponsor are those that attract publicity and media coverage. There are some specialist consultancies able to advise those considering sponsorship for the first time. The UK Sports Council has operated an advisory bureau which maintains an index of activities seeking sponsor backing and is prepared to examine and advise on draft sponsorship agreements. The exact terms of a sponsorship agreement can be a sensitive matter and it is wise to tread carefully.

Sports vary enormously in image and in the type of supporter they attract. The manager of an exclusive 'up market' product should seek polo rather than football to sponsor. Companies tend to prefer to sponsor activities whose images are perceived to match their own. Some areas appear rather 'crowded', and new entrants may be reluctant to enter the field. Thus, some quite well-known football clubs have difficulty in attracting sponsor support.

It should be remembered that individuals and teams lose as well as win: popular support can be fickle. A team can have an 'off season'. Individual sponsorship in a competitive sport can be more risky than team sponsorship. Injury can put an end to a promising career. The chart-topping musician may be a 'Mr Clean' one day and billed in tabloids as involved in a sex or drug scandal the next. A company can be at risk with sponsorship in a very public way.

A conscious sponsorship strategy should be drawn up. A typical decision relates to the issue of width versus depth. It is less risky to maintain a diversified portfolio of sponsorships but the cost can be the failure to make a real impact in any one field. Cost-effective activities should relate to the product in question. A cigarette manufacturer worried about the health risks of smoking could sponsor an out-of-doors pursuit such as rodeo riding. A company interested in reaching senior managers would favour golf sponsorship rather than greyhound racing.

Sports that attract broadcast media attention tend to attract sponsors. Poster sites and stadium advertising can allow product names to be unconsciously absorbed by those watching football or motor racing on television. It should be remembered that the broadcast media are international.

AUDIENCES RUNNING INTO HUNDREDS OF MILLIONS WATCH TELEVISION WORLD CUP MATCHES. MOTHERCARE ADVERTISED ON THE WALLS OF A WORLD CUP STADIUM IN MEXICO AT WHICH THE ENGLISH TEAM PLAYED ITS MATCHES. THE COMPANY'S AIM WAS NOT TO REACH A LOCAL AUDIENCE BUT VIEWERS IN THE UK WHO WATCHED THE MATCHES ON TELEVISION.

In some cases, legal controls can be circumvented by sponsorship activity. Thus, while tobacco advertising may be banned from television, a company manufacturing cigarettes could put its name across by sponsoring a particular league or series or by sign displays erected at outside-broadcast coverage of the activity concerned.

The actual form sponsorship takes can be varied. Sponsorship support in absolute terms is highly significant for a number of leisure activities. Financial support could be in the form of specific grant or subsidy, loss guarantee, or a cost-sharing arrangement involving joint project management. If an arrangement is to work, both parties must be open at the outset and each must benefit if agreement is to be reached. Any activity that is seeking sponsorship should be aware that many will assume it to be endorsing the products and/or services of the supporting organization.

In setting up sponsorship arrangements it is important not to be taken in by activity glamour. The likely spin-offs should not be exaggerated. A number of sports are governed by strict codes and rules and a sponsor may have to be bound by a number of these. Care should be taken not to compromise an amateur status. It is usually wise to seek the advice of the governing body of the sport concerned.

Risk should be consciously considered in sponsorship decisions. Outdoor activities can be rained off while indoor activities tend not to be affected by weather. A badly timed event can result in a product name being associated with a poor attendance. Worse still is the association with failure or a crash.

A sponsorship agreement should incorporate objectives, a timetable, an agreed division of labour and periodic liaison and reporting arrangements in a formal agreement. The detailed responsibilities of all parties should be spelt out. Confusion can arise where a division of work is not agreed. Each party could for example send separate press releases to the same media.

Question 178: As manager of the following events identify producers of products and suppliers of services you might approach with a view to the negotiation of a possible sponsorship arrangement:

    (*a*)   a national symphony orchestra
    (*b*)   a local town fête or carnival
    (*c*)   a regional chess championship
    (*d*)   horse trials
    (*e*)   national water skiing championship

(*f*)   an air display

(*g*)   a visit by an internationally known film star to his/her birth place.

19. *Social Marketing*

Not all marketing activity will be undertaken to directly benefit the party under-taking the activity. People and organizations campaign for good causes. It might be felt in the long run to benefit a company to be seen as a 'good citizen'. The motivation for social marketing can be varied. The purpose of social marketing is not to encourage a purchase but rather to alter attitudes and/or behaviour, gener-ally towards a 'third party' campaign or cause. Support of public service broad-casting could be regarded as a form of social marketing.

19.1 THE SCOPE OF SOCIAL MARKETING

Social marketing is usually more than a gift to chartiy. It implies some active involvement in a process. The purpose of social marketing is the promotion of social ideas. The basic principles of marketing are involved but may need to be tailored to the specific requirements of what is being promoted and the character-istics of the target groups.

Where social marketing is undertaken for 'spin-off' or halo benefits then, while the techniques of marketing may be used, the activity might largely involve the work and resources of a public relations department. Social causes and programmes organizations, the charity, lobby or non-profitmaking organization will consider promotional activity its mainstream work and considerable expertise may be built up in a certain areas. There are specialist consultancies able to advise on social marketing.

19.11 Causes and Campaigns

A cause programme may aim to motivate specific action such as take-up of an emergency measure, change a longer-term habit such as not fastening a seat belt on short journeys, or influence attitudes or beliefs on an issue such as the stock-piling of neutron bombs in Europe or the needs of the developing countries.

An innoculation programme will not succeed if the principles of marketing are not followed. Target groups must be made aware of a problem and a need. A product that is cost-effective will have to be made, packaged, and distributed. The product must be presented in a form acceptable to potential recipients. It may have to be advertised locally, target groups being made aware of where it can be obtained, and encouraged by point-of-delivery promotion to come forward and receive it.

A group that is not familiar with vaccinations will have to be treated differently than one which is. A campaign may focus upon early take-up by opinion formers, those others will imitate. Some incentives may need to be provided if innoculation is voluntary. The place of innoculation may have to be made less intimidating. A separate promotion may be staged, aimed at encouraging mothers to bring their children along.

A campaign can create a widespread awareness of a problem or need, but be less clear about what action can be taken. There may be little point arousing concern in a group that is in practice powerless to do anything about a particular situation. Some campaigns have created interest without providing any effective means of feedback. There will be those with questions or in search of further information. A social-marketing campaign should incorporate follow-up according to a response that is expected.

The very enthusiasm behind a social marketing campaign can confuse a target group assailed from different directions by varied and unco-ordinated promotions. Too much activity can bore. A target group may resent overt intrusion, being forced to think and challenge when they turned to a medium in the search for entertainment and reinforcement. While a group may have to be unsettled to be shaken out of their apathy, it should be remembered that, emotionally, the source of the unsettling message is likely initially to provoke hostility.

The promotion of a programme rather than a cause may require a more personal approach when the recipient of a message is being invited to participate. A programme may call for volunteers. A message seeking to encourage volunteers for project work in underdeveloped countries should make use of channels directed at promising publics, perhaps a college newspaper read by the relatively idealistic young.

A programme may offer significant benefits to participants. The advantages would need to be stressed in advertisements and promotions. Thus, a safe driving campaign promotion could appeal positively to the prospects of lower insurance premiums or, negatively, to injuries received by children as a result of the lack of skill of their parent drivers. With many programmes which benefit both the individual participant and a wider society, a crucial question is how much to charge the individual when there are both private and social benefits from the activity in question.

Social marketing recognizes that there are societal as well as individual consequences of consumption. The time dimension may be different for the individual and for society. There may be aesthetic and environmental considerations of concern to society but not to an individual. To internalize an externality a number of approaches could be adopted. Property rights could be redefined, standards set, activities prohibited or taxed or incentives given to encourage that which is felt to be socially desirable. Where the boundary lies between which activities fall within the private sector and are properly the concern of the individual and individual decision or the public sector and are legitimately the concern of government, is a political question.

THE LONDON BOROUGH OF GREENWICH FOUND ITSELF, THROUGH ITS ARTS SUPPORT, RECREATIONAL AND ADULT EDUCATIONAL ACTIVITIES AND INTERESTS, INVOLVED WITH A GREAT MANY LEISURE PURSUITS. IT WAS FOUND, PARTICULARLY DURING LONG SUMMER SCHOOL HOLIDAYS, THAT SERVICES PROVIDED WERE LARGELY UNCO-ORDINATED AND THEIR EXISTENCE WAS NOT ALWAYS APPRECIATED BY THOSE AT WHICH THEY WERE DIRECTED. A GREENWICH FESTIVAL WAS INTRODUCED. THE FESTIVAL, HELD EACH SUMMER, INTRODUCED A COMPREHENSIVE, CO-ORDINATED AND CUMULATIVE PROGRAMME COMPRISING ACTIVITIES AIMED AT A VARIETY OF PUBLICS, FROM PUNCH AND JUDY SHOWS FOR YOUNG CHILDREN TO CHAMBER MUSIC FOR THE HIGHBROW, ALL OF WHICH WERE MARKETED BY A SINGLE DOCUMENT ACTING AS BOTH BROCHURE AND CALENDAR WHICH WAS DROPPED THROUGH LETTERBOXES TO ALL HOUSEHOLDS IN THE BOROUGH.

Question 179:   Draw up a social marketing programme for a newly appointed:

- (*a*)   marketing director of a private health care scheme
- (*b*)   borough Public Health Inspector
- (*c*)   University Public Relations Officer
- (*d*)   oil company executive
- (*e*)   parish priest
- (*f*)   National Theatre Director.

19.2   PUBLIC PROGRAMMES

A marketing approach can have a major impact upon a range of public programmes. A service might be provided at an inconvenient time. Those at which it is directed may not be aware of its existence. A programme may overtly be run for the benefit of 'consumers' while in practice being organized mainly to meet the needs and interests of the 'producers', the programme staff.

The marketing orientation puts first priority upon uncovering the needs of the consumer. The problems of a service are defined in consumer need rather than production terms. Thus a hospital's major problem may appear to an administrator to be filling a plate-glass hospital with the latest piece of electronic equipment to enable senior surgeons to complete research papers. A marketing orientation in contrast may reveal that significant improvements to health might be achieved by reducing expenditure upon hospital equipment and investing more in product safety campaigns, discouraging smoking and promoting healthy diet and keep-fit classes.

In time a public programme can grow away from the needs of those at which it is targeted. These needs themselves may have changed. A programme may have been born in response to a temporary or atypical situation or problem. An educational system might have to adapt its 'product' in quantity to demographic trends and in content to a wave of immigration, perhaps of a different culture. New product demands may have arisen for education or for continuing education. Certain subjects may have become less popular. Technological developments may give rise to new subject areas and to new methods of teaching.

Organizations that do not adapt to new needs will find themselves challenged by institutions that do. A public health system with long waiting lists may find itself in competition with private medicine. Private health insurance may emerge alongside state provision. A traditional university may offer fixed course packages on a 'take it or leave it' basis which are built upon the private research interests of teachers. An alternative or non-traditional university might emerge able to recognize 'life experience', willing to allow extra-mural or distance learning and offering an individual learning programme tailored to the capabilities and personal goals of each student and drawing upon the most appropriate members of a network of supporting scholars.

The introduction of social marketing can have a significant impact upon values. Institutional values may be dominant. Individuals may have to adjust to the needs of institutions. Social marketing can promote consumer values, people centred values, the notion of the main purpose of the institution being to meet the needs of the groups that it serves rather than vice versa.

19.21 Public Programme Effectiveness

The techniques of marketing can be employed to assess the effectiveness of public programmes. A great many programmes may be felt to be a 'good thing' without having ever been systematically evaluated. The marketing approach can help to reveal the extent to which a programme is achieving its objectives and whether or not these objectives themselves are necessarily the most appropriate.

The focus of evaluation will be impact upon the target group. Many social programmes are difficult to measure and assess because other things will not have remained constant during the course of a programme. Thus a change that is observed may have been due to some other variable in which case it would have occurred if the programme had not existed.

Public programme evaluation has become a specialism in its own right. There are a number of research designs that can be used. The most rigorous approach from the point of view of reliability and validity is that which takes a population randomly selected and randomly allocated into two groups, a target and a control group. The two groups are 'measured'. The programme is then administered to the target group but not to the control group and after a suitable interval, that is thought sufficient to allow the programme to work, the two groups are 'measured' again. The differences between the target and control groups will be a measure of the impact of the programme upon the former.

In practice a simple control experiment may be very difficult to set up. Measurement of a programme at all may be regarded as a 'political' act. There could be powerful vested interests in favour of the continuance of a programme. With a programme that is felt subjectively to be effective, as with a form of medical treatment, there may be moral objections to the withholding of a treatment which is thought to be effective from members of a control group displaying the condition for which the treatment has been developed.

Question 180:   Draw up marketing criteria of effectiveness for the following programmes and set out means by which the effectiveness could be measured:

    (*a*)   coronary care units
    (*b*)   an agricultural product support programme
    (*c*)   an adult literacy programme
    (*d*)   Legal Aid
    (*e*)   Royal Air Force trainee pilot recruitment scheme.

19.3   NON-PROFIT MARKETING

Not all organizations aim to make a profit. The non-profit voluntary body may however be as interested as an organization motivated by profit in attracting income and in letting selected people know about the service it operates. Marketing skills are clearly appropriate both to putting a 'package' across to potential donors, convincing a public authority that regulatory action might be needed and in informing people of their rights and meeting their identified needs.

The non-profit organization need not necessarily be in the public sector. Private charities exist and in many societies private hospitals, schools and universities. The continued existence of these institutions depends upon the successful marketing of the services they provide. It has been suggested that this dimension has resulted in the need to enlarge the marketing concept. Against this it has been argued that whether one is marketing religion, sport or soap the same old marketing concepts apply.

Marketing in the non-profit sector does cause special problems. One may be marketing an idea, a cause rather than a tangible product. Ideas often however have their practical implications and many a new product has begun as a concept. Whether one is 'selling' a health care team, places at a graduate school, or an organization that is concerned with homelessness, success surely depends upon being flexible and precise in the definition of target groups, products and messages.

The success or failure of a birth control programme, quite apart from its intrinsic merits, assuming these can be agreed, may depend upon how it is marketed. A social welfare programme may fail due to lack of 'market' research — there might be both an embarassing overall housing surplus and a severe shortage of sheltered accommodation as a result of a failure to correctly identify demographic trends.

Any non-profit organization must devise a product or service that meets a need. It may have to be differentiated from other similar services and organizations. There may be a seasonal problem. A price may have to be established to avoid the making of a loss or to keep a loss to a level that can be covered by donations. The price itself may be used to ration a service; where demand exceeds supply a rationing device of some form may be required. There will be questions of efficiency, of the alternative uses of resources: some non-profit organizations have 'profit' products to compete with.

Rather than promoting to the world at large, identifying a specific group and offering a tailored service is often the essence of voluntary activity and this is what marketing is all about, identifying and meeting specific needs. Non-profit groups are organizations and deploy resources and generally operate within a 'market' in that there are groups and individuals beyond themselves they desire to reach. So long as these conditions exist there is scope for marketing. Efficient social marketing can promote the efficient use of resources to achieve socially desirable goals.

EXAMINATION QUESTIONS

1. Organizations have a responsibility for the social consequences of their decisions. Evaluate this statement indicating the possible areas of conflict between marketing goals and social goals.

2. Evaluate the impact of the micro-processor on UK industry and society in the next decade.

3. Is the recently fashionable concern with 'social marketing' any more than a reflection of marketing educators' distaste for the profit motive?

4. Has consumerism become a casualty to inflation?

20. *Market Research*

Effective marketing communication is two-way communication. Chapters 20 to 22 examine communications from the market. By means of market research a company can itself create structured channels for communications from the market. It needs also to be aware of the activities of competitors and of social, regulatory and economic trends that are, or could become, a significant influence upon its marketing activities. Communications from the market might suggest that some approaches be played down and others be utilized more in the marketing promotion mix.

20.1 THE MARKETING INFORMATION SYSTEM

Within a large company, senior management will devote considerable time and financial resources to the communications aspects of the marketing system, the marketing information system. More companies are coming to realize that not only do people, materials, plant and money need to be managed, but so also does information.

Breakdowns and imperfections in the marketing information system are easy to spot. Too much or too little information may be produced. It may be of the wrong kind, never delivered when needed and always appear to get into the hands of the wrong people. The organization will also have its staff who fudge figures to conceal poor performance or to gain credit.

As society becomes more complex and customer needs become ever more difficult to satisfy, an individual company can face an information explosion. An organization must be receptive to what is going on around it. It must not screen out vital information; at the same time, it must be able to refine information, to order it and present it in such a way that it can be used for analysis, decision-making, and control. The more forward-looking a company is, the more changeable its business environment, the greater its concern will be with the efficient management of information.

Question 181: At what points does information about the marketing environment enter the marketing system of the organization with which you are most familiar? Is the organization reactive or proactive?

The total-information system of a company will have many components, accounting, production, financial, and marketing. The marketing information portion comprises those areas of the total-information system which are employed to service marketing decision-makers.

Information systems generally consist of a selecting mechanism which gathers relevant information, a decision-making process which assesses this information and takes decisions in the light of the organization's agreed objectives, and an effector mechanism which puts the decisions taken into effect. A particular system might be strong or weak in one or more of these areas.

The information-gathering role is frequently overlooked in smaller organizations. There is a tendency to sit back and react to whatever turns up. An organization should go out and actively seek the information it needs. It should both initiate and respond.

Information can enter an organization at a number of points. The marketing manager may find that there are also several sources of useful information within the organization which the marketing department can plug in to. The accounting department, for example, may produce a variety of control reports on marketing performance. The analysis of sales profitability by product, area, customer, channel, or territory can be particularly valuable.

Business   Company   Marketing   Information   System   Marketing
Environment   management

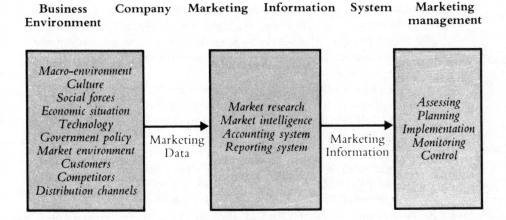

Feed back

Figure 20.1   The Marketing Information System

MAJOR US CORPORATIONS HAVE, IN SOME CASES, BUILT UP
THINK TANKS, GROUPS OF HIGHLY-QUALIFIED STAFF, WHO
DEVELOP SCENARIOS OF ALTERNATIVE FUTURES AND ATTEMPT
TO ATTACH PROBABILITIES TO MAJOR THREATS AND OPPOR-
TUNITIES WHICH MIGHT AFFECT THEIR ORGANIZATIONS. SUCH
EVALUATIONS HAVE BEEN LINKED TO COMPUTER-BASED WORLD
MODELS.

Question 182:   Compare and contrast the information systems of the following:

- (*a*)   a financial analyst
- (*b*)   a ship-based guided missile
- (*c*)   an embassy
- (*d*)   a sports complex.

20.11   Using the Information System

Before commissioning research work, a marketing manager should first check that
the information he seeks is not available elsewhere within the organization. The
corporate planning department, for example, may have accumulated information
on market trends or competitor performance. A management services department
might exist which can provide the techniques required to process one's information. An individual manager should be prepared to tap into an organization's total
information system. Sales reports can often be obtained from a variety of sources
and in differing formats. The accounts clerk may prepare one set, a salesman in
the field another. A marketing manager should develop a critical attitude towards
information: it is only as good as the credibility of its source.

There is little point generating information that is not used. From time to time,
an information audit should be carried out to determine what is no longer needed
and what new requirements have arisen which are unmet. The exception principle
should be employed, that is, control limits established and reports only made
when these are exceeded. The system then only reports the problems, where things
are going astray will stand out.

The timeliness of information is crucial. However good a report, it is useless if
it arrives after a decision has been taken. Information costs money to produce.
Even when good information arrives on time, one should always ask whether the
benefits obtained from having it justify its cost.

Managing an information system becomes even more difficult when it embraces
external organizations with dissimilar cultures.   One organization whose staff
rigidly adhere to its deadlines may rely upon information from another, say a
sales agent, which is not so concerned either with the accuracy of its information
or its timely presentation. In this type of situation, the marketing manager must
learn to assess and to take a realistic view of the credibility and capacity of external
information sources.

An information chain can only be as strong as its weakest link. Very often, reporting deficiencies in one area cannot be compensated for by accurate and detailed work elsewhere. However good an information system may appear on paper, its output will reflect the quality of its input.

> IT IS SAID THAT AMERICAN AUTHORITIES IN WASHINGTON RECEIVED PRIOR WARNING OF AN IMPENDING ATTACK BY THE JAPANESE UPON THEIR NAVAL BASE AT PEARL HARBOUR. THE MESSAGE WAS NOT UNDERSTOOD. THERE WERE CONSIDERABLE DELAYS IN ITS TRANSMISSION AND IT FAILED TO ARRIVE IN TIME IN THE HANDS OF SOMEONE ABLE TO TAKE APPROPRIATE ACTION.

Question 183: Set out what you consider to be the weak points of a marketing information system with which you are familiar. How would you remedy these?

20.12 Users and Information

An important behavioural point to bear in mind is that different executives vary enormously in their reactions to changes in the volume and type of information. Managers have distinct information styles. Some have a greater desire for information than others, are more catholic in their sources and more prepared to change these sources. Some find it less easy to be objective than others. A manager can become less tolerant of detail over time. A sudden increase of information can lead to concentration upon the minutiae and the short term.

A marketing manager should have no difficulty in accepting that information must be user-orientated. Information that is rammed down an unwilling throat is unlikely to be used effectively. It is generally a good idea to ask people what information they would like, in what form and how often. This usually gives rise to demands for more than is justified on a cost effectiveness basis, but the exercise is worth carrying out as it can identify gaps in the current information.

Question 184: Rank some executives with whom you work according to their ability to handle and cope with information and justify your ranking.

A major problem that arises when external organizations are employed stems from the impossibility of closely observing outside staff at work or even, in some cases, of knowing who actually does certain work. Behavioural problems are thus difficult to detect. Assessing a source becomes tricky when one has little idea of who is working 'at the coal face', or of the conditions and practices of work. The tendency in these situations is to judge a source on the basis of its track record. While this needs to be done, in addition every effort should be made to meet external organization staff and to assess them.

The marketing manager may also need to spend some time examining the structure of the external organizations with which he deals and the personalities of their key figures. The behaviour of certain individuals may only 'fit into place' and be understood against the background of the organizational context.

A number of large organizations have been found to lack any regular source of information on developments at the EEC headquarters in Brussels. One manager failed to read an urgent assessment of a new proposed directive that threatened to profoundly change the nature of his business, due to its being 'lost' on his desk amongst a pile of routine reports which were never read but were, for the sake of appearances, scattered over his desk for a few days before being thrown away.

Question 185: One of your salesmen has burst into your office to request information on sales over the past ten years to major customers. He believes he has uncovered a 'customer life-cycle' which might form the basis of more accurate sales forecasts. Describe your response. How would you assess the likely cost-effectiveness of the proposed exercise?

20.2 THE INFORMATION INPUT

Our initial summary diagram of the marketing system in section 13.11 showed a company receiving money and information from its customers. The money flow will be managed by the accountancy and finance function. The marketing manager will be more concerned with the information input, marketing intelligence. The manager who considers what market information he needs and then actively sets about acquiring it is engaging in market research.

20.21 Marketing Intelligence

Marketing intelligence can be carried out inside or outside of the organization. Many specialist firms are able to perform specific projects. Market intelligence is basically what, amongst all that is going on in the world, is likely to affect demand for the company's products. It can be obtained passively or actively and, if actively, by searching with varying degrees of formality. There will often be long time lags between a significant event happening and the company's identification of it.

It is frequently cost-effective to pay for rather than gather specialist information. An external expert can spread the overhead cost of a service across a number of users. An example would be the use of a Parliamentary monitoring service or the purchase of index ratings or a ratio analysis of firms in a particular industry. Contract market research such as attitude surveys might be employed. Some firms bring in information science consultants to advise them on how to more effectively evaluate, summarize, report, store and access information.

Question 186: Map out the marketing intelligence subsystem of an organization with which you are familiar. How do you account for the allocation of work inside and outside of the organization?

20.22 Selecting Intelligence Gatherers

Before entering into an external arrangement it is wise to examine samples of work undertaken by the organizations concerned, to visit their premises, meet as many of their staff as possible and ask for references and client lists. The objectives of a study and the procedure to be followed should be agreed at the outset and a written brief agreed prior to signature of any contract.

When negotiating terms it is usually a good idea to assess how important the job in question is to the organization with which one is negotiating. This gives some idea of one's bargaining position. Always obtain more than one quotation.

If one is buying specialist services it is important to be satisfied that an outside firm has the required expertise. It may have done good work in other fields, but it does not inevitably follow that it will be able to find its way around in one's own. An external company may have the nation's experts on its books. This will be an academic point however if these people are employed on other accounts. Always find out who will actually be doing the work.

Question 187: Compare the functions of the Soviet 'spy' trawler shadowing a NATO exercise with the intelligence work of the new business development manager.

20.23 Sources of Information

Customers are a major source of market information. Some companies just react to incoming suggestions, while others go out and actively seek opinions. Salesmen who should be in constant touch with customers and their requirements can suggest new methods of dealing with customer needs. It should be made clear to salesmen during their training that an important part of their job is to carry information on the company and its products to the customer and to bring back to the company information about the customer.

A company should keep a careful watch on its competitors by means of purchasing and examining their products, attending shows, reading the trade press and by talking to their past or present employees, agents and associates. Research and other associations can provide background information, so can a specific literature search and review. Other people's patents should not be overlooked as a source of information. If it is worth protecting, it is likely to have some commercial value. Technical information might be obtained from licensing consultants and patent brokers, from the monthly 'product licensing index' or from the National Research and Development Corporation.

As incoming information originates in outside sources, collecting and assessing it requires the establishment of relationships of some sort with outside organizations, if only at the level of watching them. The more resources that are available, the easier it becomes to track an information flow and to follow it back into its source, to determine how and why and under what conditions it originated. This assists the assessment of its credibility and value.

A MANAGER RESPONSIBLE FOR AN OVERSEAS SALES TERRITORY IN AFRICA FOUND THAT THE BEST SOURCE OF INFORMATION ON THE LOCAL ACTIVITIES OF COMPETITORS WAS THE MANAGER OF THE BAR IN THE AREA'S LEADING HOTEL. THE HOTEL WAS VISITED BY VIRTUALLY EVERY VISITOR OF CONSEQUENCE TO THE TERRITORY CONCERNED. THE MANAGER WAS SURPRISED ONE DAY ON BEING TOLD THAT THE BAR MANAGER'S INCOME IN 'TIPS' FROM FOREIGN COMPANIES WAS REPUTED TO BE SOME TEN TIMES HIS OFFICIAL SALARY.

Question 188: List the sources of information resorted to by your company. In each case, assess the credibility of the source, what happens to the information it provides and whether this information could be obtained from another source and, if so, the arguments for and against a change of source. How frequently are information sources reviewed and what action follows these periodic reviews?

20.3 RESEARCH

Measurement should have a purpose. Research should begin with a hypothesis to be tested. A marketor's hypothesis could be that a certain expenditure on advertising and promotion, the communication variables, has resulted in an increase in sales. Not only will the extent of the expenditure and the increase in sales need to be measured but some means will have to be developed in drawing up a research design to distinguish the advertising and promotion effects from those of other variables such as seasonal factors or competitive activity. The increase in ice-cream sales that occurs might have been stimulated in part by abnormally high temperatures.

Some exploratory research may be undertaken in order to identify problem areas and assist in the drawing up of an hypothesis. A good point with which to begin could be an existing literature. Other market research studies in libraries of business schools or available in published form might be available. Expert knowledge might be available to be tapped or similar situations may exist elsewhere from which it might be possible to learn. There is usually little point in re-inventing the wheel.

When time and resources are limited a descriptive study may be undertaken. This can be achieved by an in-depth study of a relatively small number of particular buyer—seller contexts, examining all the factors influencing a purchase. Alternatively the main influences only might be taken in a much larger number of cases and measured statistically. A descriptive study as the name suggests, describes. It can enable a prediction or forecast to be made. If an understanding of why an effect has occurred is desired then a causal study would need to be undertaken.

Question 189:   Assess the relative values of case-study (small number of cases, large number of variables) and statistical (large number of cases, small number of variables) market research approaches in respect of:

(*a*)   cans of soft drinks
(*b*)   guided missile carriers
(*c*)   private education savings plans
(*d*)   a stateman's memoirs.

Market research should be relevant and purposive, seeking to improve profitability and/or reduce costs. It should never become a ritual carried on for bureaucratic or organizational political reasons. The work of market research can be carried out by line managers or by staff specialists or by mixed teams. Elaborate techniques should not be employed to satisfy professional pride. The objective of analysis should be kept in mind which is to assist in the taking of more informed marketing decisions.

20.31   Market Research Techniques

A market researcher needs to determine what information is needed for what purpose, where it might be found and in what form, how, from whom and in what form data should be collected and when, to whom, by what means and in what form it should be presented. Information required should relate to a problem and be needed. Helpful information might reduce uncertainty and allow certain options to be dropped. Where resources are limited it may be advisable to think twice before collecting information that is required for 'interest' and for which there does not appear to be a clearly defined use.

Information can be obtained from both primary and secondary sources. Collecting or generating primary or original data can be considerably more expensive than making use of already existing secondary data. It might be a good discipline to compare the expected cost of substantial research with the difference between the expected value of a marketing decision with and without the benefit of the research in question.

In order to save resources it is generally a good idea to establish the type of data required and give some thought as to how it might be analysed and presented prior to data collection. When this is not done a great deal of effort might be expended in the collection of data which is not subsequently used.

If a certain level of reliability is desired it might also be advisable to determine what level of reliability is likely to be achieved given the sample size that can be afforded and the likely return rate of such a data collection device as a questionnaire. There is little point in commissioning research which is unlikely to have the confidence of a recipient once completed.

Question 190: How 'scientific' do you feel market research can and should be?

Question 191: Examine the possible political implications of and the political pressures that might emerge in respect of the following:

(*a*) an inconclusive market research report on an innovation that the chief executive strongly favours
(*b*) the filing away of market research findings that do not support a prevailing view in a period of a struggle for control of a company
(*c*) emergence of an obscure and dated market research report which appears to support an analysis of a market opportunity that was acted upon with disastrous consequences.

20.32 Interviews

Questions asked in interview situations should be systematically formulated and posed and responses systematically recorded. An interview can be disguised or non-disguised, structured or unstructured. The disguised interview can approach a subject indirectly, perhaps by asking a subject why friends might have purchased a product. Most interviews are open or non-disguised, the subject being asked directly his or her reasons for purchasing a product or service.

In the case of a structured interview the questions asked are standard and follow a pre-determined sequence. All responses are faithfully recorded. With an unstructured interview, an interviewer, without the encumbrance of a standard list of questions is more able to probe, to take up interesting leads and to get to know the subject.

The structured interview tends to be most suitable when large numbers of subjects are to be questioned by relatively inexperienced interviewers about a relatively straightforward consumer good purchase. Where a purchase process is more considered, and more is at stake, a more skilled interviewer may be able to interview at greater depth using the unstructured approach. A subject can be encouraged to talk, to lead the interviewer into fresh areas which might yield new insights. The commitment of the subject is clearly much greater in the case of a detailed and proficient unstructured interview. The unstructured interview can be relatively open ended.

The unstructured and disguised interview may be appropriate in sensitive areas when people are reluctant to talk about themselves. Some individuals have expectations that certain purchase motivations are looked down upon. Consumers may not want to admit that a consumer durable was bought because a nagging wife wanted to 'keep up' with a neighbour's wife who had recently acquired one. Questioned about why the neighbour bought the good in question the subject might reveal certain personal motivations.

A word or picture association test can be used in disguised interviews to probe reactions to phrases, images and symbols associated with the overt or covert attributes of a product or service. By asking subjects to complete a sentence or phrase certain attitudes may be revealed. From the results certain brand name ideas may emerge as more promising than others. Images used by a competitor may seem more appropriate to a product group in question. Over a period of time changes, following advertising and promotion campaigns, in awareness and attitudes might be disclosed. Both problems and opportunities might simultaneously emerge.

Question 192: Complete the following sentences:

    (*a*)   Smoking is . . .
    (*b*)   Compared with universities, polytechnics are . . .
    (*c*)   The government's economic policies are going to . . .
    (*d*)   Hunt saboteurs should be . . .
    (*e*)   Investment in military radar can lead to . . .
    (*f*)   Canned music in stores . . .
    (*g*)   Commercial breaks on television . . .

What do the sentences as completed above reveal about your attitudes, values and motivations?

20.33 Measurement

The questionnaire can be a relatively cheap measuring instrument, that can be systematic and comprehensive while presenting responses in a manner which can allow easy codification, processing and analysis. A good questionnaire seeks consciously to avoid questioner bias and in length, structure and language matches the interest, available time and level of understanding of the target group. A long questionnaire may not be filled in adequately without an incentive.

A questionnaire may be more acceptable in one context than another. Some people do not like being approached in a street. A direct mailed questionnaire may achieve a higher response if a stamped addressed envelope is enclosed with it. The purposes for which a questionnaire is to be used and whether or not the identity of the subject is recorded and disclosed will influence completion rates.

An individual questionnaire may have a single or a multiple purpose. A question may probe whether or not and, if so, how much of a message has been noticed, whether it has been understood and whether any action has followed, depending upon what the purpose of measurement is. If different channels or programmes are to be compared, then responses may have to be reduced to a common index such as the cost per thousand of a target group reached.

An awareness question could use an aided or an unaided approach. A subject could be presented with a specific advertisement and asked in which media it has appeared or alternatively could be asked a relatively open ended question such as a request to list commercials seen on television over the previous week. Many subjects exhibit a desire to please. The danger of presenting the object of measurement, say a specific advertisement, is that subjects are encouraged to lie and to claim to have seen the advertisement, either to please the interviewer or because this is felt to be an expected or normal response.

To avoid prompting a subject and obtaining too vague or too long a response it is sometimes possible to direct a subject by mentioning particular products and particular media without disclosing the individual brand which is the object of measurement. A questionnaire can incorporate a 'truth test'. Thus as well as identifying an advertisement a subject may be questioned about particular programmes that appeared on the radio on the evening in question. At the end of a session an actual advertisement may be presented to obtain a reaction from the subject. One advertisement may have achieved more recognition impact than another, while being successful at putting across the attributes of a product it was designed to promote.

20.34 Techniques

Meaning is difficult to measure. A start can be made by asking subjects to record their feelings by ticking a space or box between a continuum with say excellent and extremely poor at the extremes. A variety of adjectives and descriptive nouns and phrases can be mapped out in this way to allow both depth and direction of feeling to be recorded. In some questionnaires a spacial approach is used, subjects being asked to draw circles on attribute maps.

A response rate can be improved by preliminary notifications, point-of-question promotion and by follow-up techniques. A pleasant and short experience that is not onerous can encourage a response, as can a personalized approach and a covering explanation of why particular research is important. Some designs and colours elicit more of a response than others. Rewards can increase motivation but can also distort and bias a response. Only those needing the money may reply. A promise of anonymity can also provoke a higher response from the suspicious.

In order to measure attitudes a questionnaire can ask subjects whether or not they agree with certain statements. The responses obtained can be compared with the values associated with the statements. The longer the list of statements the more motivated must a subject be to complete. The addition of scales allowing subjects to indicate their strength of feeling for or against a statement can result in a lengthy questionnaire.

Responders and non-responders may have different characteristics which can introduce a source of bias. It may be necessary to attempt to correct for this by profiling both groups. There may also be a difference between early and late responders. Executive selection firms often find that those who reply at once to situations vacant advertisements are those who are unemployed or very unhappy in their current positions. Those who are more settled and busy may not have time to act until a weekend arrives.

When measuring the effectiveness of an advertisement a useful technique is to measure both those who did see and those who did not see the advertisement in question. The percentage of those seeing an advertisement who purchased the product being advertised can then be compared with the percentage of those who did not see it who purchased. A measure of the incremental effect of the advertisement can thus be obtained. How reliable and valid such measurements are will depend upon such questions as whether those who did not see an advertisement as a result of not being viewers of a programme in which an advertisement appeared are, as a group, more or less likely to purchase than the group watching the programme.

Where an assessment budget allows it control group experiments can be staged. A group can be randomly sampled (so far as is possible) and randomly allocated to groups exposed and not exposed to a message. By before and after measurement the differential impact of the message, when all else is unchanged, can be measured. By exposing messages for different lengths of time levels of comprehension can be measured. Physiological measures can detect emotional and physical responses to different stimuli.

20.35 Mathematical Techniques

Where a number of variables are present multi-variate analysis may be used. Multi-variate analysis embraces a family of techniques: multiple regression and multiple correlation, multiple discriminant analysis, principal components analysis and common factor analysis, multi-variate analysis of variance and co-variance analyses, canonical correlation analysis, cluster and profile analyses and multi-dimensional scaling.

Conjoint measurement can be particularly valuable in assessing consumer preferences, by allowing the relative importance of a number of factors present together to be assessed. Conjoint measurement can allow a company to assess the relative weight of price, place and time in a purchase decision or the relative importance to sales executives of different elements of a remuneration package.

Discriminant analysis can be used to classify consumers into groups and in so doing identifies those factors that account for the more significant differences between groups. Discriminant analysis could be used to examine the possible implication of a changing ethnic balance in a particular neighbourhood or of a change in the sex composition of a workforce.

Multiple regression tends to be used to fit a line or curve to the relationship between variables. A multiple regression package could analyse historical data and from the result predict likely sales given particular levels of advertising, promotion or income or other variables for which the historical data is available. Automatic interaction detection can allow an individual consumer to be compared with a group norm. Canonical analysis can seek to find explanations for particular variations.

Factor analysis can be used to group consumers according to such factors as personality, values or lifestyle and can be used to identify and evaluate new product opportunities.

Cluster analysis can enable variables with the greatest similarity to be separated out. A seemingly homogenous socio-economic group could be revealed through cluster analysis to be in fact composed of two or more quite distinct subgroups with different residential, educational and leisure preferences.

Where an organization wishes to compare its corporate image with that of a competitor or to compare the attributes of competing brands, multi-dimensional scaling can be used. It can enable a picture to emerge of how aspects of a product or organization are perceived by a selected group and can enable weak points to be identified for corrective action.

Question 193: Compare and contrast possible laboratory experiment measures of the following stimuli:

(*a*)   a large poster
(*b*)   a newspaper classified advertisement
(*c*)   a sign visible at the edge of a ground at a football match that is televised
(*d*)   a tape played on an independent local radio station
(*e*)   the theme and message of a magazine article
(*f*)   a cardboard package.

20.4   PRESENTATION

Much market research is very poorly presented. A report should set out clearly the problem and the research objectives. The methodology used such as sampling methods and techniques of analysis employed should be stated in order to allow a recipient to judge how much weight can be attached to the findings. The findings themselves should be clearly set out, perhaps in tabular and diagrammatic form and, alongside the conclusions and implications, should be set the limitations and recommendations.

Facts and figures do not always speak for themselves and may need to be interpreted. Where results are not required in a hurry some synthesis and refinement may be needed to pull out the main points and reduce length. Significance and confidence measures should be explained in language that can be understood by the recipient.

Question 194: Assess the likely influence upon presentation of the following considerations:

(*a*) results are needed 'yesterday'
(*b*) the results are to be published
(*c*) a major investment decision hangs in the balance and results will be considered by the board
(*d*) technical results need to be communicated to a non-specialist audience
(*e*) a group of visitors are to be shown the results during a brief tea-break in a hectic schedule.

20.5 MARKET RESEARCH ORGANIZATION

Most large companies now have their own market research organizations. Equally, there has, over the past ten years, been a considerable growth in the number and size of companies offering market research services. Some of these are generalists, while others work in specific areas such as brand-testing or sales forecasting. A number of firms carry out regular surveys and provide subscribers with periodic reports.

The ratio of internal and external work will depend upon one's inhouse skills, how soon a result is required and whether or not a project is a one-off assignment. Generally it is wiser to do leg-work internally and to employ outside experts for the more difficult tasks and for advice on policy.

The cost of market research depends upon whether one is using existing sources or commissioning original research. It will also depend upon the degree of reliability required. A larger sample will be more expensive. When carrying out original research one has to be careful that one really is measuring what is being tested. It is safest to use a control group which is equal in every respect to the experimental group except for what is being tested.

20.6 THE VALUE OF MARKET RESEARCH

The acceptability of the market research function largely depends upon the credibility of those that carry it out. Some managers consider it to be no more than fact-finding by a few clerks, the results of which always arrive late and usually cannot be relied upon. Other managers get annoyed when market researchers give answers in the form of probabilities rather than a simple yes or no. In many companies there is a suspicion of those who look into the future rather than deal with immediate problems. Stories about market researchers who have made mistakes are stored up and released as after-dinner conversation.

The design of a satisfactory survey and, particularly of a questionnaire, is usually a matter that should be left to experts. It is so easy to employ a sample that has not been randomly selected and to ask the wrong questions. When working with experts it is important to make sure that the objectives of the whole exercise are clearly understood by the researchers. They should not be lost sight of. The specialist may well have such techniques as discriminant analysis and factor analysis up his sleeve, but his work will be wasted if he does not ask relevant questions.

Question 195: You are introduced to the uncle of a foreign friend at a party who, owning a small steel plant which manufactures cheap metal toys, asks you to research your local toy market for him. Two days later a formal letter from his organization arrives asking you to submit a proposal and quote a fee. Outline the work you would undertake and establish how much you would charge for doing it.

20.7 CHANGES IN THE SYSTEM

Adaptive organizations thrive on market information. They continually monitor the environment and are always on the look out for marketing opportunities. Such opportunities, if exploited, can leave the company in a more desirable situation. They can be varied, possibly ideas for new products or markets, opportunities for improving channels of distribution or employing marketing techniques, achieving greater efficiency, or the identification of a market niche or a means of gaining a competitive advantage. It is not enough to identify a change, it must be examined and evaluated, to determine whether or not there is something in it for the company.

Changes will also occur in the wider macro-environment. The growth and distribution of income, government economic policy and, particularly, credit policy, can strongly affect the demand for a company's products. Distribution patterns will change over time as, for example, populations spread to the suburbs, or hypermarkets are set up. New sales techniques such as trading stamps and television advertising can suddenly become available. Government regulation and legislation can lead to changes of trading practice. Technological change can open new processes, provide new materials and markets as well as causing higher research and development budgets.

In Chapter 22 a number of political and social changes, for example conservation and growing demands for social responsibility, will be examined. These factors and such social forces as growing leisure time can have important consequences for an organization's future.

Changes do not affect all organizations equally. This can have important consequences for relationships with external organizations. Relative power positions can shift. Evolving market forces may strengthen one partner in a relationship and weaken another. It is therefore important to periodically review relationships, concentrating especially upon performance and negotiating position. The reason for doing this is to reduce the probability of being harmed by change and to increase the chances of capitalizing upon it.

MAJOR BANKS EMPLOY ECONOMIST CONSULTANT ADVISERS. MULTI-NATIONALS EMPLOY INTERNATIONAL RELATIONS SPECIALISTS UPON A CONSULTANCY BASIS. ONE COMPANY ENDED ITS CONTRACT WITH AN ADVISER WHO FAILED TO WARN THE COMPANY OF A COUP IN A THIRD WORLD COUNTRY. SOME TIME LATER THE COMPANY REALIZED THAT NOT ONE OF THE RECOGNIZED LEADING AUTHORITIES HAD PREDICTED THE COUP. THE EXPERT OBTAINED A MORE LUCRATIVE CONTRACT WITH A RIVAL ORGANIZATION.

Question 196: You are an editor of a television news. You employ a number of 'stringers' who report on local issues and who are prepared to cover 'sudden' events as and when required in the provinces. Two bright young graduates have written to you requesting 'stringer' positions in their areas. How would you assess the performance of the present incumbents? What would be your criteria for change?

21. *Competitors*

It is easy to overlook the fact that competitors are an external group with whom one communicates through competitive activity in the market place. This chapter examines some of the ways in which competitor activity can influence company policy.

21.1 COMPETITION

Unlike staff in certain of the other functional specialisms marketors are often engaged in a daily struggle in the marketplace with competitors. Competition can be hidden or overt. A main competitor could be the manufacturer of a substitute rather than a producer of a similar product.

How strong competition is will depend upon market structure, the number of companies in the market, their relative sizes and effectiveness and the existence of regulation, barriers to entry and economics of scale. Duopoly giants may 'slug' at one another like prize fighters. Their senior executives may employ military terminology when talking of the 'war' between the two operations. Where there is less concentration, all-out 'war' may give way to 'healthy rivalry', even some co-operation although in some states, particularly the US, this may have to fall short of collusion.

Circumstances change. Yesterday's competitor can be tomorrow's joint venture partner. Competition can be between all those products which are perceived as capable of meeting a certain need, or between similar products or between organizations supplying these similar products. A conglomerate may find its products competing with certain of the products of another company and yet in a different product area might find the two enterprises have much in common, leading perhaps to the establishment of some joint distribution arrangement.

CINEMA OPERATIONS IN CALIFORNIA BECAME OBSESSED WITH
TELEVISION.   IT WAS SEEN AS THE FILM INDUSTRY'S MAIN

COMPETITOR. THERE WERE OTHER SOURCES OF COMPETITION, HOWEVER, WHICH WERE NOT SEEN AS COMPETITION. THIS WAS BECAUSE MANY OF THE CINEMA OPERATORS DEFINED THEIR BUSINESS NARROWLY AS 'SHOWING' FILMS RATHER THAN MORE BROADLY AS PROVIDING ENTERTAINMENT.

ONE OF THE MAIN REASONS WHY FEWER MIDDLE-CLASS CALIFORNIANS WERE GOING TO THE CINEMA WAS THE ADVENT OF THE MOTOR CAR. 'CRUISING AROUND TOWN' HAD BECOME AN ALTERNATIVE WAY OF 'SPENDING' AN EVENING. THE SHREWDER CINEMA OPERATORS SAW THE MOTOR CAR THREAT AS AN OPPORTUNITY AND BUILT DRIVE-IN MOVIE THEATRES.

Question 197: List your major competitors. What forms of competitor activity do you engage in *vis-à-vis* each of them? Compare your list with a similar one you would have drawn up five years ago.

21.2 COMPETING

In a competitive situation protagonists should have clear objectives, good intelligence and be sufficiently flexible to be able to concentrate resources in order to attack competitor weak points while at the same time protecting 'home' weak spots. A mixture of offensive and defensive strategy may be employed. Information can be the key to success, allowing surprises to be achieved and defences alerted prior to 'attacks'.

A competitor might be outflanked by changing a product's image up or down market. A smaller competitor might find the giants spreading their resources so thinly that a local niche can be 'captured' by employing all available resources to exploit it.

A superior product can allow a market foothold or an alternative method of distribution. For example door-to-door selling of cosmetics originally outflanked established companies who sold similar products in stores.

In a duopoly situation firms can achieve a 'working' relationship. A balance or equilibrium can be struck as two protagonists realize that disproportionate efforts would be needed to capture small slices of each others' market share. The theory of games may be resorted to very much.

At any time a stable balance can be disturbed by the emergence of a third force. Another disturbing factor can be the lure of a new market or the prospect of innovation. The first firm to enter a new market can charge a 'creaming' price, reap benefits of larger scale production and move along the learning curve. Such a situation can lead to a classic 'race'.

In high-risk businesses the reverse of the race could be the case. Both parties might be reluctant to act for fear of the other holding back in order to learn from the mistakes of the first in the field.

Enterprise competition tends to be the most aggressive and ruthless. Competition can be direct one product versus another or more indirect, both companies seeking a given buying group, discretionary income but offering dissimilar products. One group in the market place may seek to impede another. A company may find itself 'competing' against the message of a 'good cause'.

Competition may occur in one market between enterprises but not in another. At the product level competition may be fierce, while at the market level competitors may co-operate through trade associations those interests which they have in common.

> A CLASSIC INSTANCE OF COMPETITION WAS THE GREAT NORTH AMERICAN RAILROAD 'RACE'. AS ONE COMPANY BUILT WESTWARDS ACROSS THE GREAT PLAINS ANOTHER COMPANY STARTING ON THE WEST COAST BEGAN TO LAY TRACK EASTWARDS ACROSS THE MOUNTAINS TOWARDS THE PLAINS. THE PACE OF BUILDING WAS FEVERISH. NEW RECORDS FOR THE LENGTH OF TRACK LAID IN A DAY WERE FREQUENTLY SET. THE TWO LINES MET IN UTAH AMONGST MUCH CELEBRATION.

Question 198:　　Discuss a number of forms of business competition you consider to be unacceptable and justify your selection.

21.21　Competitive Strategy

Competitive behaviour will depend upon marketing objectives and market structure. A company aiming to maximize profit may not be as concerned with loss of market share as a company aiming to maximize turnover.

Expansion may or may not be at the expense of other companies. This largely depends upon the rate of growth or shrinkage of the total market. In a competitive situation power might be sought for its own sake, competition being the 'name of the game'.

A growth strategy will depend greatly upon competitors' activity. Aiming for market penetration against an entrenched competitor might be suicidal when the competitor could be outflanked by developing new markets. Integrating backwards, forwards or horizontally might be forced in order to prevent a competitor from taking over suppliers, distributors and smaller companies. One may have to fight head on rather than take the line of least resistance and risk being trapped in a corner.

Contingency plans should be prepared to deal with a wide range of circumstances in respect of which defensive or offensive marketing action may be necessary. Events to be planned for are those the occurrence of which cannot be predicted. Examples would be a product liability suit or a significant change in legislation. A marketing department could be affected by the collapse of a product or market, a change of ownership, a tumbling price or rocketing cost, the withdrawal of all items of a particular model for testing, the loss perhaps through death of a key member of staff, industrial espionage or a strike.

On the offensive side a company could have contingency plans to take over a rival, start a lawsuit against a competitor or to initiate a round of price cutting. Contingency plans are frequently sensitive and confidential and, as they can quickly become out of date, should be reviewed annually and updated if necessary. In some cases testing or trial runs may be advisable. Action necessary must be carefully set out according to a given timetable. In some cases a contingency plan could be in the form of a decision tree.

Whether a market is entered by licensing, merger or acquisition or new product development will depend in large part upon timing. This will in turn be heavily constrained by competitor activity. Licensing may be necessary to 'beat' a competitor. The existence of the competitor could result in a higher price being paid for a licensing agreement.

The market and cash positions of competitors is of crucial importance. There is little point entering a new market if competitors have massive resources to counter any initiative one displays. A competitive struggle for market share using such techniques as price cutting can weaken all the firms in an industry.

The quality of a competitor's staff needs to be shrewdly assessed. A competent marketing manager should attempt to know as much as possible about opposite numbers in rival organizations. What sort of people are they? Do they take risks? Are they basically hungry or largely satisfied?

IN THE UK ONE MANUFACTURER OF BREAKFAST CEREAL STARTED PUTTING PLASTIC TOYS INTO CEREAL PACKETS. THE TOYS APPEALED TO CHILDREN, PARTICULARLY BOYS, WHO WERE THOUGHT TO BE A MAJOR INFLUENCE UPON WHICH BRAND OF CEREAL 'MUMS' PURCHASED.

THE TOYS BECAME EVER MORE ELABORATE AND EXTENDED TO COMPLETE SETS OF SPACEMEN AND COWBOYS AND INDIANS. THE COST OF THE TOYS BEGAN SERIOUSLY TO EAT INTO PROFIT MARGINS. PURCHASERS OF CEREALS WITHOUT BOYS TO PASS THE TOYS ON TO WERE THOUGHT TO FEEL THAT THE CEREAL MUST BE 'OVERPRICED' IF THEY WERE PAYING FOR A PLASTIC INSERT THEY DID NOT WANT. ONE MANUFACTURER DROPPED THE PRACTICE OF INSERTING PLASTIC TOYS IN CEREAL PACKETS. THE OTHER MANUFACTURERS BREATHED A SIGH OF RELIEF AND QUICKLY FOLLOWED SUIT.

Question 199: Set out the forms of competitor reaction you would expect from established firms were you to enter for the first time the following markets, in each case explaining how you would counter your competitor's likely strategies:

(*a*)   washing machine powder
(*b*)   take-away food
(*c*)   family motor car
(*d*)   soft drink
(*e*)   pop music records.

21.3 MARKET DOMINANCE

Relative product strength is extremely important. In oiligopolistic markets a marketing manager must keep a careful watch of market shares. While sales are increasing in absolute terms a company may find itself with a declining market share.

There are many advantages in having a strong market position. Marker leaders may have higher profit margins due to longer production runs and their sales may be more resilient than those of marginal suppliers whose sales may decline in an economic down turn. Sales based upon referals and word of mouth contact can grow rather like a snowball. The more successful one is the easier it may be to achieve further sales.

A strong market position also has disadvantages. When a slump affects the total market the market leader can suffer most in absolute terms. A company can become vulnerable when a high proportion of its cash flow is dependent upon a single product. A market leader can be vulnerable. A larger production line can be costly to change. Smaller operations adopting a niche strategy may cream the more profitable opportunities.

Economies of scale can give significant competitive advantages to larger selling brands. There is also frequently a learning curve effect. The longer a company has been in a business, the more experience it has accumulated and the easier it may be to identify opportunities for production cost reduction and product improvement. The competitive advantage possessed by an experienced operator can be a considerable barrier to entry.

The dominant firm in a market may not be the one with the largest volume of sales. In the long run profitability, rate of sales growth and the ability to innovate may be more important. Market power depends upon relative rather than absolute strength. A company with a 40 per cent market share, the next largest share being 30 per cent, may be in a less powerful position than the one whose market share is 25 per cent, no other company having more than 5 per cent of the market. Market strength could be measured by dividing market share by those of the next one, two or three competitors.

To be dominant a market leader may need to have a certain multiple of the sales of the next largest company in the market. The advantages of market leadership could include initiative, lower unit costs or the ability to charge a premium price. The learning curve tends to be of greatest importance with industrial and high technology goods. A television tube manufacturer may be able to bury all its competitors as a result of a price advantage.

Being 'number one' has problems. An organization can grow flabby and sluggish. A 'wait and see' strategy could be employed *vis-à-vis* newcomers, retaliatory action being taken when a new entrant has achieved a certain market share.

Building upon strength, the surplus achieved by dominance, could be employed in innovation. An existing position could be strengthened, fortified by introducing new brands to limit the market shares of new entrants.

Overspending on promotion can raise the stakes of being in the market, effectively creating a barrier to entry. By taking a short-term drop in profit prices could be cut to wipe out a newcomer and then raised again. Market power can enable a dominant firm to put 'pressure' upon distributors. A strong cash flow can be used to buy the best talent among competitor staffs.

IN ONE MARKET CLOSE TO 95 PER CENT OF ALL FURNITURE PURCHASED WAS SOLD BY A LOCAL CHAIN OF FURNITURE STORES WITH PRIME HIGH STREET LOCATIONS. THE STORE CHAIN HAD ACQUIRED A LOCAL FURNITURE MANUFACTURER AND LARGELY STOCKED UPMARKET CRAFT MADE PRODUCTS. A SMALL RETAILER ACQUIRED AN OUT OF TOWN WAREHOUSE AT THE REGIONAL RAILROAD CENTRE AND, SELLING HIS ONE HIGH STREET STORE, FINANCED THE PURCHASE OF A STOCK OF MASS PRODUCED, 'ASSEMBLE YOURSELF' IMPORTED FURNITURE. THIS WAS OFFERED ON A 'CASH AND CARRY' BASIS AT A DISCOUNT ON AN ALREADY RELATIVELY LOW PRICE. WITHIN A YEAR THE INNOVATOR HAD EXTENDED HIS CAR PARK THREE TIMES AND HAD SEIZED A THIRD OF THE REGIONAL FURNITURE MARKET.

Question 200: Explain how as a dominant firm you would assess the options you would explore in order to stave off the following competitive threats:

(*a*)   an exciting new patent by a competitor-financed small research unit promises to revolutionize the industry

(*b*)   import duties have just been removed from your product category

(*c*)   a new 'out of town' hypermarket is likely to draw shoppers away from your city centre location

(*d*)   your main rival is 'poaching' your key staff by offering salaries which are 'way out of line' with your union-negotiated differentials

(*e*)   your competitor starts to use plastic rather than glass containers.

EXAMINATION QUESTIONS

1. What does the Government mean when it refers to its 'industrial strategy'? Say whether you think the strategy is viable and describe, using examples, the affect it has had on the structure of UK industry.

2. Do you agree that in the final analysis it is how much a company spends in relation to its competitors that determines the effectiveness of its advertising?

22. *Communications from the Market*

22.1 INTERESTS IN A COMPANY

It was pointed out in Chapter 14 that there are many interests with which a company will be and ought to be communicating: existing and potential share-holders, customers and employees, distributors, creditors, local communities, opinion formers, the media and the government. Communications may well be received from all or any of these groups which may or may not be relevant to the marketor.

A reader who has examined carefully the material in this book so far as this point should know quite a lot about the nature and purpose of communications likely to be received by a marketor from the various interests in a company. The particular characteristics of individuals and groups are examined in Chapters 2 and 3 respectively. Internal communications issues are explored in Chapters 3, 4 and 5 and in areas of Chapters 11 and 12. Chapters 14 and 15 turn to external communications. Separate chapters have dealt with distributors, competitors, customers and industrial goods purchasers.

A lesson of Chapter 20 was the need for an organization to have adequate sources of information. Developments are occurring outside and inside of the company which may profoundly influence the future both for the marketor and for business generally. This chapter examines selected ongoing and unresolved debates, exploring some of the issues upon which an individual marketing manager may have to take a position.

22.2 THE CHANGING WORLD

The patterns of retailing have undergone dramatic changes with the growth of motor car ownership, the development of supermarkets, the introduction of trading stamps and in some sectors automatic vending machines. Micro-chip technology promises almost fully automated retailing organizations, a code number on a purchased good picked up at a check-out desk feeding into a computerized information system and possibly triggering a purchase if recorded stock falls below the reorder level as a result of the purchase.

In Britain the abolition of resale price maintenance has benefited the supermarkets who are now able to undercut the small shopkeeper, particularly with loss leaders. City centres have been turned into pedestrian-only precincts. Hypermarkets have developed on the outskirts of major urban areas. The trend away from personalized selling has resulted in the introduction of shops within shops in certain stores. Credit cards, direct mail, the home freezer and door-to-door selling have fundamentally altered the traditional relationship between retailer and customer.

In an era of continuing relatively high rates of inflation customers have come to terms in varying degrees with the phenomenon of regularly increasing prices. Apart from seasonal goods or items introduced at a high price as a market-skimming strategy, prices now rarely fall. The energy crisis has pushed up transportation costs which affects the great majority of goods on sale.

Along with rising prices have come allegations of 'unjustified' or 'exploitative' price increases and in some countries price controls. These cause especial problems for marketers. Price is an important part of most products and the introduction of price controls can mean that one of the most important characteristics of a product can lie beyond the control of the manufacturer.

The choices faced by consumers have become steadily more complex. Simple everyday activities involve products of great sophistication. A motor car for example is equivalent in complexity to some plant machine tools. When selecting between different makes there are a host of factors to consider. Some consumers make use of *Which*-type surveys or special reports in trade magazines to help them in their purchase decisions. Motoring magazines often carry out exhaustive tests of new cars.

If consumers are irrational and act on impulse often upon the basis of inadequate information should a government intervene to protect consumers from themselves? This question raises a number of philosophical issues concerning the role of government and the role of the market.

Will intrinsic value, performance, the ability to do the job, become more important than image and status? Perhaps economy will itself become something of a status symbol. Will the use of goods and services become more important than ownership? Will the current spate of product liability litigation continue to increase? Courts are awarding much higher damages than hitherto and drawing the responsibilities of producers ever more tightly.

In the US the Federal Trade Commission comes down hard on advertising puff. Britain has a Trade Descriptions Act. Advertising has been forced to become more honest, even factual. In the case of credit sales many countries require promotions to display the true rates of interest. The role of the government in regulating marketing activity might well increase.

Question 201:   You have just listened to a learned professor who has pointed out that as energy costs rise and communications costs fall it may soon be cheaper to take work to people who will remain in their own homes rather than to take people to their work at offices. Consider the implications of this insight for organizations with which you are familiar.

22.21   The Development of Marketing

Marketing has evolved from a preoccupation with selling products, through its integration into the larger organizations and acceptance as a management discipline to its current use as a concept that sums up an approach to business life that recognizes the prime importance of servicing customers.

Economic growth has led to more wealthy consumers with evolving needs and, while competition has existed, there has been a continuing search for efficiency and for tailoring general approaches to specific situations. Marketers have come to learn more about organizations and the behaviour of people within them and about how individuals respond to messages.

Consumers are becoming more articulate and demanding. Regulatory agencies have been placing greater responsibilities, some would say burdens, upon business. Perhaps marketing must be concerned more with quality of life and less with material quantities.

Question 202:   In the command economies of Eastern Europe goods and services are allocated by governmental authority rather than by impersonal market forces. The 'convergence' theory suggests that East and West will gradually tend together under technological imperatives. Assess the future role of marketing in Eastern Europe.

22.3   MARKETING DURING SHORTAGES

Many marketers assume that marketing is the process of increasing demand *ad infinitum*. Not so. An oil shortage, a strike, an import barrier, the technical limit to a plant size or a previous lack of capital investment can all result in demand running ahead of supplies. In such situations the marketing problem can become one of rationing, allocating short supply, questions of demand management.

As stocks fall there are a number of strategies that can be used to 'allocate' a limited output. Prices can be allowed to rise to choke off excess demand. Free marketers long argued that the world oil shortage could be largely 'resolved' by allowing the domestic US oil price to rise from its previous controlled level to the world market price.

Another strategy is to lengthen order books. Supply could be rationed according to need or preference given to large, new or existing customers. Reducing marketing effort to lessen demand pressures in the longer term can be a dangerous strategy if a shortfall in supplies is expected to be only temporary.

Shortages can lead suppliers to raise prices. Further along the production—distribution—retail chain prices will also probably have to be raised. If price rises cannot be passed on then profit margins will be squeezed.

Shortages can put severe stress upon existing arrangements and agreements. If further rises are expected then temptations to hoard may occur. Speculators may obtain control of scarce stocks. A company to whom the products concerned are marginal may cease to produce them, causing disruption and aggravating the supply problems of businesses further along the chain.

Where a shortage and price rise is expected to be more or less permanent then it may be necessary to sift through the ranks of existing companies. The socially responsible company might safeguard supplies to say hospitals or schools or the small and vulnerable company. A more entrepreneurial approach might be to 'milk' the richer customers. Allied to such strategies there should be a conscious policy of searching for replacement goods.

AT ONE NORTH AMERICAN PETROL FILLING STATION A LONG QUEUE DEVELOPED. SOME OF THE MOTORISTS HAD USED MORE FUEL GETTING TO THE STATION THAN THEY WERE LIKELY TO RECEIVE AT IT. THERE WERE SOME ACCUSATIONS OF QUEUE JUMPING. ONE OF THE MOTORISTS PULLED OUT A GUN AND SHOT ANOTHER DEAD.

22.31 Building Goodwill

How customers are treated during shortages may depend upon what is known about them. The easy-going and tolerant may fare less well than those who are noisy and likely to switch to new suppliers.

A market leader may face the prospects of lost sales to the supplier of an inferior product of a manufacturer who nevertheless does have stocks, perhaps because the product was, until shortages developed, relatively undesirable. The organization best able to manage its relations with customers during the period of shortage will be the one that understands them, their problems and preoccupations and their objectives. Meeting a need during a crisis period can result in goodwill that yields a lasting benefit.

Salesmen can play a prominent part in the creation of goodwill. They can counsel customers, find out about their problems and help them in their solution. An important part of the salesman's function is to supply information about what is happening in the market place. This role can become of greater importance in a period of difficulty. Close observation of how customers cope can lead to ideas for new products.

Question 203: An economist has just explained to you that, whenever attempts are made to ration, a black market develops and that when faced with shortages the 'best' solution is to raise the price of whatever is in short supply until demand is once again equal to the available supply. In short you are told rationing by price is better than 'arbitrary' government allocation. What do you think your government should do, if anything, about shortages of the following products or services:

(*a*)   baby milk
(*b*)   electricity
(*c*)   alligator skins
(*d*)   qualified doctors
(*e*)   imported cars.

22.32   Implications of Shortage Strategy

The change in strategy could lead to the need for new skills in the marketing department. The relative profitability of products may change causing problems as one brand manager appears to become more successful and another less so. Liaison with production may be necessary to shift production to the relatively more profitable products. Some mathematical expertise, the ability to carry out a linear programming exercise, may attract a premium.

The promotion mix may change as there might be fewer customers to reach. Sales resources may become concentrated upon key customers and long-run supply contracts negotiated during the period that suppliers are in a relatively strengthened position *vis-à-vis* customers.

Developing key accounts might mean higher level contacts and redundancy among a grass roots sales force. The key to profitability may lie in the identification of income streams and costs with particular customers and the maximization of account profitability.

Such a policy would require the appropriate identification and allocation of costs and revenues. Accounts could be ranked by turnover and profitability and management action focussed upon those falling below a cut-off level of acceptable performance.

In a seller's market the marketers must beware. Tomorrow's conditions might be different – a buyer's market and memories could be long. A substantial and prolonged shortage will affect a company generally. In these circumstances marketing policy will need to be co-ordinated with that for production and finance. Liaison with production and stock control can be particularly important.

For marketing staff in an organization that has traditionally been marketing orientated the change of roles resulting from a shortages position can be traumatic. Instead of production being required to supply whatever the marketer needs, production may now inform the marketer of what is available to sell or allocate to customers. Where a shortage is experienced across an entire economy the government might step in and regulate the distribution of supplies.

IN SOUTH AFRICA AND RHODESIA OIL BECAME EXTREMELY SHORT. BOTH COUNTRIES LACKED INDIGENOUS SOURCES OF OIL BUT HAD PLENTIFUL SUPPLIES OF COAL. RAILWAY SIDINGS AND OLD YARDS AND SHEDS WERE COMBED FOR SPARE PARTS. STEAM ENGINES, LONG ABANDONED, WERE RECONDITIONED AND PUT BACK INTO COMMISSION.

22.33   Competitor Reaction and Shortages

A company's reaction to a crisis situation will, of course, be conditioned by the response of competitors or the regulatory activities of government. A company may not wish to appear exploitative in comparison with competitors.

A price rise could be cushioned by quality reductions and the elimination of special discounts in a market in which other suppliers hold prices. It might be possible to retool in order to produce a more economical product. Where for example a particular metal is in short supply and its price has rocketed it might be possible to introduce a plastic substitute. The enterprising firm that does this may find that what was originally seen as a serious problem has given it an opportunity to steal a march on competitors.

Innovation could result in a new product manufactured that results in the more economical usage of an existing product. Substitutes are often developed in periods of stringency. Difficulty can be a great spur to innovation and creativity. Invention is frequently the child of necessity.

22.4   CRITICISMS OF MARKETING

Marketing has found a variety of criticisms. Its practices have been described as deceptive, materialistic, exploitative and manipulative. Built-in obsolescence has been condemned as wasteful of scarce resources. Poor quality and inadequate after-sales service has been condemned as has the 'artificial' stimulation of wants. Brand proliferation is criticized as extravagant.

The consumer is not always able to judge the veracity of marketing claims while in most societies there are inevitably groups that appear to have fallen behind in the race for the goods things of life. Regulation is called for to protect the consumer.

Whether society should devote so much time and effort to the acquisition of material goods at the expense of the environment is questioned as is the practice of raising expectations. Is this irresponsible when around the world so many are in need?   Marketing is concerned with the satisfaction of wants and needs rather than with the nature of needs.   What should the response of marketing be to a want that is regarded as immoral?   Should bombs be supplied to an air force automatically on receipt of an order?

Marketing has been said to encourage materialism and competitiveness, the consumption of private goods and the neglect of social ones.   It has been accused of manipulating demand, destroying culture and concentrating power.

Advocates of marketing view it as broadening, democratic, allowing innovators to break down monopolies and oligopolies, promoting choice and leading to the production of goods and services that meet the needs of consumers as expressed by the exercise of millions of individual preferences.   Whether a society invests in private or public goods and services is a political as much as an economic question. Those who mourn the pollution of culture are usually those with distinct tastes, who would prefer people to spend their incomes in different ways than they do spend when left alone.

A marketing manager inevitably faces moral dilemmas.   Should one make use of information acquired in dubious circumstances or exploit the knowledge of a salesman just recruited from a competitor?   Are sales claims exaggerated or misleading?   Should one admit to liability in the case of injuries resulting from the use of one's products?   How generous should compensation for loss of office or damages be?   Should a company offer bribes when this is the normal practice in an overseas territory but frowned upon in the country of incorporation?   Should staff be 'poached' from other companies, politicians lobbied, lakes polluted? What standards of morality are to be applied, individual standards, those of the firm or of a host country?

Question 204:   Has the world heavy-weight championship become a spectacle, acted out according to business interests rather than a genuine sporting occasion? Discuss the extent to which business sponsorship has 'destroyed' sport.

22.41   The Limits of the Market

Some would argue that a need for marketing skills does not exist in respect of public goods.   A service may be indivisible.   Such a service might, however, be complemented or augmented by private provision.   An example would be security.

Even when a public good is provided free a marketer may be called in to regulate demand.   A form of social security provision may need to be 'sold' to a target group.   Demand may have to be reduced due to the scarcity of resources.   A marketer might handle a 'save water' campaign during a drought or a 'save energy' campaign during a period of rocketing oil prices.

In the public sector there are pricing decisions to be taken.   Reducing bus fares can relieve underground congestion.   Reducing or raising prices might yield a higher total revenue, thus enabling the provision of a service to be expanded.   When cost-benefit analyses are undertaken a marketer may advise on the likely take up of a service and upon the service itself following 'market research'. In the absence of a price mechanism it is easy to provide too little or too much of a service and consumer research and attitude surveys can assume great importance.

Where consumers are not voting directly with their money, but indirectly through elected representatives, special problems of identifying consumer needs and demands arise. When voting in the marketplace people vote with their money as and when they want to vote without bothering others too much and vote in proportion to their interests. When voting politically everyone votes at once. There may be a period of years between elections. At an election issues may be confused. There is no means of expressing strength of preference. One cannot vote for items in a political programme individually. One must accept or reject a total package.

A political party and a government may seek to 'sell' policies and personalities. Some public programmes are extremely difficult to 'sell'. In a period of accelerating inflation how can one 'market' imposing the harsh economic measures thought by some to be needed to reduce inflation, such as control of the money supply, when this leads to significantly higher rates of unemployment?

In a wartime situation public bonds may need to be 'sold' to help pay for the war effort. With a health or an education campaign there may be deeply entrenched biasses to overcome, attitudes to shift.

In many developed countries populations have become deeply cynical of politicians and their policies. Those responsible for 'marketing' a public programme may face disbelief if not outright hostility.

The effectiveness of public advertising and marketing programmes may be difficult to judge in the absence of competing products and services. How would one judge the cost effectiveness of marketing the United Kingdom's public telephone service? A public advertising campaign in areas such as seat belts or smoking may have to directly confront opposition.

Public supply is not always responsive to demand. An educational system may offer a particular package of courses on a take it or leave it basis. The marketer might suggest to a public policy-maker that such a policy is 'production' rather than 'marketing' oriented. A more responsive and market oriented educational system would carry out market research to find out what the demand is for certain courses and would aim to provide those courses desired by consumers. Such courses would then need to be packaged and promoted in order to reach those who can benefit most from them. They might need to be costed and priced.

IN THE UK SOUTHEND COUNCIL PUT OUT TO TENDER ITS REFUSE COLLECTION SERVICE. PRIVATE CONTRACTORS WERE SELECTED TO COLLECT GARBAGE. THE 'PRIVATE ENTERPRISE' SOLUTION IS MORE COST-EFFECTIVE THAN MAINTAINING A MUNICIPAL SERVICE.

Question 205:   Consider both the advantages and disadvantages of extending the operations of the private sector in the following areas:

    (*a*)   education
    (*b*)   health care
    (*c*)   gas and electricity distribution
    (*d*)   postal and telephone services
    (*e*)   finding jobs for the unemployed.

22.42   The Business Response

The response of business to criticisms has included shifting the buck, blaming others, denial and concealment, bribery and corruption, public relations activity, outright attack on the credibility of critics, lobbying, the establishment of committees of enquiry, and even action to deal with the substance of criticism. The latter course is often the most effective in the long run.

Product safety is one area in which there is much scope for improvement. Many food and drug products have harmful side effects. Clothes are still often inflammable. Safety instructions could be marked more clearly on containers. Certain products such as tranquilisers, alcohol and tobacco are lethal when taken in excessive quantities. Seat belts and crash helmets could be made compulsory. Procedures could be introduced to provide the automatic recall of defective products. Testing routines could be made more stringent.

On general questions of ecology and morality the marketor has no special claims to wisdom or expertise. The marketer is just another citizen. There are limits to the area of marketing concern. Many of the world's problems have little to do with the activities of marketers.

It has become fashionable for consumers to blame marketors for supplying them with goods and services that are disapproved of. So long as exchanges are voluntary ones in a marketplace, it takes two to strike a bargain. The consumers must have expressed an initial desire for the good or service in question that was strong enough for an entrepreneur to feel that a product or service could be devised to satisfy it. The consumer cannot always blame the marketer, passing the buck for their own lack of self-management, their own irresponsibility as consumers. Consumer sovereignty implies consumer responsibility.

Planned obsolescence of clothes, cars and functions is much maligned. Companies responsible for the production of goods with limited lives may be merely responding to the desires of consumers for change. If consumers opt for conspicuous forms of consumption this is their decision, provided always that there is an opportunity for choice to be exercized.

Small market gains resulting from minor product improvements in competitive markets have been considered a wasteful use of resources. Once a basic product has been developed it could be argued that spending large sums to achieve marginal improvements to attract customers from a rival's product is not justified. Against this product variety offers choice and while changes, if only small improvements, are cumulative, over a period of time a very worthwhile change can occur. Thus today's radio may be obtained at a fraction of the real relative cost of its ancestor and is far more convenient to carry about, coming in a great variety of sizes. The product has changed gradually over a number of years as producers have sought to gain competitive advantages by introducing small changes.

Where a market exists it is likely to automatically erode barriers to entry and other signs of monopoly. While cut-throat competition, mergers and acquisitions may pose problems for businessmen, they can yield benefits to consumers. Excessive costs and prices, deceptive practices, the retailing of inferior goods and slick selling can rebound where competition is allowed and encouraged.

Much of the criticism of marketing is the result of its success. Marketing often works. It can create new centres of power and influence in society and erode existing concentrations. An existing *status quo* institution may fear the threat that aggressive marketing poses.

An emerging institution may grasp at marketing as a possible solution to problems. Many non-profit making organizations, for example are eagerly embracing the marketing concept. The marketing approach can be applied to a wide range of social situations.

Marketing is carried on within a legal framework. Laws govern competitive behaviour, product design, quality and testing, pricing practice in areas such as price-discrimination and resale price maintenance, promotion in areas such as labelling and advertising and dealing arrangements. Companies are subject to the law of the land, large ones to the laws of many lands. Critics of marketing can have recourse to the ballot box and to the courts.

Question 206:   A charity has been set up sponsored by industrial donations which places senior executives on secondment with community-based activities in need of management expertise. Your holding company has in the past donated money to the charity. You are now approached by the charity and asked if you could second a marketing manager to assess the feasibility of an inner city window box garden scheme proposed by a voluntary group for a depressed area. Set out the considerations you would weigh in coming to a decision.

22.5   CONSUMERISM

The consumer movement has regularly shifted in its focus. A wide range of ethical concerns have grown out of the movement's earlier preoccupation with such technical and relatively objective considerations as questions of weights and measures. Consumerism has become more influential and a market in its own right. Health food stores have sprung up in the wake of opposition to 'junk foods'.

Aircraft are constructed with quieter engines, motor car engines are built whose exhausts contain lower concentrations of lead pollutants. Milk suppliers have been forced to abandon plans to switch from glass to plastic containers. Nuclear power stations and airports programmes have been brought to a halt by protest lobbies. Safety lobbies have led to the redesign of some products and the withdrawal from the marketplace of others.

Consumerism has increased the relative importance of such product attributes as quality, reliability, life expectancy, safety and economy. Products with these characteristics have gained. Certain manufacturers of such products as large cars, thought to be expensive, dangerous, inefficient users of fuel and with built-in obsolescence have come under attack.

In the US, General Motors was forced to withdraw one of its models, the Corsair, as a result of pressure from a safety lobby headed by Ralph Nader. Safety and anti-pollution pressures are leading to higher costs. A marketing strategy needs to take into account consumer and environmental lobbies. Their activities need to be monitored and evaluated, their likely reactions to new products anticipated.

A numerically small group, if motivated and articulate, can be very vocal and given the fondness of much of the media for protest groups can be very influential. A business needs to take account of the interests of minorities within its customers. One of two consumers unhappy with, say, the after-sales service they have received can mushroom into a national protest movement against an industry's servicing practices.

National legislature have introduced bodies of consumer legislation. Officers of Fair Trading, Consumer Protection Advice and Action Centres, even the taking of a complaint to the Ombudsman, create avenues that can lead to public hearings and media involvement.

A variety of explanations have been put forward to account for the growth of consumerism. With basic needs satisfied people are said to adopt a more critical approach towards goods and services which cannot in any way be said to be necessities. The development of technology and large organizations is said to breed a reaction against the big and the unknown. There comes a point when pollution reaches a level that triggers a concern with the quality of life. Frustrations are created when wants are aroused more quickly than they can be satisfied, when it becomes increasingly obvious that some are so much better off than others.

THE SUNDAY TIMES NEWSPAPER PLAYED A LEADING ROLE BY MEANS OF PRESS EXPOSURE IN OBTAINING IMPROVED COMPENSATION TERMS FOR VICTIMS OF THE DRUG THALIDOMIDE. THE NEWSPAPER'S PUBLICATION OF AN 'INSIGHT' FOCUS ON THE PROBLEMS OF THE VICTIMS OF THE DRUG HELPED TO KEEP THEIR CAUSE ALIVE. THE NEWSPAPER WON A PRESTIGIOUS PRESS AWARD.

Question 207: Describe your reactions as a consumer to the following items of news:

(a) some tins of tuna fish have been found to contain poisonous levels of mercury
(b) terrorists have claimed to have randomly injected Irsraeli oranges with a deadly poison
(c) a consumer magazine reveals that washing machine A is slightly more noisy than washing machine B
(d) a friend informs you that the hotel she stayed in on a visit to Portugal was still in the process of construction
(e) the manufacturer of your car has written to you asking you to take it to your nearest garage to have its steering shaft tested.

22.51 Consumer Activities

Consumerist and protest groups typically pass through a number of stages as organizations. They are often founded by crusaders acting on a part-time and voluntary basis. An expansion of activity can lead to the establishment of some kind of formal organization and through fund-raising, the payment of salaries to full-time officials. Developments in the technology and practice of the media tend to favour the protest group.

Consumerism has created platforms for politicians, instant personalities, opportunities for media programme planners and fortunes for lawyers. Political involvement in the marketing process has led to a growing interest among marketers in the public affairs function. Among consumerists are those with a vested interest in the continuation of criticisms. Protest and complaint has for some become a way of life and, for a few, a lucrative one.

22.52 Tackling Consumerism

A marketor needs to be aware of the areas of two overlapping circles, one of which is the area of the producers concern and the other of which is the area of concern of the consumer. The area of overlap might be considerable or the two circles could merely touch. Where there is overlap there is likely to be scope for action.

A food manufacturer can date its products − a simple move which can do much to build customer goodwill. An extra-active company could obtain goodwill by seeding its waste tips or landscaping pits, perhaps opening them for community use. Companies have held open days, at which they have explained how they recycle waste.

An advertising campaign could ride on the back of consumerism, emphasizing product qualities that are highly regarded by consumerists. A greater emphasis upon post-sales activity, for example servicing or guarantee of replacement resulting from consumerist pressure, could open up new opportunities for competition. The fact that a company is responsive to consumer interests could be a main plank in its promotional activity.

Some companies have adopted statements of practice and codes of conduct and have featured this fact prominently on their packaging and in their advertisements.

Products and services are marketed but so can be organizations, arts, religion, sport, political points of view, candidates, celebrities, countries, causes and programmes. Marketing itself may need to be marketed.

22.6 CRITICISMS OF ADVERTISING

Advertising has received much criticism. Many see it as a waste or as a sinister attempt by the existing firms in a sector to erect a barrier to entry to keep out competition. Some minority groups have been very sensitive to their protrayal in advertisements.

Has advertising turned sports into spectacles, has it devalued religion? Does sex in advertising really 'exploit' women as the stickers on many advertisements suggest? There is another set of questions of course that one could ask relating to whether or not sex in advertising works. It tends to be most effective when related in some way to the product. In other cases recall tests tend to show that what is remembered is the model and not the goods.

Consumption can be viewed as a means of self-expression. People may express the sort of people they are through their purchases. In this case the image of the product in question in the eyes of others may be the crucial factor in the purchase decisions. In this it may be that the needs of others are as important as the needs of the individual consumer.

A critic of advertising might argue that advertising works by convincing people that they are in some way inadequate. It is made clear that the target individual lacks something that is desirable if only in the eyes of others and that the deficiency can be made good through purchase of the product in question.

22.61   Advertising and the Young

Concern has on occasions been expressed over the particular issue of advertising directed at the young. Children and, to a less extent, teenagers, tend not to be as critical of advertising as their adult counterparts. Knowing that children are especially receptive to advertising messages, some advertisers have aimed their advertisements at children in the hope that they will then put pressure upon their parents to purchase. Advertisers should beware that this strategy can be counter-productive, when parents become annoyed at persistent pressure that is applied to them.

Given the perception of a generation gap, many adults feel that advertising on occasions exploits the particular vulnerability of their children, leading them astray. Teenage budgets represent a tempting marketing target. The results of behavioural research to date reveals that the issue is far from straightforward. There is some evidence that to a point children imitate what they see on television. At the same time young children appear to be quite cynical when faced with certain advertisements.

22.62 Debates on Advertising

Is marketing, particularly large-scale advertising and promotion, a constraint upon competition? There is a school of thought which argues that advertising of such products as cereals and 'soap flakes' proliferates brands, and raises costs to create barriers to entry, thus enhancing the market power of existing suppliers. This enhanced market power can of course be used to increase prices and raise profit margins.

There is some evidence that advertising creates brand loyalty but this does not necessarily imply that a barrier to entry is created. Some high advertising industries are very profitable but in other profitable industries a relatively very small proportion of a product's cost is accounted for by advertising.

If anything high advertising costs tend to be related to the introduction of new products and the promotion of products in new markets. In this sense advertising is stimulating rather than reducing competition.

Is advertising annoying, irritating, unsightly and generally in poor taste? The answer to this question depends upon one's point of view. To some, the television commercial is entertaining, light relief and accepted as an integral part of television viewing, while to others it is an unwarranted intrusion. The alternative to commercial television, assuming the same number of channels were retained, would have to be greater state involvement financed through taxation, a pay as you watch meter scheme or voluntary donation/sponsored television. Given that advertising serves a number of functions those advocating its restriction need to face the question of alternatives.

The conventional wisdom in marketing is being continually eroded by initiative and experimentation. For a long time fear was thought to have no place in marketing. It has been found that fear can help to 'sell' insurance, fire protection equipment and security services, not to mention fear of lung cancer and other forms of impaired health which may lie at the core of anti-smoking campaigns.

AN IMMIGRANT PUBLISHER FOUND IT VERY DIFFICULT TO BREAK INTO THE US PUBLISHING MARKET. THERE WERE SO MANY BARRIERS TO ENTRY. THEN HE CONCEIVED OF THE IDEA OF AUTHORS PAYING FOR THE PUBLICATION OF THEIR BOOKS, SO CALLED 'VANITY PUBLISHING'. HE BUILT UP A LARGE

BUSINESS ALMOST EXCLUSIVELY AS A RESULT OF WIDESPREAD
ADVERTISING FOR MANUSCRIPTS.

22.63 Advertising Regulations

Advertising can be regulated by direct controls, for example limiting the space
devoted to advertising or the proportion of revenue devoted to it or by fiscal
means, perhaps by imposing a tax upon advertising expenditure. Taxes can distort
the mix of promotional expenditure and, when accompanied by direct controls
can, when there is excess demand as with television advertising in the UK, lead to
the tax being passed on to customers. A levy designed to reduce television
company profits was passed on to advertisers.

An advertising tax could lead to a switch of expenditure from advertising to
other aspects of the marketing mix which are less cost effective. Also to the
extent that advertising can be seen as an investment in goodwill, both direct controls and a tax result in a lower level of such advertising investment than would
otherwise be the case.

In the US the Federal Trade Commission has disallowed certain advertisements.
For example where a well-known personality is used to endorse a product the
Federal Trade Commission might veto the resulting advertisement unless the
personality concerned has particular knowledge of or some known association
with the product in question. Such limitations frequently act as a spur to
advertising creativity.

IN SCANDINAVIA THE ADVERTISEMENT OF ALCOHOLIC DRINKS
IS SEVERELY RESTRICTED. CONTRACEPTIVES ARE ADVERTISED
QUITE OPENLY, IN SOME CASES BY TAKING HALF-PAGE ADVER-
TISEMENTS IN NEWSPAPERS AND FULL PAGE ADVERTISEMENTS
IN MAGAZINES.

Question 208: Justify why any of the following forms of advertising should be
banned:

    (*a*)   girlie magazine advertisements on television
    (*b*)   slimming advertisements in women's magazines showing 'full
        frontal' nudity
    (*c*)   advertisements for sweets, ice cream and chocolate in children's
        comics
    (*d*)   tobacco advertisements in newspapers and magazines
    (*e*)   'political' advertisements.

22.7   THE   SOCIAL   ASPECTS   OF   MARKETING

The social aspects of marketing include such issues as the impact of marketing upon the structure of society, on human behaviour as well as upon the physical environment.   Its impact upon the media tends to be of special concern along with its power.

The extent to which government agencies should attempt to regulate and control marketing activity is an important issue.   Another social marketing issue is the extent to which social problems are susceptible to marketing solutions.   The crux of social marketing is the view that consumption is a social act.   Some would argue that it is a political act as well.

To understand the social aspects of marketing the marketer must know something about the social background of customers, where they live and have lived, their education and employment, incomes and consumption patterns and, importantly, their sources of consumer information.   Aggregates should be broken down into sub-publics.   Many successful businesses have adopted a niche strategy, aiming at one particular section of the market.

22.71   Social Irresponsibility

Some materials form particular disposal problems.   Many household goods come in containers which are virtually indestructible.   A few products become very dangerous as they deteriorate.   Aerosol cans often explode on incineration.   One form of packaging may be recyclable, another may not be and if thoughtlessly disposed of may cause a pollution problem for generations.   The socially responsible marketer would select the former container rather than the latter.

Waste disposal has become a major and dangerous industry.   On incineration some plastics give off toxic fumes.   Recycling is attracting its entrepreneurs – those who see problems as marketing opportunities but very often the burden is thrown upon the shoulders of local authorities.

Should the marketer satisfy the short run interests of consumers when these are incompatible with longer term welfare?   Where does the responsibility of the marketer end and that of government begin?   Lobbies and movements come and go but a vanished species is lost for all time.   Marketers face difficult trade-offs between the present and the future.   Not everyone wants a future of continued economic growth or feels it to be desirable.   Marketers are coming to acknowledge responsibilities to society at large.

Question 209:   You are the marketing manager of a company that manufacturers Napalm.   Your company's product is used in increasing quantities to incinerate villagers, most of whom are non-combatants, in a far-away country in South East Asia.   Evaluate your position.

22.72   Social Responsibility

The disadvantaged consumer has below average income and less than average ability and opportunity to shop around. Prices are often higher in inner city and rural areas.   Structural decline of traditional manufacturing industries can result in depressed regions.   Such conditions create marketing opportunities as well as problems.

Socially responsible marketing creates and markets goods and services tailored to the needs of the disadvantaged, meeting needs rather than wants, although the distinction is rather difficult to draw. Marketing need not inevitably be material-istic.   Religion, economy products, health care and sanitary products and energy saving devices can be and are marketed. A consumer rights and information service may need to be aggressively marketed if it is to reach the people it is designed to help.

A frequent criticism of marketing is that it deceives those who are unable to judge the truth of advertising claims. Such allegations are difficult to prove. While deception may allow a fast buck to be made in the short run, in the longer term, if one is aiming at repeat purchases, then honesty and value for money are often the best policies. The important issue raised is who knows best? When a government feels that it knows more than consumers about what is in their best interests, as with cigarette advertising, it can intervene in the marketplace, in this case insisting that warning notices be placed on cigarette packets.

Those who form part of the retail chain face special responsibilities. Marks and Spencer have very tight quality control procedures and insist that their products meet exacting standards.

Socially responsible marketing recognizes that many goods have long after-sales life and in their manufacture and disposal can cause harmful side effects. Social costs are frequently incurred as a result of consumption for private benefits. Recognizing the social cost of litter, many beer and soft drink can producers now manufacture cans carrying messages asking their consumers to dispose of them thoughtfully. This recognizes the responsibility of the producer not only to the consumer but to all those likely to be influenced by the consumption of the product.

Wider social responsibilities include environmental protection and equal employ-ment opportunities, and generally being 'a good citizen'. The disposable society, consuming products with built-in obsolescence, is very expensive in scarce resources terms. The energy crisis has brought consumers of many nations face-to-face with a zero-growth situation. Customers are becoming more conscious of efficiency, of value for money. Longer product life and durability may become more important.

Question 210:   As marketing director you have master-minded a nationwide advertising campaign to promote children's clothing. While you are eating your evening meal, the regional news appears on the television. It reports that a seven-year-old girl burned to death when her dress caught fire. You telephone your company's buying manager who is a personal friend. He has seen the news item and recognized the dress as one of the company's products. He tells you that the company's entire clothing range is made of highly inflammable material. Making the cloth flame-resistant would increase costs by 10 per cent. What do you do?

Efficient social marketing can promote the efficient use of resources to achieve socially desirable goals.

Question 211:   Can religion be 'sold'?

EXAMINATION QUESTIONS

1. Organizations have a responsibility for the social consequences of their decisions. Evaluate this statement, indicating the possible areas of conflict between marketing goals and social goals.

2. Evaluate the impact of the micro-processor on UK industry and society in the next decade.

3. Is the recently fashionable concern with 'social marketing' any more than a reflection of marketing educators' distaste for profit motive?

4. Has consumerism become a casualty to inflation?

Bibliography

Britt, S.H. and Boyd, H.W. Jnr (ed), *Marketing Management and Administrative Action*, 3rd Edition, McGraw-Hill Book Co. (1973).

Chisnall, P., *Marketing – A Behavioural Analysis*, McGraw-Hill Book Co. (1975).

Coulson-Thomas, C.J., *New Product Development Checklist*, Institute of Chartered Accountants (1978).

Coulson-Thomas, C.J., *Public Relations: A Practical Guide*, Macdonald and Evans (1979).

Coulson-Thomas, C.J., *Public Relations Is Your Business*, Business Books (1981).

Davis, Martyn, *The Effective Use of Advertising Media*, Business Books (1981).

Delozier, M. Wayne, *The Marketing Communication Process*, McGraw-Hill Book Company (1976) and McGraw-Hill Paperback (1978).

Doyle, P., Law, P., Weinberg, P., and Simmonds, K. (eds), *Analytical Marketing Management*, Harper & Row (1974).

Hart, N.A. and O'Connor, J. (eds), *Practice of Advertising*, Heinemann (1978).

Kotler, P., *Marketing Management, Analysis, Planning and Control*, 3rd Edition, Prentice-Hall Inc. (1976).

Mitchell, J., *Marketing and the Consumer Movement*, McGraw-Hill Book Co. (1978).

Weinberg, C., Doyle, P., Law, P., and Simmonds, K., *Advertising Management*, Harper & Row (1974).

Index

Accounts, as communication channel, 10
Advertising, 94–5, 97, 123–4, 214–37
  agencies, 223–6
  as investment, 263–4
  budgets, 259–63
  campaign elements, 256–7
  corporate image, 210–11
  criticisms, 329–31
  economics, 215–17
  effectiveness, 268–71
  effects, 217–21
    on children, 329–30
  message, 258–9
  objectives, 221–2
  outdoor, 247–8
  regulation, 331
  research into effectiveness, 227–37
  resistance to, 266
  scheduling over time, 236–7, 258
  strategy, 257–8
  types and aims, 214–15
  use of symbolism, 218–19
  see also Messages; Social marketing
Audiences, defining, 2, 3, 5
Authority, human response to, 17–18

Behaviour
  analysis of, 15–20
  factors in purchase decisions, 111–13
  'learning' factor in advertising, 219–21
  of consumers, 96–9
  within organizations, 35–41
    in relation to distribution, 178
    influenced by brand
      performance, 156
Brand loyalty, 100, 222
Brand management, 145–7
  advantages, 151
  marketing strategies, 153
  operation, 148–9
  problems, 150–1
  related to functional management, 148
Brands, 142–5
  identifying attributes, 154
  knowing when to kill, 159
  performance evaluation, 155–60
  private, policy, 143–5
Broadcasting, 206, 248–51
Buy grids, 111

Cash flows, of individual brands, 155
Character merchandising, 283–5
Charities, *see* Social marketing
Choice, within organizations, 39–40
Cinema advertising, 251
Communication, 1–14
  channels, 10–12
  electronic, 246–7
  evaluation, 12–13

  in matrix organizations, 48
  in power culture organizations, 45
  in relation to organizational tasks, 52
  in role culture organizations, 46
  mass, 238–9
  one- and two-way, 2–3
  planned approach, 3–4
  specifying objectives, 4–5
  strategy, 1–2
  with employees, 201
  with external organizations, 184–8
  with specialists, 74–6
  with variety of interests, 317
  within organizations, 41–3
  see also Marketing communication
Competition, 310–11
  advertising as restraint, 330
  market dominance, 314–15
  strategy, 311–14
  within organizations, 59
Competitions, promotional, 274, 282
Consultants, 74–5
  see also External organizations
Consumer movement, marketing
  response to, 326–9
Consumers
  behaviour, 96–9
  preferences, 99–102
  types, 98
  values, 101–2
Contract negotiation, 132–3
Control systems in organizations, 60–1
Coupons, promotional, 273–4, 276–7
Creativity, management of, 77–8
  of advertising, 227
  use of external agencies, 188
Credibility
  of advertising media, 252–3
  of advertising message, 7–8
  of authoritative sources, 17
  of salesmen, 126
  use of opinion formers, 11
Crisis, public relations in, 212–13
Cultures, influence on marketing, 22–3

Decision-making by groups, 30–1
Demand management, 104
Demographic factors, 22
Directories, advertising in, 245–6
Distribution
  channel evaluation, 169–72, 173–4
  channel selection, 165–9
  policy, 161–2
  productivity improvement, 172–8
  total-cost approach, 174, 176–7
    managers' impact on, 176
  support for, 189–90
Diversification within company, 85–7

Electronic information, 246–7
Exhibitions, trade, 281
External organizations
    advertising agencies, 223–6
    communications with, 184–8
    establishing and managing relations
        with, 188–92
    evaluating service agencies, 187–8
    managing diversity of, 186
    relationships with, 180–93

Feedback, flexibility of response to, 4

Gatekeepers, 112
Give-aways, 279
Goodwill, creation, 320
Government activities, monitoring for
    effects on company, 202–3
Groups, 26–32
    behaviour, 27–8
    characteristics, 26–7
    dynamics, 30–1
    individuals within, 28–9
    matrix organizations, 48
    selecting members, 29–30
    tensions, 31–2
    see also Teams

Hierarchy
    authority related to, 18
    of role culture organizations, 46
House journals, 201, 205
Hygiene factors, 36

Image
    character merchandising, 283–5
    corporate, 91–2, 210–12
    of products, 92–3
    public relations activities, 198–9
Individuality
    effect on groups, 28–9
    in organizations, 37–9
Industrial markets, 105–6
    characteristics of purchases, 106–9
    distributors, 167
    establishing company reputation, 118
    major purchases, 116–18
    product-associated services, 109
    selling packages of goods, 108
    see also Technical product marketing
Industrial relations, 40–1
Information
    flows to and from salesmen, 135–6
    gathering prior to purchase decision,
        110–11
    marketing, 294–8
    systems, 57
    see also Communication: channels
Innovation, management of, 78–82
    adoption of ideas, 79
    arising from crisis, 322
    teamwork, 81–2

Interviews
    market research, 302
    media techniques, 206–7

Job satisfaction, 24–6
Journals, 243–5
    see also House journals

Leadership qualities, 23–4
Lobbying, 203

Management
    control, 60–1
    of marketing specialists, 67–8
    of staff, 65–6
    theory, 35–7
Market research, 294–309
    influencing organizational changes,
        308–9
    information input, 298–300
    methods, 300–6
    organization, 307
    presentation of results, 306–7
    use of questionnaires, 303–4
    using information system, 296–8
    value, 307–8
Market share, reports on brand
    performance, 157
Marketing
    audit, 191
    control, 190–1, 195
    criticisms, 322–6
        business response to, 325–6
    demand management, 104
    development, 319
    during materials shortages, 319–22
    environment, 183–4
        changes, 317–19
    organization, 61–4
        by function, 61–2
        by market, 63
        by product, 62
        by project, 63
        market-centred, 63–4
    overseas, 130–1
    social aspects, 332–4
    structure of system, 181–3
    use of middlemen, 163–4
Marketing communications strategy,
    88–91
Marketing intelligence, 298–9
    sources, 299–300
    see also Information
Markets, as basis of marketing
    organization, 63
Matrix organization, 48–9, 51
Media, 238–55
    advertising, models, 232–6
    as communication channel, 10
    characteristics, 239–40
    conventions, 253–4
    credibility, 252–3

Media (continued)
    cultural aspects, 254–5
    multi-media advertising, 255
    planning use of, 264–5
    scheduling advertising, 265–7
    utilization in advertising
        campaigns, 226
Messages
    credibility, 7–8
    importance of relevance, 7
    perception of meaning, 6, 8
    structure, 8–9
Middlemen, 162–4
    selection, 168–9
    trade promotions, 280–2
Minorities, avoiding offence to, 201–2
Modelling, 71–4
    advertising campaigns, 267–8
    distribution options, 178
    effect of advertising on sales, 230
    market share, 103
    media advertising, 232–6
    promotion mix, 121
Motivation, 16
    in job satisfaction, 25
    management theory, 36
    of industrial purchasers, 107–8
    of salesmen, 133
Multi-variate analysis, in market
    research, 305–6

Needs, hierarchy of, 16, 36
    organizational structure to meet, 44
    person culture type of organization, 49
Newspapers, 241–3
Non-profit marketing, 292–3

Opinion formers, 11
Organizations
    characteristics and variety, 34, 43
    choices available, 39–40
    communication patterns, 41–3
    design, 54–5
        factors influencing, 57–9
    development, 53, 55–6
    effects of technology, 50–2
    formal and informal systems, 59–60
    functional, and brand management, 148
    individuals in, 37–9
    industrial relations, 40–1
    management of change, 69–71
    management theory, 35–7
    responsiveness, 58
    structure, 34–5, 44
        dictated by tasks, 52–3
    types, 45–50
        dictated by task, 54
Overseas marketing, 130–1

Packaging, in promotion mix, 122–3
Person culture type of organization,
    49–50, 51

Persuasion, 93–5
Point-of-sale promotions, 274–6
Poster advertising, 247–8
Power
    human response to, 18–19
    in relation to communication, 19
Power culture type of organization,
    45–6, 51
Preferences of consumers, 102–3
Press releases and contacts, 204–5
Price cutting, promotional, 100, 274,
    277–8
Print media, 240–6
Printed material, publicity value, 205–6
Problem solving
    by 'task culture' organizations, 47
    related to level of technology, 51
    using computer models, 72–4
Product managers, 68–9, 145–7
Products
    accounting methods, 152
    as basis of marketing
        organization, 62
    competitive strength, 314–15
    failure, management of, 158, 159–60
    image, 92–3
    new, development of, 83–5
Promotion mix, 120–1
    testing, 121–2
Public relations
    channels, 204–8
    communication role, 194–5
    departmental responsibilities, 196–7
    evaluation, 209–10
    for good publicity, 195–6
    planning, 208–9
    systematic approach, 197–8
Public services
    campaigns, see Social marketing
    limits of market, 323–4
Publics
    identification, 198
    see also Audiences
Purchase decisions, 110–19
    high risk, 114–15
    major, 116–18
Purchasers, 113–14
    analysis, 115–16
    interaction with salesmen, 134–5
    monitoring changes, 170–1

Quantity discounts, 274

Racial bias, avoidance of imputation
    of, 201–2
Radio, as advertising medium, 250–1
Recognition, human need for, 16
Reputation of company, 9
    see also Image
Rewards
    contribution to job satisfaction, 25
    human response to, 15–17

Role culture type of organization,
    46–7, 50, 51
Roles, within organizations, 19–20

Sales, measuring advertising influence
    on, 229–32
Sales management, 126–41
Sales promotion, 272–87
    sales-force, 282
    targets, 272–3
    to consumers, 273–9
    trade, 280–2
    using special opportunities, 282–3
Salesmen
    and reputation of company, 9
    characteristics, 126–7, 136
    incentives, 282
    information flows, 135–6
    interaction with buyers, 134–5
    location, 129–30
    management, 133–5
    objectives, 128
    performance assessment, 136–8
    putting across message, 127
    remuneration, 138–40
    role changes, 171
    stress, 140
    territories, 128–9
Samples, promotional, 273, 277
Satisfiers, 36
Service agencies, see External organizations
Shareholder relations, 200–1

Social marketing
    public programmes, 290–2
    scope, 288–90
Social responsibility in marketing, 332–4
Social science, insight into human
    values, 21–2
Sponsorship, 285–7
Staff management, 65–6
Status, human regard for, 19–20
Stress, 26, 140

Task culture type of organization,
    47–8, 50, 51
Tasks, dictating organizational structure,
    52–3
Teams, for innovations, 81–2
    see also Groups
Technical product marketing, 131–2
Technology, organizational effects of,
    50–2, 58
Telephone selling, 251
Television advertising, 248–50
Trading stamps, 278–9

Values, human, 20–3
    conflicts, 20–1, 40
    of consumers, 101–2
    social science aspects, 21–2
Visits from public, 207–8

Workload fluctuations, 26, 38